Honda GL1800
Gold Wing
Service and Repair Manual

by Alan Ahlstrand

(2787-1Q1)

Models covered
GL1800 Gold Wing, 2001 through 2010

ABCDE
FGHIJ
KLMNO
PQRS

ISBN-13: 978-1-56392-973-1
ISBN-10: 1-56392-973-2

Library of Congress Control Number: 2012930460
Printed in the USA

Haynes Publishing
Sparkford, Nr Yeovil, Somerset BA22 7JJ, England

Haynes North America, Inc
861 Lawrence Drive, Newbury Park, California 91320, USA

© Haynes North America, Inc. 2010, 2012

With permission from J.H. Haynes & Co. Ltd.

A book in the Haynes Service and Repair Manual Series

12-288

Contents

LIVING WITH YOUR HONDA

Introduction

Pre-ride checks

MAINTENANCE

Routine maintenance and servicing

Contents

REPAIRS AND OVERHAUL

Engine, transmission and associated systems

Chassis components

Electrical system

Wiring diagrams

REFERENCE

Index

The Birth of a Dream

by Julian Ryder

There is no better example of the Japanese post-war industrial miracle than Honda. Like other companies which have become household names, it started with one man's vision. In this case the man was the 40-year old Soichiro Honda, who had sold his piston-ring manufacturing business to Toyota in 1945 and was happily spending the proceeds on prolonged parties for his friends. However, the difficulties of getting around in the chaos of post-war Japan irked Honda, so when he came across a job lot of generator engines, he realized that here was a way of getting people mobile again at low cost.

A 12 by 18-foot shack in Hamamatsu became his first bike factory, fitting the generator motors into pushbikes. Before long he'd used up all 500 generator motors and started manufacturing his own engine, known as the "chimney," either because of the elongated cylinder head or the smoky exhaust, or perhaps both. The chimney made all of half a horsepower from its 50 cc engine but it was a major success and became the Honda A-type.

Less than two years after he'd set up in Hamamatsu, Soichiro Honda founded the Honda Motor Company in September 1948. By then, the A-type had been developed into the 90 cc B-type engine, which Mr. Honda decided deserved its own chassis, not a bicycle frame. Honda was about to become Japan's first post-war manufacturer of complete motorcycles. In August 1949 the first prototype was ready. With an output of three horsepower, the 98 cc D-type was still a simple two-stroke, but it had a two-speed transmission and, most importantly, a pressed steel frame with telescopic forks and hard tail rear end. The frame was almost triangular in profile with the top rail going in a straight line from the massively braced steering head to the rear axle. Legend has it that after the D-type's first tests, the entire workforce went for a drink to celebrate and try and think of a name for the bike. One man broke one of those silences you get when people are thinking, exclaiming "This is like a dream!" "That's it!" shouted Honda, and so the Honda Dream was christened.

Mr. Honda was a brilliant, intuitive engineer and designer, but he did not bother himself with the marketing side of his business. With hindsight, it is possible to see that employing Takeo Fujisawa - who would both sort out the home market and plan the eventual expansion into overseas markets - was a masterstroke. He arrived in October 1949 and in 1950 was made Sales Director. Another vital new name was Kiyoshi Kawashima, who along with Honda himself, designed the company's first four-stroke after Kawashima had told them that the four-stroke opposition to Honda's two-strokes sounded nicer and therefore sold better. The result of that statement was the overhead-valve 148 cc E-type, which first ran in July 1951 just two months after the first drawings were made. Kawashima was made a director of the Honda Company at 34 years old.

The E-type was a massive success, over 32,000 were made in 1953 alone, a feat of

'This is like a dream!' 'That's it' shouted Honda

mass-production that was astounding by the standards of the day given the relative complexity of the machine. But Honda's lifelong pursuit of technical innovation sometimes distracted him from commercial reality. Fujisawa pointed out that they were in danger of ignoring their core business, the motorized bicycles that still formed Japan's main means of transport. In May 1952, the F-type Cub appeared, another two-stroke despite the top men's reservations. You could buy a complete machine or just the motor to attach to your own bicycle. The result was certainly distinctive, a white fuel tank with a circular profile went just below and behind the saddle on the left of the bike, and the motor with its horizontal cylinder and bright red cover just below the rear axle on the same side of the bike. This was the machine that turned Honda into the biggest bike maker in Japan, with 70% of the market for bolt-on bicycle motors. The F-type was also the first Honda to be exported. Next came the machine that would turn Honda into the biggest motorcycle manufacturer in the world.

The C100 Super Cub was a typically audacious piece of Honda engineering and marketing. For the first time, but not the last, Honda invented a completely new type of motorcycle, although the term "scooterette'" was coined to describe the new bike which had many of the characteristics of a scooter but the large wheels, and therefore stability, of a motorcycle. The first one was sold in August 1958; fifteen years later, over nine-million of them were on the roads of the world. If ever a machine can be said to have brought mobility

Honda C70 and C90 OHV-engined models

The CB250N Super Dream became a favorite with UK learner riders of the late seventies and early eighties

The GL1000 introduced in 1975, was the first in Honda's line of Gold Wings

to the masses, it is the Super Cub. If you add in the electric starter that was added for the C102 model of 1961, the design of the Super Cub has remained substantially unchanged ever since, testament to how right Honda got it first time. The Super Cub made Honda the world's biggest manufacturer after just two years of production.

Honda's export drive started in earnest in 1957 when Britain and Holland got their first bikes; America got just two bikes the next year. By 1962, Honda had half the American market with 65,000 sales. But Soichiro Honda had already travelled abroad to Europe and the USA, making a special point of going to the Isle of Man TT, then the most important race in the GP calendar. He realized that no matter how advanced his products were, only racing success would convince overseas markets for whom "Made in Japan" still meant cheap and nasty. It took five years from Soichiro Honda's first visit to

the Island before his bikes were ready for the TT. In 1959 the factory entered five riders in the 125 class. They did not have a massive impact on the event, being benevolently regarded as a curiosity, but sixth, seventh and eighth were good enough for the team prize. The bikes were off the pace but they were well engineered and very reliable.

The TT was the only time the West saw the Hondas in '59, but they came back for more the following year with the first of a generation of bikes which shaped the future of motorcycling – the double-overhead-cam four-cylinder 250. It was fast and reliable – it revved to 14,000 rpm – but didn't handle anywhere near as well as the opposition. However, Honda had now signed up non-Japanese riders to lead their challenge. The first win didn't come until 1962 (Aussie Tom Phillis in the Spanish 125 GP) and was followed up with a world-shaking performance at the TT. Twenty-one year old Mike Hailwood

won both 125 and 250 cc TTs and Hondas filled the top five positions in both races. Soichiro Honda's master plan was starting to come to fruition; Hailwood and Honda won the 1961 250 cc World Championship. Next year Honda won three titles. The other Japanese factories fought back and inspired Honda to produce some of the most fascinating racers ever seen: the awesome six-cylinder 250, the five-cylinder 125, and the 500 four, with which the immortal Hailwood battled Agostini and the MV Agusta.

When Honda pulled out of racing in '67, they had won sixteen rider's titles, eighteen manufacturer's titles, and 137 GPs, including 18 TTs, and introduced the concept of the modern works team to motorcycle racing. Sales success followed racing victory as Soichiro Honda had predicted, but only because the products advanced as rapidly as the racing machinery. The Hondas that came to Britain in the early '60s were incredibly sophisticated. They had overhead cams where the British bikes had pushrods, they had electric starters when the Brits relied on the kickstart, they had 12V electrics when even the biggest British bike used a 6V system. There seemed no end to the technical wizardry. It wasn't that the technology itself was so amazing, but just like that first E-type, it was the fact that Honda could mass-produce it more reliably than the lower-tech competition that was so astonishing.

When, in 1968, the first four-cylinder CB750 road bike arrived, the world of motorcycling changed forever, they even had to invent a new word for it, "Superbike." Honda raced again with the CB750 at Daytona and won the World Endurance title with a prototype DOHC version that became the CB900 roadster. There was the six-cylinder CBX, the CX500T – the world's first turbocharged production bike. They invented the full-dress tourer with the GoldWing, and came back to GPs with the

Carl Fogarty in action at the Suzuka 8 Hour on the RC45

An early CB750 Four

revolutionary oval-pistoned NR500 four-stroke, a much-misunderstood bike that was more a rolling experimental laboratory than a racer. Just to show their versatility, Honda also came up with the weird CX500 shaft-drive V-twin, a rugged workhorse that powered a new industry: the courier companies that oiled the wheels of commerce in London and other big cities.

It was true, though, that Mr. Honda was not keen on two-strokes – early motocross engines had to be explained away to him as lawnmower motors! However, in 1982 Honda raced the NS500, an agile three-cylinder lightweight against the big four-cylinder opposition in 500 GPs. The bike won in its first year, and in '83 took the world title for Freddie Spencer. In four-stroke racing the V4 layout took over from the straight four, dominating TT, F1 and Endurance championships with the RVF750, the nearest thing ever built to a Formula 1 car on two wheels. And when Superbike arrived, Honda were ready with the RC30. On the roads the VFR V4 became an instant classic, while the CBR600 invented another new class of bike on its way to becoming a best-seller. The V4 road bikes had problems to start with, but the VFR750 sold world-wide over its lifetime while the VFR400 became a massive commercial success and cult bike in Japan. The original RC30 won the first two World Superbike Championships is 1988 and '89, but Honda had to wait until 1997 to win it again with the RC45, the last of the V4 roadsters. In Grands Prix, the NSR500 V4 two-stroke superseded the NS triple and became the benchmark racing machine of the '90s. Mick Doohan secured his place in history by winning five World Championships in consecutive years on it.

In yet another example of Honda inventing a new class of motorcycle, they came up with the astounding CBR900RR FireBlade, a bike with the punch of a 1000 cc motor in a package the size and weight of a 750. It became a cult bike as well as a best seller, and with judicious redesigns, it continues to give much more recent designs a run for their money.

When it became apparent that the high-tech V4 motor of the RC45 was too expensive to produce, Honda looked to a V-twin engine to power its flagship for the first time. Typically, the VTR1000 FireStorm was a much more rideable machine than its opposition, and once accepted by the market formed the basis of the next generation of Superbike racer, the VTR-SP-1.

One of Mr. Honda's mottos was that technology would solve the customers' problems, and no company has embraced cutting-edge technology more firmly than Honda. In fact, Honda often developed new technology, especially in the fields of materials science and metallurgy. The embodiment of that was the NR750, a bike that was misunderstood nearly as much as the original NR500 racer. This limited-edition technological tour-de-force embodied many of Soichiro Honda's ideals. It used the latest techniques and materials in every component, from the oval-piston, 32-valve V4 motor to the titanium coating on the windscreen, it was – as Mr Honda would have wanted – the best it could possibly be. A fitting memorial to the man who has shaped the motorcycle industry and motorcycles as we know them today.

The CX500 – Honda's first V-Twin and a favorite choice of dispatch riders

The GL1800 Gold Wing

The GL1800 is the latest in a long series of Gold Wings, beginning with the GL1000 in 1975. Honda's flagship touring motorcycle is the second Gold Wing to have an opposed 6-cylinder engine (its immediate predecessor, the GL1500, was the first).

The engine's crankshaft is mounted longitudinally in the motorcycle, with three horizontal cylinders on each side. A single overhead camshaft on each cylinder bank operates the valves through shim-under-bucket lifters. There are two valves, one intake and one exhaust, per cylinder. The camshafts are operated by a pair of timing chains.

The fuel system is a version of Honda's Programmed Fuel Injection (PGM-FI) system. It inducts air through a dual throttle body and supplies fuel through six injectors. The injectors are mounted in banks of three above each cylinder head. A number of sensors supply information to the engine management computer (engine control unit, or ECM). The ECM uses this information to control the timing and amount of fuel injected into each cylinder. The PGM-FI system includes sophisticated emission controls, including oxygen sensors or air-fuel ratio sensors in the exhaust system.

Front suspension on all models is by telescopic forks, with a damper rod design used for the left fork leg and a cartridge design used for the right fork leg. The left fork leg is equipped with an anti-dive unit. The rear suspension consists of a swingarm, single shock absorber with an automatic self-leveling system and a progressive rising rate linkage similar to that used in sport bikes and motocrossers.

The transmission is a conventional motorcycle-type five-speed. The clutch is multi-wet-plate design with hydraulic assist to reduce lever effort. The motorcycle is

2006 GL1800 Gold Wing

equipped with reverse, but the reverse system uses the starter motor, not the engine.

Final drive is by a driveshaft, which connects the engine to the final drive unit at the rear of the motorcycle.

The brakes use a pair of three-piston calipers at the front and a single three-piston caliper at the rear. All models are equipped with Honda's Linked Braking System, which ties the front and rear brakes together. In the GL1800, pulling the front brake lever operates

the upper and lower pistons in each front caliper, as well as the center piston in the rear caliper. Pressing the brake pedal operates the center piston in each front caliper, as well as the upper and lower pistons in the rear caliper. The two hydraulic systems are completely independent of each other. Anti-lock brakes (ABS) are optional.

Optional equipment on the GL1800 includes cruise control, a global positioning system and an airbag.

Acknowledgements

Our thanks to AJ Jensen for lending us his 2003 GL1800 for the disassembly photographs in this manual, as well as for cover photos; to Harry Aced for lending us his 2006 GL1800 for cover photos; to David Guy, service manager at GP Sports, Santa Clara, California, for arranging the teardown and fitting the project into his shop's busy schedule; and to Craig Wardner, service technician, for doing the mechanical work and providing valuable technical information.

About this Manual

The aim of this manual is to help you get the best value from your motorcycle. It can do so in several ways. It can help you decide what work must be done, even if you choose to have it done by a dealer; it provides information and procedures for routine maintenance and servicing; and it offers diagnostic and repair procedures to follow when trouble occurs.

We hope you use the manual to tackle the work yourself. For many simpler jobs, doing it yourself may be quicker than arranging an appointment to get the motorcycle into a dealer and making the trips to leave it and pick it up. More importantly, a lot of money can be saved by avoiding the expense the shop must pass on to you to cover its labour and overhead costs. An added benefit is the sense of satisfaction and accomplishment that you feel after doing the job yourself.

References to the left or right side of the motorcycle assume you are sitting on the seat, facing forward.

We take great pride in the accuracy of information given in this manual, but motorcycle manufacturers make alterations and design changes during the production run of a particular motorcycle of which they do not inform us. No liability can be accepted by the authors or publishers for loss, damage or injury caused by any errors in, or omissions from, the information given.

Frame and engine numbers

The vehicle identification number (VIN) is stamped into the left side of the steering head, and/or is located on a label affixed to the right side of the frame, below the exhaust pipe. The frame serial number is stamped into the right side of the steering head and the engine serial number is stamped into the right rear corner of the engine. These numbers should be recorded and kept in a safe place so they can be furnished to law enforcement officials in the event of theft.

The VIN, frame serial number, engine serial number and carburetor identification number should be kept in a handy place (such as your wallet) so they are always available when purchasing or ordering parts for your machine.

Other important identification numbers include the carburetor identification number and the color code. The carburetor identification number is stamped into the intake side of the carburetor. The color code is located on a sticker inside the fuel filler cap door. Always refer to the color code when buying painted parts such as the fuel tank, fenders or side covers.

The models covered by this manual are as follows:

Honda GL1800 Gold Wing, 2001 through 2009

The engine number location

The frame number is stamped into the right side of the steering head and also printed on a sticker located nearby

Year	Model	Initial engine number	Initial frame number
2001	Standard	SC47E-2000101	1HFSC470*1A000001
	ABS	SC47E-2000101	1HFSC474*1A000001
2002	Standard	SC47E-2100101	1HFSC470*2A100001
	ABS	SC47E-2100101	1HFSC474*2A100001
2003	Standard	SC47E-2200011	1HFSC470*3A200001
	ABS	SC47E-2200011	1HFSC474*3A200001
2004	Standard	SC47E-2300001	1HFSC470*4A300001
	ABS	SC47E-2300001	1HFSC474*4A300001
2005	Standard	SC47E-2400001	1HFSC470*5A400001
	ABS	SC47E-2400001	1HFSC474*5A400001
2006	Standard	SC47E-2500001	1HFSC47F*6A500001
	Comfort package	SC47E-2500001	1HFSC47G*6A500001
	Comfort package, GPS	SC47E-2500001	1HFSC47H*6A500001
	Comfort package, GPS, ABS	SC47E-2500001	1HFSC47L*6A500001
2007	Premium audio	Not available	1HFSC47F*7A600001
	Heated seats/grips, GPS	Not available	1HFSC47H*7A600001
	Heated seats/grips	Not available	1HFSC47L*7A600001
	Airbag	Not available	1HFSC47M*7A600001

Year	Model	Initial engine number	Initial frame number
2008	Heated seats/grips, GPS, ABS, Premium audio, Airbag	Not available	1HFSC47F*8A700001
	Premium audio, Heated seats/grips	Not available	1HFSC47H*8A700001
	Premium audio, GPS, Heated seats/grips	Not available	1HFSC47L*8A700001
	Premium audio	Not available	1HFSC47M*8A700001
2009	Comfort package, Premium audio	Not available	1HFSC47G*9A800001
	Satellite radio, GPS, Heated seats/grips, ABS, Airbag	Not available	1HFSC47H*9A800001
	Satellite radio, GPS, Comfort package, ABS	Not available	1HFSC47L*9A800001

Buying spare parts

Once you have found all the identification numbers, record them for reference when buying parts. Since the manufacturers change specifications, parts and vendors (companies that manufacture various components on the machine), providing the ID numbers is the only way to be reasonably sure that you are buying the correct parts.

Whenever possible, take the worn part to the dealer so direct comparison with the new component can be made. Along the trail from the manufacturer to the parts shelf, there are numerous places that the part can end up with the wrong number or be listed incorrectly.

The two places to purchase new parts for your motorcycle – the accessory store and the franchised dealer – differ in the type of parts they carry. While dealers can obtain virtually every part for your motorcycle, the accessory dealer is usually limited to normal high wear items such as shock absorbers, tune-up parts, various engine gaskets, cables, chains, brake parts, etc. Rarely will an accessory outlet have major suspension components, cylinders, transmission gears, or cases.

Used parts can be obtained for roughly half the price of new ones, but you can't always be sure of what you're getting. Once again, take your worn part to the breaker's yard for direct comparison.

Whether buying new, used or rebuilt parts, the best course is to deal directly with someone who specializes in parts for your particular make.

Professional mechanics are trained in safe working procedures. However enthusiastic you may be about getting on with the job at hand, take the time to ensure that your safety is not put at risk. A moment's lack of attention can result in an accident, as can failure to observe simple precautions.

There will always be new ways of having accidents, and the following is not a comprehensive list of all dangers; it is intended rather to make you aware of the risks and to encourage a safe approach to all work you carry out on your bike.

Asbestos

● Certain friction, insulating, sealing and other products - such as brake pads, clutch linings, gaskets, etc. - contain asbestos. Extreme care must be taken to avoid inhalation of dust from such products since it is hazardous to health. If in doubt, assume that they do contain asbestos.

Fire

● Remember at all times that gasoline is highly flammable. Never smoke or have any kind of naked flame around, when working on the vehicle. But the risk does not end there - a spark caused by an electrical short-circuit, by two metal surfaces contacting each other, by careless use of tools, or even by static electricity built up in your body under certain conditions, can ignite gasoline vapor, which in a confined space is highly explosive. Never use gasoline as a cleaning solvent. Use an approved safety solvent.

● Always disconnect the battery ground terminal before working on any part of the fuel or electrical system, and never risk spilling fuel on to a hot engine or exhaust.

● It is recommended that a fire extinguisher of a type suitable for fuel and electrical fires is kept handy in the garage or workplace at all times. Never try to extinguish a fuel or electrical fire with water.

Fumes

● Certain fumes are highly toxic and can quickly cause unconsciousness and even death if inhaled to any extent. Gasoline vapor comes into this category, as do the vapors from certain solvents such as trichloro-ethylene. Any draining or pouring of such volatile fluids should be done in a well ventilated area.

● When using cleaning fluids and solvents, read the instructions carefully. Never use materials from unmarked containers - they may give off poisonous vapors.

● Never run the engine of a motor vehicle in an enclosed space such as a garage. Exhaust fumes contain carbon monoxide which is extremely poisonous; if you need to run the engine, always do so in the open air or at least have the rear of the vehicle outside the workplace.

The battery

● Never cause a spark, or allow a naked light near the vehicle's battery. It will normally be giving off a certain amount of hydrogen gas, which is highly explosive.

● Always disconnect the battery ground terminal before working on the fuel or electrical systems (except where noted).

● If possible, loosen the filler plugs or cover when charging the battery from an external source. Do not charge at an excessive rate or the battery may burst.

● Take care when topping up, cleaning or carrying the battery. The acid electrolyte, even when diluted, is very corrosive and should not be allowed to contact the eyes or skin. Always wear rubber gloves and goggles or a face shield. If you ever need to prepare electrolyte yourself, always add the acid slowly to the water; never add the water to the acid.

Electricity

● When using an electric power tool, inspection light etc., always ensure that the appliance is correctly connected to its plug and that, where necessary, it is properly grounded. Do not use such appliances in damp conditions and, again, beware of creating a spark or applying excessive heat in the vicinity of fuel or fuel vapor. Also ensure that the appliances meet national safety standards.

● A severe electric shock can result from touching certain parts of the electrical system, such as the spark plug wires (HT leads), when the engine is running or being cranked, particularly if components are damp or the insulation is defective. Where an electronic ignition system is used, the secondary (HT) voltage is much higher and could prove fatal.

Remember...

✗ **Don't** start the engine without first ascertaining that the transmission is in neutral.

✗ **Don't** suddenly remove the pressure cap from a hot cooling system - cover it with a cloth and release the pressure gradually first, or you may get scalded by escaping coolant.

✗ **Don't** attempt to drain oil until you are sure it has cooled sufficiently to avoid scalding you.

✗ **Don't** grasp any part of the engine or exhaust system without first ascertaining that it is cool enough not to burn you.

✗ **Don't** allow brake fluid or antifreeze to contact the machine's paintwork or plastic components.

✗ **Don't** siphon toxic liquids such as fuel, hydraulic fluid or antifreeze by mouth, or allow them to remain on your skin.

✗ **Don't** inhale dust - it may be injurious to health (see Asbestos heading).

✗ **Don't** allow any spilled oil or grease to remain on the floor - wipe it up right away, before someone slips on it.

✗ **Don't** use ill-fitting wrenches or other tools which may slip and cause injury.

✗ **Don't** lift a heavy component which may be beyond your capability - get assistance.

✗ **Don't** rush to finish a job or take unverified short cuts.

✗ **Don't** allow children or animals in or around an unattended vehicle.

✗ **Don't** inflate a tire above the recommended pressure. Apart from overstressing the carcass, in extreme cases the tire may blow off forcibly.

✔ **Do** ensure that the machine is supported securely at all times. This is especially important when the machine is blocked up to aid wheel or fork removal.

✔ **Do** take care when attempting to loosen a stubborn nut or bolt. It is generally better to pull on a wrench, rather than push, so that if you slip, you fall away from the machine rather than onto it.

✔ **Do** wear eye protection when using power tools such as drill, sander, bench grinder etc.

✔ **Do** use a barrier cream on your hands prior to undertaking dirty jobs - it will protect your skin from infection as well as making the dirt easier to remove afterwards; but make sure your hands aren't left slippery. Note that long-term contact with used engine oil can be a health hazard.

✔ **Do** keep loose clothing (cuffs, ties etc. and long hair) well out of the way of moving mechanical parts.

✔ **Do** remove rings, wristwatch etc., before working on the vehicle - especially the electrical system.

✔ **Do** keep your work area tidy - it is only too easy to fall over articles left lying around.

✔ **Do** exercise caution when compressing springs for removal or installation. Ensure that the tension is applied and released in a controlled manner, using suitable tools which preclude the possibility of the spring escaping violently.

✔ **Do** ensure that any lifting tackle used has a safe working load rating adequate for the job.

✔ **Do** get someone to check periodically that all is well, when working alone on the vehicle.

✔ **Do** carry out work in a logical sequence and check that everything is correctly assembled and tightened afterwards.

✔ **Do** remember that your vehicle's safety affects that of yourself and others. If in doubt on any point, get professional advice.

● If in spite of following these precautions, you are unfortunate enough to injure yourself, seek medical attention as soon as possible.

Note: *The Pre-ride checks outlined in the owner's manual covers those items which should be inspected before riding the motorcycle.*

Engine oil level

Before you start:

Caution: Do not run the engine in an enclosed space such as a garage or workshop.

✔ Start the engine and let it idle for several minutes to allow it to reach normal operating temperature.

✔ Stop the engine and support the motorcycle in an upright position, using an auxiliary stand if required. Make sure it is on level ground.

✔ Leave the motorcycle undisturbed for a few minutes to allow the oil level to stabilize.

Bike care:

● If you have to add oil frequently, you should check whether you have any oil leaks. If there is no sign of oil leakage from the joints and gaskets the engine could be burning oil (see *Troubleshooting*).

The correct oil:

● Modern, high-revving engines place great demands on their oil. It is very important that the correct oil for your bike is used.

● Always top up with a good quality oil of the specified type and viscosity and do not overfill the engine.

Oil type	API grade SG or higher, meeting JASO T903 standard MA*
Oil viscosity	SAE 10W-30

*Some automotive oils contain friction modifiers than can cause motorcycle clutches to slip. Oil meeting JASO standard T903 MA is compatible with motorcycle clutches.

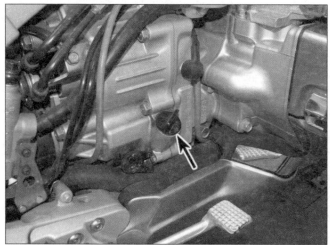

1 Remove the oil filler cap (arrow) from the right-hand side of the engine after removing the side cover. The dipstick is integral with the cap and is used to check the engine oil level. Using a clean rag or paper towel, wipe all the oil off the dipstick. Insert the clean dipstick in the filler cap hole, but do not screw it in.

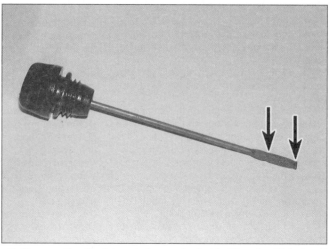

2 Remove the dipstick and observe the level of the oil, which should be somewhere in between the upper and lower lines (arrows). If the level is below the lower line, add the recommended grade and type of oil to bring the level up to the upper line on the dipstick. Do not overfill. Install the filler cap.

Coolant level

Before you start:

✔ Make sure you have a supply of coolant available – a mixture of 50% distilled water and 50% corrosion inhibited ethylene glycol antifreeze is needed.

✔ Check the coolant level when the engine is at operating temperature and idling.

✔ Support the motorcycle in an upright position on its centerstand. Make sure it is on level ground.

Bike care:

● Use only the specified coolant mixture. It is important that antifreeze is used in the system all year round, and not just in the winter. Do not top the system up using only water, as the system will become too diluted.

● Do not overfill the reservoir. If the coolant is significantly above the FULL level line at any time, the surplus should be siphoned or drained off to prevent the possibility of it being expelled out of the overflow hose.

● If the coolant level falls steadily, check the system for leaks (see Chapter 1). If no leaks are found and the level continues to fall, it is recommended that the machine be taken to a Honda dealer for a pressure test.

1 The coolant reservoir dipstick is located on the left side of the bike, beneath the side cover.

2 Remove the dipstick, wipe it clean, reinsert it, and pull it out. Coolant level should be between the upper and lower lines on the dipstick. If the coolant level is below the lower line, top the coolant level up with the recommended coolant mixture.

Suspension and steering

Suspension and Steering:

● Check that the front and rear suspension operates smoothly without binding.
● Check that the suspension is adjusted as required.
● Check that the steering moves smoothly from lock-to-lock.

Legal and safety

Lighting and signalling:

● Take a minute to check that the headlight, tail light, brake light, instrument lights and turn signals all work correctly.
● Check that the horn sounds when the switch is operated.
● A working speedometer graduated in mph is a statutory requirement in the UK.

Safety:

● Check that the throttle grip rotates smoothly and snaps shut when released, in all steering positions. Also check for the correct amount of freeplay (see Chapter 1).
● Check that the engine shuts off when the kill switch is operated.
● Check that sidestand and centerstand return springs hold the stands up securely when they are retracted.

Fuel:

● This may seem obvious, but check that you have enough fuel to complete your journey. If you notice signs of fuel leakage – rectify the cause immediately.
● Ensure you use the correct grade unleaded fuel – see Chapter 4 Specifications.

Brake and clutch fluid levels

> ⚠ *Warning: Brake hydraulic fluid can harm your eyes and damage painted surfaces, so use extreme caution when handling and pouring it and cover surrounding surfaces with rag. Do not use fluid that has been standing open for some time, as it absorbs moisture from the air which can cause a dangerous loss of braking effectiveness.*

Before you start:

✔ Support the motorcycle in an upright position on its centerstand. Turn the handlebars until the top of the front master cylinder is as level as possible. The rear master cylinder reservoir is located behind the right-hand side cover.

✔ Make sure you have the correct hydraulic fluid. DOT 4 is recommended.

✔ Wrap a rag around the reservoir being worked on to ensure that any spillage does not come into contact with painted surfaces.

Bike care:

● The fluid in the front and rear brake master cylinder reservoirs will drop slightly as the brake pads wear down.

● If any fluid reservoir requires repeated topping-up this is an indication of an hydraulic leak somewhere in the system, which should be investigated immediately.

● Check for signs of fluid leakage from the hydraulic hoses and brake system components – if found, rectify immediately (see Chapter 7).

● Check the operation of both brakes before taking the machine on the road; if there is evidence of air in the system (spongy feel to lever or pedal), it must be bled as described in Chapter 7.

1 The front brake fluid level is visible through the sight glass in the reservoir body - it must be above the LOWER reservoir line. If the fluid is below the line, remove the cap screws and lift off the reservoir cap, diaphragm plate and diaphragm. Top up with new, clean DOT 4 brake fluid, until the level is just below the upper level line cast on the inside of the reservoir. Take care to avoid spills (see WARNING above) and do not overfill. Be sure the diaphragm is correctly seated before installing the plate and cap, then tighten the screws securely.

2 The clutch fluid reservoir is mounted on the left handlebar - it's checked in the same way as the front brake reservoir, and it uses the same fluid.

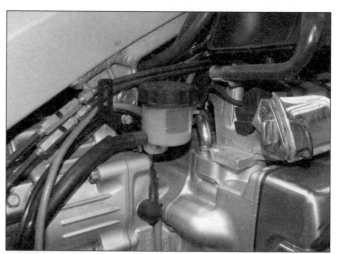

3 The rear brake master cylinder reservoir is located on the right side of the bike beneath the side cover. Fluid level should be between the upper and lower lines molded in the reservoir. If it's low, unscrew the cap/diaphragm and lift it off. Top up with new, clean DOT 4 brake fluid until the level is just below the upper line. Take care to avoid spills (see **Warning** above) and do not overfill. Install the cap/diaphragm and tighten it securely.

Tires

The correct pressures:

● The tires must be checked when **cold**, not immediately after riding. Note that low tire pressures may cause the tire to slip on the rim or come off. High tire pressures will cause abnormal tread wear and unsafe handling.

● Use an accurate pressure gauge. Many garage forecourt gauges are wildly inaccurate. If you buy your own, spend as much as you can justify on a quality gauge.

● Correct air pressure will increase tire life and provide maximum stability, handling capability and ride comfort.

Front	250 kPa (36 psi)
Rear	280 kPa (41 psi)

Tire care:

● Check the tires carefully for cuts, tears, embedded nails or other sharp objects and excessive wear. Operation of the motorcycle with excessively worn tires is extremely hazardous, as traction and handling are directly affected.

● Check the condition of the tire valve and ensure the dust cap is in place.

● Pick out any stones or nails which may have become embedded in the tire tread. If left, they will eventually penetrate through the casing and cause a puncture.

● If tire damage is apparent, or unexplained loss of pressure is experienced, seek the advice of a tire fitting specialist without delay.

Tire tread depth:

● At the time of writing UK law requires that tread depth must be at least 1 mm over the entire tread breadth all the way around the tire, with no bald patches. Many riders, however, consider 2 mm tread depth minimum to be a safer limit. Honda recommends a minimum of 1.5 mm for the front tire and 2 mm for the rear tire.

● Many tires now incorporate wear indicators in the tread. Identify the triangular pointer or

1 Check the tire pressures when the tires are cold and keep them properly inflated.

TWI mark on the tire sidewall to locate the indicator bar and renew the tire if the tread has worn down to the bar.

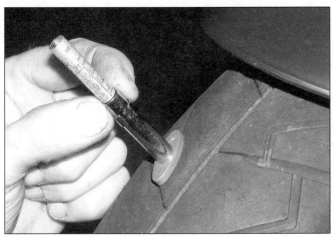

2 Measure tread depth at the center of the tire using a tread depth gauge

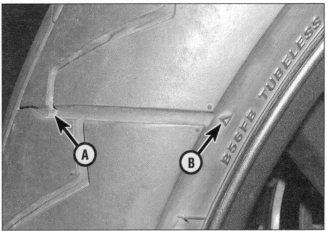

3 Tire tread wear indicator bar (A) and its location marking (B) – usually either an arrow, a triangle or the letters TWI – on the sidewall. Look for the tire information label on the chainguard or swingarm

Notes

Chapter 1
Tune-up and routine maintenance

Contents

Degrees of difficulty

Easy, suitable for novice with little experience		**Fairly easy,** suitable for beginner with some experience		**Fairly difficult,** suitable for competent DIY mechanic		**Difficult,** suitable for experienced DIY mechanic		**Very difficult,** suitable for expert DIY or professional	

Specifications

Engine

Spark plugs
  Type
    Standard .... NGK BKR6E-11 or ND K20PR-U11
    Cold weather (below 5-degrees C/41-degrees F) .... NGK BKR5E-11 or ND K16PR-U11
    Extended high-speed riding .... NGK BKR7E-11 or ND K22PR-U11
  Gap .... 1.0 to 1.1 mm (0.039 to 0.043 inch)
Engine idle speed.. 800 +/- 80 rpm
Cylinder compression pressure (at sea level)........................ See Chapter 2
Cylinder numbering (from front to rear of bike)
  Right side 1-3-5
  Left side 2-4-6

Miscellaneous

Brake pad material minimum thickness	To wear groove - see text
Brake pedal position	Not adjustable
Freeplay adjustments	
Throttle grip	2 to 6 mm (1/12 to 1/4 inch)
Clutch lever	Not adjustable
Front brake lever	Not adjustable
Minimum tire tread depth	
Front	1.5 mm (0.06 inch)
Rear	2.0 mm (0.08 inch)
Tire pressures (cold)	See *Daily (pre-ride) checks* at the front of this manual
Tire sizes	
Front	130/70R-18 (63H) or 130/70R18M/C (63H)
Rear	160/80R-16 (74H) or 180/60R16M/C (74H)
Maximum load	
US	189 kg (417 lbs)
Canada	193 kg (425 lbs)
UK and Europe	190 kg (419 lbs)

Torque specifications

Engine oil drain plug	38 Nm (27 ft-lbs)
Oil filter	26 Nm (20 ft-lbs)
Spark plugs	18 Nm (13 ft-lbs)
Final drive filler plug	12 Nm (108 ft-lbs)
Final drive drain plug	20 Nm (14 ft-lbs)

Recommended lubricants and fluids

Engine/transmission oil	
Type	API grade SG or higher meeting JASO standard MA
Viscosity	SAE 10W-40
Capacity	
With filter change	3.7 liters (3.9 US qts, 3.3 Imp qts)
Oil change only	3.6 liters (3.8 US qts, 3.2 Imp qts)
Coolant	
Type	50/50 mixture of water and ethylene glycol antifreeze containing corrosion inhibitors for aluminum engines*
Capacity	
Radiator and engine	3.53 liters (3.73 US qts, 3.11 Imp qts)
Reservoir tank	0.65 liter (0.69 US qts, 0.57 Imp qts)
Final drive oil	
Type	SAE 80 hypoid gear oil
Capacity	120 cc (4.1 US fl oz, 4.2 Imp fl oz)
Brake and clutch fluid	DOT 4 brake fluid
Fork oil	See Chapter 6

Miscellaneous

Wheel bearings	Medium weight, lithium-based multi-purpose grease
Swingarm pivot bearings	Medium weight, lithium-based multi-purpose grease
Cables and lever pivots	Chain and cable lubricant or 10W30 motor oil
Sidestand/centerstand pivots	Medium-weight, lithium-based multi-purpose grease
Brake pedal/shift lever pivots	Medium-weight, lithium-based multi-purpose grease
Throttle grip	Medium-weight, lithium-based multi-purpose grease

* *The silicate corrosion inhibitors used in automotive antifreeze/coolants may cause premature failure of the mechanical water pump seals. For this reason, be sure to use a silicate-free antifreeze, such as Honda HP coolant. Also, it's important to use only distilled water.*

1 Maintenance schedule

Note: *The pre-ride inspection outlined in the owner's manual covers checks and maintenance that should be carried out on a daily basis. It's condensed and included here to remind you of its importance. Always perform the pre-ride inspection at every maintenance interval (in addition to the procedures listed). The intervals listed below are the shortest intervals recommended by the manufacturer for each particular operation during the model years covered in this manual. Your owner's manual may have different intervals for your model.*

Daily or before riding
- [ ] Check the engine oil level
- [ ] Check the coolant level
- [ ] Check the fuel level and inspect for leaks
- [ ] Check the operation of both brakes - also check the fluid level and look for leakage
- [ ] Check the tires for damage, the presence of foreign objects and correct air pressure
- [ ] Check the throttle for smooth operation and correct freeplay
- [ ] Check the operation of the clutch - check the fluid level and look for leakage
- [ ] Make sure the steering operates smoothly, without looseness and without binding
- [ ] Check for proper operation of the headlight, taillight, brake light, turn signals, indicator lights, speedometer and horn
- [ ] Make sure the sidestand and centerstand return to their fully up positions and stay there under spring pressure
- [ ] Make sure the engine kill switch works properly

Every 4000 miles/6000 km
- [ ] Check the clutch for fluid level and leaks
- [ ] Check the brake fluid level
- [ ] Check the brake discs and pads
- [ ] Check the crankcase breather

Every 8000 miles/12000 km
- [ ] Check the operation of the brake system
- [ ] Change the engine oil and filter*
- [ ] Check the final drive oil level

- [ ] Inspect the cooling system hoses
- [ ] Check/adjust throttle cable free play
- [ ] Check the operation of the clutch
- [ ] Lubricate the clutch and front brake lever pivots
- [ ] Lubricate the throttle cables
- [ ] Lubricate the shift/brake pedal pivots and the sidestand pivots
- [ ] Check the operation of the sidestand switch
- [ ] Check the steering for looseness or binding
- [ ] Check the front forks for proper operation and fluid leaks
- [ ] Check rear suspension operation and swingarm play
- [ ] Check the tires, wheels and wheel bearings
- [ ] Check the exhaust system for leaks and check the tightness of the fasteners
- [ ] Check the cleanliness of the fuel system and the condition of the fuel lines and vacuum hoses
- [ ] Inspect the secondary air induction system
- [ ] Check all nuts, bolts and other fasteners for tightness
- [ ] Check operation of the reverse system
- [ ] Check and adjust the headlight aim (see Chapter 9)

*The initial change should be at the first 4,000 miles or 6 months, then every 8000 miles/12,000 km or 12 months)

Every 12,000 miles/18,000 km
- [ ] Replace the air filter element
- [ ] Inspect the evaporative emission control system (California models)

Every 16,000 miles/24,000 km
- [ ] Replace the spark plugs

Every 24,000 miles/36,000 km
- [ ] Change the coolant
- [ ] Change the final drive oil

Every 32,000 miles/50,000 km
- [ ] Check the valve clearances

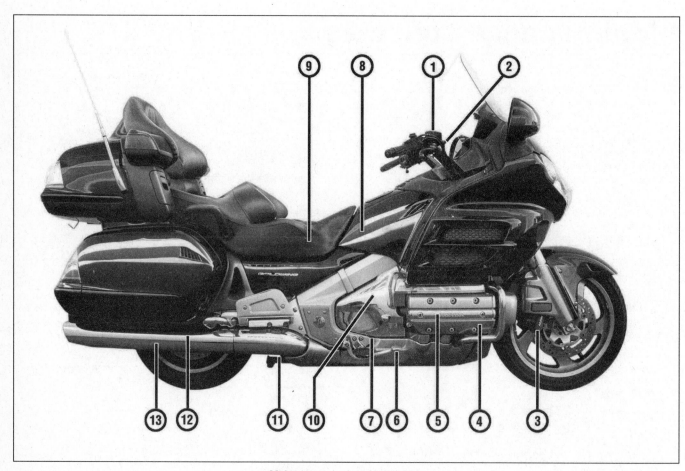

Maintenance points (right side)

1 Front brake lever and fluid level
2 Throttle cable adjuster (for minor adjustments)
3 Front brake pads (right caliper)
4 Spark plugs 1, 3 and 5 (beneath cover)
5 Valves (beneath cover)

6 Brake pedal
7 Engine oil dipstick (beneath cover)
8 Air filter (forward of the seat)
9 Fuel lines (beneath seat)
10 Rear brake master cylinder reservoir (beneath cover)

11 Coolant reservoir tank
12 Final drive oil filler and drain plugs (behind saddlebag)
13 Rear brake pads (behind saddlebag)

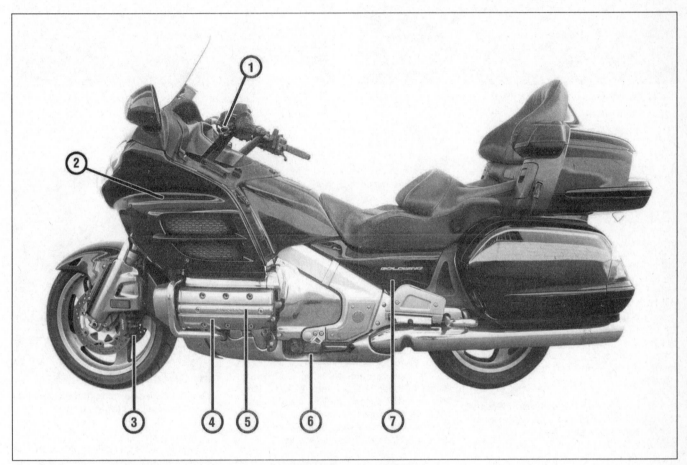

Maintenance points (left side)

1 Clutch lever
2 Throttle cable adjuster (for major
   adjustments; behind fairing)

3 Brake pads (left caliper)
4 Spark plugs 2, 4 and 6 (beneath cover)
5 Valves (beneath cover)

6 Sidestand
7 Battery (beneath cover)

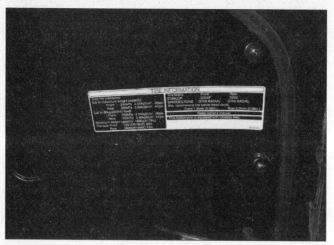

2.3a Maintenance information printed on decals includes tire pressure specifications . . .

2.3b . . . vacuum hose connections and tune-up data

2 Introduction to tune-up and routine maintenance

This Chapter covers in detail the checks and procedures necessary for the tune-up and routine maintenance of your motorcycle. Section 1 includes the routine maintenance schedule, which is designed to keep the machine in proper running condition and prevent possible problems. The remaining Sections contain detailed procedures for carrying out the items listed on the maintenance schedule, as well as additional maintenance information designed to increase reliability.

Since routine maintenance plays such an important role in the safe and efficient operation of your motorcycle, it is presented here as a comprehensive checklist. For riders who do all of their own maintenance, these lists outline the procedures and checks that should be done on a routine basis.

Maintenance information is printed on labels attached to the motorcycle (see illustrations). If the information on the labels differs from that included here, use the information on the label.

Deciding where to start or plug into the routine maintenance schedule depends on several factors. If you have a motorcycle whose warranty has recently expired, and if it has been maintained according to the warranty standards, you may want to pick up routine maintenance as it coincides with the next mileage or calendar interval. If you have owned the machine for some time but have never performed any maintenance on it, then you may want to start at the nearest interval and include some additional procedures to ensure that nothing important is overlooked. If you have just had a major engine overhaul, then you may want to start the maintenance routine from the beginning. If you have a used machine and have no knowledge of its history or maintenance record, you may desire to combine all the checks into one large service initially and then settle into the maintenance schedule prescribed.

The Sections which outline the inspection and maintenance procedures are written as step-by-step comprehensive guides to the performance of the work. They explain in detail each of the routine inspections and maintenance procedures on the check list. References to additional information in applicable Chapters is also included and should not be overlooked.

Before beginning any maintenance or repair, the machine should be cleaned thoroughly, especially around the oil filter, spark plugs, cylinder head covers, side covers, filler caps, etc. Cleaning will help ensure that dirt does not contaminate the engine and will allow you to detect wear and damage that could otherwise easily go unnoticed.

3 Fluid levels - check

1   Most of the fluid level checks on these motorcycles are included in *Daily (pre-ride)* checks at the front of this manual. In addition to the pre-ride checks, final drive oil level should be checked at the specified mileage intervals as described below.

⚠ **Warning: Be sure the exhaust system is cool before starting this procedure. You'll be working close to the right muffler and touching it may cause serious burns.**

Final drive oil level

2   Place the motorcycle on its center-stand. Clean any dirt from around the filler

3.2 Final drive filler plug (left arrow) and drain plug (right arrow)

plug, then unscrew the filler plug from the right side of the final drive (see illustration). Look or reach into the filler hole and note the oil level. It should be up to the bottom of the hole.

3   If the oil level is low, add oil of the type recommended in this Chapter's Specifications, using a funnel with a flexible tube if necessary.

4   Thread the filler plug into the hole and tighten it to the torque listed in this Chapter's Specifications.

4 Brake pads - wear check

1   The front and rear brake pads should be checked at the recommended intervals and replaced with new ones when worn beyond the limit listed in this Chapter's Specifications.

4.2a Look at the edges of the pads between the pad backing plate and brake disc (arrow) . . .

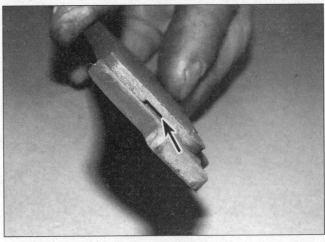

4.2b . . . if the friction material is worn so the groove (arrow) is exposed, it's time for new pads

2   To check the brake pads, look at them from the edges (see illustrations). There's a small gap between the edge of the friction material and the metal backing. If the friction material is worn near or all the way to the gap, the pads are worn excessively and must be replaced with new ones (see Chapter 7).

5 Crankcase breather - servicing

1   Remove the left engine cover (see Chapter 8).
2   Squeeze the clamp at the bottom of the drain tube and slide it up the tube (see illustration).
3   Pull the plug out of the tube and let any accumulated deposits drain out, then reinstall the plug and secure it with the clamp.

6 Brake system - general check

1   A routine general check of the brakes will ensure that any problems are discovered and remedied before the rider's safety is jeopardized.
2   Check the brake lever and pedal for loose connections, excessive play, bends, and other damage. Replace any damaged parts with new ones (see Chapter 7).
3   Make sure all brake fasteners are tight. Check the brake pads for wear (see Section 4) and make sure the fluid level in the reservoirs is correct (see Daily (pre-ride) checks at the front of this manual). Look for leaks at the hose connections and check for cracks in the hoses (see Chapter 7). If the lever or pedal is spongy, bleed the brakes as described in Chapter 7.

4   Make sure the brake light operates when the brake lever or pedal is depressed. The front and rear brake light switches are not adjustable. If the brake light doesn't come on, check the switch and replace it if necessary (see Chapter 9).

7 Engine oil/filter - change

1   Consistent routine oil and filter changes are the single most important maintenance procedure you can perform on a motorcycle. The oil not only lubricates the internal parts of the engine, transmission and clutch, but it also acts as a coolant, a cleaner, a sealant, and a protectant. Because of these demands, the oil takes a terrific amount of abuse and should be replaced often with new oil of the

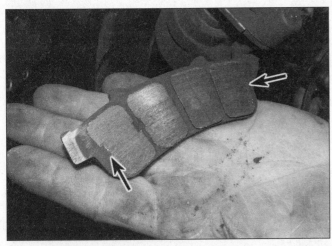

4.2c Check the pads at top and bottom - this pad wore unevenly, so the groove is exposed at one end (left arrow) while the other end still has friction material left (right arrow)

5.2 Squeeze the clamp (arrow) and slide it up the hose, then remove the plug and let any deposits drain from the hose

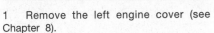

7.5a Unscrew the engine oil drain plug with a box wrench or socket - unscrew the oil filter (arrow) with a filter wrench

7.5b Taking care to avoid burns from the hot oil, remove the drain plug and sealing washer and let the oil drain into a pan

7.7 Apply a film of clean engine oil to the filter gasket

recommended grade and type. Saving a little money on the difference in cost between a good oil and a cheap oil won't pay off if the engine is damaged.

Caution: The oil should say on the label that it meets Japan Automobile Standards Organization (JASO) standard MA. Some automotive oils contain ant-friction additives that can cause motorcycle clutches to slip. Oil meeting JASO standard MA doesn't contain these additives.

2   Before changing the oil and filter, warm up the engine so the oil will drain easily. Be careful when draining the oil, as the exhaust pipes, the engine, and the oil itself can cause severe burns.

3   Place the bike on its centerstand. Remove the oil filler cap/dipstick to vent the crankcase and act as a reminder that there is no oil in the engine.

4   Remove the left engine cover and the lower front fairing panel (see Chapter 8).

5   Support the motorcycle securely over a clean drain pan. Remove the drain plug from the engine and allow the oil to drain into the pan **(see illustrations)**. Discard the sealing washer on the drain plug; it should be replaced whenever the plug is removed.

6   Unscrew the filter with a wrench or socket and a filter wrench (Honda tool no. 07HAA-PJ70100 or equivalent) **(see illustration 7.5a)**. Let the oil drain from the filter fitting.

HAYNES HiNT *As you loosen the drain plug, hold it against the engine. Once it's all the way loose, pull it away quickly so the oil won't run onto your hand.*

7   Apply a film of oil to the gasket on the new filter **(see illustration)**. Thread the filter onto the fitting and tighten it to the torque listed in this Chapter's Specifications.

8   Slip a new sealing washer over the oil drain plug, then install and tighten it to the torque listed in this Chapter's Specifications.

Avoid overtightening, as damage to the engine case will result.

9   Before refilling the engine, check the old oil carefully. If the oil was drained into a clean pan, small pieces of metal or other material can be easily detected. If the oil is very metallic colored, then the engine is experiencing wear from break-in (new engine) or from insufficient lubrication. If there are flakes or chips of metal in the oil, then something is drastically wrong internally and the engine will have to be disassembled for inspection and repair.

10   If there are pieces of fiber-like material in the oil, the clutch is experiencing excessive wear and should be checked.

11   If the inspection of the oil turns up nothing unusual, refill the crankcase to the proper level with the recommended oil and install the filler cap. Start the engine and let it idle for a few minutes (do not rev the engine). Shut it off, wait a few minutes, then check the oil level. If necessary, add more oil to bring the level up to the Maximum mark. Check around the drain plug and filter for leaks.

12   The old oil drained from the engine cannot be reused in its present state and should be disposed of. Check with your local refuse disposal company, disposal facility or environmental agency to see whether they will accept the used oil for recycling. Don't pour used oil into drains or onto the ground. After the oil has cooled, it can be drained into a suitable container (capped plastic jugs, topped bottles, milk cartons, etc.) for transport to one of these disposal sites.

8   Cooling system - inspection

⚠ *Warning: The engine must be cool before beginning this procedure.*

Note: *Refer to* Daily (pre-ride) checks *at the front of this manual and check the coolant level before performing this check.*

1   The entire cooling system should be checked carefully at the recommended intervals. Look for evidence of leaks, check the condition of the coolant, check the radiator for clogged fins and damage and make sure the fans operate when required.

2   Remove fairing panels as necessary for access to the cooling system components (see Chapter 8).

3   Examine each of the rubber coolant hoses along its entire length (see Chapter 3 for coolant hose details). Look for cracks, abrasions and other damage. Squeeze each hose at various points. They should feel firm, yet pliable, and return to their original shape when released. If they are dried out or hard, replace them with new ones.

4   Check for evidence of leaks at each cooling system joint. Tighten the hose clamps careful to prevent future leaks. If coolant has been leaking from the joints of steel or aluminum coolant tubes, remove the tubes and replace the O-rings (see Chapter 3).

5   Check the radiators for evidence of leaks and other damage. Leaks in the radiators leave telltale scale deposits or coolant stains on the outside of the core below the leak. If leaks are noted, remove the faulty radiator (see Chapter 3) and have it repaired by a radiator shop or replace it with a new one.

Caution: Do not use a liquid leak stopping compound to try to repair leaks.

6   Check the radiator fins for mud, dirt and insects, which may impede the flow of air through the radiator. If the fins are dirty, force water or low pressure compressed air through the fins from the backside. If the fins are bent or distorted, straighten them carefully with a screwdriver.

7   Remove the pressure cap **(see illustration)** by turning it counterclockwise (anticlockwise) until it reaches a stop. If you hear a hissing sound (indicating there is still pres-

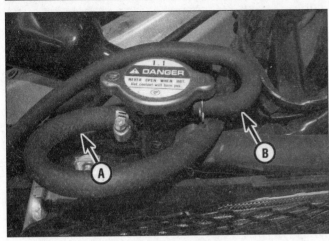

8.7a Radiator cap details

A   Siphon hose (to left radiator)
B   Overflow hose (to coolant reservoir)

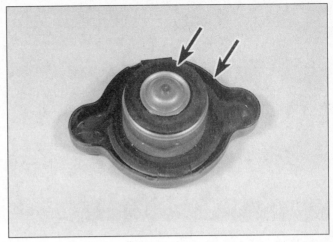

8.7b Inspect both cap gaskets (arrows)

sure in the system), wait until it stops. Now, press down on the cap with the palm of your hand and continue turning the cap counterclockwise (anti-clockwise) until it can be removed. Check the condition of the coolant in the system. If it is rust colored or if accumulations of scale are visible, drain, flush and refill the system with new coolant. Check the cap gaskets for cracks and other damage **(see illustration)**. Have the cap tested by a dealer service department or replace it with a new one. Install the cap by turning it clockwise until it reaches the first stop, then push down on the cap and continue turning until it can turn no further.

8   Check the antifreeze content of the coolant with an antifreeze hydrometer **(see illustration)**. Sometimes coolant may look like it's in good condition, but might be too weak to offer adequate protection. If the hydrometer indicates a weak mixture, drain,

flush and refill the cooling system (see Section 25).

9   Start the engine and let it reach normal operating temperature, then check for leaks again. As the coolant temperature increases, the fan should come on automatically and the temperature should begin to drop. If it doesn't, refer to Chapter 3 and check the fan and fan circuit carefully.

10   Remove the coolant reservoir (see Section 25) for access to the water pump bleed hole. The bleed hole itself can't be seen with the engine in the bike, but coolant leaking from it will run down the clutch cover **(see illustrations)**. If there is any, try to determine if the leak is simply the result of a loose hose clamp or deteriorated hose. Coolant dripping from the telltale hole behind the drain plug indicates a leaking mechanical seal; in this case the pump will have to be replaced with a new one (see Chapter 3).

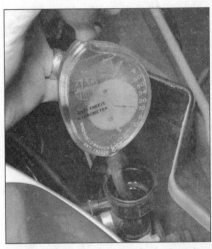

8.8 An antifreeze hydrometer is helpful in determining the condition of the coolant

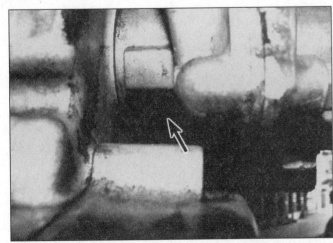

8.10a The weep hole in the bottom of the water pump (arrow) will leak coolant if the water pump seal is leaking . . .

8.10b . . . the weep hole may be impossible to see with the engine in the bike; look for coolant leakage in the general area (arrow) and down the back of the engine

9.2 Check throttle freeplay at the grip

9.3 Make minor throttle cable adjustments at the handlebar adjuster - loosen the locknut (left arrow) and turn the adjuster (right arrow)

11   If the coolant level is consistently low, and no evidence of leaks can be found, have the entire system pressure checked by a Honda dealer service department, motorcycle repair shop or service station.

9   Throttle operation and freeplay - check and adjustment

1   Make sure the throttle grip rotates easily from fully closed to fully open with the front wheel turned at various angles. The grip should return automatically from fully open to fully closed when released. If the throttle sticks, check the throttle cables for cracks or kinks in the housings. Also, make sure the inner cables are clean and well-lubricated.
2   Check for a small amount of freeplay at the grip and compare the freeplay to the value listed in this Chapter's Specifications **(see illustration)**. If adjustment is necessary, refer to the following Steps.

3   To make fine adjustments, loosen the locknut on the upper cable adjuster at the handlebar **(see illustration)**. Turn the adjuster until the desired freeplay is obtained, then retighten the locknut.
4   If major adjustment is necessary, use the lower adjuster **(see illustration)**. Refer to Chapter 8 and remove the center inner fairing panel for access. Loosen the locknut, turn the adjuster until the desired freeplay is obtained, then retighten the locknut.
5   Make sure the throttle releases all the way when the throttle grip is in the closed throttle position.

⚠️ *Warning: Turn the handlebars all the way through their travel with the engine idling. Idle speed should not change. If it does, the cables may be routed incorrectly. Correct this condition before riding the bike.*

10   Exhaust system - check

1   Periodically check all of the exhaust system joints for leaks and loose fasteners. The left and right engine covers will have to be removed to do this properly (see Chapter 8). If tightening the clamp bolts fails to stop any leaks, replace the gaskets with new ones (a procedure which requires disassembly of the system - see Chapter 4).
2   The exhaust pipe flange nuts at the cylinder heads are especially prone to loosening, which could cause damage to the head. Check them frequently and keep them tight.

11   Fuel system - check

⚠️ *Warning: Gasoline (petrol) is extremely flammable, so take extra precautions when you work on any part of the fuel system. Don't smoke or allow open flames or bare light bulbs near the work area, and don't work in a garage where a gas-type appliance (such as a water heater or clothes dryer) is present. If you spill any fuel on your skin, rinse it off immediately with soap and water. When you perform any kind of work on the fuel system, wear safety glasses and have a class B type fire extinguisher on hand.*

1   For access to the fuel lines, remove the air cleaner housing (see Chapter 4). Check the fuel tank, the lines and the throttle body for leaks and evidence of damage **(see illustration)**.
2   If the fuel lines are cracked or otherwise deteriorated, replace them with new ones.

9.4 Make major throttle cable adjustments at the mid-cable adjuster - loosen the locknut (right arrow) and turn the adjuster (left arrow)

11.1 Check the fuel lines (arrows) for cracks or deterioration

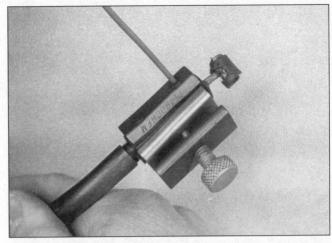

15.1 Make sure the sidestand spring is securely attached and in good condition

16.3 Lubricating a cable with a pressure lube adapter (make sure the tool seats around the inner cable)

3   If you plan to check the secondary air system (see Section 12), leave the air cleaner housing off for now. If not, reinstall it (see Chapter 4).

12 Secondary air system - inspection

1   If you haven't already done so, remove the air cleaner housing (see Chapter 4).
2   Remove the lower front fairing panel (see Chapter 8).
3   Using an inspection mirror where necessary, check the rubber hoses that connect the metal lines, check valves and control valve. Refer to Chapter 4 for complete details of the system.

13 Clutch - check and adjustment

1   The hydraulic clutch release mechanism eliminates the need for freeplay adjustment. No means of manual adjustment is provided.
2   Check the fluid level (see *Daily (pre-ride) checks* at the front of this manual). Check for fluid leaks around the master cylinder on the left handlebar. Pull back the rubber cover and inspect the fluid line connection, then follow the fluid line to the release cylinder on the rear of the engine. If leaks are found, refer to Chapter 2 for repair procedures.
3   Start the bike, release the clutch and ride off, noting the position of the clutch lever when the clutch begins to engage. If it's too close to the handlebar, there may be air in the clutch fluid (the air compresses, rather than transmitting lever force to the release mechanism). Refer to Chapter 2 and bleed the system.

14 Reverse system operation - check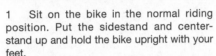

1   Sit on the bike in the normal riding position. Put the sidestand and center-stand up and hold the bike upright with your feet.
2   With the transmission in neutral, start the engine.
3   Operate the reverse switch. The reverse indicator should come on and the neutral indicator lamp should go out.
4   Make sure there's room behind the bike, then operate the starter and make sure the bike moves in reverse.
5   If the system doesn't work properly, see Chapter 9 for electrical component inspection and Chapter 2 for mechanical component inspection.

15 Sidestand - check

1   With the bike on its centerstand, raise and lower the sidestand **(see illustration)**. Check that the spring keeps it securely in the raised and lowered positions.
2   Check the centerstand in the same way as the sidestand (see Chapter 8 for details).
3   Sit on the bike in the normal riding position with the sidestand up. With the transmission in neutral, start the engine. Pull in the clutch and shift the transmission into first gear.
4   With the engine running, lower the sidestand. The engine should shut off. If not, refer to Chapter 9 and check the sidestand switch.
5   Refer to Section 16 and lubricate the sidestand and centerstand pivots.

16 Lubrication - general

1   Since the controls, cables and various other components of a motorcycle are exposed to the elements, they should be lubricated periodically to ensure safe and trouble-free operation.
2   The footpegs, clutch and brake levers, brake pedal, shift lever and sidestand pivots should be lubricated frequently. In order for the lubricant to be applied where it will do the most good, the component should be disassembled. However, if chain and cable lubricant is being used, it can be applied to the pivot joint gaps and will usually work its way into the areas where friction occurs. If motor oil or light grease is being used, apply it sparingly as it may attract dirt (which could cause the controls to bind or wear at an accelerated rate). **Note:** *One of the best lubricants for the control lever pivots is a dry-film lubricant (available from many sources by different names).*
3   To lubricate the throttle cables, disconnect the cable(s) at the lower end, then lubricate the cable with a pressure lube adapter **(see illustration)**.
4   Refer to Chapter 7 for the swingarm needle bearing lubrication procedures.

17 Tires/wheels - general check

1   Routine tire and wheel checks should be made with the realization that your safety depends to a great extent on their condition.
2   Check the tires carefully for cuts, tears, embedded nails or other sharp objects and excessive wear. Operation of the motorcycle

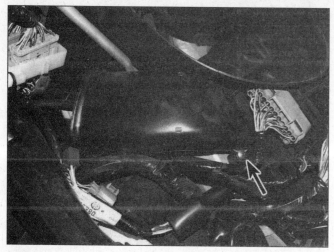

22.3a Remove the screw (arrow) and take off the left air duct

22.3b Remove the screw (arrow) and take off the right air duct

with excessively worn tires is extremely hazardous, as traction and handling are directly affected. Measure the tread depth at the center of the tire and replace worn tires with new ones when the tread depth is less than specified (see *Daily (pre-ride) checks* at the front of this manual).

3 Repair or replace punctured tires as soon as damage is noted. Do not try to patch a torn tire, as wheel balance and tire reliability may be impaired.

4 Check the tire pressures when the tires are cold and keep them properly inflated, referring to *Daily (pre-ride) checks* at the front of this manual. Proper air pressure will increase tire life and provide maximum stability and ride comfort. Keep in mind that low tire pressures may cause the tire to slip on the rim or come off, while high tire pressures will cause abnormal tread wear and unsafe handling.

5 The cast wheels used on this machine are virtually maintenance free, but they should be kept clean and checked periodically for cracks and other damage. Never attempt to repair damaged cast wheels; they must be replaced with new ones.

6 Check the valve stem locknuts to make sure they are tight. Also, make sure the valve stem cap is in place and tight. If it is missing, install a new one made of metal or hard plastic.

Caution: On 2009 and later models, which are equipped with a tire pressure monitoring system, be careful not to damage the tire pressure sensors built into the valve stems.

18 Steering head bearings - check

1 This vehicle is equipped with tapered roller type steering head bearings which can become dented, rough or loose during normal use of the machine. In extreme cases,

worn or loose steering head bearings can cause steering wobble that is potentially dangerous.

2 To check the bearings, support the motorcycle securely and block the machine so the front wheel is in the air.

3 Point the wheel straight ahead and slowly move the handlebars from side-to-side. Dents or roughness in the bearing races will be felt and the bars will not move smoothly.

4 Next, grasp the wheel and try to move it forward and backward. Any looseness in the steering head bearings will be felt as front-to-rear movement of the fork legs. If play is felt in the bearings, they should be adjusted, which is not a simple procedure on these models. Refer to Chapter 6 for details.

19 Suspension - check

1 The suspension components must be maintained in top operating condition to ensure rider safety. Loose, worn or damaged suspension parts decrease the vehicle's stability and control.

2 While standing alongside the motorcycle, lock the front brake and push on the handlebars to compress the forks several times. See if they move up-and-down smoothly without binding. If binding is felt, the forks should be disassembled and inspected as described in Chapter 7.

3 Carefully inspect the area around the fork seals for any signs of fork oil leakage. If leakage is evident, the seals must be replaced as described in Chapter 6.

4 Check the tightness of all suspension nuts and bolts to be sure none have worked loose.

5 Inspect the rear shock for fluid leakage and tightness of the mounting nuts. If leakage is found, the shock should be replaced.

6 Support the bike securely so it can't be

knocked over during this procedure. Grab the swingarm on each side, just ahead of the axle. Rock the swingarm from side to side - there should be no discernible movement at the rear. If there's a little movement or a slight clicking can be heard, make sure the pivot shaft nuts are tight. If the pivot nuts are tight but movement is still noticeable, the swingarm will have to be removed and the bearings replaced as described in Chapter 6.

7 Inspect the tightness of the rear suspension nuts and bolts.

20 Fasteners - check

1 Since vibration of the machine tends to loosen fasteners, all nuts, bolts, screws, etc. should be periodically checked for proper tightness.

2 Pay particular attention to the following:
   Spark plugs
   Engine oil drain plug
   Oil filter
   Gearshift lever
   Footpegs, sidestand and centerstand
   Engine mount bolts
   Exhaust system mounts
   Shock absorber mount bolts
   Rear suspension linkage bolts
   Front axle and clamp bolt
   Rear wheel nuts

3 If a torque wrench is available, use it along with the torque specifications at the beginning of this, or other, Chapters.

21 Headlight aim - check and adjustment

The headlight aim should be adjusted periodically so it conforms with local regu-

22.5 Move the ECM and cruise actuator to the left and tie them out of the way

22.7 Remove the air cleaner cover screws (arrow) and lift the cover off

lations, for the safety of the rider as well as oncoming drivers. For detailed adjustment procedures, refer to Chapter 9.

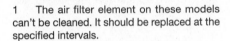

22 Air filter element - replacement

1   The air filter element on these models can't be cleaned. It should be replaced at the specified intervals.

Non-airbag models
2   Remove the fuel tank top cover inner covers for access to the air cleaner housing (see Chapter 8).
3   Remove both air ducts **(see illustrations)**.

2001 through 2005
4   Disconnect the wiring connectors for the ignition switch and intake air tempera-ture sensor (see Chapters 9 and 4). Free the cruise actuator wiring harness from its zip tie and retainer.
5   Remove the engine control module attaching screws, then lift off the ECM and cruise actuator as a unit. Move them to the left side of the motorcycle and support them out of the way with a zip tie or string wrapped around the frame **(see illustration)**.

2006 and later
6   Remove the BARO sensor (see Chap-ter 4). Free the wiring harnesses from their retainers and unplug the cruise actuator wir-ing harness and IAT sensor connectors. Take the engine control module and ABS con-trol module out of their holder, then unbolt the holder and move it off of the air cleaner cover.

All non-airbag models
7   Remove the air cleaner cover screws **(see illustration)**. Lift the cover off.
8   Lift out the filter element **(see illustra-tion)** and clean the inside of the filter hous-ing.
9   Install the new filter element by revers-ing the removal procedure. Make sure the element is seated properly in the filter hous-ing, with its TOP mark upward, before install-ing the cover **(see illustration)**.
10   Uncap the air cleaner housing drain hose **(see illustration 5.2)**. Let any deposits in the hose drain into a container, then rein-stall the cap.
11   Install all components removed for access.

Airbag models

⚠ *Warning: This procedure requires working near airbag system components. Before starting, read the airbag precautions in Chapter 9.*

12   Remove the engine control module (see Chapter 4).

22.8 Lift the air filter out of the housing

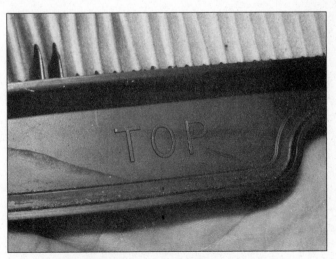

22.9 Install the filter with the TOP mark upward

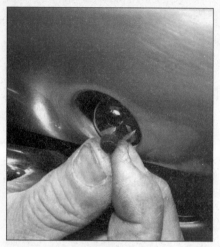

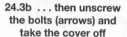
24.3b . . . then unscrew the bolts (arrows) and take the cover off

24.3a Remove the rubber plugs from the Allen bolts . . .

13 Remove the audio unit (see Chapter 9).

14 Unplug the ignition switch electrical connector (see Chapter 9).

15 Without disconnecting any airbag system electrical connectors, unbolt the airbag electronic control unit and set it aside. The airbag ECU can be identified by its bright yellow wiring connectors. Once it's unbolted, don't let the ECU hang by the wiring harness.

16 Unbolt the cruise control actuator and set it out of the way.

17 Remove the trim clip that secures the right air duct and take the duct out.

18 Unplug the wiring connector for the intake air temperature sensor (see Chapter 4).

19 Remove the air cleaner cover screws (see illustration 22.7). Move the wiring harnesses out of the way, lift the cover off and slide it to the left to remove it.

20 Complete the procedure by performing Steps 8 through 11 above.

23 Evaporative emission control system (California models) - check

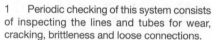

1 Periodic checking of this system consists of inspecting the lines and tubes for wear, cracking, brittleness and loose connections.

2 For access, remove the lower front fairing panel and air cleaner housing (see Chapters 8 and 4).

3 Check the lines and tubes as described in Step 1 and check the canister for obvious damage such as cracks. For further details of the system refer to Chapter 4.

24 Spark plugs - replacement

1 Make sure your spark plug socket is the correct size before attempting to remove the plugs.

2 Remove both engine covers (left and right) for access to the plugs (see Chapter 8).

3 Remove the cylinder head side covers (see illustrations).

4 Disconnect the spark plug caps from the spark plugs - if they're stuck, twist them carefully to break them free from the plugs (see illustrations). If available, use compressed air to blow any accumulated debris from around the spark plugs. Unscrew the plugs with a spark plug socket (see illustration).

5 Inspect the electrodes for wear. Both the center and side electrodes should have square edges and the side electrode should be of uniform thickness. Look for excessive deposits and evidence of a cracked or chipped insulator around the center electrode. Compare your spark plugs to the color spark plug reading chart to check for problems such as oil burning, which would indicate engine wear. Check the threads, the washer and the ceramic insulator body for cracks and other damage.

6 Before installing new plugs, make sure they are the correct type and heat range. Check the gap between the electrodes, as they are not preset. For best results, use a wire-type gauge rather than a flat gauge to

24.4a Here's the left side spark plug wire routing

24.4b Here's the right side spark plug wire routing

24.4c Twist the boot to free it and pull it off the spark plug - don't pull on the wire

24.4d Unscrew the plug with a spark plug socket, then remove the plug and washer

check the gap **(see illustration)**. If the gap must be adjusted, bend the side electrode only and be very careful not to chip or crack the insulator nose **(see illustration)**. Make sure the washer is in place before installing each plug.

7   Since the cylinder head is made of aluminum, which is soft and easily damaged, thread the plugs into the heads by hand.

HAYNES HiNT *Since the spark plugs are recessed, slip a short length of hose over the end of the plug to use as a tool to thread it into place. The hose will grip the plug well enough to turn it, but will start to slip if the plug begins to cross-thread in the hole - this will prevent damaged threads and the accompanying repair costs.*

8   Once the plugs are finger-tight, the job can be finished with a socket. If a torque wrench is available, tighten the spark plugs to the torque listed in this Chapter's Specifi-

cations. If you do not have a torque wrench, tighten the plugs finger-tight (until the washers bottom on the cylinder head) then use a wrench to tighten them an additional 1/4 turn. Regardless of the method used, do not over-tighten them.

9   Reconnect the spark plug caps and reinstall all removed components.

25 Cooling system - draining, flushing and refilling

⚠ *Warning: Allow the engine to cool completely before performing this maintenance operation. Also, don't allow antifreeze to come into contact with your skin or painted surfaces of the motorcycle. Rinse off spills immediately with plenty of water. Antifreeze is highly toxic if ingested. Never leave antifreeze*

lying around in an open container or in puddles on the floor; children and pets are attracted by its sweet smell and may drink it. Check with local authorities about disposing of used antifreeze. Many communities have collection centers which will see that antifreeze is disposed of safely. Antifreeze is also combustible, so don't store or use it near open flames.

Draining

1   Park the bike upright on a level surface and secure it so it can't fall over during this procedure.

2   Refer to Chapter 8 and remove the left engine cover and front lower fairing panel. If you're working on a non-airbag model, remove the right fairing pocket. If you're working on an airbag model, remove the right upper panel switch unit.

3   Place a large, clean drain pan under the drain fitting in the coolant hose forward of the engine **(see illustration)**.

24.6a Spark plug manufacturers recommend using a wire type gauge when checking thegap - if the wire doesn't slide between the electrodes with a slight drag, adjustment is required

24.6b To change the gap, bend the side electrode only, as indicated by the arrows, and be very careful not to crack or chip the ceramic insulator surrounding the center electrode

25.3 Unscrew the drain bolt from the fitting under the front of the engine (arrow)

25.4 Remove the drain bolt and sealing washer and let the coolant drain into a container

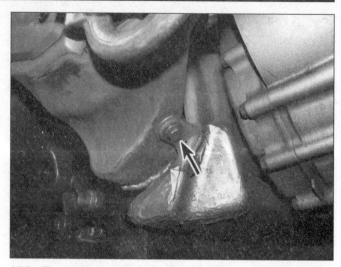

25.5a The coolant reservoir is under the bike, behind the engine - remove the reservoir bolt (arrow)

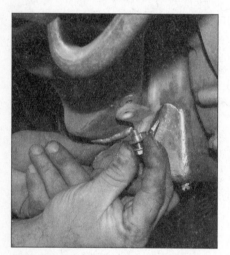

25.5b Be sure the collar is in position when you install the bolt

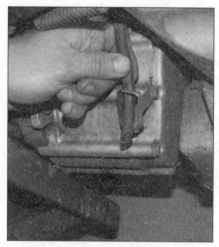

25.5c Pull the breather hose out of the retainer

4   Remove the drain bolt from the fitting and allow the coolant to drain into the pan **(see illustration)**. After removing the drain bolt, remove the pressure cap from the hose fitting above the right radiator to ensure that all of the coolant can drain **(see illustration 8.7a)**. **Note:** *The coolant will rush out with considerable force as soon as the cap is removed, so position the drain pan accordingly.*

5   Unbolt the coolant reservoir **(see illustrations)**. Slip its breather hose out of the retainer **(see illustration)** and slide the tank to the right. Release the clamp, disconnect the siphon hose and remove the reservoir from the motorcycle.

6   Remove the reservoir cap, empty the coolant and wash the reservoir out with water.

25.5d Pull the coolant bottle to the right, disengaging the post molded into the bottle from the recess in the frame near the sidestand spring

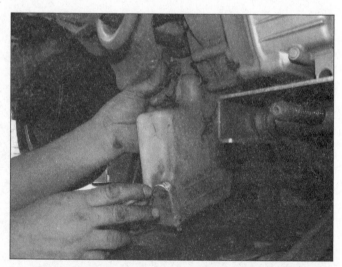

25.5e Remove the reservoir to the right side of the bike, disconnecting the breather hose as you do so

Flushing

7   Flush the system with clean tap water by inserting a garden hose in the radiator filler neck. Allow the water to run through the system until it is clear when it exits the drain bolt holes. If the radiator is extremely corroded, remove both of them (see Chapter 3) and have them cleaned at a radiator shop.

Refilling

8   Check the drain bolt gasket. Replace it with a new one if necessary.
9   Clean the drain hole, then install the drain bolt and tighten it securely, but don't overtighten it and strip the threads.
10   Fill the system with the proper coolant mixture (see this Chapter's Specifications). When the system is full (all the way up to the top of the radiator cap filler neck), start the engine. Let it idle for two to three minutes, then rev the engine three or four times to bleed out any air that remains in the system. Shut the engine off.
11   Fill the system with coolant to the top of the filler neck, then install the radiator cap.
12   Allow the engine to cool, then check the coolant level in the reservoir (see *Daily (pre-ride) checks* at the front of this manual). If the coolant level is low, add the specified mixture until it reaches the Full mark in the reservoir.
13   Check the system for leaks.
14   Do not dispose of the old coolant by pouring it down a drain. Instead, pour it into a heavy plastic container, cap it tightly and take it to an authorized disposal site or a service station.

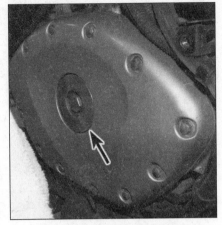

27.4a Unscrew the timing hole plug (arrow) . . .

27.4b . . . and check the condition of the O-ring (arrow)

2   Remove the filler plug, then the drain plug and let the oil drain into the pan for 10 minutes or more.
3   Reinstall the drain plug and tighten it to the torque listed in this Chapter's Specifications.
4   Add oil of the type and amount listed in this Chapter's Specifications. **Note:** *The specified capacity is approximate. Fill the final drive until the oil is at the bottom of the filler hole.*
5   Install the filler plug and tighten it to the torque listed in this Chapter's Specifications.

---

27 Valve clearances - check and adjustment

Note: *Retracting the timing chain tensioners is essential for checking the valve clearances, and requires a special tool, which can be purchased or made from a piece of metal. Read the timing chain tensioner procedure in Chapter 2 before starting this procedure.*

Check

1   Remove the left and right engine covers (see Chapter 8).
2   Remove the cylinder head side covers and disconnect the spark plug wires from the plugs (see Section 24).
3   Remove the cylinder head covers and retract the timing chain tensioners (see Chapter 2).
4   Unscrew the cap from the timing hole in the front of the engine **(see illustrations)**.
5   Look into the timing hole and locate the 1.2TF mark on the crankshaft position sensor's timing rotor **(see illustrations)**. Use a socket and ratchet to rotate the crankshaft counterclockwise until the "1.2TF" mark aligns with the mark in the timing cover. At this point, the camshaft lobes for No. 1 cylinder (at the right front corner of the engine) should point outward (away from the engine) **(see illustration 27.6a)**. If they don't, rotate the crankshaft one full turn counterclockwise, then recheck the cam lobe position again. **Note:** *Cylinders on the right side of the engine are numbered 1-3-5, starting from the front of the engine. Cylinders on the left side of the engine are numbered 2-4-6, starting from the front of the engine.*
6   Measure the valve clearances for no. 1 cylinder (at the right front corner of the

---

26 Final drive - oil change

1   Place the bike on its centerstand and place a drain pan beneath the final drive **(see illustration 3.2)**.

27.5a The timing mark on the engine front cover (arrow) . . .

27.5b . . . is aligned with the marks on the timing rotor inside the cover (cover removed for clarity)

A   *Timing mark, cylinders 1 and 2*
B   *Timing mark, cylinders 3 and 4*
C   *Timing mark, cylinders 5 and 6*

27.6a With the cam lobes pointing away from the engine, measure clearance between the cam lobe and lifter with a feeler gauge . . .

27.6b . . . all but the rearmost lobes are behind the cam bearing caps, so you'll need to insert the feeler gauge from the top (arrow)

engine) with a feeler gauge of the thickness listed in this Chapter's Specifications **(see illustrations)**. Slip the feeler gauge between the camshaft and lifter, then pull the feeler gauge out slowly - you should feel a slight drag. If there's no drag, the clearance is too loose. If there's a heavy drag, the clearance is too tight. **Note:** *The intake and exhaust valve positions are cast into the camshaft covers* **(see illustration 27.6b)**.

7   If the clearance is too loose, try measuring with thicker feeler gauges. If it's too tight, try measuring with thinner feeler gauges. Once you've found the feeler gauge that pulls out with a light drag, write its thickness down. This is the actual valve clearance.

8   Repeat the procedure on the remaining valve for no. 1 cylinder and write the reading down.

9   Cylinder no. 4 - Measure the no. 4 cylinder valve clearances. Turn the crankshaft counterclockwise 1/3 turn, until the "3.4TF" mark aligns with the index mark on the timing cover **(see illustrations 27.5a and 27.5b)**. Go over to the other side of the engine and measure the clearances of the valves on no. 4 cylinder (center cylinder on the left side), using the method described in Steps 6 through 8. Again, write the measurements down.

10   Cylinder no. 5 - Turn the crankshaft counterclockwise another 1/3 turn, until the "5.6TF" mark aligns with the index mark on the timing cover. Go over to the other side of the engine and measure the clearances of the valves on no. 5 cylinder, using the method described in Steps 6 through 8. Again, write the measurements down.

11   Cylinder no. 2 - Turn the crankshaft counterclockwise another 1/3 turn, until the "1.2TF" mark aligns with the index mark on the timing cover. Go over to the other side of the engine and measure the clearances of the valves on no. 2 cylinder, using the method described in Steps 6 through 8. Again, write the measurements down.

12   Cylinder no. 3 - Turn the crankshaft counterclockwise another 1/3 turn, until the

"3.4TF" mark aligns with the index mark on the timing cover. Go over to the other side of the engine and measure the clearances of the valves on no. 3 cylinder, using the method described in Steps 6 through 8. Again, write the measurements down.

13   Cylinder no. 6 - Turn the crankshaft counterclockwise another 1/3 turn, until the "5.6TF" mark aligns with the index mark on the timing cover. Go over to the other side of the engine and measure the clearances of the valves on no. 6 cylinder, using the method described in Steps 6 through 8. Again, write the measurements down.

14   If all of the clearances were within the ranges listed in this Chapter's Specifications, no adjustment is necessary. If any were out of the specified range, adjust as described in the following Steps.

Adjustment

Note: *You'll need an accurate micrometer for this procedure.*

15   Remove the camshaft(s), then remove the valve lifters and shims from any valves that need to be adjusted (see Chapter 2).

16   The shim size may be marked on one face of the shim, but the shim should be checked with a micrometer to see that it hasn't worn. If the shim has worn undersize, use the actual measured shim thickness, not the marked thickness, when calculating the valve clearance.

17   The new shim thickness can be calculated as follows - always try to get the clearance at the mid-point of the specified range.

18   If the valve clearance is less than specified, subtract the measured valve clearance (measured in Steps 7 through 13 above) from the specified clearance (listed in this Chapter's Specifications). Deduct the result of this calculation from the original shim thickness. For example:

Sample calculation - intake valve clearance too small

Specified clearance: 0.15 mm +/-
0.2 mm (0.006 +/- 0.001 inch)
Measured clearance: 0.08 mm
Difference: 0.07 mm
Thickness of existing shim: 2.575 mm

Correct shim thickness required is:
2.575 minus 0.07 = 2.505 mm.

19   If the valve clearance is greater than specified, subtract the specified valve clearance (measured in Steps 7 through 13 above) from the measured clearance (listed in this Chapter's Specifications). Add the result of this calculation to the original shim thickness. For example:

Sample calculation - exhaust valve clearance too large

Specified clearance: 0.22 mm +/-
0.3 mm (0.009 +/- 0.001 inch)
Measured clearance: 0.27 mm
Difference: 0.05 mm
Thickness of existing shim: 2.565 mm
Correct shim thickness required is:
2.565 plus 0.05 = 2.570 mm.

20   Obtain the correct thickness shim(s) from a Honda dealer. Where the required thickness is not exactly equal to an available shim thickness, round off the measurement to the nearest available size. Shims are available in 0.025 mm increments, with available thicknesses from 1.200 to 1.280 mm. **Note:** *If the required replacement shim thickness is greater than 1.280 mm (the thickest available), the valve is probably not seating correctly due to a build-up of carbon deposits or valve damage. Remove the cylinder head to check the valve (see Chapter 2).*

21   Lubricate the new shim with clean engine oil or molybdenum disulfide oil (a 50/50 mixture of molybdenum disulfide grease and engine oil) and install it in its recess in top of the valve (see Chapter 2). Check that the shim is correctly seated, then lubricate the lifter with engine oil or molybdenum disulfide oil and install it over the valve. Repeat the procedure for the other valves as required, then install the camshafts (see Chapter 2).

22   With the bike on its centerstand and the transmission in gear, rotate the rear wheel several turns to seat the new shim(s), then check the clearances again.

23   Once the clearances are correct, install the valve cover (see Chapter 2) and spark plugs (see Section 24).

Service record

Date	Mileage	Work performed

Service record

Date	Mileage	Work performed

Chapter 2
Engine, clutch and transmission

Contents

Degrees of difficulty

Easy, suitable for novice with little experience	**Fairly easy,** suitable for beginner with some experience	**Fairly difficult,** suitable for competent DIY mechanic	**Difficult,** suitable for experienced DIY mechanic 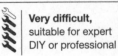	**Very difficult,** suitable for expert DIY or professional

Specifications

Cylinder compression
Standard (at 300 rpm) .... 183 kPa (201 psi)
Limit.. Not specified

Camshafts
Journal inside diameter
   Standard .... 28.000 to 28.021 mm (1.1024 to 1.1032 inches)
   Limit .... 28.05 mm (1.104 inches)

Camshafts (continued)

Journal outside diameter
    Standard .... 27.96 to 27.980 mm (1.101 to 1.1016 inches)
    Limit .... 27.959 mm (1.1007 inches)
Lobe height
    Intake
        Standard .... 41.610 to 41.690 mm (1.6382 to 1.6413 inches)
        Limit... 41.58 mm (1.637 inches)
    Exhaust
        Standard .... 41.680 to 41.760 mm (1.6409 to 1.6441 inches)
        Limit... 41.65 mm (1.640 inches)
Oil clearance
    Standard .... 0.020 to 0.062 mm (0.0008 to 0.0024 inch)
    Limit .... 0.10 mm (0.004 inch)

Lifters

Diameter
    Standard .... 28.978 to 28.993 mm (1.141 to 1.1415 inches)
    Limit .... 28.97 mm (1.1409 inches)

Cylinder head, valves and valve springs

Cylinder head warpage limit.. 0.10 mm (0.004 inch)
Valve stem bend limit .... Not specified
Valve stem diameter
    Standard
        Intake... 4.970 to 4.995 mm (0.1957 to 0.1967 inch)
        Exhaust.. 4.955 to 4.980 mm (0.1951 to 0.1961 inch)
    Limit
        Intake... 4.96 mm (0.195 inch)
        Exhaust.. 4.95 mm (0.195 inch)
Valve guide inside diameter (intake and exhaust)
    Standard .... 5.000 to 5.012 mm (0.1969 to 0.1973 inch)
    Limit .... 5.04 mm (0.198 inch)
Stem-to-guide clearance
    Intake
        Standard .... 0.005 to 0.042 mm (0.0002 to 0.0017 inch)
        Limit... 0.075 mm (0.003 inch)
    Exhaust
        Standard .... 0.020 to 0.057 mm (0.0008 to 0.0022 inch)
        Limit... 0.85 mm (0.0033 inch)
Valve guide protrusion above cylinder head (intake and exhaust) .... 11.8 to 12.0 mm (0.46 to 0.47 inch)
Valve seat width (intake and exhaust) .... 0.9 to 1.1 mm (0.035 to 0.043 inch)
Valve face width (intake and exhaust) .... Not specified
Valve spring free length (intake and exhaust)
    Standard .... 38.2 mm (1.504 inches)
    Minimum .... 37.0 mm (1.46 inches)
Valve spring bend limit .... Not specified

Cylinders

Bore diameter
    Standard .... 74.010 to 74.015 mm (2.9134 to 2.9140 inches)
    Maximum .... 74.1 mm (2.917 inches)
    Bore measuring point... Top, center and bottom of cylinder
Out-of-round limit.. 0.10 mm (0.004 inch)
Taper limit .... 0.10 mm (0.004 inch)
Surface warp limit... 0.05 mm (0.002 inch)

Pistons

Piston diameter
    Standard .... 73.970 to 73.990 mm (2.9122 to 2.9130 inches)
    Limit .... 73.85 mm (2.907 inches)
Diameter measuring point .... 10 mm (0.4 inch) from bottom of skirt
Piston-to-cylinder clearance
    Standard .... 0.010 to 0.045 mm (0.0004 to 0.0018 inch)
    Maximum .... 0.10 mm (0.004 inch)

Ring side clearance
Top ring
  Standard.. 0.025 to 0.055 mm (0.0010 to 0.0022 inch)
  Maximum... 0.10 mm (0.004 inch)
Second ring
  Standard.. 0.015 to 0.045 mm (0.0006 to 0.0018 inch)
  Maximum... 0.10 mm (0.004 inch)
Oil ring... Not specified
Ring end gap
Top ring... 0.15 to 0.30 mm (0.006 to 0.012 inch)
Second ring... 0.30 to 0.45 mm (0.012 to 0.018 inch)
Oil ring side rails.. 0.20 to 0.70 mm (0.008 to 0.028 inch)

Reverse mechanism
Reverse stopper shaft installed height................................. 6.7 to 7.3 mm (0.26 to 0.29 inch)

Primary gears
Primary driven gear boss needle bearing installed height ...... 3.5 to 4.0 mm (0.14 to 0.16 inch)

Output shaft
Shaft diameter limit .... 21.99 mm (0.866 inch)
Gear bushing inside diameter limit...................................... 22.05 mm (0.868 inch)
Gear bushing outside diameter limit.................................... 25.95 mm (1.022 inches)
Driven gear inside diameter limit... 26.03 mm (1.025 inches)

Crankshaft, connecting rods and bearings
Main bearing oil clearance
Journals 1 and 4
  Standard.. 0.012 to 0.030 mm (0.0005 to 0.0012 inch)
  Maximum... 0.06 mm (0.002 inch)
Journals 2 and 3
  Standard.. 0.020 to 0.038 mm (0.0008 to 0.0015 inch)
  Maximum... 0.06 mm (0.002 inch)
Connecting rod side clearance
  Standard.. 0.15 to 0.30 mm (0.006 to 0.012 inch)
  Maximum... 0.40 mm (0.016 inch)
Connecting rod bearing oil clearance
  Standard.. 0.028 to 0.046 mm (0.0011 to 0.0018 inch)
  Maximum... 0.06 mm (0.002 inch)
Crankshaft runout limit... 0.03 mm (0.001 inch)
Crankshaft journal taper limit... 0.003 mm (0.0001 inch)
Crankshaft journal out-of-round limit................................... 0.005 mm (0.0002 inch)
Connecting rod bearing selection
If connecting rod ID number is I or 1
  With crankshaft journal ID letter A................................... Yellow
  With crankshaft journal ID letter B................................... Green
  With crankshaft journal ID letter C................................... Brown
If connecting rod ID number is II or 2
  With crankshaft journal ID letter A................................... Green
  With crankshaft journal ID letter B................................... Brown
  With crankshaft journal ID letter C................................... Black
If connecting rod ID number is III or 3
  With crankshaft journal ID letter A................................... Brown
  With crankshaft journal ID letter B................................... Black
  With crankshaft journal ID letter C................................... Blue
Main bearing selection
If crankcase ID letter is A
  With crankshaft journal ID number 1 .... Yellow
  With crankshaft journal ID number 2 .... Green
  With crankshaft journal ID number 3 .... Brown
If crankcase ID letter is B
  With crankshaft journal ID number 1 .... Green
  With crankshaft journal ID number 2 .... Brown
  With crankshaft journal ID number 3 .... Black
If crankcase ID letter is C
  With crankshaft journal ID number 1 .... Brown
  With crankshaft journal ID number 2 .... Black
  With crankshaft journal ID number 3 .... Blue

Oil pump

Inner to outer rotor clearance
    Standard .... Less than 0.15 mm (0.006 inch)
    Limit .... 0.20 mm (0.008 inch)
Outer rotor to housing clearance
    Scavenge rotor
        Standard .... 0.15 to 0.22 mm (0.006 to 0.009 inch)
        Limit... 0.35 mm (0.014 inch)
    Feed rotor
        Standard .... 0.15 to 0.21 mm (0.006 to 0.008 inch)
        Limit... 0.35 mm (0.014 inch)
Rotor to straightedge clearance
    Standard .... 0.02 to 0.09 mm (0.001 to 0.004 inch)
    Limit .... 0.12 mm (0.005 inch)

Clutch

Friction plate thickness
    Standard .... 3.72 to 3.88 mm (0.146 to 0.153 inch)
    Minimum .... 3.5 mm (0.14 inch)
Steel plate warpage limit.. 0.30 mm (0.012 inch)
Diaphragm (clutch) spring height
    Standard .... 4.8 mm (0.11 inch)
    Minimum .... 4.6 mm (0.18 inch)
Lifter spring height
    Standard .... 2.9 mm (0.11 inch)
    Minimum .... 2.5 mm (0.10 inch)
Master cylinder bore diameter
    Standard .... 14.000 to 14.043 mm (0.5512 to 0.5529 inch)
    Limit .... 14.055 mm (0.5553 inch)
Master cylinder piston diameter
    Standard .... 13.957 to 13.984 mm (0.5495 to 0.5506 inch)
    Limit .... 13.945 mm (0.549 inch)

Transmission

Countershaft gear inside diameter (second and third)
    Standard .... 33.000 to 33.025 mm (1.2992 to 1.3002 inches)
    Limit .... 33.04 mm (1.301 inches)
Mainshaft gear inside diameter
    Fourth gear
        Standard .... 31.000 to 31.025 mm (1.2205 to 1.2215 inches)
        Limit... 31.04 mm (1.222 inches)
    Fifth gear
        Standard .... 35.000 to 35.025 mm (1.3870 to 1.3789 inches)
        Limit... 35.04 mm (1.380 inches)
Countershaft bushing outside diameter
    Standard .... 32.950 to 32.975 mm (1.2972 to 1.2982 inches)
    Limit .... 33.93 mm (1.296 inches)
Mainshaft bushing outside diameter
    Fourth gear
        Standard .... 30.950 to 30.975 mm (1.2185 to 1.2195 inches)
        Limit... 30.93 mm (1.218 inches)
    Fifth gear
        Standard .... 34.950 to 34.975 mm (1.3760 to 1.3769 inches)
        Limit... 34.93 mm (1.375 inches)
Mainshaft diameter
    At fourth gear
        Standard .... 27.987 to 28.000 mm (1.1018 to 1.1024 inches)
        Limit... 27.96 mm (1.101 inches)
    At fifth gear
        Standard .... 31.987 to 32.000 mm (1.2593 to 1.2598 inches)
        Limit... 31.96 mm (1.258 inch)
Gear to bushing clearance
    Standard .... 0.025 to 0.075 mm (0.0010 to 0.0030 inch)
    Limit .... 0.10 mm (0.004 inch)
Bushing to shaft clearance
    Standard .... 0.007 to 0.041 mm (0.0003 to 0.0016 inch)
    Limit .... 0.08 mm (0.003 inch)

Shift forks
   Bore diameter
      Standard .... 14.000 to 14.018 mm (0.5512 to 0.5519 inch)
      Limit .... 14.04 mm (0.553 inch)
   Finger thickness
      Standard .... 5.93 to 6.00 mm (0.233 to 0.236 inch)
      Limit .... 5.6 mm (0.22 inch)
Fork shaft diameter
   Standard .... 13.966 to 13.984 mm (0.5498 to 0.5506 inch)
   Limit .... 13.90 mm (0.547 inch)

Torque specifications

Cylinder head main bolts	44 Nm (33 ft-lbs) (1)
Cylinder head small bolts	Not specified
Timing chain tensioner bolts	12 Nm (108 inch-lbs)
Timing chain tensioner guide bolts	12 Nm (108 inch-lbs)
Timing chain guide bolts	12 Nm (108 inch-lbs)
Camshaft cap bolts	12 Nm (108 inch-lbs) (1)
Timing rotor/crankshaft sprocket bolt	59 Nm (44 ft-lbs) (1)
Camshaft sprocket bolts	25 Nm (19 ft-lbs) (2)
Timing chain cover (upper front cover) bolts	12 Nm (108 inch-lbs)
Cylinder head cover bolts	10 Nm (84 inch-lbs)
Oil pressure switch	12 Nm (108 inch-lbs)
Oil pump cover bolts	13 Nm (115 inch-lbs)
Clutch master cylinder clamp bolts	12 Nm (108-lbs)
Clutch hose banjo bolts	34 Nm (25 ft-lbs)
Slave cylinder bleed valve	9 Nm (78 inch-lbs)
Slave cylinder mounting bolts	Not specified
Clutch center locknut	128 Nm (94 ft-lbs) (3)
Clutch housing locknut	186 Nm (137 ft-lbs) (4)
Reverse shift shaft bolt	14 Nm (120 inch-lbs) (2)
Reverse cable bracket bolts	12 Nm (108 inch-lbs) (2)
Rear case cover bolts	24 Nm (17 ft-lbs)
Output shaft bearing holder bolts	28 Nm (21 ft-lbs)
Starter clutch bolt	74 Nm (54 ft-lbs) (5)
Oil pump driven sprocket bolt	18 Nm (156 inch-lbs) (2)
Output shaft locknut	186 Nm (137 ft-lbs) (6)
Final drive gear locknut	186 Nm (137 ft-lbs) (3, 5)
Alternator drive gear bolts	25 Nm (18 ft-lbs) (1)
Shift arm lockbolt	25 Nm (18 ft-lbs) (7)
Shift drum joint bolt	27 Nm (20 ft-lbs) (2)
Shift drum reverse lockbolt	12 Nm (108 inch-lbs) (2)
Stopper arm bolt	12 Nm (108 inch-lbs) (2)
Crankcase bolts (right side)	
10 mm shaft diameter	34 Nm (25 ft-lbs) (1)
6 mm shaft diameter	12 Nm (108 in-lbs)
Crankcase bolts (left side)	25 Nm (18 ft-lbs)
Connecting rod cap nuts	31 Nm (23 ft-lbs) (1)
Main bearing cap bolts (1)	
Stage 1	20 Nm (168 inch-lbs)
Stage 2	45-degrees additional tightening

1   *Apply engine oil to the threads and the undersides of the bolt heads.*

2   *Apply non-permanent thread locking agent to the threads.*

3   *Apply engine oil to the threads and seating surface and stake the nut.*

4   *Apply non-permanent thread locking agent to the threads and stake the locknut in two places.*

5   *Left-hand threads (tighten counterclockwise).*

6   *Stake the locknut.*

7   *Bend up the lockwasher tab.*

1 General information

The engine/transmission unit is a liquid-cooled, horizontally opposed six. The valves are operated by single overhead camshafts which are chain driven off the crankshaft. The engine/transmission assembly is constructed from aluminum alloy. The crankcase is divided vertically.

The crankcase incorporates a wet sump, pressure-fed lubrication system which uses a dual chain-driven oil pump, an oil filter, relief valve and an oil pressure switch. The scavenge portion of the pump keeps the clutch well from filling with oil and the main portion of the pump supplies oil under pressure to friction points in the engine.

Power from the crankshaft is routed to the transmission via the clutch, which is of the diaphragm spring, wet multi-plate type and rides on the rear end of the crankshaft. The clutch uses engine oil pressure, routed through the transmission mainshaft into the internal components of the clutch, to increase engagement force. This allows the clutch to have lower spring pressure, which reduces the clutch lever effort. The transmission is a five-speed, constant-mesh unit.

2 Operations possible with the engine in the frame

The components and assemblies listed below can be removed without having to remove the engine from the frame. If, however, a number of areas require attention at the same time, removal of the engine is recommended.

Alternator
Clutch
Cylinder heads
External gearshift linkage
Starter/reverse motor
Timing chains
Valve covers, rocker arms, camshafts and lifters

3 Operations requiring engine removal

It is necessary to remove the engine/transmission assembly from the frame and remove the rear engine cover or separate the crankcase halves to gain access to the following components:

Intake manifold*
Oil pump
Main oil pump
Starter clutch
Reverse shifter mechanism
Alternator drive
Primary gears
Output shaft
External and internal shift mechanisms
Crankshaft, connecting rods and bearings
Transmission shafts

*The intake manifold can be unbolted from the cylinder heads and lifted slightly to allow gasket replacement or cylinder head removal. Complete removal of the manifold requires removing the engine from the frame.

4 Major engine repair - general note

1   It is not always easy to determine when or if an engine should be completely overhauled, as a number of factors must be considered.

2   High mileage is not necessarily an indication that an overhaul is needed, while low mileage, on the other hand, does not preclude the need for an overhaul. Frequency of servicing is probably the single most important consideration. An engine that has regular and frequent oil and filter changes, as well as other required maintenance, will most likely give many miles of reliable service. Conversely, a neglected engine, or one which has not been broken in properly, may require an overhaul very early in its life.

3   Exhaust smoke and excessive oil consumption are both indications that piston rings and/or valve guides are in need of attention. Make sure oil leaks are not responsible before deciding that the rings and guides are bad. Refer to Chapter 1 and perform a cylinder compression check to determine for certain the nature and extent of the work required.

4   If the engine is making obvious knocking or rumbling noises, the connecting rod and/or main bearings are probably at fault.

5   Loss of power, rough running, excessive valve train noise and high fuel consumption rates may also point to the need for an overhaul, especially if they are all present at the same time. If a complete tune-up does not remedy the situation, major mechanical work is the only solution.

6   An engine overhaul generally involves restoring the internal parts to the specifications of a new engine. During an overhaul the piston rings are replaced and the cylinder walls are bored and/or honed. If a rebore is done, then new pistons are also required. The main and connecting rod bearings are generally replaced with new ones and, if necessary, the crankshaft is also replaced. Generally the valves are serviced as well, since they are usually in less than perfect condition at this point. The end result should be a like-new engine that will give as many trouble free miles as the original.

7   Before beginning the engine overhaul, read through all of the related procedures to familiarize yourself with the scope and requirements of the job. Overhauling an engine is not all that difficult, but it is time consuming. Plan on the motorcycle being tied up for a minimum of two weeks. Check on the availability of parts and make sure that any necessary special tools, equipment and supplies are obtained in advance.

8   Most work can be done with typical shop hand tools, although a number of precision measuring tools are required for inspecting parts to determine if they must be replaced. Often a dealer service department or motorcycle repair shop will handle the inspection of parts and offer advice concerning reconditioning and replacement. As a general rule, time is the primary cost of an overhaul so it doesn't pay to install worn or substandard parts.

9   As a final note, to ensure maximum life and minimum trouble from a rebuilt engine, everything must be assembled with care in a spotlessly clean environment.

5 Cylinder compression - check

1   Among other things, poor engine performance may be caused by leaking valves, incorrect valve clearances, leaking head gaskets, or worn pistons, rings and/or cylinder walls. A cylinder compression check will help pinpoint these conditions and can also indicate the presence of excessive carbon deposits in the cylinder heads.

2   The only tools required are a compression gauge and a spark plug wrench. Depending on the outcome of the initial test, a squirt-type oil can may also be needed.

3   Start the engine and allow it to reach normal operating temperature.

4   Place the bike on its centerstand.

5   Remove the spark plugs (see Chapter 1). Work carefully - don't strip the spark plug hole threads and don't burn your hands.

6   Disable the ignition by unplugging the primary wires from the coils (see Chapter 5). Be sure to mark the locations of the wires before detaching them. Also, disconnect the electrical connector from the fuel pump (see Chapter 4, Section 4).

7   Install the compression gauge in one of the spark plug holes **(see illustration)**.

8   Hold or block the throttle wide open.

9   Crank the engine over a minimum of four or five revolutions (or until the gauge reading stops increasing) and observe the initial movement of the compression gauge needle as well as the final total gauge reading. Repeat the procedure for the other cylinders and compare the results to the value listed in this Chapter's Specifications.

10   If the compression in all cylinders built up quickly and evenly to the specified amount, you can assume the engine upper end is in reasonably good mechanical condition. Worn or sticking piston rings and worn

5.7 A compression gauge with a threaded fitting for the spark plug hole is preferred over the type that requires hand pressure to maintain the seal

7.7 Wrapping the throttle and reverse cables with tape will prevent them from being kinked (reverse cables shown)

7.8 Tape the brake fluid reservoir out of the way

cylinders will produce very little initial movement of the gauge needle, but compression will tend to build up gradually as the engine spins over. Valve and valve seat leakage, or head gasket leakage, is indicated by low initial compression which does not tend to build up.

11 To further confirm your findings, add a small amount of engine oil to each cylinder by inserting the nozzle of a squirt-type oil can through the spark plug holes. The oil will tend to seal the piston rings if they are leaking. Repeat the test for the other cylinders.

12 If the compression increases significantly after the addition of the oil, the piston rings and/or cylinders are definitely worn. If the compression does not increase, the pressure is leaking past the valves or the head gasket. Leakage past the valves may be due to insufficient valve clearances, burned, warped or cracked valves or valve seats or valves that are hanging up in the guides.

13 If compression readings are considerably higher than specified, the combustion chambers are probably coated with excessive carbon deposits. It is possible (but not very likely) for carbon deposits to raise the compression enough to compensate for the effects of leakage past rings or valves. Remove the cylinder head and carefully decarbonize the combustion chambers (see Sections 12 and 14).

6 Engine oil pressure - check

1 Engine oil pressure can be checked with a mechanical gauge at the oil pressure switch, located at the lower front of the engine above the oil filter.

2 Refer to Chapter 9 and remove the oil pressure switch from the engine.

3 Connect a mechanical oil pressure gauge to the oil pressure switch hole, following the gauge manufacturer's instructions.

4 Start the engine and warm it to normal operating temperature. With the engine running, compare the oil pressure reading on the gauge to the value listed in this Chapter's Specifications.

5 Low oil pressure may indicate a worn oil pump, worn bearings or clogged oil lines and passages.

7 Engine - removal and installation

⚠ **Warning: Engine removal and installation should be done with the aid of an assistant to avoid damage or injury that could occur if the engine is dropped. Because the engine is very heavy (about 118 kg/261 lbs without fluids) and bulky, the jack that supports the engine during this procedure must be substantial and equipped with a support platform or cradle (a hydraulic point jack or bottle jack is not sufficient, even if you place an improvised support, such as a block of wood, on top of it). A flat jack of the type shown in Step 16 works well. If you don't have access to this type of jack, an automotive transmission jack, available from tool rental dealers, will also work. These have built-in cradles designed to support heavy transmissions. Be sure to confirm with the tool rental dealer that the jack is strong enough to support the weight of the engine. Be sure the cradle of the jack will support the motorcycle's engine securely so it can't tip to one side during removal and fall off the jack.**

Note: *You'll need a hoist to support the*

motorcycle, in addition to the jack that supports the engine. These can be rented from tool rental dealers. An engine hoist designed for heavy automotive engines can be used, as long as it has enough weight capacity to support the motorcycle. The total weight of the motorcycle is substantial - refer to the general specifications at the end of this manual. Even with the engine removed, the remaining components are extremely heavy. Be absolutely certain that the hoist can support the weight before you rely on it.

Note: *Due to the weight of the engine, you may find it easier to remove as many components as possible (such as the camshaft and cylinder heads) before removing the engine from the frame.*

Removal

1 Support the bike securely so it can't be knocked over during this procedure.

2 Disconnect the negative cable from the battery (see Chapter 1).

3 Remove the rear section of the front fender, upper and lower side covers, center inner fairing, front crash bars and front footpegs (see Chapter 8).

4 Drain the engine oil and coolant (see Chapter 1).

5 Remove the exhaust system (see Chapter 4).

6 Remove the coolant reservoir and radiator support bracket (see Chapter 3).

7 Remove the throttle body and both fuel injector covers (see Chapter 4). Cover the intake ports (below the throttle body) with a clean rag to prevent small parts and tools from falling in. **Note:** *It's a good idea to wrap the throttle and reverse cables with tape to prevent them from being kinked as the engine is removed* **(see illustration).**

8 Unbolt the rear brake fluid reservoir and bracket. Tape the reservoir up out of the way **(see illustration).**

7.16 Be sure the engine jack is adequate for the job - a flat jack like this one from K&L Supply will work

7.17 Loosen the left sub-frame bolts (arrows), but don't remove them yet

7.18 Loosen the right sub-frame bolts (arrows)

9   Disconnect the following electrical connectors:

> Crankshaft position, gear position, speed and knock sensors
> Reverse shift actuator and reverse switch
> Engine sub-wiring harnesses
> Alternator
> Starter/reverse motor
> Sidestand
> Horns

10   On California models, remove the EVAP purge control solenoid and EVAP canister (see Chapter 4).

11   Remove the coolant drain bolt fitting from the engine (see Chapter 3).

12   Disconnect the spark plug wires from the ignition coils (see Chapter 5). Remove the retainer that secures the No. 2 and No. 5 spark plug wires.

13   Drain the clutch fluid and disconnect the hose from the slave cylinder (see Section 15).

14   Detach the shift pedal linkage from the shift shaft (see Section 27). The pedal can be left bolted to the sub-frame, and the pedal and sub-frame removed together later in this procedure.

15   Unbolt the fuel hose fitting from the right fuel rail (see Chapter 4).

16   Support the engine with a jack (see illustration). The height of the jack must be adjustable so the engine can be raised or lowered slightly to relieve tension on the mounting bolts as they're removed.

17   Loosen, but don't remove, the bolts that secure the left sub-frame to the frame (see illustration).

18   Loosen, but don't remove, the bolts that secure the right sub-frame to the frame (see illustration).

19   Remove the left center engine mounting bolt and nut (see illustration).

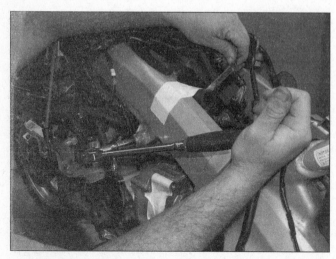

7.19a Remove the upper left center mounting bolt and nut

7.19b Label the bolts so they can be returned to the correct locations

7.20 Remove the left front nut and bolt

7.21 Remove the left rear engine mounting bolt

 HAYNES HiNT *The engine mounting bolts are slightly different sizes, so it's a good idea to label them with their locations (see illustration).*

20 Remove the left front engine mounting bolt and nut **(see illustration)**.
21 Remove the left rear engine mounting bolt **(see illustration)**.
22 Unscrew the locknut from the left center adjusting bolt, then loosen the adjusting bolt **(see illustration)**.
23 Remove the left front engine adjusting bolt locknut and loosen the adjusting bolt **(see illustration)**.
24 Remove the locknut from the left rear adjusting bolt **(see illustrations)** and loosen the adjusting bolt.
25 Remove the three bolts that secure the left sub-frame to the motorcycle and take it off, together with the shift pedal, its linkage

7.22 Use a special socket like this one to loosen the left center adjusting bolt locknut . . .

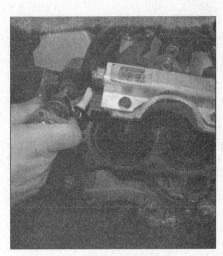

7.23 . . . left rear adjusting bolt locknut . . .

7.24a . . . and left front adjusting bolt locknut . . .

7.24b . . . then loosen the adjusting bolts with an Allen bolt bit

7.25 Unbolt the left sub-frame completely and take it off

7.26 Remove the right center mounting bolt and nut

7.27 Remove the right front mounting bolt and nut

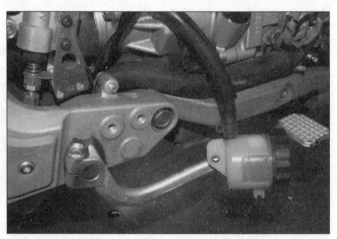

7.28 Remove the right rear mounting bolt and nut

and the sidestand **(see illustration)**.
26 Remove the right center mounting bolt and nut **(see illustration)**.
27 Remove the right front mounting bolt and nut **(see illustration)**.

28 Remove the right rear mounting bolt and nut **(see illustration)**.
29 Unbolt the right sub-frame completely and remove it from the motorcycle **(see illustration 7.18)**.

30 Support the motorcycle with a hoist.
31 Pull the rubber driveshaft boot back from the engine **(see illustration)**.
32 Move the engine forward and down, using the jack. Disengage the driveshaft as you do so **(see illustration)**. On ABS models, make sure the reverse actuator clears the ABS modulators at the front of the frame (see Section 17).
33 Lower the engine clear of the frame, and if necessary (this will depend on your jack arrangement) hoist the motorcycle for removal clearance.

Installation

Note: *If you placed any of the mounting bolts in their holes during engine removal (to help you remember where they go), remove them now.*
34 Lubricate the output shaft splines with moly-based grease. As you lift the engine into position with the jack, align the driveshaft and output shaft and slip them together.
35 Install the three left side adjusting bolts and thread them in all the way. Note that the

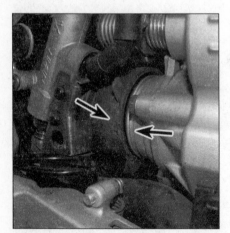

7.31 Pull the rubber driveshaft boot (left arrow) out of its groove (right arrow) and off the engine

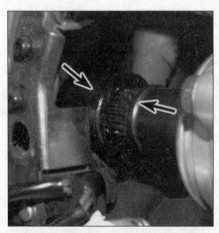

7.32 Slide the output shaft (right arrow) out of the driveshaft (left arrow) as you remove the engine

9.3a Remove the valve cover bolts (arrows) . . .

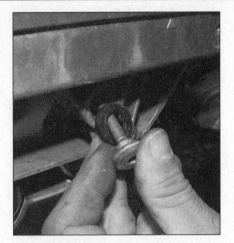

9.3b . . . and their washers

9.5 Peel the gasket off the valve cover

front and rear bolts are thicker than the center bolt.

36   Install the right sub-frame and tighten its bolts to the torque listed in this Chapter's Specifications.

37   Install the right side mounting bolts in the following order and tighten them to the torque listed in this Chapter's Specifications:

>   *Right rear*
>   *Right front*
>   *Right center*

38   Install the left sub-frame and tighten its bolts to the torque listed in this Chapter's Specifications.

39   On the left side, thread each adjusting bolt in until it touches the engine, then tighten it to the torque listed in this Chapter's Specifications. Install the locknut on the adjusting bolt and tighten it to the torque listed in this Chapter's Specifications, using the special tools described in the removal procedure. Do this in the following order:

>   *Left rear*
>   *Left center*
>   *Left front*

40   On the left side, install the engine mounting bolts and tighten them to the torque listed in this Chapter's Specifications, in the following order:

>   *Left rear*
>   *Left front*
>   *Left center*

41   The remainder of installation is the reverse of the removal steps, with the following additions:

>   a) *Use new gaskets at all exhaust pipe connections.*
>   b) *Use new sealing washers ion the clutch hydraulic system connection.*
>   c) *Use a new O-ring on the fuel feed hose.*
>   d) *Adjust the throttle cables following the procedure in Chapter 1.*
>   e) *Be sure to refill the cooling system and engine oil before starting the engine.*

8   Engine disassembly and reassembly - general information

1   Before disassembling the engine, clean the exterior with a degreaser and rinse it with water. A clean engine will make the job easier and prevent the possibility of getting dirt into the internal areas of the engine.

2   In addition to the precision measuring tools mentioned earlier, you will need a torque wrench, a valve spring compressor, oil gallery brushes, a piston ring removal and installation tool and special Honda piston ring compressors (which are described in Section 28). Some new, clean engine oil of the correct grade and type, some engine assembly lube (or moly-based grease) and a tube of RTV (silicone) sealant will also be required. Although it may not be considered a tool, some Plastigage (type HPG-1) should also be obtained to use for checking bearing oil clearances. Plastigage procedures are described in *Tools and Workshop Tips* at the end of this manual.

3   An engine support stand made from short lengths of 2 x 4s bolted together will facilitate the disassembly and reassembly procedures. The perimeter of the mount should be just big enough to accommodate the bottom of the engine oil pan.

4   When disassembling the engine, keep mated parts together (including gears, cylinders, pistons, etc. that have been in contact with each other during engine operation). These mated parts must be reused or replaced as an assembly.

5   Engine/transmission disassembly should be done in the following general order with reference to the appropriate Sections.

>   *Remove the front crankcase cover*
>   *Remove the cylinder head covers*
>   *Remove the camshaft caps, camshafts and lifters*

>   *Remove the timing chains*
>   *Remove the cylinder heads*
>   *Remove the clutch*
>   *Remove the rear crankcase cover*
>   *Remove the reverse mechanism*
>   *Remove the primary drive gears and alternator driven gear*
>   *Remove the oil pump drive chain and sprocket*
>   *Remove the starter clutch and idle gears*
>   *Remove the external shift mechanism*
>   *Separate the crankcase halves*
>   *Remove the oil pump*
>   *Remove the pistons and connecting rods*
>   *Remove the crankshaft and main bearings*
>   *Remove the transmission shafts/gears*
>   *Remove the shift drum/forks*

6   Reassembly is accomplished by reversing the general disassembly sequence.

9   Cylinder head covers - removal and installation

1   Remove the front crash bar from the side of the bike you'll be working on (see Chapter 8).

2   Remove the spark plugs (see Chapter 1).

3   Remove the cover bolts and washers **(see illustrations)**.

4   Pull the cover off the engine. If it's stuck, tap it gently with a soft faced mallet. Don't pry between the cover and engine or the gasket surfaces will be damaged.

5   Peel the rubber gasket from the cover **(see illustration)**. If it's cracked, hardened, has soft spots or shows signs of general deterioration, replace it with a new one.

6   Clean the mating surfaces of the cylinder head and cover with lacquer thinner, acetone or brake system cleaner. Apply a

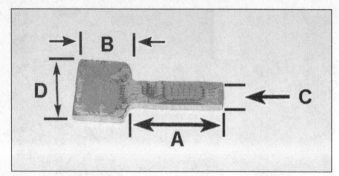

10.4a A tensioner tool can be made from sheet metal approximately 1 mm thick - here are the dimensions

A   14.28 mm (9/16-inch)   C   6.35 mm (1/4-inch)
B   At least 9.52 mm (3/8-inch)   D   9.52 mm (3/8-inch)
     (but longer will make the
     tool easier to hold and turn)

10.4b Here's the special tensioner retractor developed by K&L Supply . . .

10.4c . . . turning it clockwise retracts the tensioner and holds it in the retracted position (this is the left tensioner, located on the underside of the engine)

10.6a Here's the left camshaft sprocket in the removal position - the timing marks are aligned with the cylinder head surface, the two-fingered side of the timing rotor is outward and the single finger is inward, inside the cylinder head

10.6b Here's the left camshaft sprocket in the removal position - the timing marks are aligned with the cylinder head surface, and the M mark on the sprocket is inward, inside the cylinder head (arrow)

thin film of RTV sealant to the gasket groove in the cover, but don't put any on the head.

7   Install the gasket to the cover. Make sure it fits completely into the cover groove.

8   Position the cover on the cylinder head, making sure the gasket doesn't slip out of place.

9   Check the rubber seals on the valve cover bolts, replacing them if necessary **(see illustration 9.3b)**. Coat the seals with engine oil, then install the bolts with their seals, tightening them evenly to the torque listed in this Chapter's Specifications.

10   Install the valve cover, using a new gasket **(see illustration 9.5)**.

11   Install the crash bar.

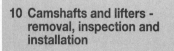

10 Camshafts and lifters - removal, inspection and installation

Note: *This procedure can be performed with the engine in the frame.*

Camshafts
Removal

1   If you're working on a left camshaft, remove the front lower fairing and left horn (see Chapters 8 and 9).

2   If you're working on a right camshaft, remove the right inner fairing (see Chapter 8).

3   Remove the cylinder head covers (see Section 9).

 The tool required to retract the timing chain tensioners is available from Honda dealers and various aftermarket suppliers. If you can't obtain one of these, you can fabricate a tool from sheet metal as shown in illustration 10.4a.

4   Remove the center bolt and sealing washer from the cam chain tensioner. Insert a tensioner tool, turn it clockwise to retract the tensioner, and lock the tensioner in the retracted position with the tool **(see illustrations)**.

5   Refer to the valve adjustment procedure in Chapter 1 and turn the engine so the 1.2TF mark is aligned with the alignment mark inside the timing cap hole.

6   Check the position of the cam sprocket marks on whichever camshaft you're removing **(see illustrations)**. The marks must be flush with the cover mating surface of the cylinder head, and the rearmost cam lobe must point away from the engine. **Note:** *The two camshafts are 180-degrees out of synch with other. This means that when the left camshaft is in the correct position for removal, the right camshaft is 180-degrees away from its removal position (its rear cam lobe will point toward the engine, not away from it). When the right camshaft is in the correct position for removal, the left camshaft is 180 degrees away from its removal position (its rear cam lobe will point toward the engine, not away from it). For this reason, you'll need to remove one camshaft, then rotate the crankshaft one full turn to*

10.7a Loosen the camshaft cap bolts (arrows) in sequence (see text) - the tightening sequence is cast into the camshaft bearing cap

10.7b With the bolts loose, tap the camshaft cap loose with a plastic screwdriver handle or similar tool . . .

10.7c . . . then pull it off the engine and locate the dowels (arrows)

10.9 Take the camshafts out of the saddles, disengage the sprocket from the chain and slip the camshaft out

position the remaining camshaft correctly for removal.

7   Unscrew the camshaft cap bolts in several stages, in a criss-cross pattern, working from the end-most bolts to the center bolts **(see illustration)**. Take the holder off **(see illustrations)**.

8   Locate the cap dowels **(see illustration 10.7c)**. They may have come off with the holder or remained in the cylinder head.

9   Remove the camshaft from the cylinder head, disengage the sprocket from the chain and pass the camshaft forward through the chain to remove it **(see illustration)**.

10   If you need to remove the remaining camshaft, rotate the crankshaft one full turn, so the 1.2 TF mark is again lined up with the alignment mark inside the timing cap hole (see the valve adjustment procedure in Chapter 1 if necessary).

Inspection

Note: *Before replacing camshafts or the cylinder head and camshaft cap because of*

damage, check with local machine shops specializing in motorcycle engine work. In the case of the camshafts, it may be possible for cam lobes to be welded, reground and hardened, at a cost far lower than that of a new camshaft. If the bearing surfaces in the cylinder head or cap are damaged, it may be possible for them to be bored out to accept bearing inserts. Due to the cost of a new cylinder head it is recommended that all options be explored before condemning it as trash!

11   Inspect the cam bearing surfaces of the head and the camshaft cap. Look for score marks, deep scratches and evidence of spalling (a pitted appearance).

12   Check the camshaft lobes for heat discoloration (blue appearance), score marks, chipped areas, flat spots and spalling **(see illustration)**. Measure the height of each lobe with a micrometer (refer to *Tools and Workshop Tips* at the end of this manual for instructions on how to use a micrometer, if necessary) and compare the results to the minimum lobe height listed in this Chapter's

10.12 Check the lobes of the camshaft for wear - here's a good example of damage which will require replacement (or repair) of the camshaft

10.14 Here's how the timing rotor fits on the left cam sprocket - its OUT mark is away from the sprocket, the timing marks are aligned, and the M mark is next to the single finger on the timing rotor

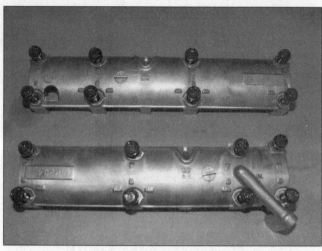

10.18 The right camshaft cap (bottom) has an oil passage, and the left camshaft cap doesn't

Specifications. If damage is noted or wear is excessive, the camshaft must be replaced.

13 Next, check the camshaft bearing oil clearances using Plastigage. This is described in *Tools and Workshop Tips* at the end of this manual. If the oil clearance is greater than specified, measure the diameter of the cam bearing journal with a micrometer (refer to *Tools and Workshop Tips* at the end of this manual for instructions on how to use a micrometer, if necessary). If the journal diameter is less than the specified limit, replace the camshaft with a new one and recheck the clearance. If the clearance is still too great, replace the cylinder head and camshaft with new parts (see the **Note** that precedes Step 11).

14 Check the timing rotor on the left camshaft **(see illustration)**. It doesn't have mechanical contact with other components, so it shouldn't be worn or damaged. If it is, remove the engine front cover (see Section 11) and check the timing pickup inside the cover for damage.

Installation

15 Make sure the crankshaft is still in the position described in Step 5. Make sure the timing rotor is installed on the left camshaft **(see illustration 10.14)**.

16 If the camshaft holder dowels aren't in their holes, install them **(see illustration 10.7c)**.

17 Make sure the bearing surfaces in the cylinder head and the camshaft cap are clean, then apply a light coat of engine assembly lube or moly-based grease to each of them.

18 Apply a coat of moly-based grease to the lobes of the camshaft. **Note:** *If you've removed both camshafts, be sure to install them on the correct sides of the engine. They're labeled R and L for right and left. The timing rotor goes on the left camshaft. The camshaft bearing caps are also different; the right one has an external oil passage* **(see illustration)**.

19 Engage the camshaft sprocket with the chain and place the camshaft in the cylinder

head bearing journals with the timing marks aligned and its rearmost lobe pointing away from the engine **(see illustration)**.

20 Position the camshaft cap on the cylinder head. Install the cap bolts and tighten them in two or three stages to the torque listed in this Chapter's Specifications, starting with the center bolts and working outward.

21 If you removed both camshafts, install the other camshaft in the same manner. However, be sure to rotate the crankshaft one full turn, so the timing marks on the camshaft already installed are 180 degrees from its installed position, and the rearmost cam lobe on the camshaft already installed points toward the engine.

22 The remainder of installation is the reverse of removal.

Valve lifters

23 The valves are opened and closed by bucket-type lifters, which are operated directly by the camshafts.

Removal

24 Remove the camshaft(s) following the procedure given above.

25 Mark the lifters with felt pen, numbering them from front to rear of the engine **(see illustration)**. Make a holder with a separate section for each lifter and shim (an egg carton will work). The parts from a wear pattern with each other and must be returned to their original locations if reused.

26 Remove the lifters with a magnet **(see illustration)**. Remove the valve adjusting shim (it may stick to the lifters or to the top of the valve stem) **(see illustrations)**.

Inspection

27 Check the camshaft and contact and side surfaces of the lifters for wear and damage such as scoring or pitting. Replace worn

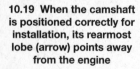

10.19 When the camshaft is positioned correctly for installation, its rearmost lobe (arrow) points away from the engine

10.25 Number the lifters with a felt pen

10.26a Pull the lifters out with a magnet . . .

or damaged lifters, and pay close attention to the lifter's cam lobe if the camshaft contact surface on the lifter shows problems.

28 Check the lifter bores in the cylinder head for wear or scoring. If you have precision measuring equipment, measure the bore and shaft diameters and compare them to the values listed in this Chapter's Specifications (refer to instructions in *Tools and Workshop Tips* at the end of this manual if necessary). Replace worn or damaged parts.

29 Check the valve adjusting shims for wear or damage. Replace worn shims. Refer to the valve adjustment procedure in Chapter 1 to select the correct shim size.

Installation

30 Stick the valve adjusting shims to their respective valves with the size number showing, using a dab of grease if necessary **(see illustration 10.26d)**. Coat the bores in the cylinder head and the outsides of the lift-

ers with oil containing molybdenum disulfide. Install the lifters, returning them to their original locations if you're using the old ones.

31 The remainder of installation is the reverse of the removal steps.

10.26b . . . and if the valve adjusting shim sticks to the inside of the lifter . . .

11 Timing chains - removal, inspection and installation

Note: *The timing chains can be removed with the engine in the frame. If the engine has been removed, ignore the steps which don't apply.*

Removal

1 Remove the camshafts (see Section 10). Leave the crankshaft positioned so the No. 1-2 cylinder timing mark is lined up with the alignment mark inside the timing hole cap.

10.26c . . . remove it with a magnet

10.26d The shim may also stick to the valve (arrow)

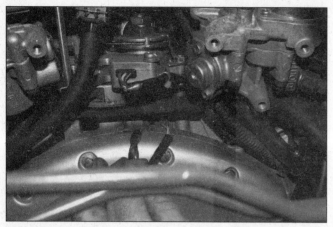

11.2a Pull the crankshaft position sensor pickup connector out to where it's visible and disconnect it

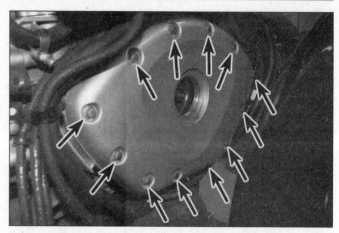

11.2b Unscrew the front cover bolts (arrows)

11.2c Tap the cover loose with a soft-faced mallet

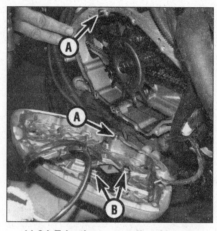

11.2d Take the cover off and locate the dowels (A). (B) are the Crankshaft Position (CKP) sensor bolts

11.4a Unscrew the right tensioner bolts all the way and lift the tensioner out of the engine

2   Unbolt the front cover from the engine, tap it loose with a soft-faced mallet and take it off **(see illustrations)**.
3   Using a felt pen, mark the chains with LEFT and RIGHT and an arrow to indicate

their direction of rotation (counterclockwise, viewed from the front of the engine).
4   Retract the timing chain tensioners as described in Section 10. Unbolt the tensioners and remove them from the engine.

The left tensioner can simply be unbolted and lowered out of the engine to remove it. Access to the right tensioner is limited by the frame, so you'll need to remove it in a specific way if the engine is installed in the

11.4b Tilt the top of the tensioner rearward, then take the tensioner out towards the front of the engine

11.4c The gasket may stay on the engine - if it does, remove it

11.5a Remove the timing rotor bolt (arrow) . . .

11.5b . . . and take off the bolt and washer

11.6a Remove the tensioner guide and chain guide bolts (arrows)

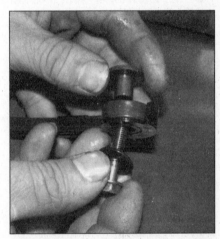

11.6b Each tensioner guide has a collar in the bolt hole

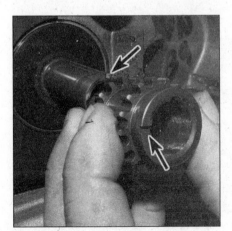

11.7 The notch on the timing chain sprocket (lower arrow) faces forward - remove the Woodruff key (upper arrow) and set it aside so it doesn't get lost

motorcycle **(see illustrations)**.
5   Remove the timing rotor from the front of the crankshaft **(see illustrations)**.
6   Unbolt the tensioner guides and chain guides, then remove them from the engine **(see illustrations)**.
7   Remove the timing chains from the sprockets. If necessary, remove the sprocket and Woodruff key from the front end of the crankshaft **(see illustration)**.

Inspection

8   Check the cam chains for wear or damage. In general, cam chains wear very little, so if one or both cam chains is worn, the engine should be checked for other wear and damage.
9   Check the sprocket teeth for wear or damage and replace the sprockets if damage is found.
10   Check the chain guides for wear or damage. Push the tensioner pistons in with your fingers and make sure they move freely. Replace the tensioners if problems are found.

Installation

11   Remove all traces of old gasket and sealer from the mating surfaces of the engine and front cover.

 HAYNES HiNT *A good way to remove old gaskets from a mating surface is to scrape with a single-edge razor blade. Be sure to hold the blade perpendicular to the surface to prevent gouging it.*

12   Install the timing chains, tensioners and sprockets by reversing the removal procedure in this Section.
13   The remainder of installation is the reverse of the removal steps, with the following additions:

   a) *Apply a small dab of sealant to the crankcase seam at the top and bottom of the cover mating surface.*
   b) *Tighten the front cover bolts evenly, in a criss-cross pattern, to the torque listed in this Chapter's Specifications.*

12 Cylinder heads - removal and installation

Caution: The engine must be completely cool before beginning this procedure, or the cylinder head may become warped.

Note: *This procedure can be performed with the engine in the frame. If the engine has been removed, ignore the steps which don't apply.*

12.7a Remove the manifold bolts on each side (left side shown)

12.7b Lift the manifold up and remove the gasket

12.7c Support the manifold with bungee cords

Removal

1   Disconnect the spark plug wires. The spark plugs can be left in if you don't plan to disassemble the head.

2   Remove the camshafts (see Section 10).

3   Remove the exhaust system, air cleaner housing and fuel rail covers (see Chapter 4).

4   Remove the radiators and their brackets (see Chapter 3).

5   Unbolt the guide plate from the front of the cylinder head (it's secured by two bolts).

6   If you're working on the left cylinder head, remove the camshaft position sensor. On both cylinder heads, detach the coolant hose fitting from the rear of the cylinder head (see Chapters 3 and 4).

7   Unbolt the intake manifold from both cylinder heads (see illustration). Lift the manifold up off the heads and support it up out of the way (see illustrations). Fuel injection components can be left attached to the manifold.

8   Unscrew the coolant temperature sensor from the left cylinder head (see Chapter 3).

9   Loosen the cylinder head bolts, 1/2 turn at a time, in a crisscross pattern (see illustration). Once all of the bolts are loose, remove the bolts and washers.

10   Take the cylinder head off the crankcase (see illustration). If the head is stuck, tap upward with a rubber mallet to jar it loose, or use two wooden dowels inserted into the intake or exhaust ports to rock the head back and forth slightly. Don't attempt to pry the head off by inserting a screwdriver between the head and the crankcase - you'll damage the sealing surfaces.

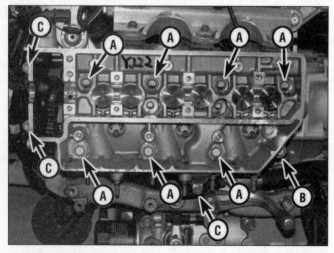

12.9 Loosen (and tighten) the cylinder head bolts in several stages, working in a criss-cross pattern

12.10 Take the cylinder head off the crankcase

A   9 mm bolts (long)   C   6 mm bolts
B   9 mm bolt (short)

12.11 Remove the dowels and coolant tube with the O-ring (arrows) and the gasket

12.12 Remove the O-ring (arrow) from the coolant tube bore

11 Lift the head gasket off the crankcase. Remove the gasket, dowel pins and coolant tube **(see illustration)**.

12 Take the coolant tube O-ring out of its bore in the crankcase **(see illustration)**.

13 Check the cylinder head gasket and the mating surfaces on the cylinder head and block for leakage, which could indicate warpage. Refer to *Tools and Workshop Tips* at the end of this manual and check the flatness of the cylinder head and its mating surface on the crankcase.

14 Clean all traces of old gasket material from the cylinder head and crankcase. Be careful not to let any of the gasket material fall into the crankcase, the cylinder bores or the coolant passages.

Installation

15 Install the O-ring, coolant tube and dowels in the crankcase **(see illustrations 12.12 and 12.11)**.

16 Lay the new gasket in place on the crankcase. Never reuse the old gasket and don't use any type of gasket sealant.

17 Carefully place the cylinder head on the crankcase, making sure the coolant tube fits into the fitting on the side of the head toward the center of the engine.

18 Coat the threads of the main bolts and the undersides of the bolt heads with molybdenum disulfide oil. Install the main head bolts and washers. Starting with the inner bolts and working outward **(see illustration 12.9)**, tighten the bolts in three stages to the torque listed in this Chapter's Specifications.

19 Install the 6 mm (small) bolts. Tighten them securely, but don't overtighten them and strip the threads.

20 The remainder of installation is the reverse of the removal steps.

21 Change the engine oil (see Chapter 1).

13 Valves/valve seats/valve guides - servicing

1 Because of the complex nature of this job and the special tools and equipment required, servicing of the valves, the valve seats and the valve guides (commonly known as a valve job) is best left to a professional.

2 The home mechanic can, however, remove and disassemble the head, do the initial cleaning and inspection, then reassemble and deliver the head to a dealer service department or properly equipped motorcycle repair shop for the actual valve servicing. Refer to Section 12 for those procedures.

3 The dealer service department will remove the valves and springs, recondition or replace the valves and valve seats, replace the valve guides, check and replace the valve springs, spring retainers and keepers/collets (as necessary), replace the valve seals with new ones and reassemble the valve components.

4 After the valve job has been performed, the head will be in like-new condition. When the head is returned, be sure to clean it again very thoroughly before installation on the engine to remove any metal particles or abrasive grit that may still be present from the valve service operations. Use compressed air, if available, to blow out all the holes and passages.

14 Cylinder head and valves - disassembly, inspection and reassembly

1 As mentioned in the previous Section, valve servicing and valve guide replacement should be left to a dealer service department or motorcycle repair shop. However, disassembly, cleaning and inspection of the valves and related components can be done (if the necessary special tools are available) by the home mechanic. This way no expense is incurred if the inspection reveals that service work is not required at this time.

2 To properly disassemble the valve components without the risk of damaging them, a valve spring compressor is absolutely necessary. This special tool can usually be rented, but if it's not available, have a dealer service department or motorcycle repair shop handle the entire process of disassembly, inspection, service or repair (if required) and reassembly of the valves.

Disassembly

3 Remove the camshaft cap if you haven't already done so (see Section 10). Store the components in such a way that they can be returned to their original locations without getting mixed up.

4 Before the valves are removed, scrape away any traces of gasket material from the head gasket sealing surface. Work slowly and do not nick or gouge the soft aluminum of the head. Gasket removing solvents, which work very well, are available at most motorcycle shops and auto parts stores.

5 Carefully scrape all carbon deposits out of the combustion chamber area. A hand held wire brush or a piece of fine emery cloth can be used once the majority of deposits have been scraped away. Do not use a wire brush mounted in a drill motor, or one with extremely stiff bristles, as the head material is soft and may be eroded away or scratched by the wire brush.

6 Before proceeding, arrange to label and store the valves along with their related components so they can be kept separate and reinstalled in the same valve guides they are removed from (labeled plastic bags work well for this).

14.7a Compress the valve spring with a spring compressor . . .

14.7b . . . and remove the keepers with a magnet

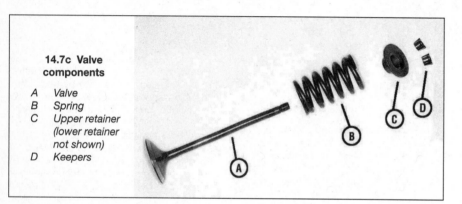

14.7c Valve components

A   Valve
B   Spring
C   Upper retainer (lower retainer not shown)
D   Keepers

7   Compress the valve spring on the first valve with a spring compressor, then remove the keepers and the spring retainer from the valve assembly **(see illustration)**. Do not compress the springs any more than is absolutely necessary. Carefully release the valve spring compressor and remove the spring and the valve from the head **(see illustrations)**. If the valve binds in the guide (won't pull through), push it back into the head and deburr the area around the keeper groove with a very fine file or whetstone.

8   Repeat the procedure for the remaining valves. Remember to keep the parts for each valve together so they can be reinstalled in the same location.

9   Once the valves have been removed and labeled, pull off the valve stem seals with pliers and discard them (the old seals should never be reused), then remove the spring seats.

10   Next, clean the cylinder head with solvent and dry it thoroughly. Compressed air will speed the drying process and ensure that all holes and recessed areas are clean.

11   Clean all of the valve springs, keepers, retainers and spring seats with solvent and dry them thoroughly. Do the parts from one valve at a time so that no mixing of parts between valves occurs.

12   Scrape off any deposits that may have formed on the valve, then use a motorized wire brush to remove deposits from the valve heads and stems. Again, make sure the valves do not get mixed up.

Inspection

13   Inspect the head very carefully for cracks and other damage. If cracks are found, a new head will be required. Check the cam bearing surfaces for wear and evidence of seizure. Check the camshafts for wear as well (see Section 10).

14   Using a precision straightedge and a feeler gauge, check the head gasket mating surface for warpage with a straightedge, referring to *Tools and Workshop Tips* at the end of this manual. If warpage exceeds the value listed in this Chapter's Specifications, the cylinder head must be machined or replaced with a new one. Minor surface imperfections can be cleaned up by sanding on a surface plate in a figure-eight pattern with 400 or 600 grit wet or dry sandpaper. Be sure to rotate the head every few strokes to avoid removing material unevenly. Also check the head mating surface on the cylinders.

15   Examine the valve seats in each of the combustion chambers. If they are pitted, cracked or burned, the head will require valve service that's beyond the scope of the home mechanic. Measure the valve seat width and compare it to this Chapter's

Specifications. If it is not within the specified range, or if it varies around its circumference, valve service work is required.

16   Clean the valve guides to remove any carbon buildup, then measure the inside diameters of the guides as described in *Tools and Workshop Tips* at the end of this manual. Record the measurements for future reference. These measurements, along with the valve stem diameter measurements, will enable you to compute the valve stem-to-guide clearance. This clearance, when compared to the Specifications, will be one factor that will determine the extent of the valve service work required. The guides are measured at the ends and at the center to determine if they are worn in a bell-mouth pattern (more wear at the ends). If they are, guide replacement is an absolute must.

17   Carefully inspect each valve face for cracks, pits and burned spots. Check the valve stem and the keeper groove area for cracks. Rotate the valve and check for any obvious indication that it is bent. Check the end of the stem for pitting and excessive wear and make sure the margin is not too thin. The presence of any of the above conditions indicates the need for valve servicing.

18   Measure the valve stem diameter with a micrometer (refer to *Tools and Workshop Tips* at the end of this manual if necessary). By subtracting the stem diameter from the valve guide diameter, the valve stem-to-guide clearance is obtained. If the stem-to-guide clearance is greater than listed in this Chapter's Specifications, the guides and valves will have to be replaced with new ones. Also check the valve stem for bending. Set the valve in a V-block with a dial indicator touching the middle of the stem. Rotate the valve and note the reading on the gauge. If the stem is bent, replace the valve.

19   Check the end of each valve spring for wear and pitting. Measure the free length **(see illustration)** and compare it to this Chapter's Specifications. Any springs that are shorter than specified have sagged and should not be reused. Stand the spring on a

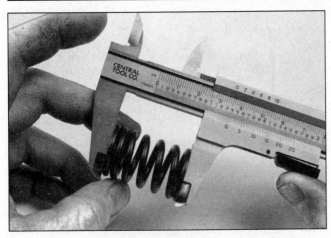

14.19a Measure the free length of the valve springs

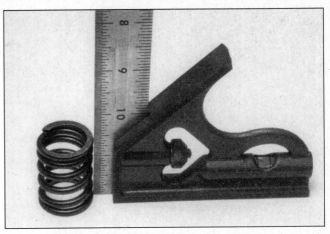

14.19b Check the valve spring for squareness

flat surface and check it for squareness **(see illustration)**.

20   Check the spring retainers and keepers for obvious wear and cracks. Any questionable parts should not be reused, as extensive damage will occur in the event of failure during engine operation.

21   If the inspection indicates that no service work is required, the valve components can be reinstalled in the head.

Reassembly

22   Before installing the valves in the head, they should be lapped to ensure a positive seal between the valves and seats. This procedure requires coarse and fine valve lapping compound (available at auto parts stores) and a valve lapping tool. If a lapping tool is not available, a piece of rubber or plastic hose can be slipped over the valve stem (after the valve has been installed in the guide) and used to turn the valve.

23   Apply a small amount of coarse lapping compound to the valve face **(see illustration)**, then slip the valve into the guide. **Note:** *Make sure the valve is installed in the correct guide and be careful not to get any lapping compound on the valve stem.*

24   Attach the lapping tool (or hose) to the valve and rotate the tool between the palms of your hands. Use a back-and-forth motion rather than a circular motion. Lift the valve off the seat and turn it at regular intervals to distribute the lapping compound properly. Continue the lapping procedure until the valve face and seat contact area is of uniform width and unbroken around the entire circumference of the valve face and seat **(see illustration)**.

25   Carefully remove the valve from the guide and wipe off all traces of lapping compound. Use solvent to clean the valve and wipe the seat area thoroughly with a solvent soaked cloth.

26   Repeat the procedure with fine valve lapping compound, then repeat the entire procedure for the remaining valves.

27   Lay the spring seats in place in the cylinder head, then install new valve stem seals on each of the guides. Use an appropriate size deep socket to push the seals into place until they are properly seated. Don't twist or cock them, or they will not seal properly against the valve stems. Also, don't remove them again or they will be damaged.

28   Coat the valve stems with assembly

lube or moly-based grease, then install one of them into its guide. Next, install the springs and retainers, compress the springs and install the keepers. **Note:** *When compressing the springs with the valve spring compressor, depress them only as far as is absolutely necessary to slip the keepers into place. Apply a small amount of grease to the keepers* **(see illustration)** *to help hold them in place as the pressure is released from the springs. Make certain that the keepers are securely locked in their retaining grooves.*

29   Support the cylinder head on blocks so the valves can't contact the workbench top, then very gently tap each of the valve stems with a soft-faced hammer. This will help seat the keepers in their grooves.

30   Once all of the valves have been installed in the head, check for proper valve sealing by pouring a small amount of solvent into each of the valve ports. If the solvent leaks past the valve(s) into the combustion chamber area, disassemble the valve(s) and repeat the lapping procedure, then reinstall the valve(s) and repeat the check. Repeat the procedure until a satisfactory seal is obtained.

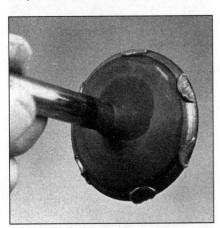

14.23 Apply the lapping compound very sparingly, in small dabs, to the valve face only

14.24 After lapping, the valve face should have a uniform, unbroken contact pattern (arrow)

14.28 A small dab of grease will help hold the keepers in place on the valve spring while the spring is released

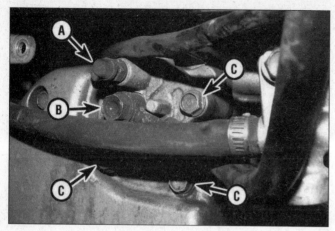

15.3 Clutch slave cylinder details

A   Bleed valve   C   Mounting bolts
B   Fluid line banjo bolt

15.7 Unplug the clutch switch and cruise cancel switch (left arrows) - remove the locknut from the pivot bolt (right arrow)

15 Clutch release mechanism - bleeding, removal, inspection and installation

Clutch bleeding

1   Place the motorcycle on its center-stand.
2   Remove the master cylinder cover and diaphragm. Place rags around the master cylinder to protect plastic and painted parts from being damaged by the clutch fluid. Top up the master cylinder with fluid to the upper level line cast inside the cylinder.
3   Remove the cap from the bleed valve **(see illustration)**. Place a box wrench over the bleed valve. Attach a vinyl tube to the valve fitting and put the other end of the tube in a container. Pour enough clean brake fluid into

the container to cover the end of the tube.
4   Squeeze the clutch lever several times until lever resistance increases, then hold the lever in. With the clutch lever held in, open the bleed valve 1/4-turn with the wrench, let air and fluid escape, then tighten the valve.
5   Slowly release the clutch lever.
6   Wait several seconds after releasing the lever, then repeat Steps 4 and 5 until there aren't any more bubbles in the fluid flowing into the container. Top off the master cylinder with fluid, then reinstall the diaphragm and cover and tighten the screws.

Master cylinder

Removal

7   Disconnect the electrical connector from the clutch switch beneath the master cylinder on the left handlebar **(see illustration)**. If the bike has cruise control, disconnect the cruise

cancel switch connector as well.
8   Place a towel under the master cylinder to catch any spilled fluid, then remove the union bolt from the master cylinder fluid line.

Caution: Brake fluid will damage paint. Wipe up any spills immediately and wash the area with soap and water.

9   Remove the master cylinder clamp bolts and take the cylinder body off the handlebar.

Overhaul

10   Remove the lever pivot bolt and nut and take off the lever **(see illustration 15.7)**.
11   Remove the cap, plate, rubber diaphragm and float from the reservoir **(see illustration)**. Remove the baffle from the bottom of the master cylinder.
12   Remove the rubber boot, pushrod and spring from the master cylinder **(see illustration)**.

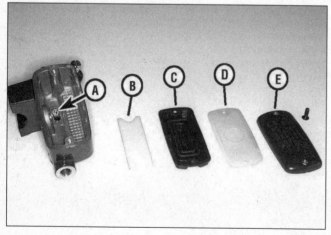

15.11 Clutch master cylinder details

A   Baffle   D   Plate
B   Float   E   Cover
C   Diaphragm

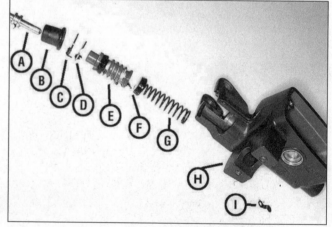

15.12 Clutch master cylinder piston details

A   Pushrod   F   Cup
B   Dust cover   G   Spring
C   Snap-ring   H   Master cylinder body
D   Retainer   I   Baffle
E   Piston

13 Remove the snap ring and retaining ring, then dump out the piston and primary cup, secondary cup and spring **(see illustration 15.12)**. If they won't come out, blow compressed air into the fluid line hole.

> ⚠ **Warning: The piston may shoot out forcefully enough to cause injury. Point the piston at a block of wood or a pile of rags inside a box and apply air pressure gradually. Never point the end of the cylinder at yourself, including your fingers.**

14 Thoroughly clean all of the components in clean brake fluid (don't use any type of petroleum-based solvent).

15 Check the piston and cylinder bore for wear, scratches and rust. If the piston shows these conditions, replace it and both rubber cups as a set. If the cylinder bore has any defects, replace the entire master cylinder.

16 Install the spring in the cylinder bore, wide end first.

17 Coat a new cup with brake fluid and install it in the cylinder, wide side first.

18 Coat the piston with brake fluid and install it in the cylinder.

19 Install the retaining ring. Press the piston into the bore and install the snap ring to hold it in place.

20 Install the rubber boot, pushrod and spring.

21 When you install the lever, align the hole in the lever bushing with the pushrod.

Installation

22 Installation is the reverse of the removal steps, with the following additions:

a) *The split between the clamp and master cylinder aligns with the punch mark on the handlebar cover.*

b) *Tighten the clamp bolts to the torque listed in this Chapter's Specifications.*

c) *Fill and bleed the clutch hydraulic system.*

d) *Operate the clutch lever and check for fluid leaks.*

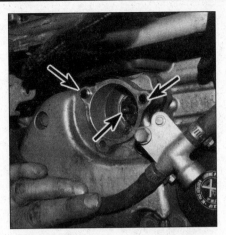

15.25a Slave cylinder dowels (upper arrows) and pushrod (lower arrow)

15.25b If you don't plan to overhaul the slave cylinder, wrap it with a zip tie so the piston doesn't pop out

Slave cylinder

Removal

23 The slave cylinder is mounted on the front of the engine near the oil filter. If the engine is in the frame, remove the front lower fairing cover (see Chapter 8) and the evaporative emission canister (California models) (see Chapter 4).

24 Place rags and a container beneath the slave cylinder to catch spilled fluid. Remove the banjo bolt and disconnect the fluid hose **(see illustration 15.3)**. Place the end of the fluid hose in the container to let the fluid drain.

Caution: Brake fluid will damage paint. Wipe up any spills immediately and wash the area with soap and water.

25 Remove the slave cylinder mounting bolts and take it off the rear cover **(see illustration 15.3)**, then locate the dowels **(see illustration)**. **Note:** *If you're not planning to disassemble the slave cylinder, wrap it with a zip tie so the spring doesn't push the piston out of the bore* **(see illustration)**.

Overhaul

26 Remove the piston and spring **(see illustration)**. If they won't come out, blow compressed air into the fluid line hole.

> ⚠ **Warning: The piston may shoot out forcefully enough to cause injury. Point the piston at a block of wood or a pile of rags inside a box and apply air pressure gradually. Never point the end of the cylinder at yourself, including your fingers.**

27 Thoroughly clean all of the components in clean brake fluid (don't use any type of petroleum-based solvent).

28 Check the piston and cylinder bore for wear, scratches and rust. If the piston shows these conditions, replace it and the seal as a set. If the cylinder bore has any defects, replace the entire slave cylinder. If the piston and bore are good, carefully remove the seal from the piston and install a new one **(see illustration)**.

29 Check the pushrod seal in the back of

15.26 Take the piston and spring out of the cylinder

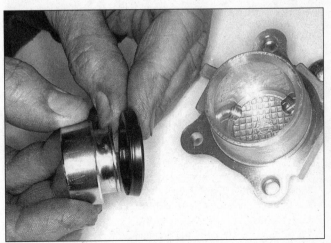

15.28 The wide side of the piston cup faces into the bore

15.29 Replace the pushrod seal if it's worn or damaged

15.30 Check the pushrod (arrow) for wear or damage and its seal for oil leaks

16.3 Free the fuel tank drain tube from the retainer

the piston and replace it if it's worn or damaged **(see illustration)**.

30 Check the end of the pushrod for wear or damage and check the pushrod seal for leakage **(see illustration)**. If the pushrod is worn or damaged, pull it out and install a new one. If the seal has been leaking, carefully pry it out and press in a new one with a socket the same diameter as the seal.

Installation

31 Installation is the reverse of the removal procedure, with the following additions:

a) *Use new sealing washers on the fluid line.*

b) *Tighten the cylinder mounting bolts and fluid line union bolt to the torques listed in this Chapter's Specifications.*

c) *Bleed the clutch (see Steps 1 through 6).*

d) *Operate the clutch and check for fluid leaks.*

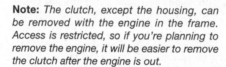

16 Clutch - removal, inspection and installation

Note: *The clutch, except the housing, can be removed with the engine in the frame. Access is restricted, so if you're planning to remove the engine, it will be easier to remove the clutch after the engine is out.*

Removal

1 Place the bike on its centerstand and drain the engine oil (see Chapter 1).

2 Remove the coolant reservoir and exhaust system (see Chapters 3 and 4).

3 Free the fuel tank drain tube from the retainer on the lower left of the clutch cover **(see illustration)**.

4 Unbolt the clutch cover from the rear of the engine **(see illustration)**. If the cover is stuck, tap it gently with a soft-faced mallet to free it. Don't pry between the cover and engine or the gasket surfaces will be damaged.

5 Locate the cover dowels. Remove the oil passage, its O-ring and the old gasket **(see illustration)**.

6 Pull the oil pickup strainer out of its tube **(see illustration)**.

Outer plate removal

7 Refer to the accompanying illustrations to remove the outer plates **(see illustrations)**.

16.4 Remove the cover bolts (arrows) and take the cover off the engine

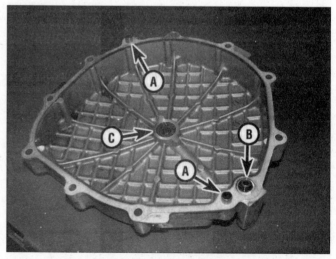

16.5 Clutch cover details

A Dowels	C Joint piece support
B Oil passage and O-ring	and snap-ring

16.6 Pull the strainer out of the engine

16.7a Here's the assembled clutch

16.7b Remove the snap-ring . . .

16.7c . . . take off lifter plate A . . .

16.7d . . . bend back the staked portion of the locknut with a hammer and punch . . .

16.7e . . . unscrew the clutch center locknut . . .

16.7f . . . remove the lockwasher . . .

16.7g . . . the spring guide . . .

16.7h . . . the diaphragm spring . . .

16.7i . . . and its spring seat

16.7j Pull the clutch center out slightly, noting how the friction plate tab locations are offset and fit into different grooves in the housing

A   Outer plate tabs (in shallow slots)
B   Inner plate tabs (in deep slots)

16.7k Pull out the clutch center, together with the plates

16.7l Remove the thrust washer from the mainshaft

16.7m Remove the snap-ring from the pressure plate . . .

16.7n . . . and take out the lifter spring . . .

16.7o . . . lifter plate B . . .

16.7p . . . and the clutch piston (arrow) - it may be held in place by its O-ring, so pull firmly if necessary, using your fingers

16.7q Take the plates and discs (clutch pack) off the clutch center, then remove the pressure plate from the clutch pack

16.8a Remove the O-ring from the clutch center

16.8b Note how the clip ring ends are installed in the clutch center

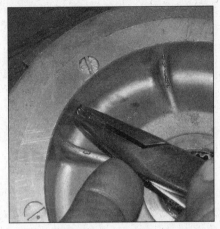

16.8c Squeeze the ends together so they'll fit through the hole

Inner plate removal

8   Refer to the accompanying illustrations to remove the inner plate, judder spring and spring seat (see illustrations).

Clutch housing removal

9   Remove the clutch center and plates as described above.
10   Bend back the staked portion of the locknut (see illustration).

TOOL TiP *You can make a tool for unstaking the nut by filing the end of a 3 mm (1/8-inch) round punch into a wedge shape.*

16.8d Carefully pry the clip ring out of its groove with a screwdriver

16.8e Remove the steel plate from the clutch center

16.8f Remove the inner friction plate (it's a different type than the other friction plates, so keep it separate)

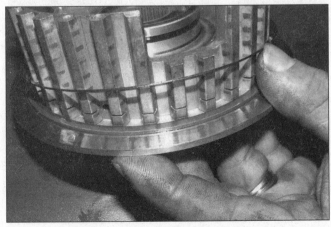

16.8g Remove the judder spring and spring seat

16.10 Bend back the staked portion of the locknut with a sharpened punch

16.11a Unscrew the clutch housing locknut

16.11b Because the nut is very tight, there's no good substitute for a 12-point, 46 mm socket

16.12 Unscrew the locknut and remove the lockwasher (arrow) - its OUT SIDE mark faces away from the engine on installation

11   Unscrew the locknut, using a special holding tool (Honda clutch center holder 07JMB-50100 or equivalent) to prevent the clutch housing from turning. You can also use an air wrench if you have one **(see illustration)**, but you'll need a holding tool later to tighten the nut. You'll also need a deep 46 mm 12-point socket **(see illustration)**. If you don't have these tools, take the engine to a dealer service department or other qualified shop and have the nut removed.

Caution: Do not insert a rod through the holes in the clutch housing to hold it. The force required to loosen the nut could damage the housing.

12   Remove the lockwasher **(see illustration)**.

13   Slide the clutch housing off the mainshaft.

Inspection

14   Check the oil passages in the clutch piston and the end of the mainshaft to make sure they're clear **(see illustrations)**. Clean the passages and blow them out with compressed air if necessary.

15   Examine the splines on both the inside and the outside of the clutch center. If any wear is evident, replace the clutch center with a new one. Check the friction surfaces on the clutch center and pressure plate for scoring, wear or signs of overheating.

16   Check the clutch housing splines for wear or damage. Check the edges of the slots in the clutch housing for indentations made by the friction plate tabs. If the indentations are deep they can prevent clutch release, so the housing should be replaced with a new one. If the indentations can be removed eas-

16.14a Check the oil passages in the clutch piston (arrows) . . .

16.14b . . . and in the mainshaft (arrow)

16.17 Measure the height of the diaphragm and lifter springs

16.19a Check the joint piece (arrow) for wear and damage

ily with a file, the life of the housing can be prolonged to an extent.

17   Measure the height of the diaphragm spring and lifter spring **(see illustration)**. Replace the spring(s) if its free height is less than the value listed in this Chapter's Specifications.

18   Check the pressure plate for wear or damage and make sure its oil passages are clear.

19   Check the joint piece in the lifter plate for wear or damage **(see illustration)**. Spin the bearing and check for rough, loose or noisy movement. If the lifter piece or bearing needs to be replaced, remove the outer snap-ring **(see illustration)** and take the joint piece out of the lifter plate **(see illustration)**. Remove the inner snap-ring **(see illustration)** and replace the bearing with a new one, referring to *Tools and Workshop Tips* at the end of this manual if necessary. Also check the joint piece support in the clutch cover **(see illustration 16.5)** and replace it if worn or damaged.

20   If the lining material of the friction plates smells burnt or if it's glazed, new parts are

16.19b Remove the outer snap-ring

required. If the metal clutch plates are scored or discolored, they must be replaced with new ones. Measure the thickness of each friction plate **(see illustration)** and compare

16.19c Remove the joint piece from the bearing . . .

the results to this Chapter's Specifications. Replace the friction plates as a set if any are near the wear limit.

21   Check the tabs on the friction plates

16.19d . . . and remove the inner snap-ring

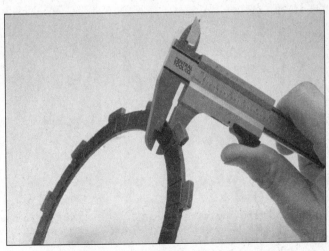

16.20 Measure the thickness of the friction plates

16.22 Check the metal plates for warpage

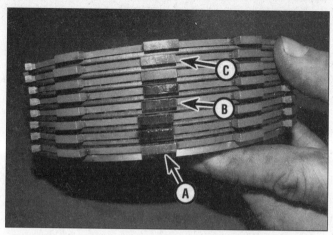

16.28 Here's the friction plate arrangement on 2003 and earlier models - on later models, all six outer plates are the same

A   Dark green tab
B   Black tabs
C   Light green tabs

for excessive wear and mushroomed edges. They can be cleaned up with a file if the deformation is not severe.

22   Lay the metal plates, one at a time, on a perfectly flat surface (such as a piece of plate glass) and check for warpage by trying to slip a feeler gauge between the flat surface and the plate **(see illustration)**. The feeler gauge should be the same thickness as the warpage limit listed in this Chapter's Specifications. Do this at several places around the plate's circumference. If the feeler gauge can be slipped under the plate, it is warped and should be replaced with a new one.

23   Check the judder spring and spring seat for wear from rubbing against each other and for damage. Replace them if problems are found.

24   Check the thrust washers for wear and damage. Replace any worn or damaged parts. Replace the locknuts with new ones.

25   Make sure the clutch pushrod isn't bent (roll it on a perfectly flat surface or use V-blocks and a dial indicator). Check the pushrod and lifter piece for wear or damage and replace them if defects are visible.

26   Clean all traces of old gasket material from the clutch cover and its mating surface on the crankcase.

Installation

27   Clean all oil from the mainshaft splines and threads, then install the clutch housing on the engine. Install the lockwasher with its OUT SIDE mark facing away from the engine. Apply non-permanent thread locking agent to the threads of the nut, then tighten it to the torque listed in this Chapter's Specifications, using one of the methods described in Step 11. Stake the nut into the mainshaft groove.

28   Identify the friction plates. There are three different kinds. The innermost friction plate has a larger internal diameter to accommodate the judder spring and spring seat. On 2001 through 2003 models, the next four can be identified by their black-colored tab and the outermost three by their green-colored tabs **(see illustration)**. On 2004 and later models, the next six friction plates are designed to fit into the deeper slots in the clutch center and the outermost disc fits into the shallow slots.

29   Coat the friction plates with clean engine oil. Install the innermost friction plate on the clutch center. Install the spring seat and judder spring inside of it, with the concave side of the judder spring facing up (away from the spring seat) **(see illustration 16.8g)**.

30   Install a metal plate on top of the friction plate and judder spring **(see illustration)**. Place one end of the clip wire into its hole and wrap it around the clutch center. As you wrap the spring around, push down on the metal plate with a ratchet handle or similar tool to compress the judder spring and expose the clip wire's groove **(see illustration)**. Once you've got the clip wire wrapped all the way around the clutch center and into the groove, push the remaining end through the hole until it latches **(see illustration 16.8b)**.

31   Install a friction plate, then a metal plate, then alternate the remaining friction and metal plates.

32   Coat a new O-ring with clean engine oil and install it in the groove in the clutch center **(see illustration 16.8a)**.

33   Install the pressure plate on the clutch center, aligning its three protrusions with the notches in the clutch center **(see illustration 16.7q)**.

34   Coat a new O-ring with engine oil and install it in the groove on the outer circumference of the clutch piston. Install the clutch piston in the pressure plate, making sure it fits in squarely and is not tilted.

16.30a Install a metal plate on top of the friction plate and judder spring, then insert the clip wire end into its hole and wrap the wire around the clutch center

16.30b Push the metal plate down with a ratchet handle to expose the clip wire's groove and wrap the wire into the groove until you can secure its free end in the hole

16.35 Align the tabs of lifter plate B with the oil holes in the pressure plate

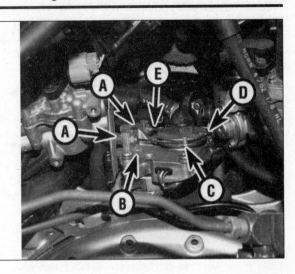

17.2 Reverse actuator details

A   Mounting nuts (two per cable, one on each side of bracket)
B   R mark
C   Reverse cable fitting (shown in Neutral position)
D   Neutral cable fitting (shown in Neutral position)
E   N mark (hidden)

35   Install lifter plate B on top of the clutch piston, aligning its three tabs with the pressure plate oil holes **(see illustration)**.
36   Make sure the friction plate tabs on the innermost friction plates are perfectly aligned with each other and the outermost plate's tabs are centered between them **(see illustration 16.28)**. If they aren't aligned they won't fit into the clutch housing slots.
37   Install the lifter spring in the pressure plate with its concave side facing away from the pressure plate **(see illustration 16.7n)**. Install the retainer ring and fit it securely into the groove **(see illustration 16.7m)**.
38   Coat the splined thrust washer with clean engine oil and install it on the mainshaft **(see illustration 16.7l)**.
39   Install the clutch pack in the clutch housing. The tabs on the innermost friction plates fit into the deep slots; the tabs on the outermost friction plate fit into the shallow slots **(see illustration 16.7j)**.
40   Install the clutch spring seat in lifter plate B with its concave side facing out **(see illustration 16.7i)**. Install the clutch spring on the spring seat with the spring's concave side toward the spring seat **(see illustration 16.7h)**. Slip the spring guide into the center

of the spring and push it onto the mainshaft **(see illustration 16.7g)**. Install the lockwasher on the mainshaft **(see illustration 16.7f)**.
41   Install a new locknut on the mainshaft. Hold the clutch from turning with the tools described in Step 11 and tighten the nut to the torque listed in this Chapter's Specifications. Stake the locknut, using the side of a chisel or other blunt tool so the lip of the locknut will be pushed into the groove and not cut.
42   Lubricate the friction surface of the lifter joint piece and clutch pushrod (the long rod that passes through the mainshaft to the front of the engine) with clean engine oil, then install them in the engine. **Note:** *The clutch pushrod is not readily visible when it's installed, so it's easy to forget to install it. Confirm that it's in position before you put the lifter plate on.*
43   Install lifter plate A on the clutch and secure it with the stopper ring **(see illustrations 16.7c and 16.7b)**.
44   Make sure the clutch cover dowels, oil passage and the oil pickup strainer are in position **(see illustration 16.7a)**. Install a new gasket. Install the cover and tighten its bolts evenly; tighten them securely, but don't strip the threads.

45   The remainder of installation is the reverse of the removal steps.
46   Fill the crankcase with the recommended type and amount of engine oil (see Chapter 1).

17 External reverse linkage - removal and installation

Cable adjustment

1   Remove the right engine cover (see Chapter 8).
2   The reverse shift actuator needs to be in the Neutral position for the next step. If you're not sure that it is, you'll need to remove the center inner fairing (see Chapter 8) and on California models, the EVAP canister (see Chapter 4). Check the positions of the cable fittings **(see illustration)**. When they're in the Neutral position, the cable fittings will be as shown in the illustration, with the neutral cable extended and the reverse cable pulled back. When they're in the Reverse position, the reverse cable will be extended and the neutral cable will be pulled back.
3   Measure the clearance between the neutral outer cable and the cable bracket at the right rear of the engine. It should be zero.
4   Measure the clearance between the reverse outer cable and the cable bracket at the right rear of the engine. It should be 0.3 to 0.8 mm (0.010 to 0.030 inch).
5   If the clearance is incorrect at either cable, loosen the adjuster locknuts and turn the adjusting nuts to correct it **(see illustration)**. Tighten the locknuts once the clearance is correct.
6   With the clearance set correctly, turn the ignition On and move the reverse switch to the on position. This should cause the pulley on the reverse actuator to rotate into the reverse position. While in the reverse position, check for clearance between the reverse

17.5 Reverse actuator cable bracket and adjusters

A   Bracket bolt (with ground cable)
B   Bracket bolt
C   Adjusters
D   Locknuts

17.6 There should be clearance (arrow) between the reverse shift arm (top) and lost motion plate (bottom)

17.10 Label the cables so they don't get mixed up

shift arm and lost motion plate on the mechanism at the right rear of the engine (**see illustration**). There should be some clearance. If not, readjust the cables as described above.

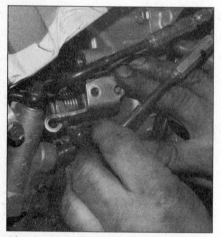

17.11 Slip the cables out of the bracket and detach them from the pulley

Cable replacement

7   Remove the right engine cover and rear master cylinder (see Chapters 8 and 7).

8   Loosen the adjuster locknuts and loosen the cable adjusters all the way (**see illustration 17.5**).

9   At the actuator, loosen the cable mounting nuts and slip the cables up out of the brackets (**see illustration 17.2**). Slip the cables out of the pulley groove and lift the cable end fittings out of the pulley.

> **HAYNES HiNT** *Attach a piece of string to the ends of the cables once they're out of the actuator pulley. When you pull the cables out, the string will follow the cable routing path so you'll know how to route it on installation.*

10   Label the cables and unbolt the cable bracket from the right rear corner of the engine (**see illustration 17.5 and the accompanying illustration**). Note that one of the bolts secures a ground cable.

11   Pull the cable housings out of the bracket (**see illustration**). Slip the cables out

of the pulley groove and lift the cable end fittings out of the pulley.

12   Installation is the reverse of the removal steps. Check the cable adjustment as described above.

Linkage removal and installation

13   Remove the rear master cylinder (see Chapter 7).

14   Unbolt the reverse cable bracket at the right rear corner of the engine (**see illustration 17.10**).

15   Remove the linkage bolt, then remove the washer, collar, lost motion spring, pulley (together with the shift cables and bracket) and lost motion plate (**see illustrations**). If you plan to disassemble the linkage further, this is a convenient time to disengage the cables from the pulley.

> ⚠ *Warning: During the next step, do not place your finger over the end of the spring or it will hit your finger as you pull the spring off.*

17.15a Remove the bolt . . .

17.15b . . . washer, collar, spring and pulley . . .

17.15c ... noting how the spring ends engage the pulley ...

17.15d ... and take them off the engine together with the lost motion plate (arrow)

17.16a Note how the pulley spring engages the tab on the rear crankcase cover (arrow) and take it off

17.16b Remove the bushing ...

17.16c ... collar ...

16   Remove the reverse shift arm (pulley) spring, bushing, collar, bearing and washer **(see illustrations)**.
17   Pry the seal out of the engine **(see illus-**tration 17.16d)**. Press in a new one with a seal driver or socket the same diameter as the seal.
18   Take the lost motion plate out of the spring and off of the reverse shift arm (pulley).
19   Pry the reverse shift arm's tab out of the spring and separate the two of them.

17.16d ... bearing ...

17.16e ... and the washer behind the bearing

20   Check all parts for wear and damage. Replace any parts that have problems.
21   Installation is the reverse of the removal steps. Assemble the reverse shift arm and lost motion plate to the spring before you install them **(see illustrations)**. Tighten the bolt to the torque listed in this Chapter's Specifications.
22   Adjust the cables as described above.

Actuator removal and installation

23   Remove the right engine cover (see Chapter 8). Remove the air cleaner housing (see Chapter 4). If you're working on a California model, remove the EVAP system purge control solenoid.
24   Loosen the cable adjusters all the way to create slack in the cables (see Chapter 1).
25   Loosen the locknuts that secure the cables to the actuator **(see illustration 17.5)**. Slip the cables out of the actuator brackets, then disconnect them from the pulley.
26   Unbolt the actuator **(see illustrations)**. Tilt the actuator down and take it out, together with the rubber baffle beneath it.

17.21a Pry the spring ends apart . . .

17.21b . . . and slip them over the lost motion plate

27   Check the rubber baffle for damage or deterioration. Replace it if necessary.
28   Clean all traces of old gasket from the mounting posts and engine **(see illustration 17.26c)**.
29   Installation is the reverse of the removal

steps. Use new gaskets. Tighten the bolts securely, but don't overtighten them and strip the threads. Connect and adjust the cables as described above.

18 Rear case cover - removal, bearing inspection and installation

Removal

1   Remove the engine from the motorcycle (see Section 7).
2   Remove the water pump (see Chapter 3).
3   Remove the external reverse linkage and the clutch (see Sections 17 and 16).
4   Disconnect the breather hose from the top of the rear case cover.
5   Unbolt the output shaft bearing holder from the engine **(see illustrations)**.
6   Reinstall the shift linkage temporarily and shift the transmission into a gear (not neutral). This is necessary so the mainshaft

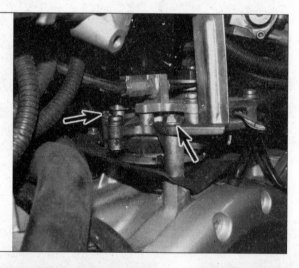

17.26a Remove the actuator bolts, two on the right side (arrows) . . .

17.26b . . . and two on the left side

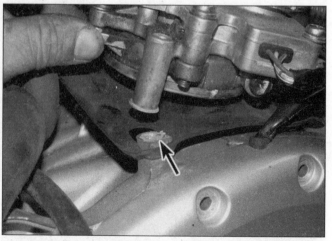

17.26c Lift the actuator up, then forward and down to remove it together with the rubber baffle - use new gaskets (arrow) at the mounting bolt locations

can be used to hold the output shaft from turning.

7   Cover the openings in the back of the crankcase with duct tape to keep metal shavings out of the engine **(see illustration)**. Grind away the staked portions of the output shaft locknut, using a die grinder or Dremel tool with a narrow grinding bit. Lock the output shaft by placing the mainshaft holder (Honda tool 07JMB-MN50200 or equivalent) over the end of the mainshaft and holding it with a wrench **(see illustration)**. Place a 12-point 30 mm socket (Honda tool 07916-MB00001 or equivalent) over the output shaft locknut, then unscrew the locknut with a breaker bar **(see illustration)**.

8   Unscrew the rear case cover bolts **(see illustration)**. Tap the cover loose with a soft-faced mallet and take it off the engine, then locate the dowel pins and remove the old gasket **(see illustration)**.

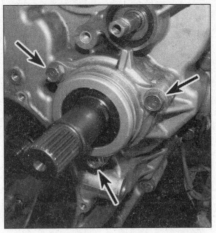

18.5a Unbolt the output shaft bearing holder (arrows)

18.5b Use a new O-ring (arrow) on installation - replace the seal if it's worn or damaged

18.7a Tape the engine openings to keep metal shavings out, and rinse them off with spray cleaner - DO NOT blow them off with an air compressor!

18.7b Use these tools to hold the mainshaft and loosen the nut

18.7c Unscrew the nut from the output shaft

18.8a Rear case cover bolts (arrows)

18.8b Remove the cover and locate the dowels (right arrows) and the oil passage and O-ring (left arrow)

18.10 The clutch pressure regulator (arrow) is installed on the inside of the cover

18.14a Drive in a new oil seal with a seal driver or socket . . .

Inspection

9 Check the cover for obvious problems, such as warpage, cracks or a damaged gasket surface, and replace it if problems are found.

10 Rotate the bearings in the cover and check them for roughness, looseness or noise **(see illustration)**. If the bearings are in bad or doubtful condition, replace them.

11 The mainshaft bearing is held in place by a pair of retainers bolted to the cover. To replace it, unbolt the retainers and tap the bearing out of its bore with a bearing driver or a socket the same diameter as the bearing outer race. Drive in a new bearing, using the same tool. Apply non-permanent thread locking agent to the retainer bolts. Place the retainers on the bearing with their OUTSIDE marks facing away from the rear cover, then install the bolts. Tighten them securely, but don't overtighten them and strip the threads.

12 The reverse shifter shaft bearing and output shaft bearing are interference (tight) fits in the cover. If either bearing needs to be replaced, tap the bearing out of its bore with a bearing driver or a socket the same diameter as the bearing outer race. Drive in a new bearing, using the same tool.

13 Check the clutch pressure regulator by pressing it into its housing with a screwdriver or similar tool **(see illustration 18.10)**. It should move freely return all the way to the top. If necessary, remove the snap-ring from the valve and take out the spring seat, spring and piston. Check all parts for wear and damage and replace as needed.

14 Replace the O-ring in the output shaft cover with a new one **(see illustration 18.5b)**. If the seal is worn or damaged, drive it out, then press in a new one with a seal driver or socket the same diameter as the seal **(see illustrations)**. Due to the amount of work involved in removing the engine, it's

18.14b . . . until it's seated all the way

a good idea to replace the seal whenever the output shaft cover is removed from the rear cover.

Installation

15 If the starter idle gears came off with the cover, remove them from the cover and install them on the back of the engine **(see illustration)**. If the alternator driven gear or its washers came off with the cover, remove them from the cover and install them on the back of the engine **(see illustration 19.2)**.

16 Apply a dab of sealant to each of the crankcase parting lines. Be sure the dowels and oil passage are in position. Lubricate a new oil passage O-ring with clean engine oil and install it on the oil passage. Install a new gasket.

17 Place the cover on the engine and finger-tighten its bolts. Then tighten the bolts evenly in stages to the torque listed in this Chapter's Specifications.

18 If the transmission is in neutral, place it in a gear. Hold the mainshaft with the tool

18.15 If the starter reduction gear and shaft came off with the cover, reinstall them on the back of the engine

described in Step 7 and install a new output shaft locknut. Tighten the locknut to the torque listed in this Chapter's Specifications, then stake it into the output shaft.

19 Coat a new output shaft bearing holder O-ring with engine oil and install it in the holder **(see illustration 18.5b)**. Install the holder on the engine and tighten its bolts to the torque listed in this Chapter's Specifications.

20 The remainder of installation is the reverse of the removal steps.

19 Alternator driven gear - removal, inspection and installation

Removal

1 Remove the rear case cover (see Section 18).

19.2 Remove the washers from the back of the alternator driven gear

19.3 Pry the drive gear teeth together with a screwdriver . . .

2   Remove the washers from the back of the alternator driven gear **(see illustration)**.

3   Place a box wrench on the starter clutch bolt and insert a screwdriver into one of the holes in the alternator drive gear **(see illustration)**. Hold the starter clutch with the wrench so it won't turn, and pry sideways with the screwdriver to align the teeth of the drive gear's two parts with each other. This will relieve tension on the alternator driven gear, so you can pull it out of the engine.

4   While holding the screwdriver in the pry position, pull the alternator driven gear out of the engine **(see illustration)**.

Inspection

5   Check the alternator driven gear for wear or damage. It can't be disassembled; replace it as a unit if problems are found.

6   Check the driven gear bearing in the back of the crankcase for loose, rough or noisy movement. If problems are found, replace it, referring to *Tools and Workshop Tips* at the end of this manual.

7   Thoroughly clean all parts in high flash point solvent and check them for wear or damage. Since needle roller bearing wear can be difficult to see, the bearings should be replaced if there's any doubt about their condition.

Installation

8   Installation is the reverse of the removal steps.

20 Starter clutch - removal, inspection and installation

Removal

1   Remove the rear case cover (see Section 18).

2   Hold the starter clutch so it won't turn by temporarily installing the clutch housing on the mainshaft and holding it with a clutch removal tool. Remove the starter clutch bolt

19.4 . . . and take the driven gear off

and washer **(see illustrations)**. **Note:** *the starter clutch bolt is marked with a counter-clockwise arrow to indicate that is has left-hand threads (turn clockwise to loosen and*

20.2a The counterclockwise arrow on the starter clutch bolt indicates that it has left-hand threads (turn clockwise to loosen)

20.2b Remove the bolt and washer . . .

20.3 ... and pull the starter clutch off the engine

21.3 Note how the starter reduction gear aligns with the other gears, then take it off

counterclockwise to tighten).
3   Pull off the starter clutch **(see illustration)**.

Inspection

4   Place the starter clutch on a bench with its gear upward and try to rotate the gear in both directions. It should turn only clockwise (viewed from the gear side). If it turns both ways or neither way, the starter clutch sprag clutch is damaged.
5   To inspect the sprag clutch and bearing, lift out the gear. Check the clutch boss on the gear (the part that fits into the sprag clutch) for wear or damage. Also check the bearing and the sprag clutch. Replace the starter clutch if problems are found.
6   Coat the bearing and sprag clutch with clean engine oil, then install the gear in the sprag clutch, turning it clockwise as you install it.

Installation

7   Installation is the reverse of the removal steps.

---

21 Starter reduction gear, primary gears and alternator drive gear - removal, inspection and installation

Removal

1   Remove the rear case cover (see Section 18).
2   Remove the alternator driven gear and starter clutch (see Sections 19 and 20).
3   Note how the starter reduction gear engages the other gears, then remove it together with its shaft **(see illustration)**.
4   Align the splines of the spline washer with those on the mainshaft, then slip the spline washer off **(see illustration)**.
5   The primary drive gear is made in two halves, which are spring loaded to keep the teeth slightly separated. This reduces gear noise. To disengage the primary drive gear from the driven gear, insert a screwdriver into the drive gear teeth and twist it to relieve the

21.4 Take the spline washer off

spring tension **(see illustration)**. Slide the driven gear off **(see illustration)**.
6   Slip the primary drive gear off the crankshaft **(see illustration)**.
7   Unbolt the alternator drive gear and take it off **(see illustrations)**.

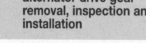

21.5a Pry the gear halves into alignment ...

21.5b ... and take the driven gear off

21.6 Remove the primary drive gear

21.7a Unbolt the alternator drive gear . . .

21.7b . . . and take it off the engine

a) Tighten the alternator drive gear bolts to the torque listed in this Chapter's Specifications.
b) Install the primary driven gear with its longer boss facing away from the engine (see illustration 21.5b).
c) Align the primary drive gear teeth while installing the driven gear (see illustration 21.5a).

22 Reverse gears and shifter shaft - removal, inspection and installation

Removal

1   Remove the rear case cover (see Section 18).
2   Pull the starter idle gear out of the engine (see illustration 21.3).
3   Take the washer and reverse idle gear off the reverse shifter shaft (see illustration).
4   Pull the reverse shifter shaft assembly out of the case (see illustration).

Inspection

8   The alternator drive gear can be inspected without removing it from the crankshaft. If it needs to be replaced due to wear or damage, or if the crankshaft will be removed from the engine, unbolt the gear and take it off.

9   Check the remaining gear teeth for wear or damage. The drive and driven gears should be replaced as a set if one of them needs to be replaced.

Installation

10   Installation is the reverse of the removal steps, with the following additions:

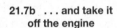

22.3 Take the washer and reverse idle gear off the shifter shaft

22.4 Remove the reverse shifter shaft from the engine

22.5a Unbolt the starter drive gear holder (arrows)

22.5b Take the drive gear off the engine and locate the dowels (arrows)

5   Unbolt the starter drive gear holder from the case, then take it off and locate the dowels **(see illustrations)**.

Inspection

6   Take the roller pin out of the shifter shaft **(see illustration)**. Slide the washer, reverse idle gear and combined shift gear and reverse shifter off.

7   Remove the snap-ring and washer and separate the reverse shifter from the shift gear, then remove the washer and bearings **(see illustration)**.

8   Thoroughly clean all parts in high flash point solvent and check them for wear or damage. Since needle roller bearing wear can be difficult to see, the bearings should be replaced if there's any doubt about their condition.

9   Spin the bearings in the starter drive gear holder and check them for wear or damage. The bearings can be replaced with a press and the appropriate size drivers. Before replacing the needle bearing, drive the stopper shaft and collar out of the holder with a hammer and punch **(see illustration 21.3)**. When installing the stopper shaft, make sure its installed height is within the range listed in this Chapter's Specifications.

Installation

10   Installation is the reverse of the removal steps, plus the following additions:

a)   *Lubricate the roller pin with grease.*
b)   *Lubricate the other parts with oil containing molybdenum disulfide.*
c)   *Install the reverse idle gear with its OUT mark facing away from the engine.*

23 Output shaft and final drive gear - removal, inspection and installation

Removal

1   Remove the primary gears (see Section 21).

2   Pull the output shaft out of the engine **(see illustration)**.

3   Grind away the staked portions of the final drive gear locknut without damaging the countershaft threads **(see illustration)**.

4   Temporarily reinstall the shift pedal and place the transmission in any gear except neutral. This will hold the countershaft so the locknut can be removed.

5   Turn the locknut clockwise to loosen (it has left-hand threads). Remove the washer from behind the locknut and pull the final drive gear off **(see illustration)**.

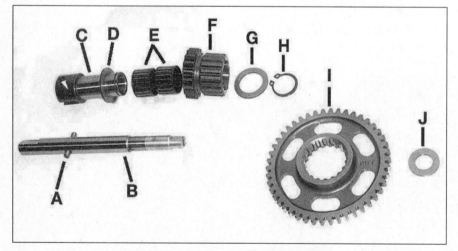

22.6 Reverse shifter shaft assembly details

A   Roller pin
B   Reverse shifter shaft
C   Reverse shifter
D   Washer

E   Needle roller bearings
F   Shift gear
G   Washer

H   Snap-ring
I   Reverse idle gear
J   Washer

22.7 Remove the snap-ring and washer and separate the shift gear from the reverse shifter

23.2 Take the output shaft out of the engine

23.3 Grind away the staked portions of the locknut (lower arrows) - the arrow mark on the nut (upper arrow) indicates that it has left-hand threads (turn clockwise to loosen)

6   Unbolt the countershaft bearing retainer from the crankcase **(see illustration)**.

Inspection

7   Check the gears for worn or damaged teeth and replace them if problems are found.
8   Check the output shaft for wear or damage, such as a broken spring. Spin the bearing on the end of the output shaft and check it for roughness, looseness or noise.
9   If problems are found, remove the snap-ring, retainer and keepers from the end of the output shaft. Place the shaft in a press and press it out of the bearing, then remove the collar, final driven gear, washer, damper lifter, spring and reverse driven gear from the shaft.
Note: *If you don't have a press, take the shaft*

to a Honda dealer for disassembly and parts replacement.
10   Measure the free length of the damper spring. Also measure the output shaft diameter at the snap-ring end, the inner and outer diameters of the collar, and the inside diameter of the reverse driven gear. If any of these measurements are not within the range listed in this Chapter's Specifications, replace the affected part.
11   Reverse Step 9 to reassemble the shaft. The dished side of the reverse driven gear faces the output shaft spring. The tab on the inner diameter of the retainer goes opposite the keyway in the shaft. The sealed side·of the ball bearing faces away from the gear.
12   Check the small oil hole in the inner diameter of the final drive gear (between the splines). Make sure it's not clogged.

13   Inspect the countershaft ball bearing in the crankcase. If it's rough, loose or noisy when you spin it, pull it out and install a new one.

Installation

14   Installation is the reverse of the removal steps, with the following additions:

a) *Install the countershaft bearing retainer with its OUT SIDE mark facing away from the crankcase and tighten its bolts to the torque listed in this Chapter's Specifications.*
b) *Coat the threads of a new locknut with non-permanent thread locking agent. Tighten the nut to the torque listed in this Chapter's Specifications (turn counterclockwise to tighten), then stake it in two places.*

23.5 Unscrew the locknut and remove the washer

23.6 Unbolt the countershaft bearing retainer

24.2a At the top, the reverse lockout linkage engages the reverse switch

24.2b At the bottom, unbolt the shift drum lock arm (arrow) . . .

24.2c . . . and take the linkage off

Make sure the return spring on the bottom of the linkage is correctly installed and in good condition **(see illustration)**. If necessary, unbolt the drum from the engine **(see illustration 24.2b)**.

4   Installation is the reverse of the removal steps. Apply non-permanent thread locking agent to the bolt threads and tighten it to the torque listed in this Chapter's Specifications.

25 Oil pump chain and sprocket - removal, inspection and installation

Removal

1   Remove the rear case cover and primary driven gear (see Sections 18 and 21).
2   Hold the crankshaft so it won't turn while you remove the oil pump sprocket bolt **(see illustration)**. One way to do this is to temporarily reinstall the clutch housing, then use it as a handle to keep the sprocket from turning.

24 Reverse lockout system - removal and installation

1   Remove the rear case cover, reverse gears and shifter shaft (see Sections 18

and 22). If necessary for access, remove the output shaft and final drive gear (see Section 23).
2   Note how the system is installed, then remove it from the rear of the crankcase **(see illustrations)**.
3   Check all parts for wear and damage.

24.3 Here's how the linkage spring is installed

25.2 Temporarily reinstall the clutch housing and use it as a handle while you unbolt the oil pump sprocket

25.3a Remove the bolt - the sprocket's OUT mark faces away from the engine

25.3b Take off the sprocket together with the driven gear boss and chain

25.4 Unbolt the baffle plate and take it off

26.4a Remove the cover bolts (arrows)

3   Once the sprocket bolt is removed, remove the holding tools. Unbolt the sprocket from the oil pump shaft and slide it off the mainshaft, together with the driven gear boss and chain **(see illustrations)**.
4   If necessary, remove the baffle plate from behind the sprocket **(see illustration)**.

Inspection

5   Check the oil pump chain for looseness between the links. If the chain flops sideways when you hold it up, replace it. If the sprocket teeth are damaged, replace the sprocket and the driven gear boss.

Installation

6   Installation is the reverse of the removal steps, with the following additions:

a) *Install the oil pump sprocket with its OUT mark facing away from the engine.*
b) *Tighten the sprocket bolt to the torque listed in this Chapter's Specifications.*

26 Front case cover - removal and installation

1   Place the transmission in neutral.
2   Drain the engine oil and coolant (see Chapter 1).
3   Remove the fairing front cover and under cover (see Chapter 8). If you're working on a California model, remove the EVAP canister (see Chapter 4).
4   Remove the cover bolts and take the cover off the engine, locate the dowels and remove the gasket **(see illustrations)**.
5   Turn the pin on the gearshift position sensor to align with the notch in the shift

26.4b Take the cover off and locate the dowels

26.5 The long end of the switch pin (lower arrow) aligns with the notch in the shift drum joint (upper arrow)

27.2 Make alignment marks on the shift linkage arm and shaft, then remove the pinch bolt (left arrow) completely - remove the Allen bolt (right arrow) to remove the pedal

27.7a Remove the bolt (arrow) and take the shift drum joint off the shift drum

27.7b Remove the drum joint and dowels

27.8 Pry the stopper lever to the left, compress the pawls against the springs to the right and pull off the shift drum cam and its dowel

drum joint **(see illustration)**.

6   Make sure the dowels are in position.

7   Place a quarter-inch wide dab of sealant across the crankcase parting lines at top center and bottom center of the gasket surface, then install a new gasket over the dowels.

8   Position the cover on the engine and install its bolts. Tighten the bolts evenly, in two or three stages, in a criss-cross pattern. Tighten the bolts securely, but don't overtighten them and damage the threads.

9   The remainder of installation is the reverse of the removal steps.

27 External shift mechanism - removal, inspection and installation ⚒

Shift pedal - removal and installation

1   Place the bike on its centerstand.

2   Look for alignment marks on the shift linkage arm and shaft **(see illustration)**. If there aren't any, make your own. Remove the pinch bolt completely and take the arm off the shaft.

3   Remove the pedal Allen bolt and slide the pedal off the shaft.

4   Installation is the reverse of the removal steps. Tighten the Allen bolt to the torque listed in this Chapter's Specifications. Tighten the pinch bolt securely, but don't overtighten it and strip the threads.

Shift mechanism
Removal

5   The stopper arm, shift drum center and cam plate are the only parts of the external shift linkage that can be removed without disassembling the crankcase. The shift arm, generally considered part of the external linkage, is bolted to components on the inside of the crankcase, so the crankcase must be disassembled to remove it.

6   Remove the front engine case (see Section 26).

7   Unbolt the shift drum joint from the shift drum **(see illustration)**. Remove the drum joint and dowels **(see illustration)**.

8   Lift the stopper arm and compress the shift arm pawls **(see illustration)**. Remove the shift drum cam and its dowel pin.

9   Remove the nut and washer from the stopper lever, then remove the stopper lever, collar and spring **(see illustration)**.

Inspection

10   Check the condition of the stopper lever and spring. Replace the stopper lever if it's worn where it contacts the shift drum. Replace the spring if it's distorted.

11   Inspect the dowels on the end of the shift drum **(see illustration)**. If they're worn or damaged, replace them. If their holes in the end of the shift drum are enlarged, you'll have to disassemble the crankcase to replace the shift drum.

27.9 Unbolt the stopper lever and remove it, its spring and collar

27.11 Make sure the dowels are in position

12 If the shift drum bearing is worn, remove the bearing retainer **(see illustration 27.7a)**. Take the bearing out of the case and install a new one.

13 Check the pawl and springs on the shift arm for wear or damage **(see illustration)**. If problems are found, the crankcase will have to be disassembled to remove the shift arm.

Installation

14 If the drum center was removed from the shift drum, install it. Be sure to reinstall the shift cam dowel as well as the shift drum joint dowels **(see illustration 27.11)**. Tighten the drum center bolt to the torque listed in this Chapter's Specifications.

15 Apply non-permanent thread locking agent to the threads of the stopper lever bolt, then install the washer, stopper lever and return spring **(see illustration)**. Make sure the stopper lever engages the neutral detent in the shift drum. Tighten the bolt securely, but

don't overtighten it and damage the threads.

16 The remainder of installation is the reverse of the removal steps, plus the following additions:

a) *Before installing the front case cover, operate the shift linkage by hand to make sure it works properly.*

b) *Fill the engine with oil and coolant (see Chapter 1).*

28 Crankcase - disassembly and reassembly

1 To examine and repair or replace the pistons, connecting rods, bearings, oil pump, crankshaft, internal shift linkage or transmission components, the crankcase must be split into two parts. Before you start, read through the procedure, paying special attention to the Honda

piston ring compressor used for assembly. Experienced Honda mechanics consider this tool essential. Even for experienced professional mechanics who use the special tool and have an assistant to help, it often takes more than one try to get the case halves together.

Disassembly

2 Remove the engine from the motorcycle (see Section 7).

3 Remove the cylinder heads, cam chains, gearshift linkage, reverse shifter, reverse locknut linkage, alternator driven gear, starter idle gear, primary gears and output shaft as described earlier in this Chapter.

4 Refer to Chapter 3 and remove the coolant hose fitting from the left side of the crankcase.

5 Unscrew four 8 mm bolts from the left side of the crankcase **(see illustration)**.

6 From the right side of the crankcase, remove eleven 6 mm bolts and eight 10 mm

27.13 Here's how the pawl spring and return spring are installed

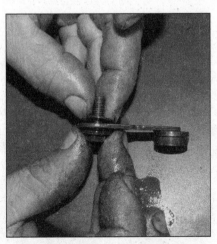

27.15 Don't forget to install the washer on the stopper lever bolt

28.5 Remove four bolts from the left side of the crankcase (arrows)

28.6a On the right side of the crankcase, remove eight 9 mm bolts (arrows) . . .

28.6b . . . two 6 mm bolts at the bottom front (arrows) . . .

28.6c . . . five 6 mm bolts along the top . . .

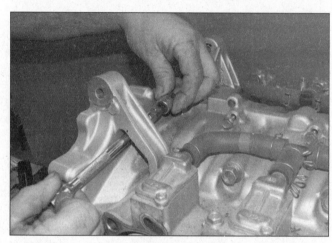

28.6d . . . to reach the rearmost top bolt, place an extension through the engine mount bracket, then attach a socket . . .

bolts (see illustrations). Loosen the bolts in several stages, working in a cross-cross pattern.

7 Place the crankcase with the left side down. Carefully separate the crankcase

halves partway, then support them with wooden blocks. Pry only at the pry points (see illustration). Do not pry against the mating surfaces.

8 Slip shop towels into the opening to

cover the transmission gears and beneath the pistons so the pistons won't fall against the engine and be damaged. If the crankcase halves won't separate easily, make sure all fasteners have been removed. Don't pry

28.6e . . . and four 6 mm bolts along the bottom

28.7 Pry only at the pry points (arrow)

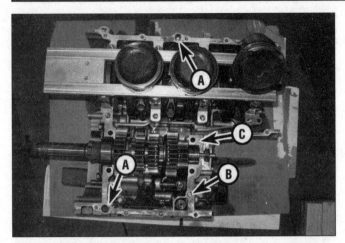

28.10 Locate the dowels (A) and oil passage (B) - on assembly, make sure the oil channel (C) is clear

28.17 Place the aluminum piston base under the no. 3 and no. 5 pistons and the plastic base under the no. 1 piston

against the crankcase mating surfaces or they will leak.

9   Lift the right crankcase half all the way off.

10   Look for the oil passage and the dowels **(see illustration)**. If they're not in one of the crankcase halves, locate them.

11   Refer to Sections 29 through 41 for information on the internal components of the crankcase.

Reassembly

12   Make sure the transmission mainshaft is correctly positioned in the right crankcase half (see Section 39). Make sure the crankshaft is fully installed, with all connecting rods, pistons and rings. The timing chain sprocket must be installed on the end of the crankshaft.

13   You'll need a pair of supports later in the procedure. Make a pair of wooden support blocks (3-3/8 by 1-1/2 by 1-1/2 inches).

14   Set the crankcase assembly on a workbench with the right side downward. Rotate the crankshaft so the no. 1 piston (forward

piston on the right side of the engine) is at the top of its travel.

15   Remove all traces of sealant from the crankcase mating surfaces. Be careful not to let any fall into the case as this is done. Check to make sure the dowel pins and oil passage are in place **(see illustration 28.10)**.

16   Slip the aluminum piston base under the no. 3 and no. 5 pistons, then release it so the pistons are supported **(see illustration 28.10)**.

17   Place the white plastic piston base under no. 1 piston **(see illustration)**.

18   Place the wooden support blocks upright on the left crankcase mating surface, one on each side of the engine.

19   Lubricate the pistons, rings and cylinder walls with clean engine oil.

20   Place a ring compressor over each piston and secure it with Velcro strips **(see illustration 28.17)**. Be sure to position the removal cords and the gaps in the ring compressors as shown, so the cords will pull the Velcro strips off after the right crankcase half

is installed over the pistons. If the cords are placed on the wrong side of the engine or the gaps are in the wrong place, it will be impossible to separate the ring compressor halves.

21   Place the supports from Step 7 on diagonally opposite corners of the engine, at the dowel locations, to support the right case half. Once the case half is on far enough that the no. 1 piston rings are in their cylinder, you'll need to stop lowering it so you can remove the ring compressor and the white plastic support tool. This will be much easier if the case half has something to rest on.

22   Lower the crankcase half straight onto the no. 1 piston until it rests on the supports **(see illustration)**. As you lower the case half, make sure the shift fork in the right case half engages the groove in the lower case half **(see illustration)**. Once it reaches the supports, remove the plastic piston base **(see illustration)**. Be very careful not to force the ring compressors off of the pistons, or you'll have to lift up the case and start over.

23   Pull the strings of the no. 1 piston's ring compressor to detach the Velcro strips. Take

28.22a Lower the crankcase half onto the support blocks

28.22b Be sure the shift fork in the upper case half fits into its gear groove

28.22c Remove the plastic piston base from no. 1 piston

28.23 Remove the ring compressor from no. 1 piston

28.25 Remove the aluminum piston base from no. 3 and no. 5 pistons

the ring compressor halves out of the crankcase **(see illustration)**.

24   Lift the case half slightly to take the weight off the support blocks, then turn the supports on their sides. Lower the right crankcase half onto the supports. At this point, the cylinders of no. 3 and no. 5 pistons (center and rear) should have slid down over the piston rings.

25   Pull the aluminum piston support tool out of the engine **(see illustration)**.

26   Pull the rear (no. 5) piston's ring compressor down until it's clear of the cylinder, then pull on its removal cords to separate the ring compressor halves and take the ring compressor out the rear of the engine **(see illustrations)**. Remove the ring compressor from no. 3 cylinder, then remove it out the rear of the engine in the same way.

27   Apply a thin, even bead of sealant to the periphery of the crankcase mating surfaces in the areas not supported by the wooden blocks. This isn't easy to do with

the crankcase halves so close together, but it's necessary to do it now (rather than earlier) to ensure that the sealant doesn't cure before the case halves are fitted together. Be sure to coat the two surfaces on either side of the clutch pushrod seal bore. Once you've applied sealant to these areas, have an assistant lift the case up while you remove the support block, then apply sealant in the areas where the support blocks were.

28   Lower the right case half onto the left case half.

29   Lubricate the threads and seating surfaces of the 10 mm bolts that go into the right case half with clean engine oil. Install all of the case bolts (10 mm and 6 mm). Tighten the bolts, in several stages and a criss-cross pattern, to the torques listed in this Chapter's Specifications.

30   Turn the mainshaft to make sure it turns freely. Also make sure the crankshaft turns freely.

31   The remainder of assembly is the reverse of disassembly.

29 Crankcase components - inspection and servicing

1   After the crankcases have been separated and the crankshaft, shift cam and forks and transmission components removed, the crankcases should be cleaned thoroughly with new solvent and dried with compressed air.

2   Remove the oil passage if it hasn't already been removed. All oil passages should be blown out with compressed air.

3   All traces of old gasket sealant should be removed from the mating surfaces. Minor damage to the surfaces can be cleaned up with a fine sharpening stone or grindstone

Caution: Be very careful not to nick or gouge the crankcase mating surfaces or leaks will result. Check both crankcase halves very carefully for cracks and other damage.

4   If any damage is found that can't be repaired, replace the crankcase halves as a set.

28.26a Remove the compressor from no. 5 piston and take it out the back of the engine

28.26b Remove the compressor from no. 3 piston and remove it the same way

30.2a Remove the oil strainer bolt (upper arrow) and mounting bolts (lower arrows)

30.2b Remove the strainer from the pump and remove its sealing ring - the small diameter of the sealing ring goes toward the pump

30 Oil pump - removal, inspection and installation

Removal

1   Refer to Section 28 and disassemble the crankcase.
2   Unbolt the strainer and pump from the left crankcase half and locate the pump dowels and O-ring **(see illustrations)**.

Inspection

3   Remove the pump assembly bolts **(see illustration)**.
4   Take the cover off the pump. Remove the scavenge rotors and drive pin **(see illustrations)**. Locate the dowels. **Note:** *If the cover won't slide off the pump shaft easily, polish the end of the shaft with 400-grit sandpaper.*

30.2c Lift the pump out of the engine and locate its dowels (arrows) - the large dowel and the small dowel in the pump recess have O-rings

30.3 Remove the pump cover bolts (arrows)

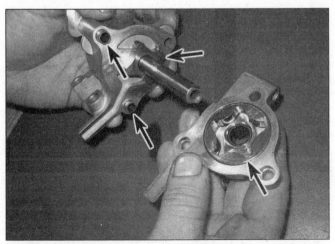

30.4a Remove the pump cover, the scavenge rotors and dowel pins

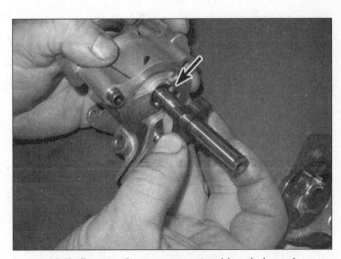

30.4b Remove the scavenge rotor drive pin (arrow)

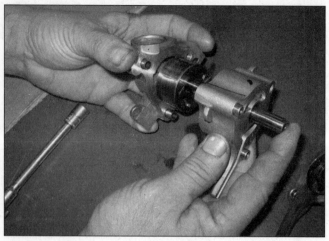

30.5a Separate the feed pump body from the pump housing

30.5b Take out the thrust washer and second drive pin (arrows)

30.7 Measure the clearance between inner and outer rotors, between outer rotors and their pump bodies and between the pump bodies and a straightedge

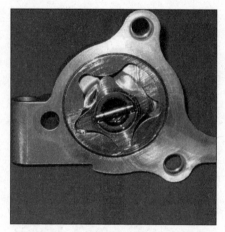

30.8 Each set of rotors has its own drive pin - be sure they're both installed

31.2a Bend back the lockwasher tab (arrow)

5   Separate the feed pump body from the pump housing **(see illustration)**. Remove the feed rotors, thrust washer and drive pin **(see illustration)**.
Take the rotors off the pump. Wash the oil pump in solvent, then dry it off.
6   Check the pump body and rotors for scoring and wear. If any damage or uneven or excessive wear is evident, replace the pump (individual parts aren't available). If you are rebuilding the engine, it's a good idea to install a new oil pump.
7   Measure the clearance between the inner and outer rotor tips and between the outer rotor and housing **(see illustration)**. Place a straightedge across the pump body and measure the gap between the straightedge and rotors with a feeler gauge. Replace the pump if any of the clearances is excessive.
8   If the pump is good, reverse the disassembly steps to reassemble it. Make sure the pins are centered in the rotor shaft so they will align with the slots in the inner rotors

(see illustration).
9   Make sure the strainer is clean.

Installation

10   Before installing the pump, prime it by pouring oil into it while turning the shaft by hand - this will ensure that it begins to pump oil quickly.
11   Installation is the reverse of removal, with the following additions:
a) *Be sure the pump-to-engine dowels and O-rings are in position.*
b) *Tighten the mounting bolts securely, but don't overtighten them and strip the threads.*

31 Internal shift linkage - removal, inspection and installation

Removal

1   Refer to Section 28 and disassemble the crankcase.

2   In the left case half, bend back the lockwasher tab and remove the shift arm bolt **(see illustrations)**.
3   On the outside of the case at the front, note how the return spring ends fit over the

31.2b Remove the lockwasher and bolt

31.3a Pull the shift arm shaft partway out of the case - note the location of the washer

31.3b Pull the shift spindle (arrow) out of the case

return spring post (see illustration 27.13). Pull the shift arm shaft partway out of the case and lift out the spindle arm (see illustrations). Then pull the shift arm shaft the rest of the way out and remove the thrust washer (see illustration 31.3a).

Inspection

4   Inspect the return spring post (see illustration 27.13). If it's worn or damaged, replace it. If it's loose, unscrew it, apply a non-permanent thread locking compound to the threads, reinstall the post and tighten it to the torque listed in this Chapter's Specifications.
5   Check the shift arm shaft for bends. If the shaft is bent, replace it. Inspect the pawls and springs on the shift shaft and replace the shaft if they're worn or damaged (see illustration 27.13).

6   Check the shift arm and shift spindle for wear at their contact points. Replace worn parts.
7   Check the shift shaft and shift spindle needle roller bearings in the crankcase (see illustration). If any of them are worn or damaged, remove it with a slide hammer puller and tap in a new one. To prevent damage to the new bearing, you'll need a shouldered drift with a small diameter the same size as the bearing inner diameter.

Installation

8   Installation is the reverse of the removal steps. Use a new lockwasher on the shift arm bolt. Tighten the bolt to the torque listed in this Chapter's Specifications and bend the lockwasher tab against the bolt.

32 Piston/connecting rod assemblies - removal, connecting rod inspection and installation

Removal

1   Remove both cylinder heads and disassemble the crankcase (see Sections 12 and 28).
2   Before removing the connecting rods from the crankshaft, measure the side clearance of each rod with a feeler gauge (see illustration). If the clearance on any rod is greater than that listed in this Chapter's Specifications, that rod will have to be replaced with a new one. If the clearance is still excessive after replacing the rod, the crankshaft will have to be replaced.

31.7 Check the three needle roller bearings for wear or damage

32.2 Measure connecting rod side clearance with a feeler gauge

32.3a Mark the cylinder number on each connecting rod

32.3b Label the pistons as well; it's a good idea to wrap them in padding so the skirts won't be damaged

32.4a Lay the right side connecting rods down so the nuts are accessible, then remove them (arrows)

32.4b Separate the caps from the connecting rods; the lines on the rod and cap (upper arrow) are a Roman numeral that indicates a bearing selection code; the letter (lower arrow) is a weight grade

3   There aren't any cylinder numbers marked on the connecting rods and caps, and it's important to reinstall them in their original locations. Using a felt pen or a center punch, mark the cylinder number on each rod and cap (see illustration). Number the pistons as well; if they're reused, they must be returned to their original cylinders (see illustration).

4   Unscrew the right side bearing cap nuts, separate the caps from the rods, then detach the rods from the crankshaft (see illustrations). If the cap is stuck, tap on the ends of the rod bolts with a soft face hammer to free them.

5   Temporarily reassemble the rods to the caps so the rods and caps don't get mixed up.

6   Unscrew the left side bearing cap nuts and separate the caps from the rods (see illustration). If the engine is still on a workbench with its left side facing down, lay it flat. Tap gently on the studs of the connecting rods with a wooden hammer handle to push the pistons out of their bores, then carefully remove the rods without scratching the cylinders. Temporarily reassemble the rods to the caps so the rods and caps don't get mixed up.

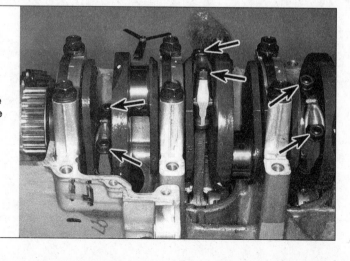

32.6 Remove the cap nuts from the left connecting rods (arrows)

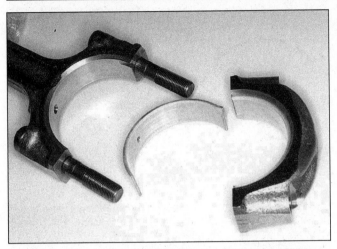

32.8 Align the rod and bearing oil holes. Fit the bearing tabs into the notches

32.10 Gently tap the pistons in with a wooden hammer handle

Connecting rod inspection

7   Check the connecting rods for cracks and other obvious damage. Have the rods checked for twisting and bending at a dealer service department or other motorcycle repair shop.

Installation

8   Wipe off the bearing inserts, connecting rods and caps. Install the inserts into the rods and caps, using your hands only, making sure the tabs on the inserts engage with the notches in the rods and caps **(see illustration)**. When all the inserts are installed, lubricate them with engine assembly lube or moly-based grease. Don't get any lubricant on the mating surfaces of the rod or cap.

9   Place short pieces of vinyl hose over the connecting rod studs to prevent them from damaging the crankshaft.

10   On the right side of the engine, place the ring compressors over the rings **(see illustration)**. Insert the connecting rods into the correct bores, making sure the oil holes and piston top marks are in the correct rela-

tionship. Assemble each connecting rod to its proper journal, referring to the previously applied cylinder numbers. The lines present at the rod/cap seam on one side of the connecting rod should fit together perfectly when the rod and cap are assembled **(see illustration 32.4b)**. If it doesn't, the wrong cap is on the rod. Fix this problem before assembling the engine any further.

11   When you're sure the rods are positioned correctly, lubricate the threads of the rod bolts and the undersides of the rod nuts with molybdenum disulfide grease and tighten the nuts to the torque listed in this Chapter's Specifications **(see illustration)**. **Note:** *Snug both nuts evenly, in several stages, to the specified torque.*

12   Turn the rods on the crankshaft. If any of them feel tight, tap on the bottom of the connecting rod caps with a hammer - this should relieve stress and free them up. If it doesn't, recheck the bearing clearance.

13   As a final step, recheck the connecting rod side clearances (see Step 2). If the clearances aren't correct, find out why before proceeding with engine assembly.

33 Cylinders - inspection

1   Don't attempt to separate the liners from the cylinder block.

2   Check the cylinder walls carefully for scratches and score marks.

3   Using the appropriate precision measuring tools, check each cylinder's diameter. Measure parallel to the crankshaft axis and across the crankshaft axis, at the top, center and bottom of the cylinder. Average the measurements and compare the results to this Chapter's Specifications. If the cylinder walls are tapered, out-of-round, worn beyond the specified limits, or badly scuffed or scored,

have them rebored and honed by a dealer service department or a motorcycle repair shop. If a rebore is done, oversize pistons and rings will be required as well.

4   As an alternative, if the precision measuring tools are not available, a dealer service department or motorcycle repair shop will make the measurements and offer advice concerning servicing of the cylinders.

5   If they are in reasonably good condition and not worn to the outside of the limits, and if the piston-to-cylinder clearances can be maintained properly, then the cylinders do not have to be rebored; honing is all that is necessary.

6   To perform the honing operation you will need the proper size flexible hone with fine stones, or a bottle brush type hone, plenty of light oil or honing oil, some shop towels and an electric drill motor. Hold the crankcase half in a vise (cushioned with soft jaws or wood blocks) when performing the honing operation. Mount the hone in the drill motor, compress the stones and slip the hone into the cylinder. Lubricate the cylinder thoroughly, turn on the drill and move the hone up and down in the cylinder at a pace which will produce a fine crosshatch pattern on the cylinder wall with the crosshatch lines intersecting at approximately a 60-degree angle. Be sure to use plenty of lubricant and do not take off any more material than is absolutely necessary to produce the desired effect. Do not withdraw the hone from the cylinder while it is running. Instead, shut off the drill and continue moving the hone up and down in the cylinder until it comes to a complete stop, then compress the stones and withdraw the hone. Wipe the oil out of the cylinder and repeat the procedure on the remaining cylinders. Remember, do not remove too much material from the cylinder wall. If you do not have the tools, or do not desire to perform the honing operation, a dealer service department or motorcycle repair shop will generally do it for a reasonable fee.

32.11 Tighten the rod cap nuts to the specified torque

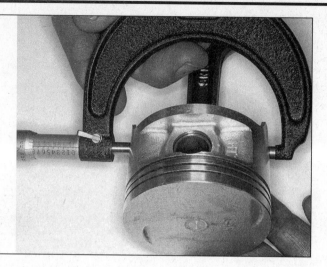

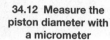
34.12 Measure the piston diameter with a micrometer

7   Next, the cylinders must be thoroughly washed with warm soapy water to remove all traces of the abrasive grit produced during the honing operation. Be sure to run a brush through the bolt holes and coolant passages and flush them with running water. After rinsing, dry the cylinders thoroughly and apply a coat of light, rust-preventative oil to all machined surfaces.

34 Pistons - inspection, removal and installation

1   The pistons are pressed into the connecting rods and are a slip fit in the pistons.
2   Refer to Section 32 and remove the piston/connecting rod assemblies.

Inspection

3   Before the inspection process can be carried out, the pistons must be cleaned and the old piston rings removed.
4   Using a piston ring installation tool, carefully remove the rings from the pistons. Do not nick or gouge the pistons in the process.
5   Scrape all traces of carbon from the tops of the pistons. A hand-held wire brush or a piece of fine emery cloth can be used once most of the deposits have been scraped away. Do not, under any circumstances, use a wire brush mounted in a drill motor to remove deposits from the pistons; the piston material is soft and will be eroded away by the wire brush.
6   Use a piston ring groove cleaning tool to remove any carbon deposits from the ring grooves. If a tool is not available, a piece broken off the old ring will do the job. Be very careful to remove only the carbon deposits. Do not remove any metal and do not nick or gouge the sides of the ring grooves.
7   Once the deposits have been removed, clean the pistons with solvent and dry them thoroughly. Make sure the oil return holes below the oil ring grooves are clear.

8   If the pistons are not damaged or worn excessively and if the cylinders are not rebored, new pistons will not be necessary. Normal piston wear appears as even, vertical wear on the thrust surfaces of the piston and slight looseness of the top ring in its groove. New piston rings, on the other hand, should always be used when an engine is rebuilt.
9   Carefully inspect each piston for cracks around the skirt, at the pin bosses and at the ring lands.
10   Look for scoring and scuffing on the thrust faces of the skirt, holes in the piston crown and burned areas at the edge of the crown. If the skirt is scored or scuffed, the engine may have been suffering from overheating and/or abnormal combustion, which caused excessively high operating temperatures. The oil pump and cooling system should be checked thoroughly. A hole in the piston crown, an extreme to be sure, is an indication that abnormal combustion (preignition) was occurring. Burned areas at the edge of the piston crown are usually evidence of spark knock (detonation). If any of the above problems exist, the causes must be corrected or the damage will occur again.
11   Measure the piston ring-to-groove clearance by laying a new piston ring in the ring groove and slipping a feeler gauge in beside it. Check the clearance at three or four locations around the groove. Be sure to use the correct ring for each groove; they are different. If the clearance is greater than specified, new pistons will have to be used when the engine is reassembled.
12   Check the piston-to-bore clearance by measuring the bore (see Section 33) and the piston diameter. Make sure that the pistons and cylinders are correctly matched. Measure the piston across the skirt on the thrust faces at a 90-degree angle to the piston pin, at the distance from the bottom of the skirt listed in this Chapter's Specifications (see illustration). Subtract the piston diameter from the bore diameter to obtain the clearance. If it is greater than specified, the cylinders will have to be rebored and new oversized pistons and rings installed. If the appropriate precision

measuring tools are not available, the piston-to-cylinder clearances can be obtained, though not quite as accurately, using feeler gauge stock. Feeler gauge stock comes in 12-inch lengths and various thicknesses and is generally available at auto parts stores. To check the clearance, select a feeler gauge of the same thickness as the piston clearance listed in this Chapter's Specifications and slip it into the cylinder along with the appropriate piston. The cylinder should be upside down and the piston must be positioned exactly as it normally would be. Place the feeler gauge between the piston and cylinder on one of the thrust faces (90-degrees to the piston pin bore). The piston should slip through the cylinder (with the feeler gauge in place) with moderate pressure. If it falls through, or slides through easily, the clearance is excessive and a new piston will be required. If the piston binds at the lower end of the cylinder and is loose toward the top, the cylinder is tapered, and if tight spots are encountered as the feeler gauge is placed at different points around the cylinder, the cylinder is out-of-round. Repeat the procedure for the remaining pistons and cylinders. Be sure to have the cylinders and pistons checked by a dealer service department or a motorcycle repair shop to confirm your findings before purchasing new parts.

Removal

13   The pistons are secured in the rods by a press fit. Separating the pistons from the rods requires a press and special tools and should be done by a Honda dealer or motorcycle service shop.

Installation

14   Install the pistons on the connecting rods so that when the assembly is installed in the engine, the connecting rod oil jets will face down and the L or R marks will be upward (see illustration 32.4b).

35 Piston rings - installation

1   Before installing the new piston rings, the ring end gaps must be checked.
2   Lay out the pistons and the new ring sets so the rings will be matched with the same piston and cylinder during the end gap measurement procedure and engine assembly.
3   Insert the top (No. 1) ring into the bottom of the first cylinder and square it up with the cylinder walls by pushing it in with the top of the piston. The ring should be about one inch above the bottom edge of the cylinder. To measure the end gap, slip a feeler gauge between the ends of the ring (see illustration) and compare the measurement to the Specifications.
4   If the gap is larger or smaller than speci-

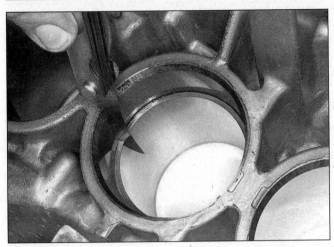

35.3 Check the ring end gap near the bottom of the cylinder

35.5 If the end gap is too small, clamp a file in a vise and file the ring ends (from the outside in only) to enlarge the gap slightly

35.9a Installing the oil ring expander - make sure the ends don't overlap

35.9b Installing an oil ring side rail - don't use a ring installation tool to do this; the left cylinder bank's oil ring expanders have a tab on one end that fits in the notch in the upper side of the ring groove

fied, double check to make sure that you have the correct rings before proceeding.

5   If the gap is too small, it must be enlarged or the ring ends may come in contact with each other during engine operation, which can cause serious damage. The end gap can be increased by filing the ring ends very carefully with a fine file (see illustration). When performing this operation, file only from the outside in.

6   Excess end gap is not critical unless it is greater than the limits listed in this Chapter's Specifications. Again, double check to make sure you have the correct rings for your engine.

7   Repeat the procedure for each ring that will be installed in the first cylinder and for each ring in the remaining cylinders. Remember to keep the rings, pistons and cylinders matched up.

8   Once the ring end gaps have been checked and corrected, the rings can be installed on the pistons.

9   The oil control ring (lowest on the piston) is installed first. It is composed of three separate components. Slip the expander into the groove, then install the upper side rail (see illustrations). Note: The upper side rail on each left piston's oil ring has a raised tab at one end. This fits into a notch in the upper

side of the oil ring groove, just to one side of the L mark on top of the piston. Do not use a piston ring installation tool on the oil ring side rails as they may be damaged. Instead, place one end of the side rail into the groove between the spacer expander and the ring land. Hold it firmly in place and slide a finger around the piston while pushing the rail into the groove. Next, install the lower side rail in the same manner.

10   After the three oil ring components have been installed, check to make sure that both the upper and lower side rails can be turned smoothly in the ring groove.

11   Install the second (middle) ring next. It can be distinguished from the top ring by its profile (see illustration). Do not mix the top and middle rings.

12   To avoid breaking the ring, use a piston ring installation tool and make sure that the identification mark is facing up. Fit the ring into the middle groove on the piston. Do not expand the ring any more than is necessary to slide it into place.

13   Finally, install the top ring in the same manner. Make sure the identifying mark is facing up.

14   Repeat the procedure for the remaining pistons and rings. Be very careful not to confuse the top and second rings.

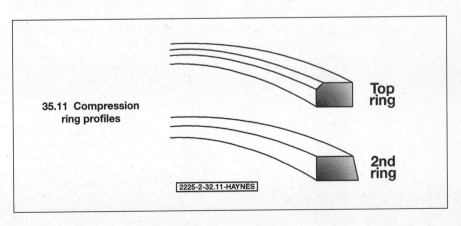

35.11 Compression ring profiles

Top ring

2nd ring

2225-2-32.11-HAYNES

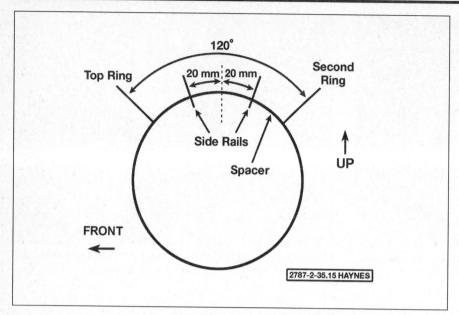

35.15 Piston ring details

37.2 Roll the bearings sideways to free it from the connecting rod and cap

15   Once the rings have been properly installed, stagger the end gaps, including those of the oil ring side rails **(see illustration)**.

36 Main and connecting rod bearings - general note

1   Even though main and connecting rod bearings are generally replaced with new ones during the engine overhaul, the old bearings should be retained for close examination as they may reveal valuable information about the condition of the engine.
2   Bearing failure occurs mainly because of lack of lubrication, the presence of dirt or other foreign particles, overloading the engine and/or corrosion. Regardless of the cause of bearing failure, it must be corrected before the engine is reassembled to prevent it from happening again.
3   When examining the bearings, remove the main bearings from the case halves and the rod bearings from the connecting rods and caps and lay them out on a clean surface in the same general position as their location on the crankshaft journals. This will enable you to match any noted bearing problems with the corresponding side of the crankshaft journal.
4   Dirt and other foreign particles get into the engine in a variety of ways. It may be left in the engine during assembly or it may pass through filters or breathers. It may get into the oil and from there into the bearings. Metal chips from machining operations and normal engine wear are often present. Abrasives are sometimes left in engine components after reconditioning operations such as cylinder honing, especially when parts are not thor-

oughly cleaned using the proper cleaning methods. Whatever the source, these foreign objects often end up imbedded in the soft bearing material and are easily recognized. Large particles will not imbed in the bearing and will score or gouge the bearing and journal. The best prevention for this cause of bearing failure is to clean all parts thoroughly and keep everything spotlessly clean during engine reassembly. Frequent and regular oil and filter changes are also recommended.
5   Lack of lubrication or lubrication breakdown has a number of interrelated causes. Excessive heat (which thins the oil), overloading (which squeezes the oil from the bearing face) and oil leakage or throw off (from excessive bearing clearances, worn main oil pump or high engine speeds) all contribute to lubrication breakdown. Blocked oil passages will also starve a bearing and destroy it. When lack of lubrication is the cause of bearing failure, the bearing material is wiped or extruded from the steel backing of the bearing. Temperatures may increase to the point where the steel backing and the journal turn blue from overheating.
6   Riding habits can have a definite effect on bearing life. Full throttle low speed operation, or lugging the engine, puts very high loads on bearings, which tend to squeeze out the oil film. These loads cause the bearings to flex, which produces fine cracks in the bearing face (fatigue failure). Eventually the bearing material will loosen in pieces and tear away from the steel backing. Short trip driving leads to corrosion of bearings, as insufficient engine heat is produced to drive off the condensed water and corrosive gases produced. These products collect in the engine oil, forming acid and sludge. As the oil is carried to the engine bearings, the acid attacks and corrodes the bearing material.

7   Incorrect bearing installation during engine assembly will lead to bearing failure as well. Tight fitting bearings which leave insufficient bearing oil clearances result in oil starvation. Dirt or foreign particles trapped behind a bearing insert result in high spots on the bearing which lead to failure.
8   To avoid bearing problems, clean all parts thoroughly before reassembly, double check all bearing clearance measurements and lubricate the new bearings with engine assembly lube or moly-based grease during installation.

37 Connecting rod bearings - removal, inspection and installation

Removal
1   Refer to Section 32 and remove the connecting rod/piston assemblies from the engine.
2   Remove the rod bearing inserts from one rod at a time. Roll the bearing inserts sideways to separate them from the rods and caps **(see illustration)**. Keep them in order so they can be reinstalled in their original locations. Wash the parts in solvent and dry them with compressed air, if available.

Inspection
3   Examine the connecting rod bearing inserts. If they are scored, badly scuffed or appear to have been seized, new bearings must be installed. Always replace the bearings in the connecting rods as a set. If they are badly damaged, check the corresponding crankshaft journal. Evidence of extreme heat, such as discoloration, indicates that lubrication failure has occurred. Be sure to thoroughly check the main oil pump and its pressure relief valve, as well as the scavenging pump and all oil holes and passages, before reassembling the engine.

37.5 Measure crankpin diameter at several points to check for out-of-roundness and at both ends to check for taper

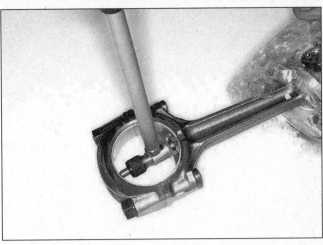

37.6 Measure the assembled connecting rod bearings with a bore gauge

37.7a The six letters on the end of the crankshaft (A) are used to select connecting rod bearings; the four numbers (B) are used to select main bearings

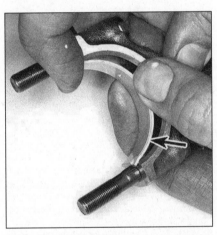

37.7b The bearing color codes are on the edge of the bearing near the tang (arrow)

38.2 Each main cap is numbered 1-2-3-4, with a punch mark next to the number of the cap (arrow); the arrowhead with the numbers cast in it points to the top of the engine

Clearance check

4   If you don't have a micrometer and a bore gauge, connecting rod bearing clearance can be checked inexpensively with Plastigage. Refer to *Tools and Workshop Tips* at the end of this manual.

5   If you have a micrometer, check the crankpin journal diameter at a number of points around the journal's circumference to determine whether or not the journal is out-of-round **(see illustration)**. Take the measurement at each end of the journal to determine if the journal is tapered. If any journal is tapered or out-of-round or bearing clearance is beyond the maximum listed in this Chapter's Specifications, replace the crankshaft.

6   Install the bearings and connecting rod cap and tighten the cap bolts to the torque listed in this Chapter's Specifications. Measure the inside diameter of the assembled bearing with a bore gauge **(see illustration)**. If the clearance is excessive and the crankpin

diameter is within the Specifications, select new bearings as described below.

Connecting rod bearing selection

7   Each connecting rod has a Roman numeral or an Arabic number stamped across its parting line, ranging from 1 to 3 **(see illustration 32.4b)**. There's a corresponding letter on the end of the crankshaft **(see illustration)**. Using the letter and number together, refer to this Chapter's Specifications to select the correct bearing color code for each connecting rod. The color codes are stamped on the edge of the bearing near the locating tab **(see illustration)**.

8   Repeat the bearing selection procedure for the remaining connecting rods.

Installation

9   Refer to Section 32 for bearing and connecting rod installation.

38 Crankshaft and main bearings - removal, inspection, main bearing selection and installation

Removal

1   Before removing the crankshaft check the endplay, using a dial indicator mounted in-line with the crankshaft. Honda doesn't provide endplay specifications, but if the endplay is excessive (more than a few thousandths of an inch), replace the thrust bearings.

2   Look for main bearing cap number marks **(see illustration)**. If you don't see any, make your own.

3   Unbolt the connecting rods from the crankshaft (see Section 32). The left connecting rods and pistons don't need to be removed from the cylinders.

38.4a Lift the bolts to this point and use them to rock the caps free of the crankcase

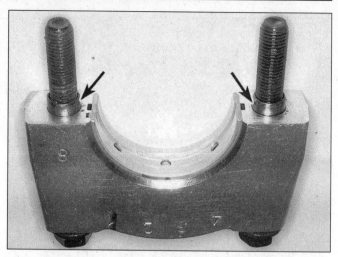

38.4b This type of dowel (arrow) is used on early models; on later models, the dowels are solid and go alongside the bolt holes

4   Unbolt the main bearing caps. Use the bolts as levers to rock the caps from side-to-side to free them from the engine, then lift them out **(see illustration)**. Note the locations of the cap dowels **(see illustration)**. On early models, the dowels are the hollow type and they go in the bolt holes. On later models, the dowels are solid and fit in holes in the bearing caps and crankcase, alongside the bolt holes.

5   Lift the crankshaft out and set it on a clean surface **(see illustration)**.

6   The main bearing inserts can be removed from their saddles by pushing their centers to the side, then lifting them out **(see illustration)**. Keep the bearing inserts in order. The main bearing oil clearance should be checked, however, before removing the inserts (see Step 11).

Inspection

7   Clean the crankshaft with solvent, using a rifle-cleaning brush to scrub out the oil passages. If available, blow the crank dry with compressed air. Check the main and connecting rod journals for uneven wear, scoring and pits. Rub a copper coin across the journal several times - if a journal picks up copper from the coin, it's too rough. Replace the crankshaft.

8   Check the crankshaft for cracks and other damage. It should be magnafluxed to reveal hidden cracks - a dealer service department or motorcycle machine shop will handle the procedure.

9   Steps 9 though 11 require precision measuring equipment. You can have the measurements done by a dealer or motorcycle repair shop. Measure the main bear-

ing journals with a micrometer. Compare the readings with the values listed in this Chapter's Specifications.

10   Assemble the main caps and bearings and tighten them to the specified torque. Measure the inside diameter of the bearing bore with a bore gauge. Once you've done this, remove the caps.

11   Check the main bearing clearance with Plastigage, referring to *Tools and Workshop Tips* at the end of this manual.

Main bearing selection

12   The clearance should be within the range listed in this Chapter's Specifications.

13   Use the number marks on the crankshaft and on the case to determine the bearing sizes required. The first four numbers on the crankshaft are the main journal numbers, starting with the front journal **(see illustration**

38.5 Lift the crankshaft out of the bearing saddles

38.6 Be sure the bearing tabs engage the notches (upper arrow) and the thrust bearing oil grooves face away from the crankcase (lower arrow)

38.13a The Arabic numerals indicate the journal number; the Roman numerals above them are used, together with the crankshaft numbers, to select main bearings

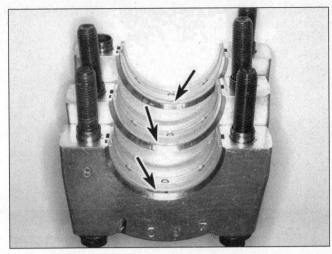

38.13b The bearing color codes are painted on the sides of the bearings (arrows)

38.2). These correspond with the numbers on the front of the left crankcase half **(see illustration)**. Use these numbers and this Chapter's Specifications to determine the correct bearing color code for each journal. The color codes are painted on the edges of the bearings **(see illustration)**.

Installation

14 Clean the bearing saddles in the case halves, then install the bearing inserts and thrust bearings in the case **(see illustration 38.6)**. When installing the bearings, use your hands only - don't tap them into place with a hammer.
15 Lubricate the bearing inserts and thrust bearings with engine assembly lube or moly-based grease.
16 Carefully lower the crankshaft into place **(see illustration 38.5)**.
17 Make sure the main bearing cap dowels

are in position. Install the caps in their correct locations, referring to the number marks **(see illustrations 38.2)**. Be sure the arrow marks on the caps point to the top of the engine.
18 Lubricate the threads and the underside of the bolt heads with clean engine oil, then finger-tighten the bolts.
19 Tighten the bolts in several stages, in a criss-cross pattern, to the torque listed in this Chapter's Specifications.
20 Turn the crankshaft. It should turn easily by hand. If it doesn't, there's a problem; find and fix it before assembling the engine further. You may have forgotten to lubricate the bearing inserts; the bearings may be the wrong size; or a bearing cap may be in the wrong location or installed backwards (with its arrow pointing to the bottom of the engine). Any of these can cause bearing damage when the engine is first started, or may prevent it from turning at all.

21 If the crankshaft turns freely, continue with assembly.

39 Transmission shafts, shift drum and forks - removal and installation

Removal

1 Remove the engine and separate the case halves (see Sections 7 and 28). Remove the external shift linkage, shift drum bearing retainer, the final drive gear and its bearing retainer (see Sections 27 and 23).
2 Pull the clutch pushrod out of the mainshaft (if you haven't already done so **(see illustration)**. Lift out the mainshaft **(see illustration)**. If it's stuck, use a soft-face hammer and gently tap on the bearings on the ends of the shaft to free it.

39.2a Pull the clutch pushrod out of the mainshaft

39.2b Lift the mainshaft out of the crankcase

39.3a Remove the shift shaft bearing retainer

39.3b Before removing the shift shaft, note the marks on the shift forks - R for rear, C for center and F for front

39.3c Pull the shift shaft out of the case . . .

39.3d . . . removing the forks as you go

39.3e It's a good idea to reassemble the forks on the shafts as soon as they're removed

39.4a The reverse drum lock is secured to the case by a bolt

39.4b Slip a screwdriver through the shift drum to hold it while unscrewing the bolt

3   Unbolt the retainer that secures the front end of the fork shaft (see illustration). Note the position marks (F, C and R for front, center and rear) on the shift forks (see illustration). Grip the inside of the fork shaft with snap-ring pliers or a similar tool, pull it out of the crankcase and lift the forks away from the gears (see illustrations). It's a good idea to reassemble the forks to the shaft right away so you don't forget how they go (see illustration).
4   Unbolt the drum rotor from the front end of the countershaft (see illustrations). Pull the shift drum forward out of the case (see illustration).

39.4c Pull the shift drum out of the case

39.5a The countershaft is installed in the case like this

39.5b Push the countershaft partway out to free the bearing

39.5c Remove the bearing completely

39.6 Remove first gear from the countershaft

39.7 Tilt the countershaft and lift it out of the case

5   Pull the front countershaft bearing out of the case **(see illustrations)**.
6   Pull the countershaft forward to clear its rear bearing, then take first gear off the shaft and remove it from the crankcase **(see illustration)**.

7   Tilt the countershaft and lift it out of the case **(see illustration)**.
8   Refer to Section 40 for information pertaining to shift drum and fork inspection and Section 41 for information pertaining to transmission shafts.

Installation

9   Installation is the reverse of the removal steps, with the following additions:

 a) *Be sure the mainshaft bearing locating pin engages the hole in the bearing outer race* **(see illustration 39.2b)**.

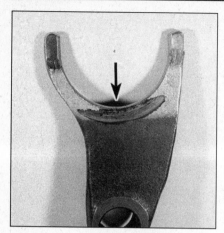

40.3 An arc-shaped burn mark like this means the fork was rubbing against a gear, probably due to bending or worn fork ears

b) *Install the shift forks in the correct locations, facing the proper direction* **(see illustrations 39.3b and 39.3e).**
c) *Engage the shift fork pins with the shift drum grooves* **(see illustration 39.3c).**

10   Make sure the gears are in the neutral position. When they are, it will be possible to rotate the transmission shafts independently of each other.

40 Shift drum and forks - inspection

1   Check the edges of the grooves in the shift drum for signs of excessive wear. If the grooves are worn, replace the shift drum.
2   Check the bearing at each end of the shift drum for wear and damage. Spin the bearings and check for roughness, looseness or noise. If problems are found, replace

41.2 The assembled transmission shafts mesh like this

the worn or damaged bearings.
3   Check the shift forks for distortion and wear, especially at the fork fingers and pins. Check for an arc-shaped burn mark on the fork **(see illustration)**. If the forks are discolored or severely worn they are probably bent. If damage or wear is evident, check the shift fork groove in the corresponding gear as well. Inspect the shaft bore for excessive wear and replace any defective parts with new ones.
4   Check the shift fork shaft for evidence of wear, galling and other damage. Make sure the shift forks move smoothly on the shaft. If the shaft is worn or bent, replace it with a new one.

41 Transmission shafts - disassembly, inspection and reassembly

Note: *When disassembling the transmission shafts, place the parts on a long rod or*

thread a wire through them to keep them in order and facing the proper direction.
1   Remove the shafts from the case (see Section 39).
2   Before you start, mesh the assembled shafts, noting how they're assembled and how they fit together **(see illustration)**.

Mainshaft
Disassembly
3   Slide the parts off the mainshaft, keeping them in order **(see illustration)**. Use snap-ring pliers to remove the snap-rings.

Inspection
4   Wash all of the components in clean solvent and dry them off. Rotate the bearings, feeling for tightness, rough spots and excessive looseness and listening for noises. If any of these conditions are found, replace the bearing.
5   Check the gear teeth for cracking and other obvious damage. Check the gear bushings and the surface in the inner diameter of each gear for scoring or heat discoloration. If the gear or bushing is damaged, replace it. If you have precision measuring equipment, measure the inside diameters of the removable gears and compare the measurements with the values listed in this Chapter's Specifications. Replace worn gears.
6   Inspect the dogs and the dog holes in the gears for excessive wear. Replace worn or damaged gears as a set with their mating gear on the countershaft.
7   Measure the bushing outside diameters at the smooth sections **(see illustration)**. Use this measurement, together with the gear inside diameter, to calculate gear-to-bushing clearance.
8   Place the shaft in V-blocks and check runout with a dial indicator. Replace the shaft if runout exceeds the value listed in this Chapter's Specifications.
9   Check the mainshaft bearings for wear or damage. Spin the bearings by hand and

41.3 Mainshaft details

41.7 Check the slots (left arrow) and dogs (right arrow) for wear, especially at the corners; rounded corners (top) can cause the transmission to jump out of gear - new gears (bottom) have sharp corners

check for loose, rough or noisy movement. Replace worn or damaged bearings. The center bearing on the mainshaft is secured by a 12-point nut, but it can't be replaced separately. Replace the mainshaft as a unit if the bearing is worn or damaged.

Reassembly

10   Lubricate the components with engine oil before assembling them.

11   Assembly is the reverse of the disassembly procedure. The washers and snap-rings have a sharp side and a rounded side. Install them with the sharp side away from the component they're securing, and align the snap-ring gap with a groove in the shaft. Refer to *Tools and Workshop Tips* at the end of this manual if necessary.

Countershaft

Disassembly

12   Slide the parts off the end of the shaft and place them in order **(see illustration)**.

Inspection

13   Refer to Steps 4 through 9 above to inspect the countershaft components.

Reassembly

14   Assembly is the reverse of the disassembly procedure. Lubricate the components with engine oil before assembling them. Install snap-rings as described in Step 11 above.

41.12 Countershaft details

42 Initial start-up after overhaul

1   Make sure the engine oil level is correct and the cooling system is full, then remove the spark plugs from the engine. Place the engine kill switch in the Off position and unplug the primary wires from the coils.

2   Turn on the key switch and crank the engine over with the starter several times to build up oil pressure. Reinstall the spark plugs, connect the wires and turn the switch to On.

3   Make sure there is fuel in the tank.

4   Start the engine and allow it to run at a moderately fast idle until it reaches operating temperature.

5   Check carefully for oil leaks and make sure the transmission and controls, especially the brakes, function properly before road testing the machine. Refer to Section 43 for the recommended break-in procedure.

43 Recommended break-in procedure

1   Any rebuilt engine needs time to break in, even if parts have been installed in their original locations. For this reason, treat the machine gently for the first few miles to make sure oil has circulated throughout the engine and any new parts installed have started to seat.

2   Even greater care is necessary if the cylinders have been rebored or a new crankshaft has been installed. In the case of a rebore, the engine will have to be broken in as if the machine were new. This means greater use of the transmission and a restraining hand on the throttle until at least 500 miles have been covered. There's no point in keeping

to any set speed limit - the main idea is to keep from lugging the engine and to gradually increase performance until the 500 mile mark is reached. These recommendations can be lessened to an extent when only a new crankshaft is installed. Experience is the best guide, since it's easy to tell when an engine is running freely. The following recommendations, which Honda provides for new motorcycles, can be used as a guide:

a) *Don't lug the engine (full throttle at low engine speeds).*

b) *0 to 600 miles (0 to 1000 km): Keep sustained engine speed below 4,000 rpm.*

c) *600 to 1000 miles (1000 to 1600 km): Don't run the engine for long periods above 5000 rpm, or at all above 5500 rpm. Rev the engine freely through the gears, but use full throttle only for very short periods. Change engine speeds often.*

d) *Above 1000 miles (1600 km): Full throttle can be used. Don't exceed maximum recommended engine speed (redline).*

3   If a lubrication failure is suspected, stop the engine immediately and try to find the cause. If an engine is run without oil, even for a short period of time, severe damage will occur.

Notes

Chapter 3
Cooling system

Contents

Degrees of difficulty

Easy, suitable for novice with little experience	Fairly easy, suitable for beginner with some experience	Fairly difficult, suitable for competent DIY mechanic	Difficult, suitable for experienced DIY mechanic	Very difficult, suitable for expert DIY or professional

Specifications

General

Coolant type	See Chapter 1
Mixture ratio	See Chapter 1
Cooling system capacity	See Chapter 1
Radiator cap pressure rating	108 to 137 kPa (16 to 20 psi)
Thermostat rating	
Opening temperature	76 to 80-degrees C (169 to 176-degrees F)
Fully open at	90-degrees C (194-degrees F)
Valve travel (when fully open)	Not less than 8 mm (5/16 inch)

General (continued)

Engine Coolant Temperature (ECT) sensor resistance

    2001 through 2005

At 80-degrees C (176-degrees F)	47 to 57 ohms
At 120-degrees C (248-degrees F)	14 to 18 ohms

    2006 and later

At 80-degrees C (176-degrees F)	2.1 to 2.7 k-ohms
At 120-degrees C (248-degrees F)	0.6 to 0.8 k-ohms

Torque specifications

Water pump cover bolts	13 Nm (120 inch-lbs)
Water pump-to-engine bolts	13 Nm (120 inch-lbs)
Engine coolant temperature sensor	25 Nm (18 ft-lbs)

1 General information

The models covered by this manual are equipped with a liquid cooling system which utilizes a water/antifreeze mixture to carry away excess heat produced during the combustion process. The cylinders are surrounded by water jackets, through which the coolant is circulated by the water pump. The coolant passes through hoses, around the cylinders and to the thermostat. When the engine is warm, the thermostat opens and allows coolant to flow into the radiators, where it is cooled by the passing air, routed through another hose and back to the water pump, where the cycle is repeated. The water pump is mounted to the back of the crankcase and driven by the oil pump shaft.

Two electric fans, one mounted on each radiator, provide a flow of cooling air through the radiators. When the coolant temperature reaches a specified point, the Engine Coolant Temperature (ECT) sensor sends an electrical signal to the engine control module, which grounds the fan relay, which in turn switches electrical current to the fan motors.

The ECT sensor, threaded into the left cylinder head, also controls the coolant temperature gauge on the instrument cluster.

The entire system is sealed and pressurized. The pressure is controlled by a valve which is part of the radiator cap. By pressurizing the coolant, the boiling point is raised, which prevents premature boiling of the coolant. An overflow hose, connected between the radiator and reservoir tank, directs coolant to the tank when the radiator cap valve is opened by excessive pressure. The coolant is automatically siphoned back to the radiator as the engine cools.

Many cooling system inspection and service procedures are considered part of routine maintenance and are included in Chapter 1.

 The coolant hoses on these motorcycles are secured by screw-type hose clamps. When you loosen one of them, slide the clamp up the hose and tighten it slightly. This will make it easy to remember where the clamp belongs, especially if you're disconnecting several hoses. It will also make it easy to remember which way the clamp screw should face. That's important on these motorcycles, which have a complicated arrangement of numerous coolant hoses fitted into a small space.

 Warning: Do not allow antifreeze to come in contact with your skin or painted surfaces of the motorcycle. Rinse off spills immediately with plenty of water. Antifreeze is highly toxic if ingested. Never leave antifreeze lying around in an open container or in puddles on the floor; children and pets are attracted by its sweet smell and may drink it. Check with local authorities about disposing of used antifreeze. Many communities have collection centers which will see that antifreeze is disposed of safely.

 Warning: Do not remove the pressure cap from the radiator when the engine and radiator are hot. Scalding hot coolant and steam may be blown out under pressure, which could cause serious injury. To open the pressure

cap, wait until the engine has cooled. Place a thick rag, like a towel, over the radiator cap and slowly rotate the cap counterclockwise to the first stop. This procedure allows any residual pressure to escape. When the steam has stopped escaping, press down on the cap while turning counterclockwise and remove it.

2 Radiator cap - check

If problems such as overheating and loss of coolant occur, check the entire system as described in Chapter 1. The radiator cap opening pressure should be checked by a dealer service department or service station equipped with the special tester required to do the job. If the cap is defective, replace it with a new one.

3 Coolant reservoir - removal and installation

This procedure is done as part of routine cooling system flushing. Refer to Chapter 1, Section 25.

4 Cooling fan and coolant sensor - check and replacement

1   The fan circuit consists of the engine coolant temperature (ECT) sensor, fuse and relay. Power is supplied by the fuse to the relay, which in turn supplies power to the fans. If neither fan works, the problem is most likely in the fuse, relay, or engine coolant temperature sensor. The engine control unit may also be at fault, since it grounds the relay coil. If only one fan works, the problem is most likely in the wiring to the non-working fan motor or the motor itself.

4.4a Locate the fan wiring connectors inside the boot

4.4b You may need to free the harness from its retainers to get enough slack to unplug the connector

Check

2   If the engine is overheating and the cooling fans aren't coming on, first check the fan fuse (see Chapter 9 for fuse location and checking procedures). If the fuse is blown, check the fan circuit for a short to ground (see the *Wiring diagrams* at the end of this book). Check that the battery is fully charged.

3   If the fuses and battery are good, check the fan relay (see Chapter 9). Swap another of the relays in the relay box (with the same part number) for the fan relay and see if that solves the problem. If it does, replace the fan relay with a new one.

4   If the fuse and relay are good, follow the wiring harness from each fan motor in turn to the electrical connector and unplug the connector **(see illustrations)**. Using two jumper wires, apply battery voltage to the terminals in the fan motor side of the electrical connector. If the fan doesn't work, replace the motor.

5   If the fan does come on, the problem lies in the ECT sensor or the wiring that connects the components. Refer to the wiring diagrams at the end of this manual and check the wiring for breaks or bad connections.

6   Before replacing the ECT, test it as follows.

7   Refer to Steps 16 through 22 to remove the sensor from the engine.

8   Suspend the sensor in a pan of coolant (50/50 mixture of antifreeze and water) so just the threads are covered.

> ⚠ *Warning: Antifreeze is poisonous. DO NOT use a cooking pan for this test!*

Don't let the sensor body sink into the coolant and don't let the sensor touch the sides of the pan (there must be at least 1-1/2 inches [40 mm] clearance between the sensor and the bottom of the pan). Connect an ohmmeter between the green-black wire's terminal and sensor body.

9   Heat the coolant to the operating temperature listed in this Chapter's Specifications. Hold the temperature at this range for three minutes before checking continuity. Let the coolant cool down and note the ohmmeter readings as it cools. The resistance should increase as the temperature decreases. If the readings aren't within the specified ranges, replace the sensor.

10   If the sensor is good, the engine control unit may be defective. Since this is an expensive part that can't be returned once purchased, further testing should be done by a dealer service department or other qualified shop. Reinstall the sensor as described below.

Replacement
Fan motor

> ⚠ *Warning: The engine must be completely cool before beginning this procedure.*

11   Remove the radiator (see Section 8).
12   Remove the bolts securing the fan shroud to the frame **(see illustration)**. Separate the fan and shroud from the radiator.
13   Unscrew the fan nut and take the fan

4.12 Remove the fan shroud mounting bolts (arrows) and take the shroud off the radiator

4.13a Remove the fan nut . . .

4.13b . . . and the collar from the motor shaft

4.14 Remove the motor mounting screws (arrows)

4.15 The flats in the fan mounting hole align with the flats on the motor shaft (arrows)

nut threads. Refill the cooling system (see Chapter 1).

Engine Coolant Temperature (ECT) sensor

⚠ *Warning: The engine must be completely cool before beginning this procedure.*

16   If you're working on a non-airbag model, remove the engine control module bracket (see Chapter 4).

17   If you're working on an airbag model, remove the radio (see Chapter 9) and the right air intake duct (see Chapter 4).

18   Remove the radiator mounting brackets (see Section 8 and **illustration 13.2** in Chapter 4).

19   Depressurize the fuel lines, then unbolt the fuel hose fitting from the left fuel rail (see Chapter 4).

20   Unplug the wiring connector from the ECT sensor **(see illustrations)**.

21   Unbolt the intake manifold (see Chapter 2) and lift it for access to the ECT sensor.

and collar off the motor **(see illustrations)**.

14   Unbolt the fan motor from the shroud **(see illustration)**

15   Installation is the reverse of the removal steps. Be sure to install the collar. Align the

flats in the fan mounting hole with the flats on the motor shaft **(see illustration)**. Use non-permanent thread locking agent on the fan

4.20a Disconnect the wiring connector from the ECT sensor on top of the left cylinder head (arrow) . . .

4.20b . . . for access to the sensor terminals

4.22a Unscrew the sensor with a 15 mm deep socket . . .

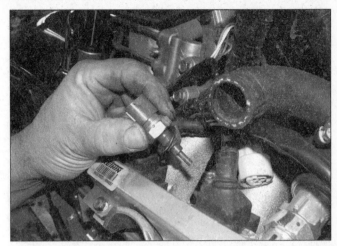

4.22b . . . and lift the sensor and its sealing washer out of the cylinder head

6.3a The rails on the thermostat fit into the slots in the housing (arrows)

6.3b Remove the sealing ring from the thermostat - on installation, use a new sealing ring and slip the edge of the thermostat securely into the sealing ring groove

22   Refer to Chapter 1 and drain the cooling system. Unscrew the ECT sensor, using a 15 mm deep socket, from the left cylinder head and remove its sealing washer **(see illustrations)**.
23   Installation is the reverse of the removal steps. Use a new sealing washer and tighten the sensor to the torque listed in this Chapter's Specifications. Connect the electrical connector to the switch.
24   The remainder of installation is the reverse of the removal steps.
25   Refill the cooling system (see Chapter 1).

5   Coolant temperature gauge and sender unit - check and replacement

Check

1   If the engine has been overheating but the coolant temperature gauge hasn't been indicating a hotter than normal condition, begin with a check of the coolant level (see

Chapter 1). If it's low, add the recommended type of coolant and be sure to locate the source of the leak.
2   Check the other gauges (speedometer, tachometer and fuel gauge). If they aren't working, check the power and ground lines to the instrument cluster, referring to the wiring diagrams at the end of this manual.
3   If the other gauges work properly, remove the bracket from the top of the left radiator (see Section 8) and disconnect the wiring connector from the engine coolant temperature sensor (see Section 4).
4   With the ECT sensor disconnected, turn the ignition On and watch the gauge.
5   If the gauge needle moves to H (hot), the ECT sensor may be defective. Test it as described in Section 4.
6   If the gauge stays at C (cold), the gauge may be defective. To confirm the problem, check the green/black wire between the ECT sensor and the instrument cluster gray connector for a short. If there is no short, the

gauge is probably bad. Replacement of the temperature gauge requires replacement of the entire instrument cluster. Since this is an expensive component that can't be returned once it's ordered, have your diagnosis confirmed by a dealer service department or other qualified shop.

Replacement
ECT sensor
7   Refer to Section 4 for this procedure.

Temperature gauge
8   The temperature gauge is removed and installed as a unit with the instrument cluster. Refer to Chapter 9 for the cluster replacement procedure.

6   Thermostat - removal, check and installation

Warning: The engine must be completely cool before beginning this procedure.

Removal
1   If the thermostat is functioning properly, the coolant temperature gauge should rise to the normal operating temperature quickly and then stay there, only rising above the normal position occasionally when the engine gets abnormally hot. If the engine does not reach normal operating temperature quickly, or if it overheats, the thermostat should be removed and checked, or replaced with a new one.
2   Remove the water pump cover from the water pump (see Section 7). **Note:** *If you're planning to remove just the thermostat, remove the three cover bolts. There's no need to remove the three water pump-to-engine bolts.*
3   Lift the thermostat out of the water pump cover and remove its sealing ring **(see illustrations)**.

6.11 Be sure the jiggle valve (arrow) is upward (toward the bypass hose fitting), or it may not be possible to bleed all the air out of the cooling system

7.2 Disconnect the bypass hose (top arrow), inlet hose (center arrow) and outlet hose (bottom arrow, hidden beneath starter motor)

Check

4 Remove any coolant deposits, then visually check the thermostat for corrosion, cracks and other damage. If it was open when it was removed, the thermostat is defective.

5 To check the thermostat operation, submerge it in a container of coolant (50/50 antifreeze and water) along with a thermometer. The thermostat should be suspended so it does not touch the sides of the container.

> ⚠ **Warning: Antifreeze is poisonous. DO NOT use a cooking pan to test the thermostat!**

6 Gradually heat the water in the container with a hot plate or stove and check the temperature when the thermostat first starts to open.

7 Compare the opening temperature to the values listed in this Chapter's Specifications.

8 Continue heating the water until the valve is fully open.

9 Measure how far the thermostat valve

has opened and compare that to the value listed in this Chapter's Specifications.

10 If these specifications are not met, or if the thermostat doesn't open while the coolant is heated, replace it with a new one.

Installation

11 Install the thermostat into the water pump cover. Align the thermostat rails with the channels inside the housing **(see illustration 6.3a)**. **Note:** *Make sure the bleed valve is installed upward* **(see illustration)**. *Otherwise, it may not be possible to bleed all the air out of the cooling system.*

12 Install a new O-ring in the groove in the water pump cover and install a new thermostat seal. Fit the seal groove around the edge of the thermostat **(see illustration 6.3b)**.

13 Refer to Section 7 and install the water pump cover.

14 The remainder of installation is the reverse of the removal steps. Fill the cooling system with the recommended coolant (see Chapter 1).

7 Water pump - removal, inspection and installation

> ⚠ **Warning: The engine must be completely cool before beginning this procedure.**

Removal

1 Refer to Chapter 1 and drain the cooling system. Remove the alternator and starter motor (see Chapter 9).

2 Disconnect the coolant hoses from the water pump **(see illustration)**.

3 Loosen the three cover bolts and remove the three mounting bolts **(see illustration)**. Pull the pump out of the engine **(see illustration)**.

4 Remove the cover from the water pump **(see illustrations)**.

Inspection

5 Check the shaft seal for leaks (indicated by coolant leaking from the telltale

7.3a Loosen the cover bolts (silver) and remove the mounting bolts (gold) . . .

7.3b . . . then take the water pump off the engine - on installation, align the drive tab with the slot in the oil pump bolt (arrows)

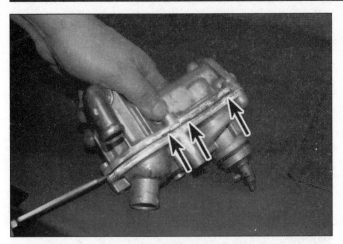

7.4a Insert a screwdriver into the pry points (arrows) and pry the cover loose . . .

7.4b . . . then separate the cover from the water pump

hole). Replace the water pump if the seal has been leaking. The mechanical seal can't be replaced separately.

6   Try to wiggle the pump impeller back-and-forth and in-and-out. Check the impeller blades for corrosion. If you can feel movement or the impeller blades are heavily corroded, the water pump must be replaced.

7   If the impeller blades are heavily corroded, flush the system thoroughly (it would also be a good idea to check the internal condition of the radiators).

8   Remove the cover O-ring from its groove with a pointed tool and install a new one **(see illustration 7.4b)**.

9   Install the cover and tighten the bolts securely, but don't overtighten them and strip the threads.

Installation

10   Installation is the reverse of the removal steps with the following additions:

Caution: Do not tighten the water pump bolts until the pump body is seated firmly against the engine. Pulling the water pump onto the engine by tightening the bolts may damage the pump drive lug or shaft.

a) Align the drive lug on the end of the water pump shaft with the drive slot in the starter clutch bolt inside the engine **(see illustration 7.3b)**.

b) Tighten the mounting bolts to the torque listed in this Chapter's Specifications.

---

8   Radiators - removal and installation

⚠ *Warning: The engine must be completely cool before beginning this procedure.*

1   Place the bike on its centerstand.

2   Drain the cooling system (see Chapter 1).

3   Remove the fuel tank top cover, intake air duct and front fairing panel (see Chapter 8).

Non-airbag models

Left radiator

4   If you're working on a 2006 model, remove the ventilation air duct (it's secured by a single trim clip).

5   Free the wiring harness from the top of the radiator, either by removing the retainer bracket screws (2005 and earlier) or undoing the retainer band (2006 and later).

6   Disconnect the drain hose (small) and coolant hose (large) from the bottom of the radiator. Disconnect the siphon hose (small) and coolant hose (large) from the top of the radiator **(see illustrations)**. Note: *Refer to the Haynes Hints in Section 9 for tips on hose removal.*

8.6a There are two inlet hoses (bottom and center arrows) at the front of each radiator - on the left radiator, the siphon hose (top arrow) runs to the coolant filler neck on the right radiator

8.6b The outlet hose at the lower rear of each radiator (arrow) runs to a Y-fitting, and from there to the water pump

8.7a Remove the mounting bolts (arrows) . . .

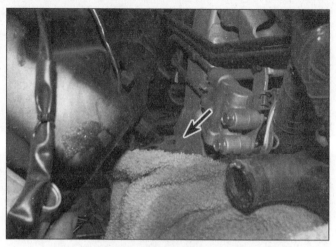

8.7b . . . lift the radiator support post out of its grommet (arrow) . . .

8.7c . . . and disconnect the fan motor connector (arrow)

7   Remove the two mounting bolts from the top of the radiator **(see illustration)**. Lift the radiator mounting post out of its grommet. Lean the radiator away from the motorcycle, unplug its wiring connector and take the radiator off **(see illustrations)**.

8   Inspect the radiator mounting grommet. Replace it if it's cracked or deteriorated.

9   Installation is the reverse of the removal steps. Tighten the radiator mounting bolts to the torque listed in this Chapter's Specifications.

10   Fill the cooling system with the recommended coolant and bleed out the air (see Chapter 1).

Right radiator

11   Remove the trim clips or screw that secure the intake air duct.

12   Free the wiring harness from the top of the radiator, either by removing the retainer bracket screws (2005 and earlier) or undoing the retainer band (2006 and later). Disconnect the fan motor wiring connector.

13   Disconnect the drain hose (small) and coolant hose (large) from the bottom of the

radiator. Disconnect the siphon hose (small) and coolant hose (large) from the top of the radiator.

14   Remove the mounting bolts from the top of the radiator **(see illustration 8.7a)**. Lift the radiator mounting post out of its grommet **(see illustration 8.7b)** and remove the radiator from the motorcycle.

15   Inspect the radiator mounting grommet. Replace it if it's cracked or deteriorated.

16   Installation is the reverse of the removal steps. Tighten the radiator mounting bolts to the torque listed in this Chapter's Specifications.

17   Fill the cooling system with the recommended coolant and bleed out the air (see Chapter 1).

Airbag models

Left radiator

 Warning: This procedure requires working near the airbag. Before beginning work, read the airbag precautions in Chapter 9.

18   Remove the top left fuel tank cover and front fairing (see Chapter 8).

19   Remove the engine control module (see Chapter 4).

20   Remove the trim clip that secures the left air duct and remove the air duct from the motorcycle.

21   Unbolt the fan motor wiring harness retainer from the top of the radiator. Free the harness from its retainer, then unplug its connector (white connector with two pins).

22   Disconnect the coolant hoses from the radiator **(see illustrations 8.6a and 8.6b)**.

23   Remove the two mounting bolts from the top of the radiator **(see illustration 8.7a)**. Lift the radiator mounting post out of its grommet and take the radiator off **(see illustration 8.7b)**.

24   Inspect the radiator mounting grommet. Replace it if it's cracked or deteriorated.

25   Installation is the reverse of the removal steps. Tighten the radiator mounting bolts to the torque listed in this Chapter's Specifications.

26   Fill the cooling system with the recommended coolant and bleed out the air (see Chapter 1).

Right radiator

27   Remove the front fairing (see Chapter 8).

28   If you're working on a 2009 or later model, remove the tire pressure monitoring system receiver (see Chapter 9).

29   Free the fan motor wiring harness from its retainers and unplug the connector (white with two pins).

30   Unbolt the filler neck. If you're working on a 2006 through 2008 model, remove one bolt. If you're working on a 2009 or later model, remove two bolts and the bracket that secures the tire pressure monitoring receiver.

31   Disconnect the hoses from the front of the radiator. Lift the radiator mounting posts out of their grommets. Lean the radiator away from the engine, disconnect the lower coolant hose and remove the radiator from the motorcycle.

32   Inspect the radiator mounting grommet. Replace it if it's cracked or deteriorated.

33   Installation is the reverse of the removal steps. Tighten the radiator mounting bolts to the torque listed in this Chapter's Specifications.

34   Fill the cooling system with the recommended coolant and bleed out the air (see Chapter 1).

9   Coolant hoses - removal and installation

 Warning: The engine must be completely cool for this procedure.

9.2a Slide the clamp partway up the hose and retighten it with its head in the same location as it is when the clamp is installed

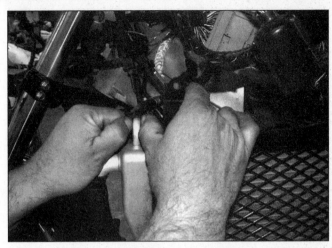

9.2b Try to push hoses off fittings with your thumbs, using even pressure on both sides

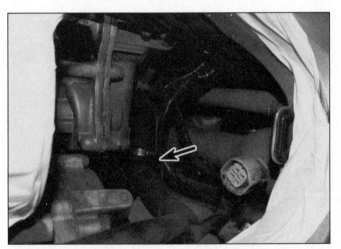

9.4a The water pump outlet hose connects to a Y-fitting, which branches to two hoses (viewed through the left side of the frame, with the alternator removed for clarity) . . .

9.4b . . . the hoses run to the inlet fitting on the bottom of each cylinder head (arrow, left side of engine shown)

1   Refer to Chapter 1 and drain the cooling system.
2   When you disconnect coolant hoses, especially small ones, try to avoid using tools. Instead, push on both sides of the hose with your thumbs **(see illustrations)**. This will place even pressure on the hose fitting so it doesn't crack.

> **HAYNES HiNT** *When you loosen a hose clamp, don't take it all the way off if you don't have to - slide it partway up the hose and retighten it slightly, with its head in the installed position. That way, you'll know which way the clamp head faces when you reconnect the hose.*

3   For access to the coolant hoses, you'll need to remove the seat, fuel tank top cover and fairing (see Chapter 8).
4   Coolant leaves the water pump through a single large hose that branches into two other large hoses **(see illustration)**. These

run to fittings on the bottom of each cylinder head **(see illustrations)**. Coolant is routed through the fittings into the cylinder head

and through the engine. The small hose connected to each of these fittings runs around the engine to the drain fitting at the front cen-

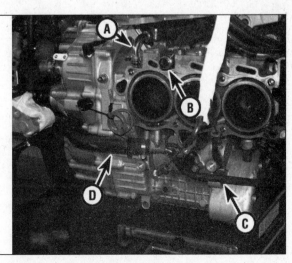

9.4c Right side coolant hose details (left side similar, cylinder head removed for clarity)

A   Bypass outlet fitting and hose to water pump (cold engine)
B   Outlet fitting and hoses to radiator (warm engine)
C   Hose to drain bolt fitting
D   Inlet hose from water pump to inlet fitting

9.4d The coolant drain hose (right arrow) is routed over the support rail to the drain bolt fitting (left arrow)

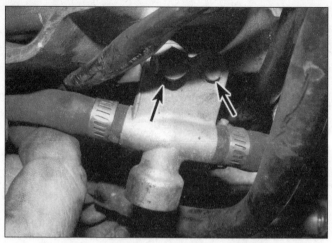

9.4e The drain bolt fitting is secured by a bolt (left arrow) and located by a dowel (right arrow)

ter of the engine **(see illustrations)**.

5   Each radiator has two inlet hoses at the front and an outlet hose at the rear **(see illustrations 8.5a and 8.5b)**. The outlet hoses meet at a Y-fitting under the fuel tank, and a single hose runs from the Y-fitting to the large inlet fitting on the water pump **(see illustration)**. The bypass hoses run from fittings at the top rear of each cylinder head to a Y-fitting under the fuel tank, and a single hose runs from the Y-fitting to the small inlet fitting on the top left of the water pump.

6   A small-diameter siphon hose runs from the top front corner of the left radiator, across the motorcycle, to the radiator filler neck on the right radiator **(see illustration 8.6a and the accompanying illustration)**.

9.4f Drain bolt fitting, hoses and inlet fittings - note that the right hose is longer than the left hose

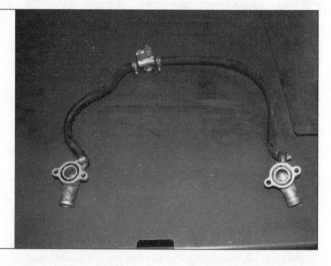

9.5 The radiator outlet hoses meet at this Y-fitting under the fuel tank, and a single hose connects the Y-fitting to the water pump

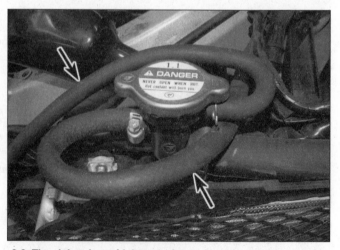

9.6 The siphon hose (right arrow) runs from the top front corner of the left radiator - the overflow hose (left arrow) runs to the reservoir tank

Chapter 4
Fuel, exhaust and emission control systems

Contents

Degrees of difficulty

Easy, suitable for novice with little experience	**Fairly easy,** suitable for beginner with some experience	**Fairly difficult,** suitable for competent DIY mechanic	**Difficult,** suitable for experienced DIY mechanic	**Very difficult,** suitable for expert DIY or professional 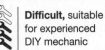

Specifications

Programmed Fuel Injection (PGM-FI) system

System type	Sequential, multi-point fuel injection
Idle speed...	630 to 770 rpm
Fuel pressure...	50 psi (343 kPa)
Fuel pump flow (12 volts supplied power)................................	133 cc (4.5 US fl oz, 4.7 Imperial oz) in 10 seconds
Manifold pressure at idle...	400 to 450 mm Hg (15.7 to 17.7 inches Hg)
Intake air pressure sensor resistance....................................	2.2 to 2.7 k-ohms
Throttle position sensor resistance	4 to 6 k-ohms
Fuel injector resistance..	11.1 to 12.3 ohms
Camshaft position sensor peak voltage..................................	0.7 V or higher
Crankshaft sensor peak voltage..	0.7 V or higher

Torque specifications

Pressure regulator fitting bolts	10 Nm (84 inch-lbs)
Fuel supply hose fitting bolts to fuel rail	10 Nm (84 inch-lbs)
Fuel rail mounting bolts	10 Nm (84 inch-lbs)
Fuel rail end fitting	33 Nm (25 ft-lbs)
Fuel rail end plug	12 Nm (108 inch-lbs)
Pulse air check valve cover bolts	10 Nm (84 inch-lbs)
Crankshaft Position (CKP) sensor bolts	12 Nm (108 in-lbs)
Oxygen/air/fuel ratio sensors	31 Nm (23 ft-lbs)
Knock sensors	31 Nm (23 ft-lbs)
Gear position switch mounting bolts	Not specified
Vehicle speed sensor mounting bolts	Not specified
Exhaust pipe to manifold nuts	12 Nm (108 inch-lbs)
Exhaust pipe clamp bolts	27 Nm (20 ft-lbs)
Exhaust pipe mounting bolts	27 Nm (20 ft-lbs)
Muffler clamp bolts	27 Nm (20 ft-lbs)
Exhaust system front cover nuts	
2001 through 2005	12 Nm (108 inch-lbs)
2006 and later	Not specified
Exhaust system rear cover screws	14 Nm (120 inch-lbs)

1 Programmed Fuel Injection (PGM-FI) system - general information

1   The Programmed Fuel Injection (PGM-FI) system is a sequential multiport system. This means that there is a fuel injector in each intake port, and that these fuel injectors inject fuel into the intake ports in the cylinder firing order (1-4-5-2-3-6). The injectors are turned on and off by the Engine Control Module (ECM). When the engine is running, the ECM constantly monitors engine operating conditions with an array of information sensors, calculates the correct amount of fuel, then varies the interval of time during which the injectors are open. Sequential multiport systems provide much better control of the air/fuel mixture ratio than earlier fuel injection systems, and are therefore able to produce more power, better mileage and lower emissions.

2   The PGM-FI system uses the ECM and an array of information sensors to determine and deliver the correct air/fuel ratio under all operating conditions. The PGM-FI system consists of three sub-systems: air induction, electronic control and fuel delivery. The PGM-FI system is also closely interrelated with ECM-controlled emission control systems.

Air induction system

3   The air induction system consists of the air filter assembly, the air intake ducts, the throttle body, the intake manifold and several sensors.

4   **Throttle body** - The downdraft throttle body contains two throttle plates, one for each bank of cylinders, which regulate the amount of air entering the intake manifold. The throttle plates are opened and closed by the accelerator and decelerator cables.

5   **Throttle Position (TP) sensor** - Mounted on the throttle body, this sensor is a potentiometer that monitors the opening angle of the throttle plate and sends a variable voltage signal to the Engine Control Module (ECM).

6   **Manifold Absolute Pressure (MAP) sensor** - Located on the throttle body. The MAP sensor measures intake manifold pressure and vacuum and generates a variable voltage signal that's proportionate to the pressure or vacuum. The ECM uses this data to calculate the load on the engine.

7   **Intake Air Temperature (IAT) sensor** - The IAT sensor relays a voltage signal to the ECM that varies in accordance with the temperature of the incoming air in the air cleaner housing. The ECM uses this data to calculate how rich or lean the air/fuel mixture should be.

8   **Idle Air Control (IAC) valve** - When the engine is idling, the Idle Air Control (IAC) valve maintains the correct idle speed by regulating the amount of air that bypasses the (closed) throttle plate in response to a command from the ECM. The IAC valve is activated and controlled by the ECM in response to the running conditions of the engine (cold or warm running).

Fuel system

9   The fuel system consists of the fuel tank, an electric fuel pump (located in the fuel tank), the fuel rail and the fuel injectors. Programmed Fuel Injection (PGM-FI) is a sequential multiport system, which means that the fuel injectors deliver fuel directly into the intake ports of the cylinders in firing order sequence (1-4-5-2-3-6).

10   All models are equipped with a vacuum-operated fuel pressure regulator. The regulator, which is attached to the left fuel rail, senses intake manifold vacuum as well as fuel pressure. It uses this information to maintain fuel pressure at a steady 50 psi above intake manifold vacuum.

Exhaust system

11   The exhaust system consists of two sections, one for each side of the bike. Each section consists of an exhaust manifold, catalytic converter and muffler. The left and right sections of the exhaust system are connected by integral crossover pipes on the downstream side of the catalytic converters. Oxygen sensors or air/fuel ratio sensors are mounted in the exhaust system. These detect the richness of the fuel mixture and signal the ECM to adjust it as needed.

Electronic control system

12   Fuel delivery in the PGM-FI system is controlled by the Engine Control Module (ECM). This is a computer that receives information from a number of sensors and uses the information to control both the timing and the amount of fuel delivered to the engine. It does this by opening and closing the fuel injectors.

Basic input sensors

13   **Camshaft Position (CMP) sensor** - The CMP sensor produces a signal that the ECM uses to identify the number 1 cylinder and to time the firing sequence of the fuel injectors. There is one CMP sensor, mounted on the front end of the left camshaft.

14   **Crankshaft Position (CKP) sensor** - The sensor produces a signal that the ECM uses to determine the position of the crankshaft. The CKP sensor is located inside the engine front cover.

15   **Throttle Position (TP) sensor** - The TP sensor is a potentiometer that receives a constant voltage input from the ECM and sends back a voltage signal that varies in relation to the opening angle of the throttle plate inside the throttle body. This voltage signal tells the ECM when the throttle is closed, half-open, wide open or anywhere in between. The ECM uses this data, along with information from other sensors, to calculate injector pulse width (the interval of time during which an injector solenoid is energized by the ECM). The TP sensor is located on the throttle body, on the end of the throttle plate shaft. If the TP sensor is defective on any of these models you must replace the throttle body. The TP sensor cannot be adjusted or replaced separately.

16   **Manifold Absolute Pressure (MAP) sensor** - The MAP sensor, which is located on the throttle body, monitors the pressure or vacuum downstream from the throttle plate, inside the intake manifold. The MAP sensor measures intake manifold pressure and vacuum on the absolute scale - from zero instead of from sea-level atmospheric pressure (14.7 psi). The MAP sensor converts the absolute pressure into a variable voltage signal that changes with the pressure. The ECM uses this data to determine engine load so that it can alter the ignition advance and fuel enrichment.

Correction input sensors

17   **Engine Coolant Temperature (ECT) sensor** - The ECT sensor is a thermistor (temperature-sensitive variable resistor) that sends a voltage signal to the ECM, which uses this data to determine the temperature of the engine coolant. The ECT sensor helps the ECM control the air/fuel mixture ratio and ignition timing. The ECT sensor is located on top of the left cylinder head

18   **Intake Air Temperature (IAT) sensor** - The IAT sensor monitors the temperature of the air inside the air cleaner housing and sends a signal to the ECM. The IAT sensor is located on top of the air cleaner housing.

19   **Barometric pressure (BARO) sensor** - The BARO sensor, mounted to the right of the air cleaner housing (next to the cruise actuator, if equipped), measures atmospheric pressure and signals this information to the ECM, which uses it to compensate for changes in altitude (the thinner air at higher altitudes won't absorb as much gasoline into vapor as sea-level air, so the fuel mixture must be leaner).

20   **Vehicle speed sensor** - The vehicle speed sensor provides the Engine Control Module (ECM) with information about the speed of the motorcycle.

21   **Gear position switch** - The gear position switch tells the ECM what gear the transmission is in, so the ECM can select the correct ignition map. These motorcycles have separate ignition maps for neutral, first gear, second gear and third through fifth gears.

Control input sensors

22   **Oxygen or air/fuel ratio sensors** - An oxygen sensor is a galvanic battery that generates a small variable voltage signal in proportion to the difference between the oxygen content in the exhaust stream and the oxygen content in the ambient air. The ECM uses the voltage signal from the oxygen sensors to maintain a stoichiometric air/fuel ratio of 14.7:1 by constantly adjusting the on-time of the fuel injectors. The air/fuel ratio sensors used on later models are similar to oxygen sensors, but operate over a wide range of air/fuel ratios. They're mounted upstream of the catalytic converters. Since they must be warm to work properly, they're heated electrically.

23   **Knock sensors** - The knock sensor is a piezoelectric crystal that oscillates in pro-

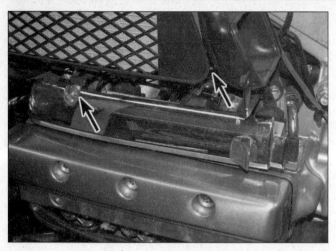

3.6a Remove the screws (arrows) . . .

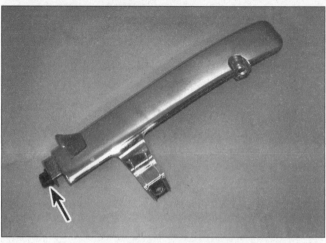

3.6b . . . and pull the cover forward to disengage the tab at the rear end (arrow)

portion to engine vibration. The term piezo-electric refers to the property of certain crystals that produce a proportional, repeatable voltage output when subjected to a certain level of mechanical stress. The oscillation of the piezoelectric crystal produces a voltage output that is monitored by the ECM, which retards the ignition timing when the oscillation exceeds a certain threshold. When the engine is operating normally, the knock sensor oscillates consistently and its voltage signal is steady. When detonation occurs, engine vibration increases, and the oscillation of the knock sensor exceeds a design threshold. Detonation is an uncontrolled explosion, after the spark occurs at the spark plug, which spontaneously combusts the remaining air/fuel mixture, resulting in a pinging or slapping sound. If allowed to continue, the engine could be damaged. There are two knock sensors, located in the underside of the cylinder head on each side of the engine.

Engine Control Module (ECM)

24   The ECM is located under the fuel tank top cover. The ECM is the brain of the engine management system. It receives information from all of the information sensors described above, processes all of this data, and issues commands to the output actuators. The ECM is a complex and expensive component, and new ECMs must be programmed with a Honda Diagnostic Scan (HDS) tool before the motorcycle will run, so it is impossible to replace an ECM at home. If a Diagnostic Trouble Code (DTC) indicates a problem with the ECM (a very rare and unlikely occurrence), we recommend that you have the ECM serviced and, if necessary, replaced by a Honda dealer service department.

Output actuators

25   **EVAP canister purge control solenoid** - The EVAP canister purge valve is normally closed, but when ordered to do so by the ECM, it allows the fuel vapors that are stored in the EVAP canister to be drawn into the

intake manifold, where they're mixed with intake air, then burned along with the normal air/fuel mixture.

26   **Fuel injectors** - The fuel injectors spray a fine mist of fuel into the intake ports, where it is mixed with incoming air. Each injector consists of a spray nozzle, a valve that opens and closes the nozzle, and an inductive coil that opens and closes the valve under ECM control. The timing of injector opening and the duration of opening (which controls fuel mixture richness) can be very precisely controlled by electrical signals from the ECM.

27   **Ignition coils** - The ignition coils are under the control of the Engine Control Module (ECM). There is no separate ignition control module. The coils are located inside the front area of the frame. For more information about the ignition coils, see Chapter 5.

28   **Fan control and fuel pump relays** - The fan control relay and fuel pump relay are under the control of the ECM. When signaled to do so, the relays switch on the cooling fan or the fuel pump. For more information about relays, see Chapter 9.

2   Fuel pressure relief procedure

Warning: Gasoline is extremely flammable, so take extra precautions when you work on any part of the fuel system. Don't smoke or allow open flames or bare light bulbs near the work area, and don't work in a garage where a gas-type appliance (such as a water heater or clothes dryer) is present. Since gasoline is carcinogenic, wear latex gloves when there's a possibility of being exposed to fuel, and, if you spill any fuel on your skin, rinse it off immediately with soap and

water. Mop up any spills immediately and do not store fuel-soaked rags where they could ignite. The fuel system is under constant pressure, so, if any fuel lines are to be disconnected, the fuel pressure in the system must be relieved first. When you perform any kind of work on the fuel system, wear safety glasses and have a Class B type fire extinguisher on hand.

Warning: Be sure to disconnect the battery (see Chapter 9) before disconnecting any fuel lines.

Honda does not specify a procedure for relieving residual fuel pressure when disconnecting fuel lines, only that you have shop rags handy to catch any spilled fuel. Observe the precautions described in the **Warnings** above. In addition, wear eye protection and catch any spilled fuel in an approved gasoline container.

3   Fuel pump/fuel pressure - check

Warning: Gasoline is extremely flammable, so take extra precautions when you work on any part of the fuel system. See the Warning in Section 2.

General checks

1   Verify that there is fuel in the fuel tank.
2   Verify that the fuel pump actually runs. Turn the ignition switch to ON - you should hear a brief whirring noise for a few seconds as the pump comes on and pressurizes the system. **Note:** *If you can't hear the pump, open the fuel filler neck cap, then have an assistant turn the ignition switch to ON while you listen to the pump through the fuel filler neck.*

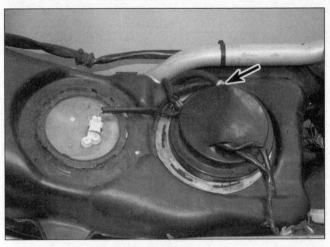

3.7 Place rags over the plug at the front of the left fuel rail (arrow), hold the fitting with one wrench and remove the plug with another wrench

4.2 Cap off the fuel return fitting (arrow) as soon as the hose is disconnected

Fuel pump/fuel pressure test

3   To measure the fuel pressure, you'll need a fuel pressure gauge capable of reading pressures in excess of 50 psi (343 kPa). You will also need some fuel hose.
4   Before disconnecting any fuel line fittings, relieve the fuel system pressure (see Section 2), then disconnect the cable from the negative terminal of the battery (see Chapter 9).
5   Remove the front fairing (see Chapter 8).
6   Unbolt the cover from the left fuel rail **(see illustrations)**.
7   Place rags over the plug in the front end of the left fuel rail and unscrew the plug. Connect the fuel pressure gauge to the fuel system **(see illustration)**.
8   Pinch off the fuel pressure regulator vacuum hose **(see illustration 3.7)**.
9   Reconnect the battery.
10   Start the engine and let it warm up until it's idling at its normal operating temperature.
11   Note the indicated fuel pressure reading on the gauge and compare it with the value listed in this Chapter's Specifications.
12   If the indicated pressure is within the specified range, the system is operating correctly.
13   If the indicated pressure is lower than the specified range, the fuel filter might be clogged or the fuel pump or fuel pressure regulator might be defective (see Sections 4 and 14).
14   After the test is complete, relieve the system fuel pressure (see Section 2).
15   Disconnect the cable from the negative battery terminal.
16   Remove your fuel pressure testing rig, then install the plug in the end of the fuel rail, using a new sealing washer. Tighten the plug to the torque listed in this Chapter's Specifications.
17   Reconnect the cable to the negative

battery terminal (see Chapter 9). Start the engine and check for fuel leaks.
18   Reinstall the fuel rail cover and front fairing.

Fuel flow test

19   Remove the seat (see Chapter 8).
20   Have a vacuum cap ready to cap off the fuel return fitting on top of the fuel tank. Disconnect the hose and place the cap over the fitting as soon as the hose is disconnected.
21   Place the disconnected end of the fuel return hose in an approved gasoline container.
22   Check that the ignition switch and engine kill switch are in the OFF positions.
23   Turn the ignition switch to ON, then turn the kill switch to ON. The fuel pump should run for about two seconds, then stop.
24   Once the fuel pump stops running, turn the kill switch to OFF, then back to ON, so the fuel pump runs for another two seconds. Each time the pump runs, fuel will flow from the return hose into the container.

25   Turn the kill switch off, then back on, three more times, for a total of five on times (10 seconds fuel pump running time). Measure the total amount of fuel that flowed from the return hose and compare the amount to the value listed in this Chapter's Specifications.
26   If the fuel flow is insufficient, check the return and feed hose for clogging. Also check the fuel filter and the pickup screen (see Section 4). If these are OK, check the fuel pressure regulator and fuel pump (see Sections 14 and 4).

<table><tr><td>**4**</td><td>**Fuel pump and filter - removal and installation**</td><td></td></tr></table>

1   Remove the seat (see Chapter 8).
2   Disconnect the wiring connector from the fuel level sender **(see illustration)**.
3   Pull the rubber cap off the fuel pump cover and disconnect the fuel pump wiring connector **(see illustration)**. Disconnect the fuel return line.

4.3 Unplug the fuel pump wiring connector (right arrow) and unbolt the fuel feed hose fitting (left arrow)

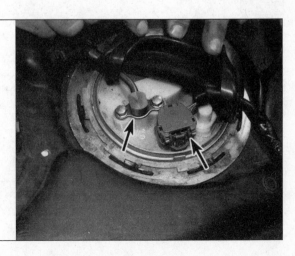

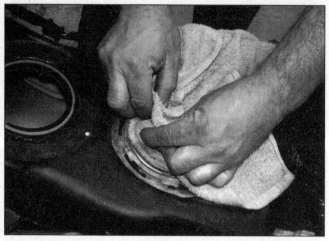

4.4a Place rags over the feed hose fitting to catch residual fuel . . .

4.4b . . . lift the fitting straight up and remove its O-ring (arrow)

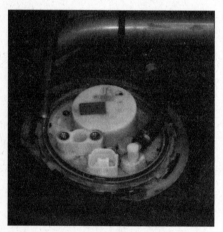

4.5 Tap the retainer ring counterclockwise with a brass or hardwood drift

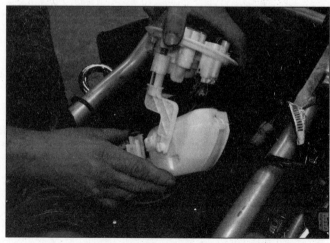

4.6 Lift off the retainer ring and the retainer plate beneath it (arrow)

hammer and drift if you're careful **(see illustration)**. The drift should be made of brass or hardwood (not steel) to prevent sparks.

6 Lift off the retainer ring and the retainer plate beneath it **(see illustration)**.

7 Lift out the pump, together with the fuel filter and strainer **(see illustrations)**. You'll need to tilt and turn the assembly to clear the opening.

8 Remove the sealing ring from the opening **(see illustration 4.7a)**.

9 Check the stainless steel mesh screen and the filter for clogging. They aren't available separately, so the pump assembly will need to be replaced as a unit if any problems are found.

10 Installation is the reverse of the removal steps, with the following additions:

a) *Use a new sealing ring if the old one is compressed, brittle or deteriorated.*

b) *Use a new O-ring, lubricated with clean engine oil, on the fuel feed hose fitting. Push the fitting straight down when you install it.*

4 Place shop rags over the fuel feed hose fitting **(see illustration)**. Unbolt the fitting from the fuel pump cover and lift it straight up **(see illustration)**.

5 Unscrew the retainer ring. Honda makes a special tool for this, but you can also use a

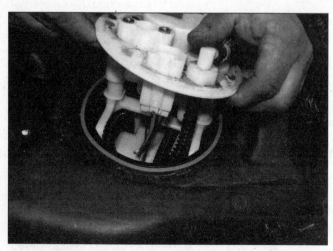

4.7a Remove the fuel pump/filter unit out of the tank . . .

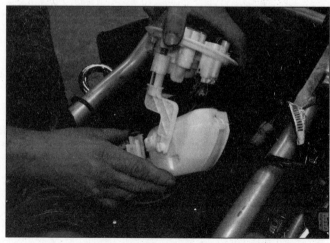

4.7b . . . turning and tilting it as needed for clearance

5.4 Unscrew the fuel filler cap and lift the drain tray (arrow) over the filler neck

5.5 Disconnect the fuel tank breather hose

5 Fuel tank - removal and installation

⚠ *Warning: Gasoline is extremely flammable, so take extra precautions when you work on any part of the fuel system. See the Warning in Section 2.*

1   The fuel tank is mounted beneath the seat and is held in place by four bolts.

2   Remove the seat and fuel tank top cover (see Chapter 8).

3   Remove the battery, battery box and fuse block (see Chapter 9).

4   Unscrew the fuel tank cap and lift the drain tray off over the filler neck **(see illustration)**. Reinstall the cap.

5   Disconnect the fuel tank breather hose **(see illustration)**.

6   Unplug the electrical connectors for the fuel pump and the fuel level sensor (see Sec-

5.7a Remove two bolts and washer at the front of the tank (arrows) . . .

tion 4). Disconnect the fuel feed and return lines.

7   Remove the mounting bolts at the four corners of the tank and remove their washers **(see illustrations)**. The two rear bolts also

secure the seat bracket.

8   Working on the left side of the bike, tilt the left side of the tank up and lift the tank out of the frame **(see illustration)**.

9   Before installing the tank, check the

5.7b . . . and two at the rear - inspect the mounting bushings

5.8 Lift the tank up from the left side and angle its rear section out of the frame

5.9a Inspect the mounting pads on the lower bracket (arrows) . . .

5.9b . . . and on the frame (arrows)

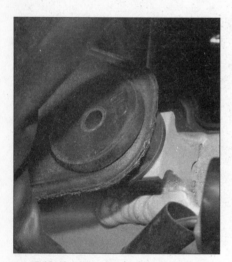

5.10 If you removed the mounting bushings, install them with their UP marks upward

condition of the hoses, bolt hole rubber bushings and rubber mounting dampers **(see illustrations)**; if they're hardened, cracked, or show any other signs of deterioration, replace them.

10 When replacing the tank, reverse the above procedure. Make sure the tank seats properly and does not pinch any control cables or wires. If the mounting bushings were removed, install them with the UP marks upward **(see illustration)**.

6 Fuel tank - cleaning and repair

1 All repairs to the fuel tank should be carried out by a professional who has experience in this critical and potentially dangerous work. Even after cleaning and flushing of the fuel system, explosive fumes can remain and ignite during repair of the tank.

2 If the fuel tank is removed from the vehicle, it should not be placed in an area where sparks or open flames could ignite the fumes coming out of the tank. Be especially careful inside garages where a gas-type appliance is located, because it could cause an explosion.

7 Air filter housing - removal and installation

1 Remove the air filter element (see Chapter 1). .

2 Remove the fuel tank (see Section 5).

3 Disconnect the crankcase breather hoses from the lower rear of the air cleaner housing **(see illustration)**.

4 Loosen the air horn screws all the way **(see illustration)** (the air horns can't be removed completely at this point).

5 Remove the lower front fairing panel (see Chapter 8). Pull the air cleaner housing

7.3 Disconnect the crankcase breather hoses (arrows) from the air cleaner housing

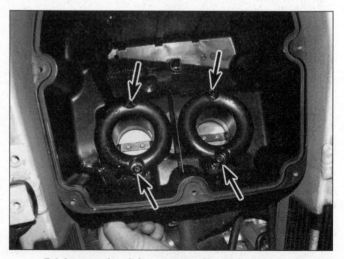

7.4 Loosen the air horn screws (arrows) all the way

7.5 At the front of the bike, pull up the air cleaner housing drain hose to provide some slack

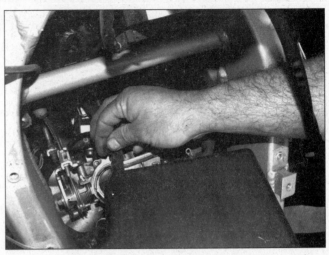

7.6a Slide the clamp down the drain hose . . .

7.6b . . . and disconnect it from the air cleaner housing (lower arrow). Disconnect the pulse air hose as well (upper arrow)

7.7 The gasket (arrow) may stick to the air cleaner housing or stay on the throttle body

drain hose up into its retainer to create slack in the hose (see illustration).

6　Lift the air cleaner housing for access to the drain hose and secondary air hose (see illustrations). Squeeze the clamps and slide them down the hoses, then work the hoses off their fittings.

7　Lift the air cleaner housing out of the frame and remove the gasket between the bottom of the air cleaner housing and the top of the throttle body (see illustration).

8　If you need to remove the air horns, twist them to align their tabs with the openings on the air cleaner housing, then take them out.

9　Installation is the reverse of the removal steps, with the following additions:

a) Install a new gasket on top of the throttle body (see illustration).

b) If you remove the air horns, install them in their original locations. They are labeled R for right and L for left (see illustration).

7.9a Install a new gasket on the throttle body (arrow) and make sure it seats evenly in the groove

7.9b Install the air horns on the correct side of the air cleaner housing - they're labeled R for right (arrow) and L for left

8.3a Insert a long screwdriver under the upper right frame rail and loosen the right clamp (arrow) . . .

8.3b . . . repeat the procedure on the left side (arrow) to loosen the left clamp

8.3c Lift the throttle body up

8.4a Disconnect the fuel pressure regulator hose

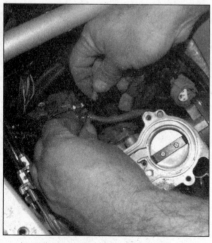

8.4b Disconnect the EVAP hose at the T-fitting

8 Throttle body - removal and installation

1   Remove the air cleaner housing (see Section 7).
2   Remove both radiators (see Chapter 3).
3   Loosen the insulator clamps and pull the throttle body up out of the insulators **(see illustrations)**.
4   Disconnect the vacuum hose that runs to the fuel pressure regulator **(see illustration)**. If you're working on a California model, disconnect the single hose that connects to the EVAP hoses at the T-fitting **(see illustration)**.
5   Disconnect the wiring connectors for the MAP sensor, throttle position sensor and idle air control valve.
6   Refer to Section 9 and disconnect the throttle cables (and cruise cable if equipped).
7   Lift the throttle body out and remove the

insulators **(see illustration)**. Cover the openings in the intake manifold with clean rags to keep out dirt, small parts, etc.
8   The MAP sensor and IAC valve can be replaced separately. The throttle position sensor is a permanent part of the throttle body; if it has failed, the entire throttle body must be replaced. Do not turn any screws marked with white paint **(see illustrations)**. These are set at the factory and can't be adjusted.
9   Installation is the reverse of the removal steps, with the following additions:

a) *Position the insulator notches to the rear* **(see illustration 8.7)**.
b) *Make sure the BODY UP marks on the insulators are upward* **(see illustration)**.
c) *Position the gap in the left clamp straight toward the front of the bike, and the gap in the right clamp 25-degrees to the right* **(see illustration 8.7)**.

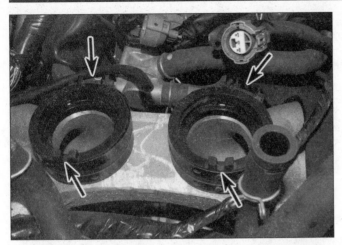

8.7 Position the throttle body with the insulators notches (lower arrows) toward the rear; the gap in the left clamp (upper left arrow) faces straight forward and the gap in the right clamp (upper right arrow) faces 25-degrees to the right of center

8.8a Do not turn screws coated with white paint (arrows) . . .

d) Tighten the clamps so the gap between the ends is 12 +/- 1 mm (0.47 +/- 0.04 inch).

9 Throttle and cruise control cables - removal and installation

1   Perform Steps 1 through 5 of Section 8. Lift the throttle body for access to the cables. The throttle cables (and cruise cable if equipped) are located on the left end of the throttle body **(see illustration)**.

2   Measure the protrusion of each cable housing from the bracket **(see illustration)**. Record this number and use it during installation to position the cables at their original

8.8b . . . including these that secure the throttle position sensor (arrows)

8.9 Install the throttle body insulators with the BODY UP marks (arrow) upward

9.1 Throttle body connection details

1	Throttle and cruise cables	4	EVAP vacuum hose
2	Fuel pressure regulator vacuum hose	5	MAP sensor
3	Pulse air control solenoid	6	Throttle position sensor
		7	Idle air control valve

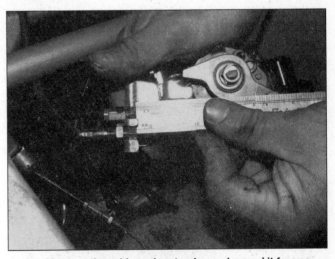

9.2 Measure the cable end protrusion and record it for use on installation

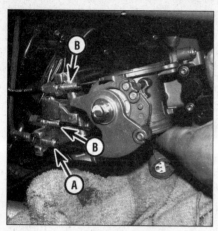

9.3a Cruise control cable (A) and throttle cables (B)

9.3b Loosen the nuts, slip the cable housing out of the bracket, slip the cable out of the pulley groove . . .

9.3c . . . and slip the cable end plug sideways out of the pulley

adjustment positions. This will make final adjustment easier.

3   Loosen the accelerator cable mounting nuts and slip the cables out of their brackets **(see illustrations)**. Rotate the cables so they align with the slots in the pulley and slip them out **(see illustration)**.

4   Loosen the cable locknuts at the throttle grip **(see illustration)**.

5   Remove the handlebar switch mounting screws and separate the halves of the handlebar switch (see Chapter 9).

6   Detach the accelerator and decelerator cables from the throttle grip pulley. Remove the cables, noting how they are routed.

7   Take the throttle grip off the handlebar. Clean the handlebar and apply a light coat of multi-purpose grease.

8   The cruise cable is replaced as a unit with the cruise actuator. If you plan to install a new cruise cable, refer to Chapter 9.

9   Route the cables into place. Make sure they don't interfere with any other compo-

nents and aren't kinked or bent sharply.

10   Lubricate the ends of the cables with multi-purpose grease and connect them to the pulleys at the throttle body and at the throttle grip.

11   Install the cable housings in the bracket and secure them with the locknuts. Adjust the cruise cable position with the locknut and adjusting nut so the distance from the end of the cable fitting to the bracket is 34 mm (1.34 inches) **(see illustration)**.

12   Follow the procedure outlined in Chapter 1, *Throttle operation/grip freeplay - check and adjustment*, to adjust the throttle cables. Refer to the cruise control section in Chapter 9 to adjust the cruise cable (if equipped).

13   Turn the handlebars back and forth to make sure the cables don't cause the steering to bind. With the engine idling, turn the handlebars back and forth and make sure idle speed doesn't change. If it does, find and fix the cause before riding the motorcycle.

14   Install components removed for access.

10 Idle speed adjustment

1   Idle speed adjustment is not a routine procedure on these motorcycles. It's done only if idle speed changes over time and there are no trouble codes that would indicate a problem. The throttle body controls half of the idle air flow into the engine (the other half is controlled by the idle air control valve). Throttle body air flow is adjusted with a pair of adjusting screws **(see illustration)**.

2   Before adjusting the idle speed, use the motorcycle's self-diagnostic capability to check for trouble codes (see Section 12). Correct any problems you find before proceeding. The charging system must be in good condition and the motorcycle's battery fully charged.

9.4 Unscrew the throttle cable nuts at the housing (arrows)

9.11 Adjust the cruise control cable fitting so the gap between the bracket and the end of the housing (between the arrows) is as specified (see text)

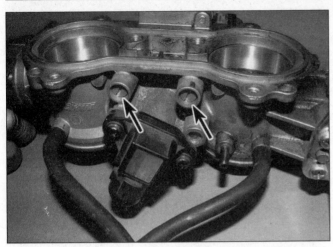

10.1 Idle speed is adjusted with these screws (arrows)

10.9 This fuel delivery setup from K&L Supply includes a variable pressure fuel pump and an auxiliary fuel tank, which make it possible to run the engine without the bike's fuel tank and pump installed

3 Place the motorcycle on its center-stand. Place the transmission in neutral, start the engine, and let it warm up to its normal operating temperature.

4 Let the engine idle and check the idle speed. It should be between 630 and 770 rpm. If it's too high or too low, check for problems and make adjustments as described below.

Idle speed too low

5 Shut off the engine and remove the left engine cover (see Chapter 8).

6 With the ignition switch in the Off position, unplug the black connector from the engine control module (22 pins on 2005 and earlier models; 33 pins on 2006 and later models). Also unplug the 4-pin connector from the back of the alternator (see Chapter 9).

7 Connect an ohmmeter between the black wire terminals in the two connectors. There should be continuity. If not, check the black wire for breaks or bad connections and repair them.

10.12 Disconnect the idle air control valve (lower arrow) and cover the air passages (upper arrows)

8 If there is continuity, remove the air cleaner housing (see Section 7).

9 Connect an auxiliary fuel supply so you can run the engine with the air cleaner housing removed. One way to do this is to reinstall the fuel tank temporarily. Another is to use an external fuel source such as the one available from K&L Supply **(see illustration)**. This has its own fuel container and an adjustable-pressure fuel pump that can be used to run the engine with the fuel tank removed.

10 Connect the electrical connectors for the ECM, BARO sensor and Intake Air Temperature (IAT) sensor.

11 Start the engine and let it idle. If it's cooled down, let it warm up to operating temperature.

12 Unplug the wiring connector for the Idle Air Control (IAC) valve **(see illustration)**. Cover the air passages in the throttle body with duct tape and check the idle speed. It should decrease. If it doesn't, replace the IAC valve with a new one.

13 If idle speed drops, increase it to 500 to 600 rpm by turning the air screws evenly **(see illustration 10.1)**. If this doesn't bring the idle speed up, remove the throttle body, unscrew the air screws all the way and clean the air screw passages. Reinstall the air screws, recheck idle speed and adjust it as necessary.

Idle speed too high

14 Start with the engine cool enough that the temperature gauge needle is below the C mark. Let the bike cool overnight if necessary.

15 Run the engine at idle until the radiator cooling fan comes on, then shut it off. Restart the engine right away and check the idle speed after 10 to 20 seconds. If it's within the range listed in this Chapter's Specifications, no further work is needed.

16 If the idle speed is too high, remove the air cleaner housing (see Section 7). Check the fuel pressure regulator hose and EVAP

vacuum hoses **(see illustration 10.12)**. Follow the regulator hose to the regulator on the left fuel rail. Follow the EVAP hoses from the T-fitting to the solenoid at the front of the bike between the frame rails. Make sure they're securely connected and in good condition. If they aren't, connect or replace them as needed.

17 If you haven't already done so, remove the air cleaner housing (see Section 7).

18 Connect an auxiliary fuel supply so you can run the engine with the air cleaner housing removed. One way to do this is to reinstall the fuel tank temporarily. Another is to use an external fuel source such as the one available from K&L Supply **(see illustration 10.9)**. This has its own fuel container and an adjustable-pressure fuel pump that can be used to run the engine with the fuel tank removed.

19 Connect the electrical connectors for the ECM, BARO sensor and intake air temperature sensor.

20 Start the engine and let it idle. If it's cooled down, let it warm up to operating temperature.

21 Cover the air passages in the throttle body with duct tape and check the idle speed. It should range from 500 to 600 rpm. If it does, skip to Step 23

22 If the idle speed is above the specified range, turn the air screws inward evenly until it drops to within the specifications. If it doesn't drop to within the specifications, even with the air screws turned all the way inward, replace the throttle body with a new one. If it does, go to Step 23.

23 Shut the engine off. Remove the duct tape from the air passages and clean away all traces of adhesive.

24 Start the engine and recheck the idle speed. It should be 1500 to 1600 rpm. If not, replace the IAC valve (see Section 23). If it is within the specified range, shut the engine off. Connect the electrical connector to the IAC valve, start the engine and recheck idle

12.4 The diagnostic connector is located beneath the seat

speed. If it's now within the range of 630 to 770 rpm, the system is OK. If it's still too high, replace the IAC valve with a new one (see Section 23).

11 Programmed Fuel Injection (PGM-IF) system - check

Note: *The following procedure is based on the assumption that the fuel pump is working and the fuel pressure is adequate (see Section 3). If it isn't, you can use a variable-pressure auxiliary pump like the one from K&L Supply* **(see illustration 10.9)**.

1 Check all electrical connectors that are related to the system. Check the ground wire connections for tightness. Loose connectors and poor grounds can cause many problems that resemble more serious malfunctions.

2 Verify that the battery is fully charged. The Engine Control Module (ECM), information sensors and output actuators (the fuel injectors are output actuators) depend on a stable voltage supply in order to meter fuel correctly.

3 Inspect the air filter element (see Chapter 1). A dirty or partially blocked filter will severely impede performance and economy.

4 Check all fuses related to the fuel system (see Chapter 9). If you find a blown fuse, replace it and see if it blows again. If it does, look for a wire shorted to ground in the circuit(s) protected by that fuse.

5 Check the air induction system between the throttle body and the intake manifold for air leaks, which will cause a lean air/fuel mixture ratio (when the mixture ratio becomes excessively lean, the engine will begin misfiring). Also inspect the condition of all vacuum hoses connected to the intake manifold and to the throttle body. A loose or broken vacuum hose will allow false (unmetered) air into the intake manifold. The Manifold Absolute Pressure (MAP) sensor and the ECM can compensate for some false air, but if it's excessive, especially at idle and during other

high-intake-manifold-vacuum conditions, the engine will misfire.

6 Remove the air cleaner housing from the throttle body and look for dirt, carbon, varnish, or other residue in the throttle body, particularly around the throttle plate. If it's dirty, clean it with a clean shop towel. The throttle plates and bores are coated with a molybdenum sealant. Be careful not to remove it.

7 With the engine running, place an automotive stethoscope against each injector, one at a time, and listen for a clicking sound that indicates operation. If you don't have a stethoscope, touch the tip of a long screwdriver against each injector and listen through the handle.

8 If you can hear the injectors operating, but the engine is misfiring, the electrical circuits are functioning correctly, but the injectors might be dirty or clogged. Try a commercial injector cleaning product (available at auto parts stores). If cleaning the injectors doesn't help, the injectors probably need to be cleaned professionally, or replaced.

9 If an injector is not operating (it makes no sound), disconnect the injector electrical connector and measure the resistance across the injector terminals with an ohmmeter. Compare your measurement with the resistance values of the other injectors. If the resistance of the non-operational injector is well outside the range of resistance of the other injectors, replace it.

10 If the injector is not operating, but the resistance reading is within the range of resistance of the other injectors, the ECM or the circuit between the ECM and the injector might be faulty.

12 Self-diagnosis system and trouble codes

Scan tool information

1 Hand-held scanners are handy for analyzing the engine management system used on these motorcycles. However, they're not strictly necessary - the self-diagnosis system can also signal DTCs by flashing the Malfunction Indicator Light (MIL) on the instrument cluster.

2 With the advent of self-diagnosis systems, specially designed scanners were developed. Honda makes one, and they're available from aftermarket suppliers as well. Aftermarket scan tools, which can diagnose many different makes, are a logical choice for independent shops. For the home mechanic working on a Gold Wing, it's more cost-effective to extract trouble codes using the Malfunction Indicator Light (MIL). **Note:** *An aftermarket generic scanner should work with any model covered by this manual. Before purchasing a generic scan tool, verify that it will work properly with the self-diagnosis system you want to scan. If necessary, of course, you*

can always have the codes extracted by a dealer service department or an independent repair shop with a professional scan tool.

Self-diagnosis system general description

3 All models are equipped with an onboard self-diagnosis system. This system consists of an on-board computer known as the Engine Control Module (ECM), and information sensors, which monitor various functions of the engine and send data to the ECM. This system incorporates a series of diagnostic monitors that detect and identify fuel injection and emissions control systems faults and store the information in the computer memory. This system also tests sensors and output actuators, diagnoses drive cycles, freezes data and clears codes.

4 This powerful diagnostic computer can be accessed using a scan tool, or code reader, plugged into the Data Link Connector (DLC) located under the seat **(see illustration)**. The ECM is located beneath the fuel tank top cover. The ECM is the brain of the electronically controlled fuel and emissions system. It receives data from a number of sensors and other electronic components (switches, relays, etc.). Based on the information it receives, the ECM generates output signals to control various relays, solenoids (fuel injectors) and other actuators. The ECM is specifically calibrated to optimize the emissions, fuel economy and driveability of the motorcycle.

5 It isn't a good idea to attempt diagnosis or replacement of the ECM or emission control components at home while the motorcycle is under warranty. Because of a federally mandated extended warranty that covers the emissions system components and because any owner-induced damage to the ECM, sensors and/or control devices might void this warranty, take the vehicle to a dealer service department if the ECM or a system component malfunctions.

Obtaining and clearing Diagnostic Trouble Codes (DTCs)

6 All models covered by this manual are equipped with on-board diagnostics. When the ECM recognizes a malfunction in a monitored emission control system, component or circuit, it turns on the Malfunction Indicator Light (MIL) on the instrument cluster. The ECM will continue to display the MIL until the problem is fixed and the Diagnostic Trouble Code (DTC) is cleared from the ECM's memory. A code reader or scan tool is a convenient way to access any DTCs stored in the ECM, but you can also access the codes with the MIL and a simple jumper wire.

Accessing the DTCs

7 If you have a scan tool, follow the manufacturer's instructions to access the DTCs. If you're using a Honda scan tool,

plug into the diagnostic connector, which is located beneath the seat at the upper edge of the relay box. Then follow the instructions included with the tool to extract the DTCs.

8   If you don't have a scan tool, remove the seat and locate the diagnostic connector at the upper edge of the relay box. Remove the cap from the connector (if equipped).

9   If you're working on a 2001 through 2003 model, connect the terminals of the diagnostic connector to each other with a short length of wire. If you're working on a 2004 or later model, connect the terminals for the brown and green wires to each other with a short length of wire.

10   Turn the ignition switch to On. If there are no trouble codes stored, the MIL will come on and glow steadily. If there are trouble codes, the MIL will blink to indicate them.

11   The ECM blinks to indicate the number of the diagnostic code. Single-digit numbers are indicated by the number of blinks: for example, diagnostic code 7 is indicated

by seven blinks. Two-digit numbers are indicated by a combination of long blinks (1.3 seconds each) and short blinks (0.5 seconds each), for example: diagnostic code 25 is indicated by two long blinks followed by five short blinks.

12   Once you have extracted all of the stored DTCs, look them up on the accompanying DTC chart.

13   After troubleshooting the source of each DTC, make any necessary repairs or replace the defective component(s).

Clearing the DTCs

14   If you read the DTCs with a scan tool, clear the DTCs with the scan tool, following the instructions provided by the tool's manufacturer.

15   If you used the MIL to read the DTCs, clear them using the check connector. With the sidestand down and ignition switch in the Off position, short the terminals of the check connector together (if you haven't already done so). Turn the ignition switch to On and

remove the jumper wire. The MIL will light up for approximately 5 seconds. During this time, reconnect the jumper wire to the check connector. **Note:** *The jumper wire must be connected during the 5-second period while the MIL is on.* If the codes clear, the MIL will go from a steady glow to blinking.

Diagnostic Trouble Codes

16   The accompanying table is a list of the Diagnostic Trouble Codes (DTCs) that can be accessed by a do-it-yourselfer working at home (the Honda scan tool will access more detailed codes on 2004 and later models; for example, it will indicate whether sensor voltage is too low or too high, where the blink method only indicates that sensor voltage is not within specifications). If the problem persists after you have checked and repaired the connectors, wire harness and vacuum hoses (if applicable) for an emission-related system, component or circuit, have the vehicle checked by a dealer service department or other qualified repair shop.

Diagnostic Trouble Codes

Blinks	Problem area	Causes	Symptom(s)
None	ECM	Defective ECM	Engine will not start
None	ECM circuits		
1	MAP sensor voltage	MAP sensor or circuit	None - normal operation
6 (2006-on)	BARO sensor voltage	BARO sensor or circuit	Rough idle at high altitude
7	ECT sensor voltage	ECT sensor or circuit	Hard starting when cold
8	TP sensor voltage	TP sensor or circuit	Poor acceleration
9	IAT sensor voltage	IAT sensor or circuit	None - normal operation
10 (2003 and earlier)	BARO sensor voltage	BARO sensor or circuit	Rough idle at high altitude
11	No VSS signal	VS sensor or circuit	None - normal operation
12	No. 1 injector	No. 1 injector or circuit	Engine won't start
13	No. 2 injector	No. 2 injector or circuit	Engine won't start
14	No. 3 injector	No. 3 injector or circuit	Engine won't start
15	No. 4 injector	No. 4 injector or circuit	Engine won't start
16	No. 5 injector	No. 5 injector or circuit	Engine won't start
17	No. 6 injector	No. 6 injector or circuit	Engine won't start

Diagnostic Trouble Codes (continued)

Blinks	Problem area	Causes	Symptom(s)
18	No CMP sensor signal	CMP sensor or circuit	Engine won't start
19	No CKP sensor signal	CKP sensor or circuit	Engine won't start
21	Right O2 sensor	Right O2 sensor or circuit	None - normal operation
22	Left O2 sensor	Left O2 sensor or circuit	None - normal operation
23	Right O2 sensor heater	Right O2 sensor or circuit	None - normal operation
24	Left O2 sensor heater	Left O2 sensor or circuit	None - normal operation
25	Right knock sensor	Right knock sensor or circuit	None - normal operation
26	Left knock sensor	Left knock sensor or circuit	None - normal operation
29	IACV	IACV or circuit	Hard starting, rough idle, stalling
33	ECM EEPROM	ECM or PROM chip defective	Normal running, codes not stored
36	Right AF ratio sensor	Right AF ratio sensor or circuit	None - normal operation
37	Left AF ratio sensor	Left AF ratio sensor or circuit	None - normal operation
38	Right AF ratio sensor heater	Right O2 sensor or circuit	None - normal operation
39	Left AF ratio sensor heater	Left O2 sensor or circuit	None - normal operation
41	GP sensor	GP sensor or circuit	None - normal operation
55	AF ratio sensor circuit	AF sensor circuit	None - normal operation

13.2 Unbolt the right fuel injector cover (A) and radiator bracket (B) for access to remove the fuel injectors

13 Fuel injectors and fuel presure regulator - removal and installation

Fuel injector(s)

1   Remove the radiator from the side of the bike you're working on (see Chapter 3).

2   Remove the injector cover from the side of the bike you're working on **(see illustrations 3.6a and 3.6b or the accompanying illustration)**.

3   Unbolt the radiator bracket and lift it out of the way **(see illustration 13.2 and the accompanying illustration)**.

4   Place shop rags over the fitting at the front end of the left fuel rail **(see illustration)**. Hold the fitting with one wrench and unscrew the plug with another wrench.

5   Check the injector wiring connectors for labels that indicate the cylinder number **(see illustration)**. If you don't see the labels, make your own. Disconnect the connectors from the injectors.

6   If you're working on the right side, unbolt the two fuel feed hoses from the fuel rail **(see illustration 13.5)**.

7   If you're working on the left side, remove two bolts that secure the fuel feed hose and two bolts that secure the pressure regulator fitting **(see illustration)**.

8   Disconnect the feed hose fitting(s) from the fuel rail and remove the O-ring **(see illustration)**. Remove the O-ring from the base of the pressure regulator fitting.

9   Clean all debris from the area around the injectors with spray cleaner or compressed air.

10   Unbolt the fuel rail **(see illustration 13.7 or the accompanying illustration)**. Lift it off the intake manifold together with the injectors. Cover the injector ports with clean shop rags to keep out dirt.

11   Remove the clip from the injector(s) you're removing. Work the injector free of the fuel rail.

13.3 **Left side radiator bracket bolts (arrows)**

13.4 **Camshaft position sensor (left arrow) and fuel rail plug (right arrow)**

12   Installation is the reverse of the removal steps, with the following additions:

a) *Use new O-rings on the injectors, fuel feed hoses, and on the left side, the fuel pressure regulator fitting. Lubricate the O-rings with clean engine oil.*

b) *Install the injectors into the fuel rail, then push the fuel rail and injectors into position on the intake manifold.*

13.5 **Look for a cylinder number label on each injector harness (arrow) and make your own labels if they're not visible**

13.7 **On the left side, unbolt the fuel feed hose fitting (left arrows) and fuel pressure regulator fitting (right arrows)**

13.8 **Pull the fittings out of the fuel rail and remove the O-rings**

13.10 **On the right side, unbolt the fuel feed hose fittings (arrows)**

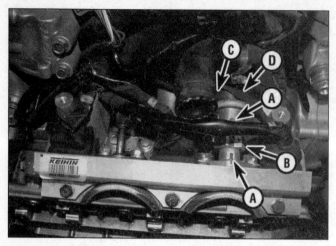

13.15 Fuel pressure regulator installation details

A   Alignment lugs
B   Nut
C   Vacuum hose
D   Fuel return hose (hidden)

14.1 The BARO sensor (arrow), which may be labeled as a MAP sensor, is outside the air cleaner housing

c) Tighten the fuel rail bolts, fuel feed hose bolts and pressure regulator fitting bolts to the torque listed in this Chapter's Specifications.
d) Fill and bleed the cooling system (see Chapters 1 and 3).

Fuel pressure regulator

13   Remove the left radiator (see Chapter 3). Unbolt the radiator bracket and lift it out of the way (see illustration 13.3).
14   Place shop rags over the fitting at the front end of the fuel rail and unscrew the plug (see illustration 13.4).
15   Grip the pressure regulator body firmly with one hand so it won't turn and unscrew the nut (see illustration).
16   Lift the regulator off the fuel rail, then disconnect the vacuum hose and fuel return hose (see illustration 13.3).
17   Pull the joint fitting out of the fuel rail. Remove the O-rings, coat new ones with clean

engine oil and install them on the joint fitting. Push the joint fitting back into the fuel rail.
18   Connect the vacuum hose and fuel return line to the regulator.
19   Push the regulator into position and tighten its nut with fingers (don't use a wrench yet). Align the lugs on the regulator body and the fitting in the fuel rail. Hold the regulator firmly with one hand so it won't turn and tighten the nut to the torque listed in this Chapter's Specifications.

14 Barometric Pressure (BARO) sensor - removal and installation

1   The BARO sensor on non-airbag models is mounted on the right side of the air cleaner housing, next to the cruise actuator (see illustration). On airbag models, it's mounted behind the ignition switch.

2   Remove the fuel tank top cover (air bag models) or center front top cover (airbag models) (see Chapter 8).
3   Unplug the wiring connector from the BARO sensor. Remove its mounting screw and take it off. Note: Honda motorcycles often use a MAP sensor to perform the function of the BARO sensor. The BARO sensor may have the word MAP on it, but you can tell it's the BARO sensor by its location (the actual MAP sensor is mounted on the throttle body).
4   Installation is the reverse of the removal steps.

15 Manifold Absolute Pressure (MAP) sensor - removal and installation

1   Remove the air cleaner housing (see Section 7).
2   Disconnect the EVAP hoses and secondary air supply hose and move them out of the way (see illustration 9.1 and the accompanying illustration).
3   Remove the MAP sensor screws (see illustration) (if necessary, loosen the throttle body clamps and lift it partially as described in Section 8).
4   Take the MAP sensor off the throttle body and remove its O-ring.
5   Installation is the reverse of the removal steps. Use a new O-ring.

16 Intake Air Temperature (IAT) sensor - removal and installation

1   Remove the fuel tank top cover (see Chapter 8).
2   Detach the ECM support bracket and

15.2 Location of the pulse air control solenoid (upper arrow) and idle air control valve (lower arrow)

15.3 Remove the MAP sensor screws (arrows)

16.3 Disconnect the IAT sensor (arrow) and work it free of the grommet (2001 through 2005 shown)

19.4a There's a knock sensor (arrow) on each side of the engine, on the underside of the cylinder head (exhaust system removed for clarity)

set it aside, together with the ECM (see the air filter replacement procedure in Chapter 1).
3   Unplug the connector from the IAT sensor. Work the IAT sensor free of the grommet in the air cleaner cover **(see illustration)**.
4   Installation is the reverse of the removal steps.

17 Camshaft Position (CMP) sensor - removal and installation

1   Remove the left fuel injector cover (see Section 13).
2   Disconnect the connector from the cam position sensor **(see illustration 13.4)**.
3   Remove the single bolt the secures the CMP sensor and take it out of the engine.
4   Installation is the reverse of the removal steps.

18 Crankshaft Position (CKP) sensor - check and replacement

Check
1   Make sure the motorcycle's battery is fully charged. Remove the air cleaner housing (see Section 7).
2   Locate the 2-pin red connector that runs to the CKP sensor and disconnect it (it's on top of the engine near the front).
3   Connect a peak voltage tester or a voltmeter with a peak voltage adapter to the sensor side of the connector (positive to yellow wire and negative to white-yellow wire).
4   Make sure the transmission is in neutral and turn the ignition switch to the On position (but don't start the engine).

5   Crank the engine with the starter and measure the peak voltage. If it's as specified, the CKP sensor is OK. If it's low, or there's no voltage at all, the sensor is probably defective.
6   If the sensor tests OK but there's a stored trouble code, follow the wires from the sensor connector to the ECM and check them for breaks or bad connections.

Replacement
7   Remove the lower front cover from the engine (see *Timing chains - removal and installation* in Chapter 2).
8   Unbolt the crankshaft position sensor and wiring harness retainer from the inside of the cover **(see illustration 11.2d** in Chapter 2). Pull the wiring harness grommet out of its notch in the edge of the cover and remove the sensor, together with the wiring harness and grommet.
9   Installation is the reverse of the removal steps. Tighten the sensor bolts to the torque listed in this Chapter's Specifications.

19 Knock sensors - removal and installation

1   There are two knock sensors, one on each side of the engine.
2   Remove the lower front exhaust cover from the side of the bike you're working on (see Section 28).
3   Remove the lower front fairing panel (see Chapter 8).
4   Unplug the electrical connector from the knock sensor and unscrew the knock sensor from the engine **(see illustrations)**.
5   Installation is the reverse of the removal steps. Tighten the knock sensor to the torque listed in this Chapter's Specifications.

19.4b Location of the right side knock sensor (right arrow) and the vehicle speed sensor (left arrow)

20 Vehicle speed sensor - removal and installation

1   Remove the fuel tank top cover (see Chapter 8).
2   Remove the forward exhaust heat shield from the right side of the bike (see Section 28).
3   Disconnect the electrical connector from the speed sensor **(see illustration 19.4b)**. Free the wring harness from its retainer (you may need to remove the brake fluid reservoir to this - if you do, leave the hose connected to the reservoir).
4   Unbolt the speed sensor from the engine and pull it out. Remove the sensor O-ring.
5   Installation is the reverse of the removal steps. Use a new O-ring, coated with clean engine oil. Tighten the bolts securely, but don't overtighten them and strip the threads.

21.2a Unbolt the holder bracket on the left side (arrows) . . .

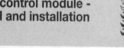

21.2b . . . and on the right side (arrows), then lift the holder up

21 Engine control module - removal and installation

1   Remove the fuel tank top cover (non-airbag models) or left top cover (airbag models) (see Chapter 8).

2   If you're removing the ECM for access to other components, remove the holder mounting screws and lift the holder off, together with the ECM (and cruise/reverse module on 2001 through 2005 models) **(see illustrations)**. Set the ECM aside.

3   If you're removing the ECM completely on a 2001 through 2005 model, disconnect the electrical connectors from the cruise/reverse control module **(see illustration)**.

4   On all models, disconnect the electrical connectors from the ECM **(see illustration)**. Remove the ECM from the holder and take it out.

5   Installation is the reverse of the removal steps.

22 Oxygen or air/fuel ratio sensors - general precautions and replacement

General precautions

Note: *Because it is installed in the exhaust pipe, which contracts when it cools off, an oxygen or air/fuel ratio sensor might be very difficult to loosen when the engine is cold. Rather than risk damage to the sensor or its mounting threads, start and run the engine for a minute or two, then shut it off. Be careful not to burn yourself during the following procedure.*

1   Be particularly careful when servicing an oxygen or air/fuel ratio sensor.

The sensors have a permanently attached pigtail and an electrical connector that cannot be removed. Damaging or removing the pigtail or electrical connector will render the sensor useless.

Keep grease, dirt and other contaminants

away from the electrical connector and the louvered end of the sensor.

Do not use cleaning solvents of any kind on an oxygen or air/fuel ratio sensor.

These sensors are extremely delicate. Do not drop a sensor, throw it around or handle it roughly.

Make sure that the silicone boot on the sensor is installed in the correct position. Otherwise, the boot might melt and prevent the sensor from operating correctly.

Replacement

2   The oxygen sensors or air/fuel ratio sensors are screwed into the exhaust pipe behind the catalytic converter on each side of the bike.

3   If you're working on a non-airbag model, remove the fuel tank top cover (see Chapter 8). If you're working on an airbag model, remove the left top cover or right top cover, depending on which sensor you want to remove. Also remove the trim clip that secures the ventilation air duct and take the air duct out. Remove the rear exhaust pipe cover (see Section 28).

4   Follow the wiring harness from the sensor up to the connector, then unplug the connector **(see illustrations)**. Free the harness from any retainers.

5   Unscrew the sensor from the exhaust pipe. Use an oxygen sensor socket if you have one - these have a slot in the side to accommodate the wiring harness. If you don't have the special socket, slip a box wrench over the sensor harness, then down onto the sensor.

6   If you're going to install the old sensor, apply anti-seize compound to the threads of the sensor to facilitate future removal. If you're going to install a new oxygen sensor, it's not necessary to apply anti-seize compound to the threads. The threads on new sensors already have anti-seize compound on them.

7   Installation is the reverse of removal.

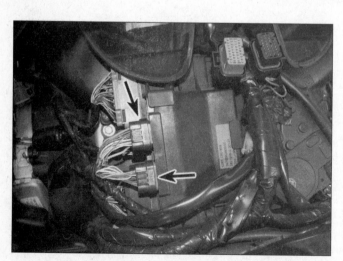

21.3 Disconnect the cruise/reverse control unit connectors (arrows) . . .

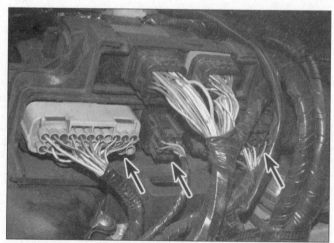

21.4 . . . and the ECM connectors (arrows) (2001 through 2005 shown)

22.4a Location of the right side oxygen sensor connector (2001 through 2005 models, later models similar)

22.4b Location of the left side oxygen sensor connector - the harness can be identified by its woven covering

23.3 Remove the screws (arrows) and take the idle air control valve and its gasket off the throttle body

Be sure to tighten the oxygen sensor to the torque listed in this Chapter's Specifications.

23 Idle Air Control (IAC) valve - removal and installation

1   Remove the air cleaner housing (see Section 7).
2   Disconnect the electrical connector from the IAC valve (see illustration 16.2).
3   Remove the IAC valve mounting screws and take it off the throttle body (see illustration). Remove the rubber gasket.
4   Installation is the reverse of the removal steps. Use a new gasket and fit it into the groove on the throttle body. One of the openings in the gasket is slightly offset so it will only go one way.

24 Gear position sensor - removal and installation

1   Remove the engine front cover (see Chapter 2, Section 11).
2   Unbolt the sensor from inside the cover (see illustration 11.2d in Chapter 2).
3   Installation is the reverse of the removal steps. Tighten the bolts securely, but don't overtighten them and strip the threads.

25 Pulse secondary air (PAIR) system - check and component replacement

1   The PAIR system uses exhaust gas pulses to suck fresh air into the exhaust ports, where it mixes with hot combustion gases.

The additional oxygen provided by the fresh air allows combustion to continue for a longer time, reducing unburned hydrocarbons in the exhaust. Check valves allow the flow of air into the ports and prevent exhaust gas from flowing into the system (see illustration). There are two sets of three check valves, one for each cylinder head. The PAIR control solenoid valve shuts off the flow of air into the system during deceleration to prevent backfiring.

Check

2   Remove the air filter (see Chapter 1). Check for carbon in the air hose intake port in the bottom of the air cleaner housing (see illustration). If there is carbon in the port, remove and inspect the check valves as described below. This requires removing the engine from the motorcycle and removing the intake manifold from the engine.
3   Remove the air cleaner housing (see Section 7). Check the control solenoid hoses

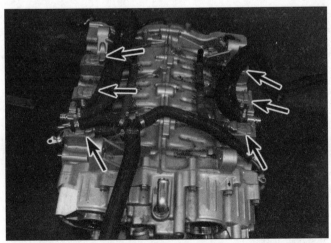

25.1 There are six check valves (arrows) on top of the engine, connected by hoses

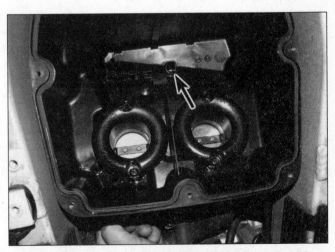

25.2 If there's built-up carbon in the air intake port (arrow), inspect the check valves

26.3a Disconnect the hose on the left side of the EVAP canister (arrow) . . .

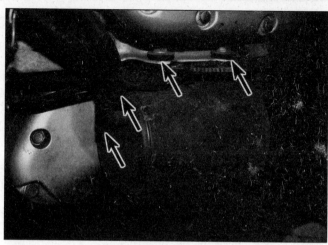

26.3b . . . and on the right side (lower arrows), then remove the mounting bolts (upper arrows)

for loose connections, damage and deterioration (see illustration 16.2). Tighten or replace loose or damaged hoses.

4   Reconnect the ECM connectors (if they were disconnected), as well as the IAT sensor and BARO sensor connectors. Connect an auxiliary fuel supply (either reinstall the tank temporarily or use an auxiliary setup) (see illustration 10.9).

5   Warm the engine to normal operating temperature.

6   Place a finger over the end of the disconnected air supply hose (see illustration 16.2). Rev the engine slightly. There should be suction at the end of the hose. If not, the control solenoid may be defective or the hose may be clogged.

7   To check the control solenoid, disconnect its electrical connector, remove the three hoses, remove the mounting screws and take it out (see illustration 16.2). Blow air into the hose fitting nearest the electrical connector. It should flow from both of the other fittings. Connect a 12-volt battery to the electrical terminals (positive to the black/yellow wire's

26.5 The EVAP control solenoid is mounted inside the front of the frame

terminal; negative to the orange/green wire's terminal). Again, try to blow air into the hose fitting nearest the electrical terminal. Air should not flow from either of the other fittings. If it does, replace the solenoid with a new one.

Component replacement

8   Access to the hoses and check valves on top of the engine requires removal of the engine from the motorcycle and removal of the intake manifold from the engine (see Chapter 2). To remove check valves from the cylinder heads, unbolt the covers and lift them off (see illustration 25.1). Take the check valves out of their seats in the top of the crankcase. If there is any clearance between the reed portion of the valve and its seat, if the reed is damaged or weak, or if the rubber seat is damaged or deteriorated, replace the reed valve.

9   Installation is the reverse of the removal steps.

26 Evaporative emission control (EVAP) system - check and component replacement

1   The evaporation control system used on California models prevents fuel vapor from escaping into the atmosphere. When the engine isn't running, the vapor is stored in a canister mounted low on the front of the motorcycle, then routed into the combustion chambers for burning when the engine starts.

2   The hoses should be checked periodically for loose connections, damage and deterioration. Tighten or replace the hoses as needed.

3   To remove the canister, disconnect the hoses. Remove the mounting bolts and lower the canister away from the bracket (see illustrations).

4   Inspect the rubber mounting bushings and replace them if they're cracked or deteriorated. Bolt the canister to its bracket and reconnect the hoses.

5   To check the solenoid, remove the center inner fairing (see Chapter 8). Disconnect the electrical connector and hoses and lift the solenoid out of its rubber mount (see illustration).

6   Try to blow air into the bottom hose fitting. It should not flow from the other fitting. Connect a 12-volt battery to the electrical terminals (positive to the black/yellow wire's terminal; negative to the yellow/black wire's terminal). Again, try to blow air into the bottom hose fitting. Air should now flow from the other fitting. If it flows when it shouldn't, or doesn't flow when it should, replace the solenoid with a new one.

7   Installation is the reverse of the removal steps.

27 Crankcase emission control system - check and component replacement

1   The crankcase emission control system routes blow-by gases from the crankcase into the air cleaner housing. On these models, the system consists of a hose running from the top of the crankcase to a Y-fitting, and from there two hoses run to the air cleaner housing (see illustration).

2   To check the system, remove the fuel tank (see Section 5). Check the hoses for damage, deterioration and loose connections. Reconnect or replace the hoses as needed.

3   At periodic intervals, remove the plug from the air cleaner housing drain hose and drain any accumulated deposits (see Chapter 1).

27.1 The crankcase emission hose (lower arrow) runs from a fitting on the back of the engine to two hoses (upper arrows) that connect to the air cleaner housing

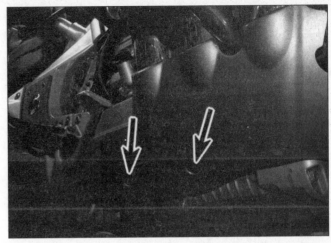

28.2a Remove two nuts and washers (arrows) that secure the lower front exhaust pipe cover (right side shown; left side identical)

28 Exhaust system - removal and installation

Removal

1   Remove the lower front fairing panel (see Chapter 8).
2   Remove two nuts and washers that secure the lower front cover **(see illustration)**. Remove the bolt at the front end of the cover **(see illustration)**. Lower the front of the cover off the crash bar, pull the cover forward to disengage its slots from the tabs at the rear, then take it off **(see illustrations)**.
3   Remove the fiber washers from the cover studs **(see illustration)**.

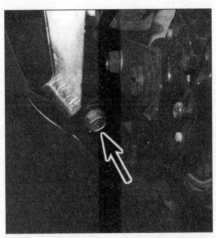

28.2b Remove the bolt at the front end of the cover (arrow)

28.2c Lower the front of the cover until the slot (arrow) clears the crash bar

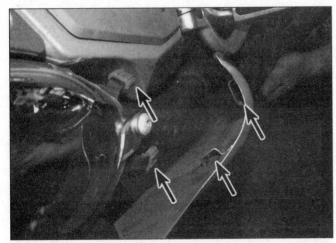

28.2d Pull the cover forward to disengage its slots from the tabs (arrows) and take the cover off

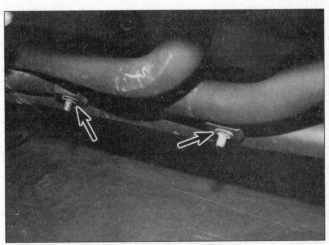

28.3 There are fiber washers on the studs (arrows), in addition to the fiber washers under the cover nuts

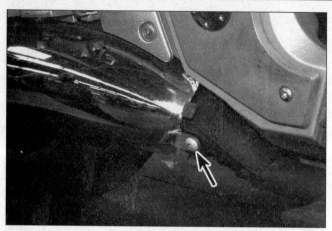

28.4a Remove the Allen screw and washer at the front end of the rear cover . . .

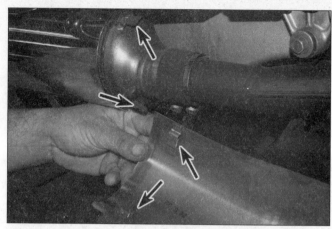

28.4b . . . and slide the cover forward to disengage the tabs from the slots (arrows)

4   Remove the Allen bolt and washer at the front of the lower rear cover **(see illustration)**. Pull the cover forward to disengage its slots from the tabs at the rear, then take it off **(see illustration)**.

5   Remove the center mounting bolts and washer. Loosen the clamp bolts at the front of the muffler and at the crossover pipe **(see illustration)**.

6   Loosen the muffler bolt **(see illustration)**.

> **HAYNES HiNT**
>
> *Leave this bolt in place for the time being to support the rear end of the exhaust system while the front end is detached from the engine.*

28.5 Unscrew the center hanger bolt (A) and loosen the crossover clamp bolts (B) and muffler clamp bolts (C)

28.6 Loosen the muffler hanger bolt, but don't remove the bolt and washer yet

28.7a Remove the header nuts (arrows) and lower the header away from the engine

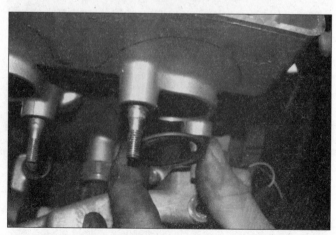

28.7b Remove the gasket from the exhaust ports

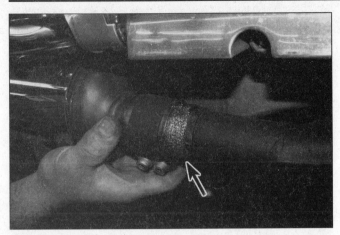

28.8 Remove the muffler bolt and washer completely, then slide the muffler back, separate it from the exhaust pipe and remove the gasket (arrow)

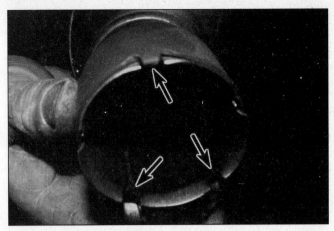

28.9 On installation, align the clamp tabs with the slots on the pipe (arrows)

7   Remove the nuts that secure the header to the cylinder head **(see illustration)**. Lower the header until the pipes clear the exhaust ports, then remove the gaskets from the ports **(see illustration)**.

8   Remove the muffler bolt and washer completely and lower the muffler. Separate the crossover and muffler joints and remove the gaskets **(see illustration)**.

9   Installation is the reverse of the removal steps. Use new gaskets at the joints and at the cylinder head. Position the clamp tabs in the slots of the pipe **(see illustration)**. Tighten the exhaust system nuts and bolts to the torques listed in this Chapter's Specifications.

Notes

Chapter 5
Ignition system

Contents

Degrees of difficulty

Easy, suitable for novice with little experience	**Fairly easy,** suitable for beginner with some experience	**Fairly difficult,** suitable for competent DIY mechanic	**Difficult,** suitable for experienced DIY mechanic	**Very difficult,** suitable for expert DIY or professional

Specifications

Arcing distance.. 6 mm (1/4 inch)
Ignition coil peak voltage.. 2.5 to 5.0 volts
Ignition timing... Not adjustable
Spark plugs .... See Chapter 1

1 General information

This motorcycle is equipped with a battery operated, fully transistorized, breakerless ignition system. The system consists of the following components:

Engine Control Module (ECM)
Crankshaft Position (CKP) sensor and
*   timing rotor*
Battery and relay
Ignition coils
Spark plugs
Ignition (main) and engine kill (stop)
*   switches*
Primary and secondary circuit wiring

The transistorized ignition system functions on the same principle as a breaker point DC ignition system with the CKP sensor, timing rotor and engine control module performing the tasks previously associated with the breaker points and mechanical advance system. As a result, adjustment and maintenance of ignition components is eliminated (with the exception of spark plug replacement). The Crankshaft Position sensor is an integral part of the programmed fuel injection (PGM-FI) system and is covered in Chapter 4.

There are three ignition coils, each operating a pair of cylinders. The coils are triggered by integral igniters. At the appropriate time, the ECM sends a 5-volt signal to the igniter built into each coil. The igniter voltage is stepped to ignition voltage by the coil and travels through the spark plug wire to the spark plug.

2.12 A simple spark gap testing fixture can be made from a block of wood, a large alligator clip, two nails, a screw and a piece of wire

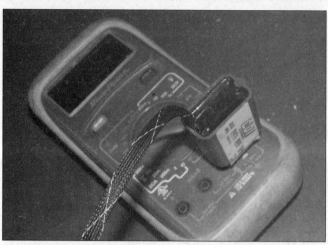

3.1 Testing the ignition coils requires a peak voltage tester - this model is an adapter that plugs into a standard voltmeter

The ignition timing is controlled by the ECM, which adjusts the timing for various riding conditions, taking into account engine rpm, throttle position, coolant and air temperature, intake manifold vacuum and transmission gear position.

Because of their nature, the individual ignition system components can't be repaired. If ignition system troubles occur, and the faulty component can be isolated, the only cure for the problem is to replace the part with a new one. Keep in mind that most electrical parts, once purchased, can't be returned. To avoid unnecessary expense, make very sure the faulty component has been positively identified before buying a replacement part.

2 Ignition system - check

⚠ *Warning: Because of the very high voltage generated by the ignition system, extreme care should be taken when these checks are performed.*

1 If the ignition system is the suspected cause of poor engine performance or failure to start, a number of checks can be made to isolate the problem.
2 Make sure the engine kill switch is in the Run position.

Engine will not start

⚠ *Warning: Don't remove one of the spark plugs from the engine to perform this check - atomized fuel being pumped out of the open spark plug hole could ignite, causing severe injury!*

3 Disconnect one of the spark plug wires, connect the wire to a spare spark plug and lay the plug on the engine with the threads contacting the engine. If necessary, hold the spark plug with an insulated tool. Crank the engine over and make sure a well-defined, blue spark occurs between the spark plug electrodes.
4 If no spark occurs, repeat the same test on the other ignition coils.
5 If one coil fails to produce spark, but the others do spark, the problem is most likely in the non-sparking coil, its plug wire cap or its primary wires. Make sure all electrical connectors are clean and tight, including the spark plug caps. Check for water inside the spark plug caps. Check all wires for shorts, opens and correct installation.
6 Check the battery voltage with a voltmeter. If the voltage is less than the value listed in the Chapter 9 Specifications, recharge the battery.
7 Check the ignition fuse and the fuse connections. If the fuse is blown, replace it with a new one; if the connections are loose or corroded, clean or repair them.
8 Refer to Chapter 9 and check the ignition relay, ignition switch, engine kill switch, neutral switch and sidestand switch.
9 Refer to Section 3 and check the ignition coil peak voltage.
10 Refer to Chapter 4 and check the Crankshaft Position (CKP) sensor peak voltage.

Engine starts but misfires

11 If the engine starts but misfires, make the following checks before deciding that the ignition system is at fault.
12 The ignition system must be able to produce a spark across a six millimeter (1/4-inch) gap (minimum). A simple test fixture **(see illustration)** can be constructed to make sure the minimum spark gap can be jumped. Make sure the fixture electrodes are positioned six millimeters apart.
13 Connect one of the spark plug wires to the protruding test fixture electrode, then attach the fixture's alligator clip to a good engine ground/earth.
14 Crank the engine over (it will probably start and run on the remaining cylinders) and see if well-defined, blue sparks occur between the test fixture electrodes. If the minimum spark gap test is positive, the ignition coil for that cylinder (and its companion cylinder) is functioning properly. Repeat the check on one of the spark plug wires that is connected to the other coils. If the spark will not jump the gap during either test, or if it is weak (orange colored), refer to Steps 3 through 10 of this Section and perform the component checks described.

3 Ignition coils - check and replacement

1 The ignition coils on these models are tested by measuring peak voltage. This requires either a voltmeter that will measure peak voltage or a special adapter that plugs into a standard voltmeter **(see illustration)**. The tester must have an impedance of at least 10 mega-ohms per volt. These adapters can be expensive, so if you don't have one, it may be more cost-effective to have the coils tested by a dealer service department or other qualified shop.
2 Make sure the battery is fully charged (see Chapter 9 if necessary). An undercharged battery can cause inaccurately low peak voltage readings, even if there's nothing wrong with the coils.
3 Remove the seat and center inner fairing (see Chapter 8). Disconnect the electrical connector for the fuel pump (see Chapter 4).
4 Unplug the connector from the coil being tested **(see illustration)**. Connect the tester to the ignition coil signal wire as follows:
   a) No. 1 and 2 - positive to yellow/white wire and negative to ground

3.4 Unplug the primary connector (arrows) from the top of the coil being tested

1 Coil for cylinders 1 and 2
2 Coil for cylinders 3 and 4
3 Coil for cylinders 5 and 6

3.11a Disconnect the spark plug wires from the underside of the coil (arrows) - center coil shown

b) No. 3 and 4 - positive to yellow/blue wire and negative to ground
c) No. 5 and 6 - positive to yellow/red wire and negative to ground

5   Make sure the transmission is in Neutral. Turn the ignition switch to the On position and crank the engine, using the starter. Compare the peak voltage reading to the value listed in this Chapter's Specifications.

6   If peak voltage is within the specified limits, but the coil isn't making any sparks, check the coil's power and ground wires for breaks or bad connections. If the wires are good, check the spark plug wire(s). If they're good, the coil is probably defective.

7   If there's no peak voltage, confirm that the battery is fully charged and that the peak voltage tester is the correct type. Check the ignition coil signal wire (refer to Step 4 for colors). Refer to Chapter 9 and check the wiring for the sidestand switch and gear position sensor.

8   If none of the above checks have

located the problem, refer to Chapter 4 and test the Crankshaft Position sensor.

9   If the problem still hasn't been located, the problem may be with the engine control module. Since this is a very expensive component that usually can't be returned once purchased, further testing should be done by a dealer service department or other qualified shop.

Removal and installation

10   For access to the coils, remove the front lower fairing (all models) and EVAP purge solenoid (California models) (see Chapters 8 and 4).

11   Disconnect the spark plug wires from the coil you want to remove **(see illustration)**. Look for number labels on the wires **(see illustration)** and make your own labels with tape if they aren't visible. Unplug the coil primary circuit electrical connectors **(see illustration 3.4)**

12   Unbolt the individual coil(s) from the

bracket and remove them from the motorcycle.

13   Installation is the reverse of removal. Make sure the primary circuit electrical connectors are attached to the proper terminals and the plug wires to the correct plugs.

4   Spark plug wires - removal and installation

1   Remove the ignition coils (see Section 3).

2   Remove the retainer that secures the No. 2 and No. 5 plug wires from its bracket **(see illustration)**.

3   Remove the spark plug covers. Label the spark plug wires with their cylinder numbers **(see illustration 3.11b)**, then disconnect the wires from the spark plugs (see Chapter 1 if necessary).

3.11b Look for number marks on the spark plug wires (arrow) - if the marks aren't visible, make your own marks

4.2 Free the spark plug wires from the retainers on the front of each cylinder head

4.4a Remove the lower inner engine cover bolts (arrows) . . .

4.4b . . . and take the cover off the engine

4   Remove the lower inner engine cover **(see illustrations)**. Free the plug wires from the retainers and remove the wires from the motorcycle.
5   Installation is the reverse of the removal steps.

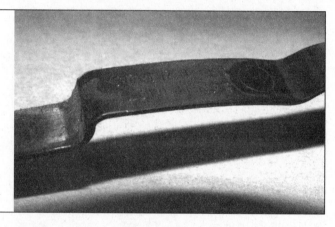

4.4c The cover is labeled left or right for the side of the engine it goes on

5   Engine control module - check, removal and installation

Check

1   The ECM is checked by process of elimination (when all other possible causes have been checked and eliminated, the ECM is at fault). Because the ECM is expensive and can't be returned once purchased, consider having a Honda dealer test the ignition system before you buy a new ECM.

Removal and installation

Note: *If the motorcycle is equipped with an airbag, refer to the airbag precautions in Chapter 9 before beginning work.*

2   Remove the top cover from the fuel tank (see Chapter 8).
3   If you're working on an airbag model, free the ECM wiring harness from its retainer. Unbolt the ECM hold-down and take it off.
4   If you're working on a 2001 through 2005 model, unplug the wiring connectors from the reverse/cruise module and remove it from its mounts **(see illustration)**.
5   Unplug the electrical connectors (2001

through 2005 models have two large connectors with a small one in between them; 2006 and later models have two large connectors). Take the ECM out **(see illustration)**. **Note:** *One of the large connectors is gray and the other is black. The sockets they plug into are the same color as the connectors.*
6   Installation is the reverse of the removal steps. Be sure to plug the large ECM connectors into the correct sockets.

5.4 Unplug the electrical connectors (arrows) and remove the reverse-cruise module from on top of the ECM

5.5 Unplug the electrical connectors (arrows) and remove the engine control module

Chapter 6
Steering, suspension and final drive

Contents

Degrees of difficulty

| Easy, suitable for novice with little experience | | Fairly easy, suitable for beginner with some experience | | Fairly difficult, suitable for competent DIY mechanic | | Difficult, suitable for experienced DIY mechanic | | Very difficult, suitable for expert DIY or professional | |

Specifications

Fork spring length (2001 through 2005)
    Standard .... 335.3 mm (13.2 inches)
    Limit .... 328.6 mm (12.94 inches)
Fork spring length (2006 and later)
    2006 non-airbag models
        Standard .... 335.3 mm (13.2 inches)
        Limit .... 328.6 mm (12.94 inches)
    2006 airbag models, all 2007 and later models
        Standard .... 334.9 mm (13.19 inches)
        Limit .... 328.2 mm (12.92 inches)
Fork oil capacity
    Left fork .... 529 +/- 2.5 cc (17.9 +/- 0.08 US fl oz, 18.6 +/- 0.09 Imp oz)
    Right fork .... 485 +/- 2.5 cc (16.4 +/- 0.08 US fl oz, 17.1 +/- 0.09 Imp oz)
Fork oil level (fully compressed) .... 128 mm (5.0 inches) below top of fork tube
Fork oil type.. Pro Honda Suspension Fluid SS-8 (10W) or equivalent
Fork tube runout limit .... 0.2 mm (0.01 inch)

Torque specifications

Handlebar mounting bolts	26 Nm (20 ft-lbs)
Upper triple clamp bolts	26 Nm (20 ft-lbs)
Lower triple clamp bolts	29 Nm (22 ft-lbs)
Front fork caps	
2001 through 2005	23 Nm (17 ft-lbs)
2006 and later	22 Nm (16 ft-lbs)
Fork damper rod Allen bolt	20 Nm (14 ft-lbs) (1)
Fork damper rod locknut (right fork leg only)	20 Nm (14 ft-lbs)
Anti-dive plunger unit to case Allen bolts	4 Nm (35 inch-lbs) (2)
Anti-dive plunger case to fork leg	Not specified
Steering stem upper nut (above triple clamp)	103 Nm (76 ft-lbs)
Steering stem adjusting nut	
Initial torque	
2001 through 2005	27 Nm (20 ft-lbs)
2006 and later	28 Nm (21 ft-lbs)
Final torque	Same as initial torque
Rear shock absorber bolts/nuts	42 Nm (31 ft-lbs)
Rear suspension linkage bolts/nuts	
Tie-rods to shock arm	64 Nm (47 ft-lbs)
Shock arm to swingarm	64 Nm (47 ft-lbs)
Final drive unit mounting nuts	88 Nm (65 ft-lbs)
Swingarm pivot bolts	
Right side	108 Nm (80 ft-lbs)
Left side	34 Nm (25 ft-lbs)
Swingarm pivot bolt locknut	
Indicated torque with Honda special tool	98 Nm (72 ft-lbs)
Actual applied torque	108 Nm (80 ft-lbs)

(1) Use non-permanent thread locking agent on the threads.
(2) Replace the bolts with new ones.

2.2 Remove the screws (arrows) and lift off the center handlebar cover

2.4 Remove the bolts (arrows) and lift the handlebar off

1 General information

The steering system on these motorcycles consists of a two-piece handlebar, bolted to the upper triple clamp, and a steering stem, which rides in a steering head attached to the front portion of the frame. All models use caged ball bearings in the steering head.

The front suspension consists of conventional coil spring, hydraulically damped telescopic forks with an anti-dive unit.

The rear suspension consists of a single nitrogen-filled shock absorber and a swingarm. The shock is connected to the swingarm through a progressive rising rate linkage that increases effective stiffness as the swingarm rises. All models have an on-board preload adjustment system that allows suspension preload to be changed at the touch of a switch.

The final drive uses a shaft and bevel gears to transmit power from the transmission to the rear wheel.

2 Handlebars - removal and installation

1   Remove the instrument cluster (see Chapter 9).
2   Remove the center cover **(see illustration)**.
3   Remove the cover from the handlebar you're planning to remove.
4   If the handlebars must be removed for access to other components, such as the forks or the steering head, simply unbolt the handlebar and lift it off the upper triple clamp **(see illustration)**. It's not necessary to disconnect the cables, wires or hoses, but it is a good idea to support the assembly with a piece of wire or rope, to avoid unnecessary strain on the cables, wires and the brake or clutch hose.
5   If the handlebars are to be removed completely, refer to Chapter 2 for clutch master cylinder removal procedures, Chapter 7 for the brake master cylinder removal procedures, Chapter 5 for the throttle cable removal procedure and Chapter 9 for the switch removal procedure.
6   Check the handlebars for cracks and distortion and replace them if any undesirable conditions are found. When installing the handlebars, tighten the bolts to the torque listed in this Chapter's Specifications.

3 Forks - removal and installation

Removal

⚠ **Warning: This procedure requires removal of some airbag components on models so equipped. Before beginning work, refer to the airbag precautions in Chapter 9.**

1   Support the bike securely so it can't be knocked over during this procedure. Place a jack under the engine and raise it slightly to lift the front tire off the ground.
2   Remove the front fender (see Chapter 8).
3   If you're working on an airbag model, remove the crash sensors at the front wheel and detach the crash sensor wiring harness retainer from the left fork leg.
4   Remove the brake calipers and front wheel (see Chapter 7).

5   Remove the combination meter (see Chapter 9).
6   Remove the handlebar center cover **(see illustration 2.2)**.
7   If you're removing the left fork leg, unbolt the anti-dive plunger **(see illustration)** and the secondary master cylinder and brake line fitting bolt (see Chapter 7).
8   Remove any wiring harness clamps or straps from the fork tubes. If you're working on an airbag model, unbolt the crash sensor support bracket.
9   If the fork will be disassembled after removal, read through the disassembly procedure (see Section 4), paying special attention to the damper rod bolt removal steps. If you don't have the necessary special tool or a substitute for it, you can loosen the damper rod bolt before the fork is disassembled, while the spring tension will keep the damper rod from spinning inside the fork tube.

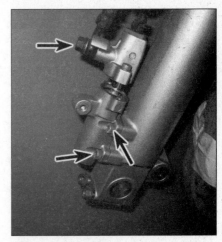

3.7 Unbolt the anti-dive plunger from the case - the banjo bolt (upper arrow) and case bolts (lower arrows) need not be removed

3.10 Unscrew the cap (arrow) from the top of the fork; the cap seam should be flush with the top of the triple clamp on installation

3.11a Loosen the upper and lower triple clamp bolts (arrows) . . .

3.11b . . . and twist and pull the fork leg downward out of the triple clamps

10   If you plan to disassemble the forks after removal, loosen the fork caps (but don't remove them yet) **(see illustration)**.
11   Loosen the fork upper and lower triple clamp bolts **(see illustrations)**, then slide the fork tubes down and remove the forks from the motorcycle.

Installation

12   Slide each fork leg into the lower triple clamp.
13   Slide the fork legs up, installing the tops of the tubes into the upper triple clamp. Position the top of the fork tube flush with the top of the upper triple clamp.
14   The remainder of installation is the reverse of the removal procedure, with the following additions:

a) *Before installing the anti-dive plunger case (left fork only), clean all dirt from the mating surfaces on the plunger case and the cylinder on the fork leg. Lubricate the tip of the anti-dive plunger with silicone grease.*
b) *Tighten all fasteners to the torques listed in this Chapter's Specifications and the*

Chapter 7 Specifications. Use new bolts for the secondary master cylinder and anti-dive plunger case.

15   Pump the front brake lever several times to bring the pads into contact with the discs.

---

4   Forks - disassembly, inspection and reassembly

Left fork leg

Disassembly

1   Remove the forks following the procedure in Section 3. Work on one fork leg at a time to avoid mixing up the parts. The left and right fork legs are different designs, but some parts may look similar enough to cause confusion if the fork legs are disassembled at the same time.
2   Remove the fork cap (it should have been loosened before the forks were removed) **(see illustration 3.10)**.

⚠ *Warning: The fork cap is under spring tension. Be sure to point the end of the fork away from yourself while you remove the cap.*

Remove the spacer, spring seat and spring **(see illustration)**.

HAYNES HiNT *To prevent damage to the fork caps, place a piece of duct tape over the cap's hex fitting, then push the wrench down on top of it (see illustration).*

3   Invert the fork assembly over a container and extend and compress it several times to drain the oil.
4   Pry the dust seal from the outer tube **(see illustration)**.
5   Pry the retaining ring from its groove in the outer tube **(see illustration)**.
6   Unscrew the Allen bolt at the bottom of the outer tube and remove the copper washer **(see illustration)**.

4.2b To keep from scratching the fork cap, place a piece of duct tape over the hex, then push the socket or wrench down on top of it

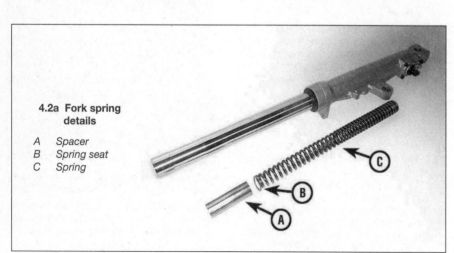

4.2a Fork spring details

A   Spacer
B   Spring seat
C   Spring

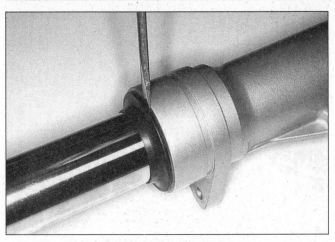

4.4 Pry the dust seal from its bore

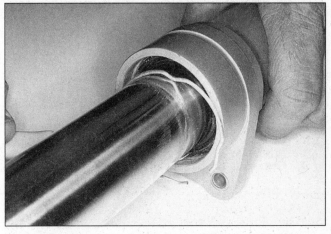

4.5 Pry the retainer from its bore without scratching the fork tubes

4.6a Unscrew the Allen bolt and remove the sealing washer; use a new sealing washer on assembly

4.6b To make a long Allen bolt bit, cut off a 6 mm Allen wrench and slip it into a 6 mm socket

TOOL TiP *Allen bit sockets are generally not long enough to reach in and engage the head of the damper rod bolt. You can make your own tool by cutting off a 6 mm Allen wrench and slipping it into a 6 mm socket (see illustration).*

7   Hold the outer tube and yank the inner tube away from it, repeatedly (like a slide hammer), until the seal and outer tube guide bushing pop loose **(see illustration)**.
8   Remove the stopper ring, oil lock valve, spring and spring seat from the damper rod **(see illustration)**.

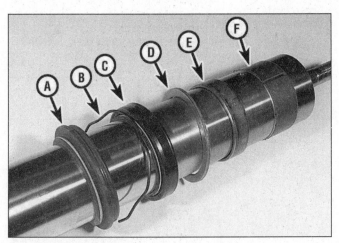

4.7 Seal and bushing details

A	Dust seal	D	Backup ring
B	Retainer	E	Outer tube bushing
C	Oil seal	F	Inner tube bushing

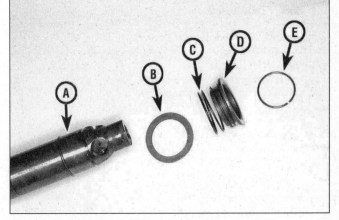

4.8 Oil lock valve details (left fork leg)

A	Damper piston	D	Oil lock valve
B	Spring seat	E	Stopper ring
C	Spring		

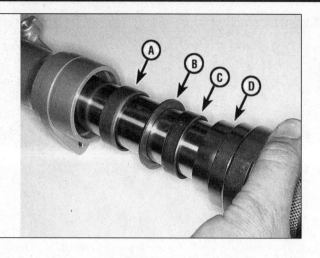

4.22a Drive the bushing into the outer fork seal bore like this

A   New bushing
B   Backup ring
C   Old bushing (used as a spacer)
D   Fork seal driver

4.22b If you don't have a seal driver, a section of pipe can be used the same way the seal driver would be used - as a slide hammer (be sure to tape the ends of the pipe so it doesn't scratch the fork tube)

9   Slide the oil seal, backup ring and slider bushing (larger bushing) from the inner tube.
10   Remove the anti-dive unit (see illustration 3.7).

Inspection

11   Clean all parts in solvent and blow them dry with compressed air, if available. Check the inner and outer fork tubes and the damper rod for score marks, scratches, flaking of the chrome and excessive or abnormal wear. Look for dents in the tubes and replace them if any are found. Check the fork seal seat for nicks, gouges and scratches. If damage is evident, leaks will occur around the seal-to-outer tube junction. Replace worn or defective parts with new ones.
12   Check the bushings for scoring, scratches or excessive wear. Replace them if they're scored or scratched, or if the Teflon coating has worn away from more than three-quarters of the surface, exposing the copper. If the bushings need to be replaced, pry them apart at the slit and take them off the fork tube. Install new ones, prying them just enough so they fit over the tube.
13   Check the inner circumference of the backup ring and replace it if it looks bent or distorted.
14   Have the inner fork tube checked for runout at a dealer service department or other repair shop.

 Warning: If it is bent, it should not be straightened; replace it with a new one.

15   Measure the overall length of the fork spring(s) and check for cracks and other damage. Compare the length to the minimum length listed in this Chapter's Specifications. If it's defective or sagged, replace the springs in both forks with new ones. Never replace the spring(s) in only one fork.
16   Check the Teflon rings on the damper rod and replace them if they're worn or damaged.
17   Inspect the anti-dive plunger for leaking brake fluid. Replace it if problems are found.

Reassembly

18   Install the rebound spring on the damper rod. Install the damper rod in the inner fork tube, then let it slide slowly down until it protrudes from the bottom of the inner fork tube.
19   Install the spring seat, spring, oil lock valve and stopper ring on the damper rod (see illustration 4.8).
20   Install the inner fork tube in the outer fork tube.
21   Temporarily install the fork spring and cap bolt. Apply non-permanent thread locking agent to the damper rod bolt, then install the bolt and tighten it to the torque listed in this Chapter's Specifications.
22   Slide the slider bushing down the inner tube, then slide the backup ring on behind it. Using a fork seal driver (Honda tool or equivalent) and a used slider bushing placed on top of the slider bushing being installed, drive the bushing into place until it's fully seated (see illustration). If you don't have access to one of these tools, it is highly recommended that you take the assembly to a Honda dealer service department or other motorcycle repair shop to have this done. It is possible, however, to drive the bushing into place using a section of pipe and an old guide bushing (see illustration). Wrap tape

around the ends of the pipe to prevent it from scratching the fork tube. Once you've installed the new bushing, remove the old one that was used as a spacer.
23   Lubricate the lips and the outer diameter of the oil seal with the recommended fork oil (see Chapter 1) and slide it down the inner tube, with the seal lip facing into the outer fork tube. Drive the seal into place with the same tool used to drive in the slider bushing (see illustration). If you don't have access to these, it is recommended that you take the assembly to a Honda dealer service department or other motorcycle repair shop to have the seal driven in. If you are very careful, the seal can be driven in with a hammer and a drift punch. Work around the circumference of the seal, tapping gently on the outer edge of the seal until it's seated. Be careful - if you distort the seal, you'll have to disassemble the fork again and end up taking it to a dealer anyway!
24   Install the retainer ring, making sure it's completely seated in its groove.
25   Install the dust seal, making sure it seats completely. The same tool used to drive in

4.23 Drive the oil seal in with the same tool used to install the bushing

4.27 **Measure fork oil level with a vernier caliper, ruler or steel tape measure**

4.33a **Unscrew the fork cap and pull the spring spacer partway out to expose the locknut (arrow)**

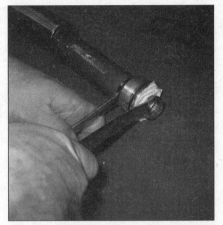

4.33b **Hold the fork cap with a wrench and unscrew the locknut (away from the fork cap)**

the oil seal can be used for the dust seal.

26 Install the anti-dive assembly (if equipped).

27 Add the recommended type and amount of fork oil. Pump the fork up and down several times, then measure oil level with the spring removed and the fork fully compressed **(see illustration)**.

28 Install the fork spring, with the closer-wound coils at the bottom. Install the spring seat and spacer.

29 Install the O-ring and fork cap.

30 Install the fork by following the procedure outlined in Section 3. If you won't be installing the fork right away, store it in an upright position.

Right fork leg

Disassembly

31 Remove the forks following the procedure in Section 3. Work on one fork leg at a time to avoid mixing up the parts. The left and right fork legs are different designs, but some parts may look similar enough to cause confusion if the fork legs are disassembled at the same time.

32 Unscrew the fork cap from the fork tube (it should have been loosened before the forks were removed) **(see illustration 3.10)**.

> Warning: *The fork cap is under spring tension. Be sure to point the end of the fork away from yourself while you remove the cap.*

33 Slip an open-end wrench between the fork cap and spring seat and place it on the damper rod locknut **(see illustrations)**. Hold the fork cap with a socket or wrench and turn the locknut to loosen it, then unscrew the fork cap from the damper rod shaft.

34 Remove the spacer, spring seats and springs.

35 Place the fork assembly over a container and extend and compress it several times to drain the oil **(see illustration)**.

36 Pry the dust seal from the outer tube

(see illustration 4.4).

37 Pry the retaining ring from its groove in the outer tube **(see illustration 4.5)**.

38 Unscrew the Allen bolt at the bottom of the outer tube and remove the sealing washer **(see illustration 4.6)**. Take the cartridge out of the top of the fork.

39 Hold the outer tube and yank the inner tube away from it, repeatedly (like a slide hammer), until the seal and outer tube guide bushing pop loose **(see illustration 4.7)**. Separate the fork tube and slider.

40 Remove the oil lock piece **(see illustration)**.

41 Slide the oil seal, backup ring(s) and slider bushing (larger bushing) from the inner tube. 2001 through 2005 models and 2006 non-airbag models have a single backup ring. 2006 airbag models and all 2007 and later models have two backup rings.

Inspection

42 This is basically the same as for the left fork leg (Steps 11 through 17 above).

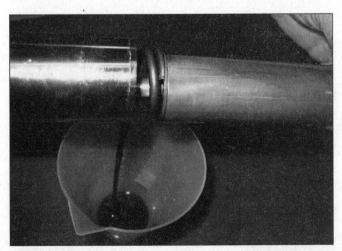

4.35 **Pour the fork oil out of the upper fork tube into a container**

4.40 **Place the oil lock piece onto the bottom end of the inner fork tube**

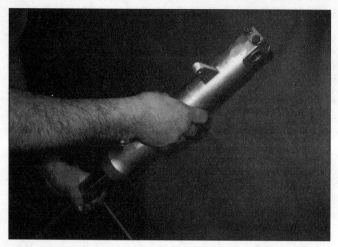

4.45a Hold the inner and outer fork tubes tightly together to keep the oil lock piece from falling out of position

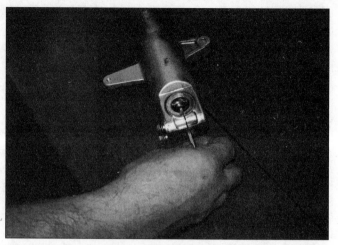

4.45b The head of the damper rod bolt should still be exposed like this when you start to thread it in; if it goes all the way into the fork, the oil lock piece is out of position

Reassembly

43   Install the cartridge in the inner fork tube, then let it slide slowly down until it protrudes from the bottom of the inner fork tube.

44   Install the oil lock piece on the cartridge **(see illustration 4.40)**.

45   Install the inner fork tube in the outer fork tube. Hold the tubes tightly together to prevent the oil lock piece from falling out of position **(see illustration)**. Slide the cartridge into the inner tube all the way.

 HAYNES HiNT *When installing the Allen bolt in the bottom of the fork leg, the head should still be visible when it contacts the cartridge (see illustration). If the head goes all the way into the tube before it's threaded in, the oil lock piece has fallen out of position. Disassemble the fork leg again and reposition the oil lock piece.*

46   Temporarily install the fork spring, spring seat, spacer and fork cap. Apply non-permanent thread locking agent to the damper rod bolt, then install the bolt and tighten it to the torque listed in this Chapter's Specifications. Remove the fork cap, spring seat, spacer and spring.

47   The remainder of assembly and installation are the same as for the left fork leg, described above.

---

5   Steering head bearings - check, adjustment and lubrication

⚠️ *Warning: This procedure requires removal of some airbag components on models so equipped. Before beginning work, refer to the airbag precautions in Chapter 9.*

Check

Note: *This procedure requires an accurate spring scale.*

1   Remove the front fairing (see Chapter 8).

2   Support the motorcycle securely with the front wheel off the ground. Center the front wheel.

3   Connect a spring scale to one of the fork legs between the upper and lower triple clamp. Hold the scale so it's aimed straight to the rear of the motorcycle.

4   Pull on the scale, keeping it at the same angle to the upper triple clamp. Note the reading as the triple clamp just starts to move and compare it to the value listed in this Chapter's Specifications. If it's not within the specified range, make sure that there's no drag from cables or wires that could affect the reading. If there isn't, adjust the bearings as described below.

Adjustment

5   Remove the instrument cluster and turn signal cancel unit (see Chapter 9).

6   Remove the top cover inner covers (see Chapter 8).

7   Detach the air baffle plate from the front forks.

8   Detach the instrument cluster support bracket, the throttle cable guide and all hose retainers from the upper triple clamp.

9   Unbolt the handlebars (see Section 2), lift them off the triple clamp and support them from above.

10   Loosen the steering stem nut **(see illustration)** while the front forks are securely installed, then remove the front forks (see Section 3).

11   Unscrew the steering stem nut and remove the upper triple clamp.

12   Bend back the lockwasher tabs and

5.10 Remove the steering stem upper nut and lift the triple clamp off

5.12a Bend the lockwasher tabs away
from the locknut . . .

5.12b . . . then undo the locknut with this special tool or an
adjustable spanner wrench . . .

unscrew the steering stem locknut (see illustrations).

13   Carefully tighten the steering stem nut to the initial torque listed in this Chapter's Specifications (see illustration). Loosen the nut just until it's hand tight (not all the way) and retighten to the final torque listed in this Chapter's Specifications.

14   Turn the steering stem from lock-to-lock five times, then retighten to the final torque.

15   Again, turn the steering stem from lock-to-lock five times. Finish by tightening to the final torque.

16   Turn the steering from lock-to-lock and check for binding. If there is any, remove the bearings for inspection (see Section 6).

17   If the steering operates properly, install a new lockwasher with its tabs in the slots of the steering stem nut. Tighten the locknut with fingers, then tighten it further with the locknut wrench so its slots align with those of the steering stem nut (don't allow the steering stem nut to turn). Do not tighten the locknut more than 1/4-turn (90-degrees) with the tool.

18   Bend two of the lockwasher tabs into locknut slots.

19   Recheck the steering head bearings for play as described in Chapter 1. If necessary, repeat the adjustment procedure. Reinstall all parts previously removed. Tighten the steering stem nut, triple clamp bolts and handlebar bolts to the torques listed in this Chapter's Specifications.

Lubrication

20   Periodic cleaning and repacking of the steering head bearings is recommended by the manufacturer. Refer to Section 6 for steering head bearing lubrication and replacement procedures.

6   Steering head bearings - replacement

Warning: This procedure requires removal of some airbag components on models so equipped. Before beginning work, refer to the airbag precautions in Chapter 9.

1   If the steering head bearing adjustment (see Section 5) does not remedy excessive play or roughness in the steering head bearings, the entire front end must be disassembled and the bearings and races replaced with new ones.

2   Remove the front wheel (see Chapter 7), the front forks (see Section 3), the handlebars (see Section 2) and the front

5.12c . . . and take the locknut and lockwasher off

5.13 Undo or tighten the steering stem adjusting nut with the
same tool used on the locknut

6.5a Lower the steering stem out the bottom of the steering head . . .

6.5b . . . and lift the upper bearing out of the top

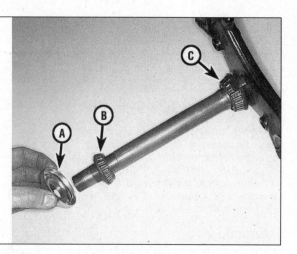

6.5c The bearings fit on the steering stem like this

A Cover
B Upper bearing
C Lower bearing and grease seal

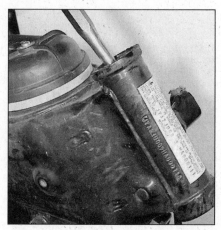

6.8 Drive out the bearing races with a hammer and drift

fender (see Chapter 8).

3 Refer to Section 5 and remove the upper triple clamp, steering stem locknut and steering stem lockwasher.

4 Remove the steering stem bearing adjusting nut **(see illustration 5.13)**.

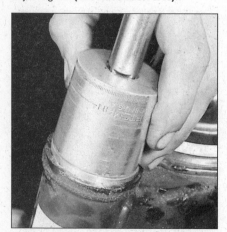

6.9 Drive in the bearing races with a bearing driver or socket the same diameter as the bearing race

5 Lower the steering stem and lower triple clamp assembly out of the steering head, then remove the dust seal, upper bearing and the upper bearing's inner race **(see illustrations)**. If it's stuck, gently tap on the top of the steering stem with a plastic mallet or a hammer and a wood block.

6 Clean all the parts with solvent and dry them thoroughly, using compressed air, if available. If you do use compressed air, don't let the bearings spin as they're dried - it could ruin them. Wipe the old grease out of the frame steering head and bearing races.

7 Examine the races in the steering head for cracks, dents, and pits. If even the slightest amount of wear or damage is evident, the races should be replaced with new ones.

8 To remove the outer bearing races, drive them out of the steering head with a hammer and long rod **(see illustration)**. A slide hammer with the proper internal-jaw puller will also work.

9 Since the races are an interference fit in the frame, installation will be easier if the new races are left overnight in a refrigerator. This will cause them to contract and slip into place in the frame with very little effort. When

installing the races, tap them gently into place with a hammer and a bearing driver, punch or a large socket **(see illustration)**. Do not strike the bearing surface or the race will be damaged.

10 Check the bearings for wear. Look for cracks, dents, and pits in the races and flat spots on the bearings. Replace any defective parts with new ones. If a new bearing is required, replace both of them as a set.

11 Don't remove the lower bearing race from the steering stem unless it, or the grease seal underneath, must be replaced. To remove the bearing from the steering stem, carefully tap between the bearing and steering stem with a hammer and punch. You can also use a bearing splitter and puller setup (these can be rented). Tap the lower bearing race onto the steering stem with a hammer and piece of pipe the same diameter as the bearing inner race **(see illustration)**. Don't tap against the rollers or outer race or the bearing will be ruined. As an alternative, take the steering stem to a Honda dealer or motorcycle repair shop for bearing replacement.

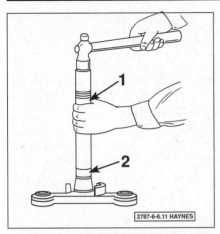

6.11 Drive the grease seal and bearing lower race on with a hollow driver (or an equivalent piece of pipe)

1 Driver
2 Bearing and grease seal

6.14 Work the grease completely into the rollers or balls

7.3 Unplug the connectors and remove the self-leveling actuator (arrow)

12 Check the grease seal under the lower bearing and replace it with a new one if necessary.

13 Inspect the steering stem/lower triple clamp for cracks and other damage. Do not attempt to repair any steering components. Replace them with new parts if defects are found.

14 Pack the bearings with high-quality grease (Honda specifies urea-based extreme pressure multi-purpose grease such as Shell Stamina EP-2) **(see illustration)**. Coat the outer races with grease also.

15 Insert the steering stem/lower triple clamp into the steering head. Install the upper bearing, inner race and steering stem nut. Refer to Section 5 and adjust the bearings.

16 The remainder of installation is the reverse of removal.

---

7   Rear shock absorber - removal, inspection and installation

Removal

1 Place the bike on its centerstand. Remove the fuel tank (see Chapter 4) and the right saddlebag (see Chapter 8).

2 Support the swingarm so it can't drop.

3 Unplug the electrical connectors for the angle sensor and actuator motor from the self-leveling actuator **(see illustration)**. You'll need to free the motor connector from the fender to disconnect it.

4 Unbolt the actuator and its support bracket **(see illustration 7.3)**.

5 Remove the shock absorber lower bolt and nut **(see illustration)**.

6 Remove the shock absorber upper bolt and nut **(see illustration)**. Take the shock absorber out, together with the self-leveling actuator.

Caution: If you're going to re-use the shock, store it upright to prevent fluid loss.

Inspection

7 Check the shock, actuator and connecting hose for signs of oil leaks and visible wear or damage. If any problems are found, replace the shock and actuator as an assembly.

8 Inspect the pivot hardware at the top and bottom of the shock and replace any worn or damaged parts.

Installation

9 Installation is the reverse of the removal procedure, with the following additions:

a) *Position the shock absorber with the actuator hose fitting toward the left side of the bike.*

b) *Install the upper and lower shock absorber bolts from the left side of the bike, then install the nuts on the bolts and tighten them to the torque values listed in this Chapter's Specifications.*

7.5 Remove the shock absorber lower bolt and nut (arrows) - the bolt head goes to the left

7.6 Remove the shock absorber upper bolt and nut (arrows) - the bolt head goes to the left

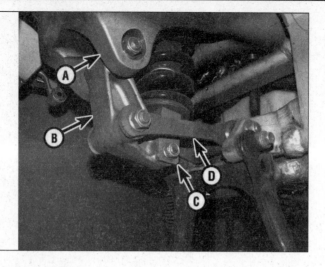

8.3 Rear suspension linkage details

A   Swingarm
B   Shock link
C   Shock absorber lower end
D   Tie rods

8 Rear suspension linkage - removal, inspection and installation

Removal

1   Support the bike so it can't be knocked over during this procedure.
2   Remove the exhaust system (see Chapter 3).
3   Unbolt the lower end of the shock absorber from the suspension linkage **(see illustration)**.
4   Remove the linkage mounting bolts and take the linkage out from under the motorcycle.

Inspection

5   Remove the pivot bushings from the shock arm. Check the bushings and dust seals for wear and damage and replace them as necessary.
6   Check the needle roller bearings inside the shock link and shock arm for wear or damage. Replace the bearings as described below if problems are found.

7   Press the bearings out with a press and shouldered drift.
8   Lubricate the rollers of the new bearings with multi-purpose grease and press them in, using the same tools, with the marked sides of the bearings facing out. Installed depth is 5.5 mm (0.220 inch) below the edge of the bore.

Installation

9   Installation is the reverse of the removal steps. Install the bolts from the left side of the bike and tighten the nuts to the torque listed in this Chapter's Specifications.

9 Final drive unit - removal, inspection and installation

Removal

1   Place the bike on its centerstand. Remove the right muffler and rear wheel (see Chapters 4 and 7).

2   Unbolt the brake hose retainer from the right side of the swingarm. If the motorcycle is equipped with ABS, remove the speed sensor (see Chapter 7 if necessary).
3   Remove the rear brake caliper, leaving the hoses connected (see Chapter 7).
4   Place a jack beneath the final drive unit to support it. Strap the final drive unit to the jack so it can't fall.
5   Remove the mounting nuts and washers (two on each side) **(see illustration)**. Separate the unit from the swingarm **(see illustration)**.
6   To remove the joint shaft from the final drive unit, grasp the forward end of the shaft and wiggle it in a circle while pulling it away from the final drive unit **(see illustrations)**. The stopper ring will provide some resistance, then the driveshaft should pull free of the final drive unit. **Note:** *If you remove the joint shaft as described in this step, you'll need a new stopper ring.*
7   The joint shaft oil seal should be replaced whenever the joint shaft is removed **(see illustrations)**. Slip the joint shaft off the driveshaft.

Inspection

8   Look into the oil filler hole and check for obvious signs of wear or damage such as broken gear teeth. Also check the seals for signs of leakage. Slip the joint shaft into its splines and turn the pinion by hand.
9   Final drive overhaul is a complicated procedure that requires several special tools, for which there are no readily available substitutes. If there's visible wear or damage, or if the differential rotation is rough or noisy, take it to a Honda dealer for disassembly and further inspection.
10   While the final drive unit is removed, check for play in the swingarm bearing (see Section 10).

Installation

11   Installation is the reverse of the removal steps, with the following additions:

9.5a Remove the four mounting nuts (arrows, two upper nuts shown)

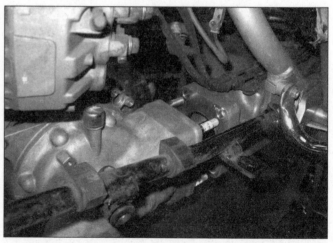

9.5b Pull the final drive unit and driveshaft rearward

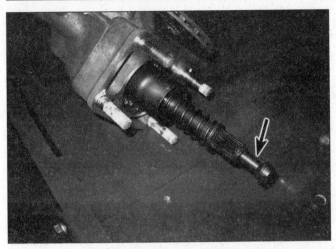

9.6a Grasp the joint shaft (arrow), wiggle it in a circle to disengage the lock ring . . .

9.6b . . . and pull it out of the final drive unit

9.7a To replace the oil seal, you'll need to remove the snap-ring (arrow) . . .

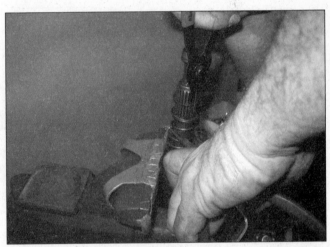

9.7b . . . slip a pair of needle-nosed pliers between the coils of the spring and push firmly downward until the snap-ring is exposed, then remove the snap-ring, spring seat and spring

9.7c Install a new seal with its open side toward the rear of the shaft and pack the groove with grease . . .

9.7d . . . then push the seal all the way on with fingers

9.11 Install a new stopper ring in the joint shaft groove

11.3 Remove the Allen bolts (arrows) and take the swingarm pivot bolt cover off the frame (there's one on each side of the bike)

11.8a This is the Honda tool used to loosen and tighten the swingarm locknut . . .

a) Install a new joint shaft oil seal on the shaft with its wide side toward the thick part of the shaft. Pack the seal groove with molybdenum disulfide grease.

b) Install a new stopper ring on the joint shaft (see illustration). Push the joint shaft into the final drive unit until the stopper ring locks in place. Check this by pulling on the joint shaft.

c) Lubricate the splines of the joint shaft with Honda moly 60 grease or equivalent.

d) Install the final drive unit loosely, aligning the joint shaft with the driveshaft. Tighten the nuts to the torque listed in this Chapter's Specifications.

e) Check the final drive unit oil level (see Chapter 1).

11.8b . . . this aftermarket equivalent will also work, but it isn't possible to hold the pivot bolt while tightening the locknut, so you'll need to mark the position of the pivot bolt relative to the frame with a felt pen

11.8c Once the locknut is loose, unscrew it from the pivot bolt

10 Swingarm bearings - check
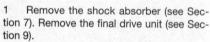

1   Remove the shock absorber (see Section 7). Remove the final drive unit (see Section 9).

2   Grasp the rear of the swingarm with one hand and place your other hand at the junction of the swingarm and the frame. Try to move the rear of the swingarm from side-to-side. Any wear (play) in the bearings should be felt as movement between the swingarm and the frame at the front. The swingarm will actually be felt to move forward and backward at the front (not from side-to-side). If any play is noted, the bearings should be replaced with new ones (see Section 12).

3   Next, move the swingarm up and down through its full travel. It should move freely, without any binding or rough spots. If it does not move freely, refer to Section 12 for servicing procedures.

11 Swingarm and driveshaft - removal and installation

Note 1: *Loosening and tightening the pivot bolt locknut on the left side of the swingarm requires a special wrench or equivalent. Before starting, read the procedure, paying attention to the special tools required. If you don't have access to the special Honda tools or equivalents, have the locknut unscrewed (and later tightened) by a Honda dealer or other shop equipped with the special tools.*
Note 2: *You'll need a new stopper ring and seal for the joint shaft in the final drive unit (see Section 9).*

Removal

1   Remove the final drive unit (see Section 9).

2   Remove the shock absorber (see Section 7) and set it aside. The suspension leveling actuator can be left installed.

3   Unbolt the swingarm pivot cover from each side of the bike (see illustration).

4   Unbolt the brake hose retainer from the swingarm (see the brake hose section of Chapter 7 if necessary).

5   Remove the rear brake light/cruise cancel switch (see Chapter 7).

6   Remove the stopper (round, light-colored plastic disc) from the underside of the swingarm.

7   Unbolt the shock link from the shock arm (see Section 8).

8   Remove the locknut from the left pivot bolt, using Honda tool 07ZMA-MCA0100, 07ZMA-MCA0101 or equivalent (see illustrations). While you're undoing the locknut, hold the pivot bolt from turning with a 17 mm Allen bolt bit. These are available from tool stores.

9   Unscrew the swingarm pivot bolts with the Allen bolt bit (see illustrations).

10   Disengage the front end of the driveshaft

11.9a Use an Allen bolt bit in a socket to hold the left pivot bolt while you loosen and tighten the locknut

11.9b A multi-sized hex bolt bit, made by Motion Pro, is available through dealers and from K&L Supply

11.10 Disengage the front end of the driveshaft boot (arrow) from the back of the engine (viewed from above with starter motor removed for clarity)

11.11 Pull the driveshaft rearward out of the swingarm

11.13 Install the driveshaft in the swingarm with the universal joint toward the front of the motorcycle

boot from the back of the engine **(see illustration)**.

11 Pull the driveshaft rearward out of the swingarm **(see illustration)**. Pull the swingarm rearward to separate it from the frame and remove it from the motorcycle. **Note:** *You can remove the driveshaft and swingarm together.*

12 Check the pivot bearings in the swingarm for dryness or deterioration (see Section 12). Lubricate or replace them as necessary.

Installation

13 Lubricate the universal joint splines with moly-based grease. Install the driveshaft in the swingarm with the universal joint toward the engine **(see illustration)**. Lubricate the splines on the front end of the driveshaft with moly-based grease.

14 Place the boot over the driveshaft, with its wide end on the swingarm and one tab straight up.

15 Remove the joint shaft from the final drive unit (if you haven't already done so) and slip it into the driveshaft to use as a handle during installation.

16 If the swingarm bearings aren't installed, install them now (see Section 12).

17 Lift the swingarm into position and slide it forward, fitting the front end of the driveshaft over the engine output shaft and aligning the splines. Slide the swingarm forward until its bearing holes align with the pivot holes in the bike's frame.

18 Grease the tips of the pivot bolts and thread them into their holes, making sure the tips fit into the swingarm bearings **(see illustration)**. Thread the bolts in until they're seated, but don't torque the pivot bolts yet.

19 Tighten the left pivot bolt to the torque listed in this Chapter's Specifications. Tighten the right pivot bolt after tightening the left pivot bolt. The right pivot bolt's specified torque is much lower than that of the left

11.18 On installation, grease the pivot bolt tips and make sure they engage the swingarm bearings

12.3 The swingarm rides on a pair of tapered roller bearings

pivot bolt. **Note:** *The swingarm pivot bolts and locknut must be tightened in the specified sequence and to the correct torque settings.*

20   Raise and lower the swingarm several times to seat the bearings, then retighten the right pivot bolt to its specified torque.

21   Thread the locknut onto the left pivot bolt as far as you can with fingers. Then place the special wrench on the locknut and install a torque wrench in the special wrench's square hole. Hold the pivot bolt with the 17 mm Allen bolt bit so it won't turn, then tighten the locknut to the torque listed in this Chapter's Specifications. **Note:** *The special wrench increases the torque applied to the nut, so the specified torque is less than the actual applied torque. The length and design of the torque wrench also affect the amount of torque applied to the nut. Use a beam-type torque wrench (not a click-stop type), 20 inches long.*

22   The remainder of installation is the reverse of the removal steps.

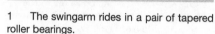

12 Swingarm bearings - replacement

1   The swingarm rides in a pair of tapered roller bearings.

2   Remove the swingarm from the motorcycle (see Section 11).

3   Take the bearings and outer seals out of the swingarm **(see illustration)**.

4   Clean all the parts with solvent and dry them thoroughly, using compressed air, if available. If you do use compressed air, don't let the bearings spin as they're dried - it could ruin them. Wipe the old grease out of the swingarm and bearing races.

5   Examine the races in the swingarm for cracks, dents, and pits. If even the slightest amount of wear or damage is evident, the races should be replaced with new ones. If one race (or one bearing) needs to be replaced, replace both of the bearings, as well as their races and seals, as a set.

6   To remove the bearing races, drill a 1/2-inch hole through the inner grease holder of one bearing. Insert a long rod through the hole and tap it with a hammer to drive the opposite grease holder and bearing race out. Remove the rod, turn the swingarm over, insert the rod through the hole the first bearing was removed from, then drive the remaining grease holder and bearing out.

7   Since the races are an interference fit in the swingarm, installation will be easier if the new races are left overnight in a refrigerator. This will cause them to contract and slip into place in the frame with very little effort. When installing the races, tap them gently into place with a hammer and a bearing driver, punch or a large socket. Do not strike the bearing surface or the race will be damaged.

8   Check the bearings for wear. Look for cracks, dents, and pits in the rollers and flat spots on the bearings. Replace any defective parts with new ones. If a new bearing is required, replace both of them, and the bearing races and seals, as a set.

9   Before installing the bearings, pack them with moly-based grease (1 to 1.5 grams; 0.4 to 0.5 oz) so the spaces between the rollers are filled with grease. Also grease the seal lips.

Chapter 7
Brakes, wheels and tires

Contents

Degrees of difficulty

Easy, suitable for novice with little experience		**Fairly easy,** suitable for beginner with some experience		**Fairly difficult,** suitable for competent DIY mechanic		**Difficult,** suitable for experienced DIY mechanic	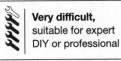	**Very difficult,** suitable for expert DIY or professional	

Specifications

Brakes

Brake lever and pedal freeplay... See Chapter 1
Brake fluid type .... See Chapter 1
Front brake disc thickness
    Standard .... 4.5 mm (0.18 inch)
    Minimum* .... 3.5 mm (0.14 inch)
Rear brake disc thickness
    Standard .... 11.0 mm (0.43 inch)
    Minimum* .... 10.0 mm (0.39 inch)
Disc runout limit .... 0.3 mm (0.01 inch)
Pad friction material thickness .... See Chapter 1
Front caliper-to-bracket gap .... 0.7 mm (0.028 inch)
Refer to marks stamped into the disc (they supersede information printed here)

Wheels and tires

Wheel runout limit
    Radial (up-and-down) .... 2.0 mm (0.08 inch)
    Axial (side-to-side) .... 2.0 mm (0.08 inch)
Axle runout limit... 0.2 mm (0.01 inch)
Tire pressures.. See *Daily (Pre-ride) checks* at the front of this manual
Tire sizes .... See Chapter 1

Torque specifications

Front calipers

Left caliper lower mounting bolt	31 Nm (22 ft-lbs)	
Left caliper upper mounting bolt (secondary master cylinder clevis bolt)	25 Nm (19 ft-lbs)	
Right caliper mounting bolts	31 Nm (22 ft-lbs)	
Pad retaining pins	17 Nm (13 ft-lbs)	
Caliper slide pin	13 Nm (81 inch-lbs)	
Caliper bracket pin	23 Nm (24 ft-lbs) (1)	
Caliper frame bolts	32 Nm (24 ft-lbs) (2)	

Rear caliper

Pin bolt	27 Nm (20 ft-lbs)
Mounting bolts	45 Nm (33 ft-lbs)
Caliper bracket pin	23 Nm (17 ft-lbs) (1)
Caliper frame bolts	32 Nm (24 ft-lbs) (2)
Pad retaining pin	17 Nm (13 ft-lbs)
Bleed valves (all)	6 Nm (52 inch-lbs)
Delay valve mounting bolts	12 Nm (81 inch-lbs)
Proportional control valve mounting bolts	12 Nm (81 inch-lbs)
Anti-dive plunger to case	4 Nm (35 inch-lbs)
Anti-dive case to fork leg	Not specified
Front brake disc mounting bolts	40 Nm (29 ft-lbs)
Rear brake disc mounting screws	9 Nm (78 inch-lbs)
Union (banjo fitting) bolts	34 Nm 25 ft-lbs)
Metal line flare nuts	17 Nm (12 ft-lbs)

Master cylinder mounting bolts

Front and rear	12 Nm (81 inch-lbs)
Secondary	31 Nm (22 ft-lbs)
Front brake lever pivot bolt	1 Nm (8 inch-lbs)
Front brake lever pivot bolt locknut	6 Nm (52 inch-lbs)
Wheel speed sensor bolts (ABS models)	12 Nm (81 inch-lbs)

Front axle

Axle bolt	59 Nm (43 ft-lbs)
Axle pinch bolts	22 Nm (16 ft-lbs)

(1) Use non-permanent thread locking agent on the threads.
(2) Replace the bolts with new ones.

1 General information

The models covered by this manual are equipped with hydraulic disc brakes on the front and rear. All models use a pair of three-piston calipers at the front and one three-piston caliper at the rear, which are connected through a sophisticated version of Honda's Linked Braking System.

Anti-lock brakes (ABS) are optional. The ABS system used on these motorcycles incorporates speed sensors in the front and rear wheels, electric actuators for the two hydraulic systems and a control module.

All models are equipped with cast aluminum wheels, which require very little maintenance and allow tubeless tires to be used. The tire pressure monitoring system used on 2009 and later models requires special wheels, which should not be replaced with wheels not designed for the system.

Caution: Disc brake components rarely require disassembly. Do not disassemble components unless absolutely necessary. If any hydraulic brake line connection in the system is loosened, the entire system should be disassembled, drained, cleaned and then properly filled and bled upon reassembly. Do not use solvents on internal brake components. Solvents will cause seals to swell and distort. Use only clean brake fluid, brake cleaner or alcohol for cleaning. Use care when working with brake fluid as it can injure your eyes and it will damage painted surfaces and plastic parts.

Linked braking system

Unlike conventional motorcycle braking systems, which have completely separate controls for the front and rear brakes, this system applies some braking force to all three calipers (two front and one rear) whenever the rider operates the brake lever or pedal.

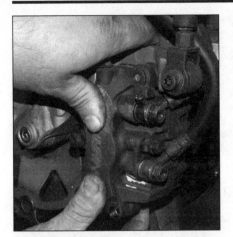

2.2 Push the caliper inward to press the pistons in and make room to remove the pads

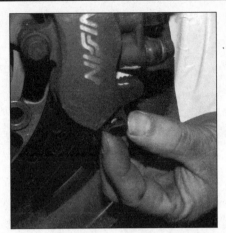

2.3a Remove the pad pin plug from the bottom of the caliper . . .

2.3b . . . and unscrew the pad pin with an Allen wrench (this is the left front caliper)

All three calipers are linked hydraulically. There are two separate hydraulic circuits, one operated by the brake lever and the other by the pedal. The lever circuit incorporates the upper and lower pistons of the right front caliper and the center piston of the left front caliper. The pedal circuit incorporates the center piston of the right front caliper, the upper and lower pistons of the left front caliper and all three pistons of the rear caliper.

The front brake lever operates the front calipers directly, using hydraulic pressure from the front master cylinder. In addition, the front brake lever operates the rear caliper indirectly; as the left front caliper squeezes the brake disc, the caliper's motion operates the secondary master cylinder on the left fork leg, which sends hydraulic pressure to the proportional control valve, and from the proportional control valve to the upper and lower pistons of the rear caliper.

The brake pedal operates the center piston of the rear caliper directly, using hydraulic pressure from the rear master cylinder. In addition, the rear master cylinder's hydraulic pressure operates the center piston of the right front caliper as well as the upper and lower pistons of the left front caliper. A delay valve slows the transfer of hydraulic pressure to the front calipers to reduce front-end dive. The secondary master cylinder also uses the motion of the left front caliper to transfer hydraulic pressure to the center piston in the rear master cylinder, just as it does when the brake lever is applied.

The secondary master cylinder also uses the left front caliper's motion to transfer hydraulic pressure to the anti-dive unit on the left fork leg.

The calipers, front master cylinder and rear master cylinder are basically the same as those used with conventional braking systems, and are covered in other Sections in this Chapter. Components unique to the linked braking system are the secondary master cylinder, delay valve and proportional control valve.

Anti-lock braking system (ABS)

The ABS system is designed to prevent wheel lock-up, which can lead to a loss of control, during heavy or panic braking. It works by controlling the brake line pressure so it doesn't rise suddenly enough to cause either wheel to lock up.

The system monitors the rotational speed of each wheel. When the speed of either wheel drops suddenly, indicating that the wheel is about to lock up, the system momentarily releases the hydraulic pressure to the wheel, then restores it.

2 Brake pads - replacement

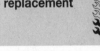

⚠️ *Warning: When replacing the front brake pads always replace the pads in BOTH calipers - never just on one side. Replace*

the anti-squeal shims and pad spring whenever the pads are replaced. Also, the dust created by the brake system is harmful to your health. Never blow it out with compressed air and don't inhale any of it. An approved filtering mask should be worn when working on the brakes.

1　Place the bike on its centerstand. If you're replacing front brake pads, refer to Chapter 8 and remove the brake disc covers.

2　Remove the cap from the front and rear master cylinder reservoirs and siphon out some fluid. Push the pistons into the caliper as far as possible, while checking the master cylinder reservoirs to make sure they don't overflow (see illustration). If you can't depress the pistons with hand pressure, the pistons may be seized. If the pistons stick, remove the caliper and overhaul it as described in Section 3.

3　Remove the pad pin plugs, then unscrew the pad pins (see illustrations).

2.3c Here's the pad pin plug on the right front caliper

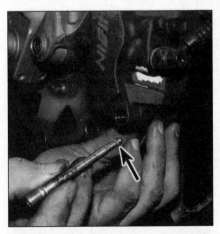

2.3d Coat the stopper ring on the pad pin (arrow) with silicone grease before you install it

2.4a Remove the outer pad . . .

2.4b . . . and the inner pad . . .

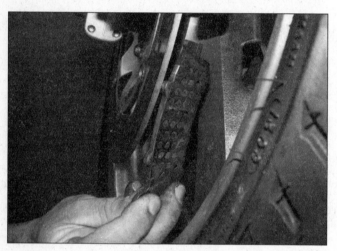

2.4c . . . with its shim

2.4d Lower the pads out of the right front caliper

4   Lower the pads out of the caliper (see illustrations).

5   Check the condition of the brake discs (see Section 4). If they are in need of machining or replacement, follow the procedure in that Section to remove them. If they are okay, deglaze them with sandpaper or emery cloth, using a swirling motion.

6   If you're replacing front pads, make sure the shim is in place on the pad nearest the wheel (see illustration 2.4c). On front or rear pads, make sure the retainer is in place on the bracket (see illustrations).

7   Lubricate the stop ring on the inner end of each pad pin with silicone grease (see illustration 2.3c).

8   Install the pads and make sure they fit correctly in the retainers (see illustration 2.6a or 2.6b). Press the pads down against the spring and install the pad pin. Thread the pin in and tighten it to the torque listed in this Chapter's Specifications.

9   Install the pin plug.

10   Refill the master cylinder reservoir (see Chapter 1) and install the diaphragm and cover. Operate the brake lever or pedal several times to bring the pads into contact with the disc.

11   If you're working on the front calipers, reinstall the disc brake covers (see Chapter 8).

12   Check the operation of the brakes carefully before riding the motorcycle.

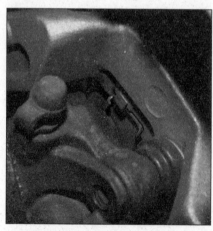

2.6a Here's how the pad fits into the retainer on front calipers . . .

2.6b . . . and on the rear caliper

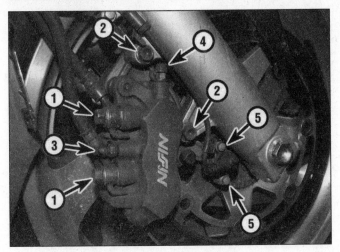

3.4 Right front caliper details

1 Caliper banjo bolts
2 Caliper upper mounting bolt
3 Lower bleed valve
4 Upper bleed valve
5 Wheel speed sensor bolts (ABS models)

3.5 Replace the caliper mounting bolts with new ones whenever they're removed

 3 Brake calipers - removal, overhaul and installation

 Warning: If a caliper indicates the need for an overhaul (usually due to leaking fluid or sticky operation), ALL THREE calipers should be overhauled and all old brake fluid flushed from the system, since the calipers . Also, the dust created by the brake system is harmful to your health. Never blow it out with compressed air and don't inhale any of it. An approved filtering mask should be worn when working on the brakes. Do not, under any circumstances, use petroleum-based solvents to clean brake parts. Use brake cleaner or denatured alcohol only!

Removal

Warning: This procedure requires working near the airbag system components on models so equipped. Before beginning work, read the airbag precautions in Chapter 9.

Note: If you're just removing the caliper for access to other components, leave the brake hoses connected. Once the caliper is unbolted, support it so it doesn't hang by the hoses.

1 Support the bike securely so it can't be knocked over during this procedure.

2 Remove the brake pads from the caliper being removed (see Section 2).

Right front caliper

3 If the motorcycle is equipped with ABS, free the wiring harness retainer and detach the wheel speed sensor from the caliper bracket **(see illustration 3.4).**

4 With a clean rag handy to catch spills, remove the brake hose banjo fitting bolts and separate the hoses from the caliper **(see illustration).** Discard the sealing washers. Place the end of the hoses in a container and operate the brake lever to pump out the fluid. Once this is done, wrap a clean shop rag tightly around the hose fittings to soak up any drips and prevent contamination.

5 Unscrew the caliper mounting bolts **(see illustration 3.4 and the accompanying illustration).**

Left front caliper

6 With a clean rag handy to catch spills, remove the brake hose banjo fitting bolts and separate the hoses from the caliper **(see illustration).** Discard the sealing washers. Place the end of the hoses in a container and operate the brake lever to pump out the fluid. Once this is done, wrap a clean shop rag tightly around the hose fittings to soak up

3.6 Left front caliper details

1 Caliper lower mounting bolt
2 Caliper lower banjo bolt
3 Caliper lower bleed valve
4 Caliper upper banjo bolt
5 Caliper upper mounting bolt/secondary master cylinder clevis bolt
6 Secondary master cylinder lower mounting bolt
7 Secondary master cylinder upper mounting bolt
8 Secondary master cylinder upper banjo bolt
9 Secondary master cylinder lower banjo bolt
10 Caliper upper bleed valve
11 Anti-dive unit banjo bolt
12 Anti-dive unit bleed valve

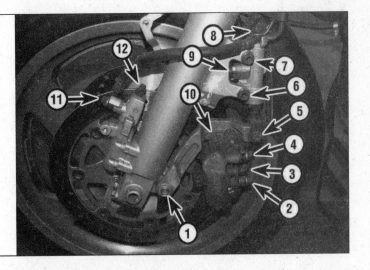

3.7a Unscrew the lower mounting bolt, then use it as handle to remove the bushing

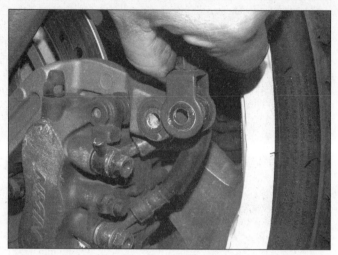

3.7b Unscrew the upper mounting bolt, then slide the secondary master cylinder's clevis off the bushing so you can inspect it

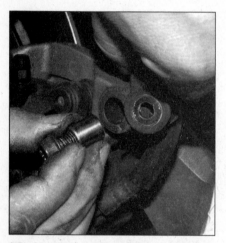

3.7c Use the mounting bolt as a handle to pull the bushing out

3.8 Take the caliper off the brake disc and support it so it doesn't hang by the brake hoses

any drips and prevent contamination.

7   Unscrew the caliper mounting bolts and push the pivot collars out of the bolt holes **(see illustration 3.6 and the accompanying illustrations)**.

8   Lift off the caliper, together with the mounting bracket **(see illustration)**.

9   Take a look at the pivot bearings in the fork leg, as well as its dust seals **(see illustration)**. Also inspect the pivot bushing in the caliper bracket **(see illustration 3.7c)**. If the bearing shows any signs of wear or damage, replace it as described below. If he bushing is worn or damaged, replace the caliper bracket.

Rear caliper

10   With a clean rag handy to catch spills, remove the brake hose banjo fitting bolts and separate the hoses from the caliper **(see illustration)**. Discard the sealing washers. Place the end of the hoses in a container

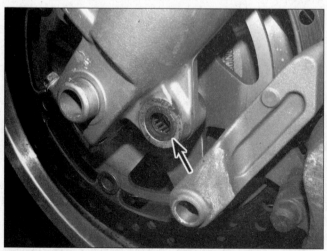

3.9 Inspect the bearing and seals in the caliper lower mounting bolt hole (arrow)

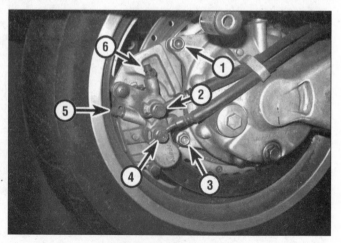

3.10 Rear caliper details

1	Upper mounting bolt	4	Lower banjo bolt
2	Upper banjo bolt	5	Lower bleed valve
3	Lower mounting bolt	6	Upper bleed valve

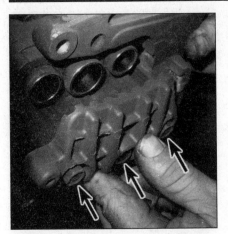

3.11 Remove the caliper frame bolts to overhaul the caliper (arrows, rear caliper shown) - use new bolts on assembly

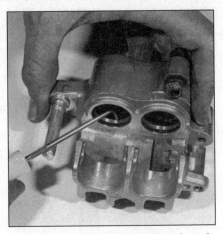

3.15 Remove the dust (outer) seals and piston (inner) seals on all three bores; be careful not to scratch the surface of the bores

4.3 Set up a dial indicator with the probe touching the surface of the disc, turn the wheel slowly and measure runout

and operate the brake lever to pump out the fluid. Once this is done, wrap a clean shop rag tightly around the hose fittings to soak up any drips and prevent contamination.

11   Unscrew the caliper mounting bolts **(see illustration 3.10)**. Take the caliper off, together with the mounting bracket **(see illustration)**.

Caliper overhaul

12   Clean the exterior of the caliper with denatured alcohol or brake system cleaner.
13   Pull the bracket off of the caliper and take the pad spring out of the pad cavity.
14   Push the pistons out of the caliper with compressed air. Disconnect the hose from the caliper. Place a few rags against the caliper frame to act as a cushion, then use compressed air, directed into the fluid inlet, to remove the pistons. Use only enough air pressure to ease the pistons out of the bore. If a piston is blown out, even with the cushion in place, it may be damaged.

 Warning: Never place your fingers in front of the piston in an attempt to catch or protect it when applying compressed air, as serious injury could occur.

Once the pistons have extended far enough to contact the caliper frame, remove the bolts, separate the frame from the caliper body and remove the pistons the rest of the way. **Note:** *If the bike's hydraulic system is in reasonably good condition, it can be used to remove the pistons from the calipers. Leave the fluid hose connected and remove the caliper and pads. Pump the lever or pedal a few times to force the pistons out of the caliper. If necessary, unbolt the caliper frame to provide clearance to remove the pistons all the way.*
15   Using a wood or plastic tool, remove the dust seals and piston seals **(see illustration)**. Metal tools may cause bore damage.
16   Clean the pistons and the bores with denatured alcohol, clean brake fluid or brake

system cleaner and blow dry them with filtered, unlubricated compressed air. Inspect the surfaces of the pistons for nicks and burrs and loss of plating.
17   Check the caliper bores. If surface defects are present, the caliper must be replaced. If the caliper is in bad shape, the master cylinder should also be checked.
18   Lubricate new piston seals with clean brake fluid and install them in their grooves in the caliper bore. Make sure they aren't twisted and seat completely.
19   Lubricate new dust seals with clean brake fluid and install them in their grooves, making sure they seat correctly.
20   Lubricate the pistons with clean brake fluid and install them into the caliper bores. Using your thumbs, push the pistons all the way in, making sure they don't get cocked in the bores.
21   Check the rubber pin boots for damage or deterioration and replace them if necessary. it's a good idea to replace the pin boots whenever the caliper is disassembled. Pack the groove(s) inside each boot with silicone grease and apply a thin coat of the same grease to the pins. Slip the boots onto the pins.

Pivot bearing replacement (left caliper)

22   If the pivot bearing in the left caliper's lower bolt hole (in the fork leg) is worn or corroded, it will need to be replaced.
23   Remove the caliper from the fork leg as described above. Remove the fork leg from the motorcycle (see Chapter 6).
24   Pry the grease seals out of the caliper bracket or fork leg. Drive the bearing out of the bore with a hammer and drift.
25   Lubricate the new bearing with multipurpose grease. Install the new bearing with a shouldered drift (14 mm narrow diameter and 16 mm wide diameter). This will support the bearing as it's being installed. Carefully press the bearing into the bore until it's

recessed 3.5 mm (0.14 inch) below the bearing bore.
26   Coat the lips of new grease seals with grease and install one on each side of the bearing. Reinstall the fork leg.

Installation

27   Bolt the caliper to the fork leg and tighten the bolts to the torque listed in this Chapter's Specifications.
28   Attach the fluid hoses to the calipers, using new sealing washers. Tighten the banjo bolts to the torque listed in this Chapter's Specifications.
29   Refer to Section 2 and install the brake pads.
30   Fill the master cylinder with the recommended brake fluid (see Chapter 1) and bleed the system (see Section 12). Check for leaks.
31   Check the operation of the brakes carefully before riding the motorcycle.

4   Brake discs - inspection, removal and installation

Inspection

1   Support the bike securely so it can't be knocked over during this procedure, with the wheel to be checked off the ground.
2   Visually inspect the surface of the disc(s) for score marks and other damage. Light scratches are normal after use and won't affect brake operation, but deep grooves and heavy score marks will reduce braking efficiency and accelerate pad wear. If the discs are badly grooved they must be machined or replaced.
3   To check disc runout, mount a dial indicator to a fork leg or the swingarm, with the plunger on the indicator touching the surface of the disc about 1/2-inch from the outer edge **(see illustration)**. Slowly turn the wheel and

4.4a Use a micrometer to measure the thickness of the disc at several points

4.4b Minimum thickness (lower arrow) and a directional indicator (upper arrow) are stamped into the disc

watch the indicator needle, comparing your reading with the limit listed in this Chapter's Specifications. If the runout is greater than allowed, check the hub bearings for play (see Section 17). If the bearings are worn, replace them and repeat this check. If the disc runout is still excessive, it will have to be replaced.

4   The disc must not be machined or allowed to wear down to a thickness less than the minimum allowable thickness, stamped on the disc and listed in this Chapter's Specifications **(see illustration)**. The thickness of the disc can be checked with a micrometer **(see illustration)**. If the thickness of the disc is less than the minimum allowable, it must be replaced.

Removal

5   Remove the wheel (see Section 15 for front wheel removal or Section 16 for rear wheel removal).

Caution: Don't lay the wheel down and allow it to rest on one of the discs - the disc could become warped. Set the wheel on wood blocks so the disc doesn't support the weight of the wheel.

6   Mark the relationship of the disc to the wheel, so it can be installed in the same position.

7   If you're working on a front wheel, look for L and R marks on the left and right front discs. If you don't see them, make your own. If you're working on the right front wheel or the rear wheel of an ABS model, remove the Torx bolts that retain the pulser ring to the wheel **(see illustration)**. On all models, remove the Allen head bolts that retain the disc to the wheel **(see illustration 4.7a and the accompanying illustration)**. Loosen the bolts a little at a time, in a criss-cross pattern, to avoid distorting the disc. Once all the bolts are loose, take the disc off.

8   If you're working on a rear wheel, remove the wheel and brake caliper (see Sections 15 and 16). Remove the Phillips screws that secure the disc to the final drive unit and take it off **(see illustration)**.

Installation

9   Position the disc on the wheel, aligning the previously applied matchmarks (if you're reinstalling the original disc). Make sure the arrow mark on the disc faces away from the wheel and points in the direction of forward wheel rotation **(see illustration 4.4a)**. If you're installing a front disc, make sure the disc with the L mark goes on the left side of the bike and the disc with the R mark goes on the right side.

10   Install NEW Allen bolts, tightening them a little at a time, in a criss-cross pattern, until the torque listed in this Chapter's Specifications is reached. If you're working on an

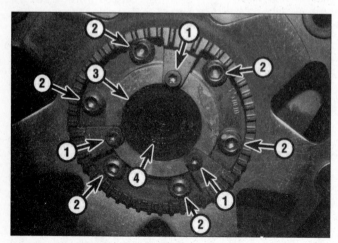

4.7a Right front brake disc and wheel bearings

1   *Sensor rotor mounting bolts (ABS models)*
2   *Brake disc mounting bolts*
3   *Grease seal*
4   *Wheel bearing*

4.7b Left front brake disc and wheel bearings

1   *Brake disc mounting bolts*
2   *Grease seal*
3   *Wheel bearing*

of clear plastic hose to the valve. Place the open end of the hose in a clear container so you can see the fluid flowing into it. Have an assistant pull the brake lever 5 to 10 times in quick succession, then hold it in. Open the bleed valve 1/4 turn, let fluid flow out of the hose and tighten the bleed valve. Continue this until fluid flows from the valve.

15   Keep an eye on the fluid level in the master cylinder reservoir as it's being bled and top up as soon as it becomes low. If the fluid level is allowed to drop below the master cylinder intake port, air will be sucked into the system and you'll have to start over.

16   Perform Step 13 or 14 at the lower bleed valve of the left front caliper. Again, keep an eye on the fluid level in the master cylinder.

Bleeding

17   Bleeding is done without a bleeder tool, even if you have one. Perform Steps 14 and 15 in the following order:

  a) *Right front caliper upper bleed valve*
  b) *Left front caliper lower bleed valve*

18   Replace the reservoir cover, wipe up any spilled brake fluid and check the entire system for leaks. **Note:** *If bleeding is difficult, it may be necessary to let the brake fluid in the system stabilize for a few hours (it may be aerated). Repeat the bleeding procedure when the tiny bubbles in the system have settled out.*

Brake pedal hydraulic system

Draining

19   A brake bleeder tool is required to drain the fluid completely.

20   Remove the right side cover, brake disc covers and the rear section of the front fender (see Chapter 8). Unscrew the cap from the rear master cylinder reservoir. Refer to *Daily (Pre-ride) checks* at the front of this manual if necessary.

21   Uncover the upper bleed valve of the left front caliper (**see illustration 3.4**). Slip a box wrench over the valve, connect the bleeder tool to the bleed valve, open the valve and pump the bleeder tool until all of the fluid is drained from the valve.

22   Repeat Step 7 until all of the fluid is drained from the system.

23   Connect the bleeder tool or hose to the lower bleed valve of the left front caliper (**see illustration 3.6**). Repeat Step 7 until all of the fluid is drained from the system.

24   Fill and bleed the system as described below.

Filling

25   Fill the master cylinder reservoir with DOT 4 brake fluid from a sealed container.

26   Bleed air from the master cylinder by pressing and releasing the brake pedal several times in a row.

27   If you have a brake bleeder, uncover the lower bleed valve of the right front caliper (**see illustration 3.4**). Slip a box wrench over the valve, connect the bleeder to the bleed valve, open the valve and pump the bleeder

tool until fluid flows from the valve. Close the valve and disconnect the bleeder.

28   If you don't have a brake bleeder, uncover the lower bleed valve of the right front caliper (**see illustration 3.4**). Slip a box wrench over the valve and connect a length of clear plastic hose to the valve. Place the open end of the hose in a clear container so you can see the fluid flowing into it. Have an assistant pump the brake pedal 5 to 10 times in quick succession, then hold it in. Open the bleed valve 1/4 turn, let fluid flow out of the hose and tighten the bleed valve. Continue this until fluid flows from the valve. **Note:** *There may be a lot of resistance to pedal movement when the bleed valve is open - this is caused by the delay valve. Make sure you push the pedal all the way to the bottom of its travel.*

29   Keep an eye on the fluid level in the master cylinder reservoir as it's being bled and top up as soon as it becomes low. If the fluid level is allowed to drop below the master cylinder intake port, air will be sucked into the system and you'll have to start over.

30   Continue filling the system, pumping fluid out of the following bleed valves in order:

  a) *Lower bleed valve on the rear caliper* (**see illustration 3.10**).
  b) *Anti-dive plunger bleed valve* (**see illustration 3.6**).
  c) *Rear caliper upper bleed valve* (**see illustration 3.10**).

Bleeding

31   Bleeding is done without a bleeder tool, even if you have one. Perform Steps 28 and 29, in the following order:

  a) *Right caliper lower bleed valve*
  b) *Lower bleed valve on the rear caliper*
  c) *Anti-dive plunger bleed valve*
  d) *Rear caliper upper bleed valve*

32   Replace the reservoir cap, wipe up any spilled brake fluid and check the entire system for leaks. **Note:** *If bleeding is difficult, it may be necessary to let the brake fluid in the system stabilize for a few hours (it may be aerated). Repeat the bleeding procedure when the tiny bubbles in the system have settled out.*

13 Wheels - inspection and repair

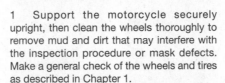

1   Support the motorcycle securely upright, then clean the wheels thoroughly to remove mud and dirt that may interfere with the inspection procedure or mask defects. Make a general check of the wheels and tires as described in Chapter 1.

2   Raise the wheel to be checked off the ground, then attach a dial indicator to the fork slider or the swingarm and position the stem against the side of the rim. Spin the wheel slowly and check the side-to-side

(axial) runout of the rim, then compare your readings with the value listed in this Chapter's Specifications. In order to accurately check radial runout with the dial indicator, the wheel would have to be removed from the machine and the tire removed from the wheel. With the axle clamped in a vise, the wheel can be rotated to check the runout.

3   An easier, though slightly less accurate, method is to attach a stiff wire pointer to the fork or the swingarm and position the end a fraction of an inch from the wheel (where the wheel and tire join). If the wheel is true, the distance from the pointer to the rim will be constant as the wheel is rotated. **Note:** *If wheel runout is excessive, refer to the appropriate Section in this Chapter and check the wheel bearings very carefully before replacing the wheel.*

4   The wheels should also be visually inspected for cracks, flat spots on the rim and other damage. Since tubeless tires are involved, look very closely for dents in the area where the tire bead contacts the rim. Dents in this area may prevent complete sealing of the tire against the rim, which leads to deflation of the tire over a period of time.

5   If damage is evident, or if runout in either direction is excessive, the wheel will have to be replaced with a new one. Never attempt to repair a damaged cast aluminum wheel.

14 Wheels - alignment check

1   Misalignment of the wheels, which may be due to a cocked rear wheel or a bent frame or triple clamps, can cause strange and possibly serious handling problems. If the frame or triple clamps are at fault, repair by a frame specialist or replacement with new parts are the only alternatives.

2   To check the alignment you will need an assistant, a length of string or a perfectly straight piece of wood and a ruler graduated in 1/64 inch increments. A plumb bob or other suitable weight will also be required.

3   Support the motorcycle in a level position, then measure the width of both tires at their widest points. Subtract the smaller measurement from the larger measurement, then divide the difference by two. The result is the amount of offset that should exist between the front and rear tires on both sides.

4   If a string is used, have your assistant hold one end of it about half way between the floor and the rear axle, touching the rear sidewall of the tire.

5   Run the other end of the string forward and pull it tight so that it is roughly parallel to the floor. Slowly bring the string into contact with the front sidewall of the rear tire, then turn the front wheel until it is parallel with the string. Measure the distance from the front tire sidewall to the string.

15.4a Loosen the right side axle pinch bolts (arrows) . . .

15.4b . . . loosen the axle bolt with a box wrench or socket . . .

6   Repeat the procedure on the other side of the motorcycle. The distance from the front tire sidewall to the string should be equal on both sides.

7   As was previously pointed out, a perfectly straight length of wood may be substituted for the string. The procedure is the same.

8   If the distance between the string and tire is greater on one side, or if the rear wheel appears to be cocked, refer to Chapter 6, *Swingarm bearings - check*, and make sure the swingarm is tight.

9   If the front-to-back alignment is correct, the wheels still may be out of alignment vertically.

10   Using the plumb bob, or other suitable weight, and a length of string, check the rear wheel to make sure it is vertical. To do this, hold the string against the tire upper sidewall and allow the weight to settle just off the floor. When the string touches both the upper and lower tire sidewalls and is perfectly straight, the wheel is vertical. If it is not, place thin spacers under one leg of the centerstand.

11   Once the rear wheel is vertical, check the

front wheel in the same manner. If both wheels are not perfectly vertical, the frame and/or major suspension components are bent.

15 Front wheel - removal, inspection and installation

Removal

1   Place the bike on its centerstand. Raise the front wheel off the ground by placing a floor jack, with a wood block on the jack head, under the engine. Don't place the jack under the oil filter.

2   Remove the brake disc covers and the forward section of the front fender (see Chapter 8).

3   On airbag models, remove the left brake pads (see Section 2). On all models, remove both front calipers, leaving the brake hoses connected (see Section 3). Tie each caliper to a support such as the handlebars with a piece of wire so it doesn't hang by the brake hose. **Note:** *Slip a piece of wood between*

the pistons or pads of the removed calipers so the pads won't be squeezed together if the brake lever is accidentally pulled or the pedal is accidentally pressed.

4   Loosen the axle pinch bolts on the bottom of the right fork leg and unscrew the axle bolt **(see illustrations)**.

5   Loosen the axle pinch bolts on the bottom of the left fork leg **(see illustration)**. Thread the axle bolt partway back in and tap on it with a soft-faced mallet to break the axle loose **(see illustration)**. Support the wheel, then pull out the axle **(see illustrations)** and carefully lower the wheel away from the forks.

6   Remove the spacer from each side **(see illustrations)**.

HAYNES HiNT *Slip the spacers back onto the axle temporarily so you remember how they fit during installation (see illustration).*

Set the wheel aside.

Caution: Don't lay the wheel down and allow it to rest on one of the discs - the disc could become warped. Set the

15.4c . . . and unscrew the bolt

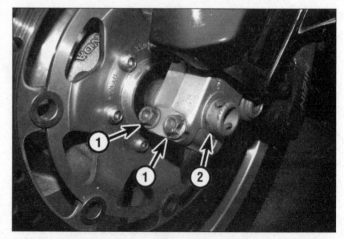

15.5a Loosen the left side axle pinch bolts (1); on installation, insert the axle up to the index line (2)

15.5b Thread the bolt partway into the right side of the axle and tap with a soft-faced mallet to free the axle

15.5c Slip a screwdriver shaft into the axle holes, twist it to free the axle . . .

wheel on wood blocks so the disc doesn't support the weight of the wheel.

Note: *Don't operate the front brake lever with the wheel removed.*

Inspection

7   Set the axle in a pair of V-blocks, rotate it and check runout with a dial indicator. If the axle is corroded, remove the corrosion with fine emery cloth.
8   Check the condition of the wheel bearings (see Section 17).

Installation

9   Place the spacers in the wheel hub **(see illustrations 15.6a and 15.6b)**. Note the spacer with the flange goes in the right side of the wheel.
10   Position the wheel between the fork legs, making sure the directional arrow on the tire points in the direction of forward rotation.
11   Start the axle into the left fork leg. Lift the wheel so the hub aligns with the axle, then slip the axle in until its index line is flush

15.5d . . . and pull the axle out while supporting the wheel

with the outside of the fork leg **(see illustration 15.5a)**. Tighten the axle pinch bolts in the left fork leg to the torque listed in this Chapter's Specifications.

15.6a The right side spacer (arrow) has a flange on the outer end . . .

12   Install the axle bolt on the right side of the axle and tighten it to the torque listed in this Chapter's Specifications.
13   Tighten the pinch bolts on the right side

15.6b . . . the left side spacer (arrow) does not have a flange

15.6c It's a good idea to store the spacers on the axle while it's out, so you can remember how they go

16.2 Remove the nuts and take the rear wheel off the studs

17.5a This tool is used to remove the front wheel bearings

17.5b Place the split portion into the bearing like this . . .

of the axle to the torque listed in this Chapter's Specifications.

14   If the bike is equipped with ABS, measure the gap between the pulser ring and sensor with a feeler gauge. Turn the wheel and measure the gap at several points. The gap can't be adjusted; if it's not within the range listed in this Chapter's Specifications, check for damaged or incorrectly installed parts.

15   The remainder of installation is the reverse of the removal steps.

16   After all parts are installed, loosen the left axle pinch bolts. Straddle the bike, squeeze the front brake lever and pump the forks up and down several times (this will seat the axle). The front brake should operate well enough to hold the bike securely while you do this.

17   Tighten the left axle pinch bolts to the torque listed in this Chapter's Specifications.

16 Rear wheel - removal, inspection and installation

Removal

1   Remove the rear section of the rear fender (see Chapter 8). If you're working on a Canadian model, remove the cross brace behind the wheel.

2   With the wheels on the ground, have an assistant sit on the bike and hold the brake pedal down. Loosen the wheel nuts **(see illustration)**.

3   Place the bike on its centerstand and support it with the rear wheel off the ground. The support must be stable, so the bike can't be knocked over, and located so it won't interfere with removal of the wheel.

4   Remove the wheel nuts. Pull the wheel off its studs, lower it away from the motorcycle, and roll it clear.

Caution: Don't lay the wheel down and allow it to rest on the brake disc or pulser ring (ABS models) - they could become

warped. Set the wheel on wood blocks so the disc or the pulser ring doesn't support the weight of the wheel. Do not operate the brake pedal with the wheel removed.

Inspection

5   This is the same as for front wheels, described in Section 15.

Installation

6   Installation is the reverse of the removal steps. Tighten all fasteners to the torques listed in this Chapter's Specifications.

7   Check the operation of the brakes carefully before riding the motorcycle.

17 Wheel bearings - replacement

1   This procedure applies to the front wheel bearings. The rear wheel is supported by bearings inside the final drive unit land doesn't have conventional wheel bearings.

2   Support the bike securely so it can't be knocked over during this procedure and remove the wheel, pulser ring (ABS models) and brake discs (see Sections 15 and 4). Remove the spacer from each side of the wheel.

3   Set the wheel on blocks so as not to allow the weight of the wheel rest on the brake disc.

4   Pry the grease seal out of the each side of the wheel **(see illustration 4.7a or 4.7b)**.

5   A common method of removing wheel bearings is to insert a metal rod (preferably a brass drift punch) through the center of one hub bearing and tap evenly around the inner race of the opposite bearing to drive it from the hub. The bearing spacer will also come out. On these motorcycles, it's generally not possible to tilt the rod enough to catch the opposite bearing's inner race. In this case,

17.5c . . . and pass the wedge end of the rod through the hub into the split portion, then tap on the end of the rod to lock the split portion to the bearing and drive the bearing out of the hub

use a bearing remover tool consisting of a shaft and remover head **(see illustration)**. The head, which has a 20 mm diameter, fits inside the bearing **(see illustration)**, then the wedge end of the shaft is tapped into the groove in the head to expand the head and lock it inside the bearing. Tapping on the shaft from this point will force the bearing out of the hub **(see illustration)**.

6   Lay the wheel on its other side and remove the remaining bearing using the same technique. **Note:** *The bearings must be replaced with new ones whenever they're removed, as they're almost certain to be damaged during removal.*

7   Thoroughly clean the hub area of the wheel. Install the bearing into the recess in the hub. Using a bearing driver or a socket large enough to contact the outer race of the bearing, drive it in until it's completely seated **(see illustration)**.

8   Turn the wheel over and install the bearing spacer and bearing, driving the bearing into place as described in Step 7.

17.7 Drive in new bearings and seals with a bearing driver like this one or with a socket the same size as the bearing outer races

19.3 The rear ABS sensor is bolted to the swingarm

9   Install a new dust seal on each side of the front wheel. It should be possible to push the seals in with even finger pressure, but if necessary use a seal driver, large socket or a flat piece of wood to drive the seals into place.

10   Clean off all grease from the brake discs using acetone or brake system cleaner.

11   Refer to Section 15 and install the wheel.

18 Tubeless tires - general information

1   Tubeless tires are used as standard equipment on this motorcycle. They are generally safer than tube-type tires but if problems do occur they require special repair techniques. In addition, special removal and installation techniques are required on 2009 and later models to prevent damage to the tire pressure sensors built into the air vales.

2   The force required to break the seal between the rim and the bead of the tire is substantial, and is usually beyond the capa-bilities of an individual working with normal tire irons.

3   Also, repair of the punctured tire and replacement on the wheel rim requires special tools, skills and experience that the average do-it-yourselfer lacks.

4   For these reasons, if a puncture or flat occurs with a tubeless tire, the wheel should be removed from the motorcycle and taken to a dealer service department or a motorcycle repair shop for repair or replacement of the tire. The accompanying illustrations can be used to replace a tubeless tire in an emergency.

19 Anti-lock brakes - general information

The optional anti-lock braking system consists of three main components: pulser rings/wheel sensors, modulators and the control module. Repairs to the ABS system are complicated and should be done by a dealer service department or other qualified shop. The system is designed to dis-able itself if it detects a problem, leaving the motorcycle with standard (non-ABS) brakes. If the ABS warning light on the instrument cluster comes on and stays on, take the bike in for service immediately.

Pulser rings and wheel sensors

Each wheel has a metal ring with square teeth on it and a magnetic sensor mounted to a fixed location near the ring. The teeth move past the magnetic sensor as the wheel rotates. As each tooth passes the sensor, the sensor generates a voltage pulse, which is sent to the control unit. As the wheel rotates faster, the time between the voltage pulses becomes shorter; as the wheel rotates slower, the time between the voltage pulses becomes longer. The control unit detects this information and uses it to calculate how quickly the wheel is losing speed.

The wheel sensors can easily be removed when necessary for the removal of other components **(see illustration 3.4 and the accompanying illustration)**. The pulser rings are secured to the right front and rear brake discs by Allen bolts - to remove them, remove the disc(s) as described in Section 4 and remove the Allen bolts that secure the sensor ring to the disc.

Modulators

There are two modulators, one in the hydraulic circuit controlled by the brake pedal and the other in the hydraulic circuit controlled by the brake lever **(see illustration)**. Each has an electrically-powered control valve that regulates brake line pressure. The control valve uses an electric motor to turn a crankshaft, which turns a cam that opens or closes a spring-loaded valve in the hydraulic line. The valve allows full hydraulic pressure under normal braking conditions. When the control unit senses that one of the wheels is about to lock up, it opens the control valve to release brake line pressure so the wheel keeps turning.

19.4 The rear ABS modulator (shown) is located inside the fairing at the left front corner of the frame; the front ABS modulator is in the right front corner

19.5 The ABS control module is mounted at the rear of the motorcycle on 2001 through 2005 models (shown); on 2006 and later models, it's under the fuel tank top cover

Control module

The control module (see illustration) senses the voltage inputs from the wheel speed sensors and uses this information to operate the control valves in the modulators. The control module can respond to system inputs at an extremely high rate of speed, sensing impending lockup, operating the modulator(s) to release brake line pressure, holding the pressure at a level that will allow the wheel to keep turning, then restoring full pressure. The control module contains two central processing units, which run constant diagnostic checks on each other so that any failure of the system can be detected. If a failure is detected, the module stores a trouble code. It also shuts off the ABS. This causes the spring-loaded valves in the modulators to open fully, so that normal braking (without the ABS function) is maintained.

TIRE CHANGING SEQUENCE - TUBELESS TIRES

Deflate tire. After releasing beads, push tire bead into well of rim at point opposite valve. Insert lever next to valve and work bead over edge of rim.

Use two levers to work bead over edge of rim. Note use of rim protectors.

When first bead is clear, remove tire as shown.

Before installing, ensure that tire is suitable for wheel. Take note of any sidewall markings such as direction of rotation arrows.

Work first bead over the rim flange.

Use a tire lever to work the second bead over rim flange.

Notes

Chapter 8
Fairing and bodywork

Contents

Degrees of difficulty

Easy, suitable for novice with little experience		**Fairly easy,** suitable for beginner with some experience		**Fairly difficult,** suitable for competent DIY mechanic		**Difficult,** suitable for experienced DIY mechanic		**Very difficult,** suitable for expert DIY or professional	

1 General information

This Chapter covers the procedures necessary to remove and install the fairing and other body parts. Since many service and repair operations on these motorcycles require removal of the fairing and/or other body parts, the procedures are grouped here and referred to from other Chapters.

In the event of damage to the fairing or other body part, it is usually necessary to remove the broken component and replace it with a new (or used) one. The material that the fairings are composed of doesn't lend itself to conventional repair techniques. There are, however, some shops that specialize in plastic welding, so it would be advantageous to check around first before throwing the damaged part away. When you order new body parts, refer to the color label inside the filler cap lid to make sure the new parts match the bike.

1.3a If the clip has a pin in the center, push it in partway . . .

1.3b . . . and pull the clip out

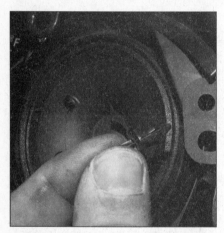

1.3c To install the clip, position the pin like this . . .

1.3d . . . insert the clip in the hole and push the pin in until it's flush with the head of the clip

1.3e If the clip has a protruding head like this . . .

There are two basic types of trim clip that retain body panels on these models, one with a center pin that's flush with the head and one with a center pin that protrudes. For details of how to remove and install each type, refer to the accompanying illus- trations (see illustrations).

Shouldered Allen bolts are used in a number of locations on the bodywork. There

1.3f . . . pull it up and pull the clip out

1.3g Position the head like this, insert the clip in the hole and push the head down

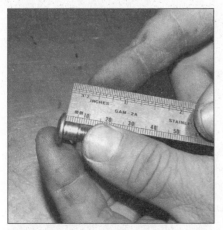

1.4 Measure the shoulder length of each Allen bolt as you remove it and write the length down so the bolts can be returned to the correct holes

2.1a Remove the Allen bolts (arrows) and take the handles off

2.1b The handle nuts can be removed once the handles have been removed

2.2a Lift the seat cushion at the back . . .

2.2b . . . pull it away from the frame . . .

are numerous different shoulder lengths. It's a good idea to measure them **(see illustration)** and write the measurements down so the bolts can be returned to the correct locations.

2 Seat - removal and installation

1   Unscrew the Allen bolts and take the handles off **(see illustration)**. The Allen bolt nuts can be removed once the bolts are out **(see illustration)**.

2   Lift up the back of the seat and pull it rearward to disengage the hook at the front from the top compartment **(see illustrations)**. If the bike has a seat heater, unplug its wiring connector.

3   Installation is the reverse of the removal steps. It's possible to install the grab handles upside down, so refer to the R and L (right

and left) marks to make sure they're installed on the correct sides of the bike **(see illustration)**. The grip area on each grab handle should be horizontal, not diagonal.

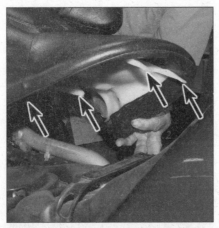

2.2c . . . and disengage the hooks at the front (arrows) from the retaining strap

2.3 The handles are marked L and R for left and right sides of the bike

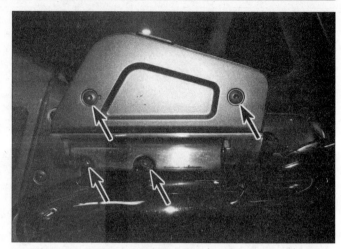

3.1 The front footpeg brackets are secured by Allen bolts (upper arrows), the footrest pivot pin is secured by a cotter pin (lower arrow)

3.2 Remove the mounting bolts (lower arrows) to remove a rear footrest; remove the Allen bolts (upper arrows) to remove the pad

3 Footrests - removal and installation

1   To remove a front footrest, either unbolt its bracket from the frame or remove the clip and slide out the pivot pin **(see illustration)**.
2   To remove a rear footrest, remove the Allen bolts and take the footrest off **(see illustration)**. If necessary, unbolt the rubber pad from the footrest.
3   Installation is the reverse of the removal steps.

4 Front fender and brake disc covers - removal and installation

1   Remove the fender front section mounting bolts **(see illustration)**. The lower bolt on each side has a rubber washer.
2   Lift the fender off.

4.1 The front portion of the fender is secured by two Allen bolts on each side (arrows); the lower bolt on each side has a rubber washer

3   Remove the disc brake cover bolts **(see illustration)**. On airbag models, the bolts have rubber washers. Take the covers off **(see illustration)**.
4   Remove the trim clip and two bolts that

secure the fork cover and take it off **(see illustrations)**.
5   To remove the rear fender section, unbolt the delay valve, but leave it in position (see Chapter 7). Remove the three remaining

4.3a Remove the disc brake cover bolts . . .

4.3b . . . and take the cover off

4.4a Remove the trim clip from the center rear side of the fork cover . . .

4.4b . . . and the bolts . . .

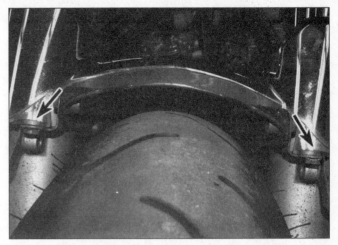

4.4c . . . there's a bolt on each side (arrows) . . .

4.4d . . . and lift the cover off

4.5a Remove the bolt at the right front . . .

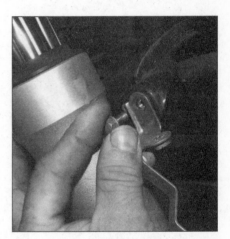

4.5b . . . at the left front . . .

fender bolts **(see illustrations)**. Spread the brake hoses (the rubber hoses that run down to the calipers) apart to create removal clearance, lower the fender down onto the tire

so it clears the crossover brake lines, slide it back, then take the rear fender section off **(see illustration)**.

6   Installation is the reverse of the removal

steps. On the fender rear section, the longer bolts go in the forward holes. On the front section, the longer bolts go in the lower holes.

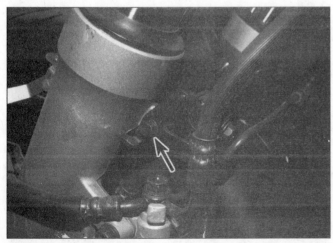

4.5c . . . and at the left rear . . .

4.5d . . . then spread the brake hoses, lower the fender onto the tire and withdraw it to the rear

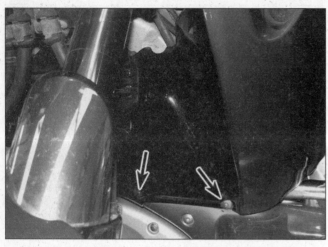

5.1a The center inner fairing is secured by bolts and trim clips (arrows)

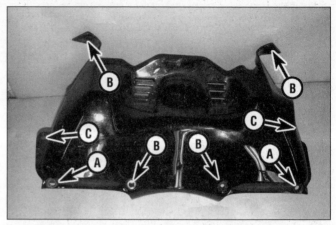

5.1b Fastener locations - center inner fairing

A   Allen bolts
B   Trim clip locations (all models)
C   Trim clip locations (2001 through 2005 only)

5.2 Pull the panel forward and remove it to the left side of the bike (to the right, viewed from the front)

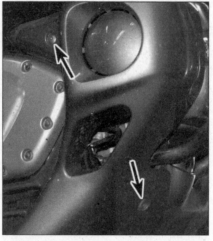

5.5 The fairing under cover is secured by upper and lower Allen bolts on each side (arrows)

5 Fairing front and under covers - removal and installation

Front cover

1   Remove two trim clips and two bolts from the lower edge of the center inner fairing **(see illustrations)**.
2   Place rags on the fender to protect it from scratches. Remove a trim clip from each side of the panel (2001 through 2005 only), and one trim clip from upper corner **(see illustration 5.1b)**. Ease the panel out and to the left side of the bike **(see illustration)**.
3   Installation is the reverse of the removal steps.

Under cover

4   Remove the front cover as described above.

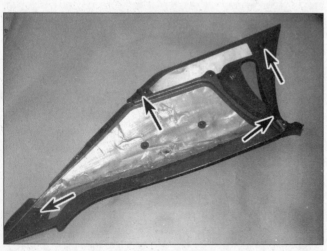

6.2a Pull the posts (arrows) . . .

6.2b . . . out of the grommets on the frame (arrows)

6.4 Remove the Allen bolts (arrows) and lift the cover off

7.2a Pull the lower edge of the cover away from the frame to disengage the post from the grommet . . .

5   Remove two bolts from the top of the cover and one bolt from each lower side **(see illustration)**. Take the cover off.
6   Installation is the reverse of the removal steps.

6   Rear side covers - removal and installation

Upper side covers

1   Refer to Section 2 and remove the seat.
2   Reach behind the cover and slowly pull the two rear posts out of the rubber grommets on the frame **(see illustrations)**. Pull the center post out of the grommet on the frame and the front post out of the grommet in the fuel tank top cover.
3   Installation is the reverse of the removal

steps. Push the posts into the grommets firmly but carefully.

Lower side covers

4   To remove one of the lower side covers, unscrew the Allen bolts and lift it off **(see illustration)**.
5   Installation is the reverse of the removal steps.

7   Front side covers - removal and installation

Upper side covers

1   Remove the seat and the rear side cover (see Sections 2 and 6).
2   To remove the left cover, pull the lower post out of the grommet on the frame **(see**

illustration). Pull the rear edge out to detach the rear tab from the frame grommet **(see illustration)**. Slide the cover rearward to disengage the tab from the grommet at the front, then take the cover off **(see illustration)**.
3   To remove the right cover, pull the cover outward to free the posts at the rear and bottom from their grommets on the frame, then slide it rearward to disengage the grommet in the cover from the tab on the fuel injector cover **(see illustration)**.
4   Installation is the reverse of the removal steps.

Lower side covers

⚠️ *Warning: These covers protect the exhaust system and can get very hot. To prevent burns, make sure the engine is completely cool before removing the covers.*

7.2b . . . pull the rear edge out to disengage the tab from the grommet on the frame . . .

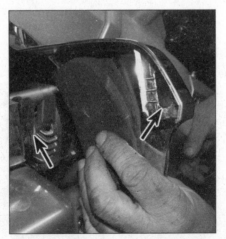

7.2c . . . and pull the cover rearward to disengage the tab and grommet at the front (arrows)

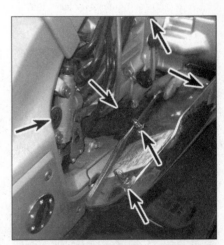

7.3 To remove the right cover, pull the posts out of the grommets (lower arrows) and disengage the tab from the grommet at the front (upper arrows)

7.6 Remove the nuts and fiber washers from the underside of the cover (arrows) . . .

7.7 . . . remove the bolt at the front . . .

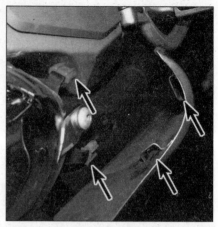

7.8a . . . disengage the slots and tabs at the rear . . .

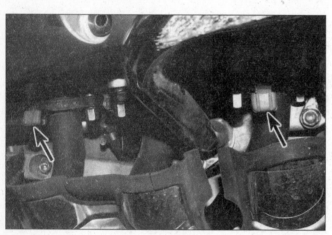

7.8b . . . and the slots and tabs at the top . . .

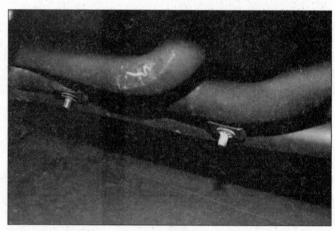

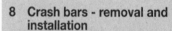

7.9 . . . then take the cover off and remove the washers from the studs

5   Remove the lower front fairing panel (see Section 5).

6   Remove the nuts and fiber washers from the underside of the cover (see illustration).

7   Remove the bolt at the front of the cover (see illustration).

8   Disengage the tabs at the rear and top of the cover and take it off (see illustrations).

9   Installation is the reverse of the removal steps. Don't forget to reinstall the fiber washers over the studs before you install the cover (see illustration).

8   Crash bars - removal and installation

1   To remove the front crash bars, remove the fairing (see Section 11). Undo two lower bolts and one upper bolt and take the bars off (see illustrations).

8.1a Remove the upper front bolt . . .

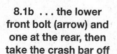

8.1b . . . the lower front bolt (arrow) and one at the rear, then take the crash bar off

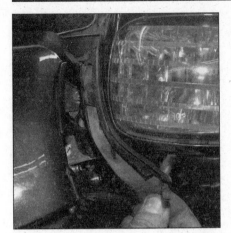

9.1 Disengage the mirror boot from the fairing

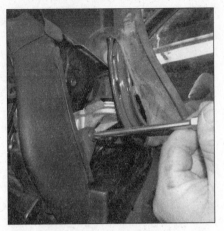

9.2a On 2005 and earlier models, remove the screw . . .

9.2b . . . and trim clip (arrow) that secure the mirror cover . . .

2   To remove a rear crash bar, remove the rear lower side covers (see Section 6). Remove the bolts and take the bar off.
3   Installation is the reverse of the removal steps.

9   Rearview mirrors - removal and installation

1   Disengage the mirror boot tabs and take the boot off **(see illustration)**.
2   If you're working on a 2005 or earlier model, remove the screw and trim clip that secure the mirror cover **(see illustrations)**. Unhook the cover tabs from the slots in the mirror boot **(see illustration)**. Take the cover off. Pull gently downward on the cover to disengage the upper tab **(see illustration)**.

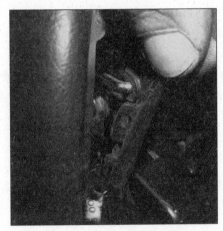

9.2c . . . disengage the tabs at the side . . .

3   Remove the screws and mirror stay. Note that the stays are marked R and L for left and right side of the bike **(see illustra-**

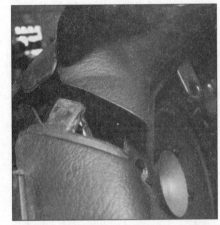

9.2d . . . and at the top to remove the mirror boot

tions). Unplug the turn signal connector and take the mirror off.
4   Installation is the reverse of the removal steps.

9.3a Remove the bracket screws (arrows) and take the mirror off

9.3b The brackets are marked R and L for right and left sides of the bike

10.2a Remove the windshield trim mounting bolt from each side of the bike . . .

10.2b . . . and remove the washer and grommet; the wide side of each grommet faces the washer

10.4a Note how the holder tab and fairing tab engage each other (arrow) . . .

10 Windshield - removal and installation

1   Disengage the mirror boot tabs on both sides of the bike (see Section 9).
2   Rotate the mirrors forward to expose the windshield trim mounting bolts (one on each side of the bike) **(see illustration)**. Remove the washers and rubber grommet from each bolt hole **(see illustration)**.
3   Disengage the windshield trim mounting pins (two at the front and one on each side) from the grommets. Carefully spread the trim panel so the bolt holes clear the bolt bosses, then take the trim panel off the bike.
4   Note how the holder plate tabs fit against the fairing stay **(see illustration)**. Remove the bolt at the front of the holder plate and the nut on each side, then lift the

holder plate off the bike **(see illustrations)**.
5   Have an assistant support the windshield so it doesn't fall when the last fastener is removed. Remove the screw, at each lower corner **(see illustration)**. On 2001 and 2002 models, remove two additional screws toward the center of the windshield. Remove the bolts at the lower center and lift the windshield off **(see illustration)**. Note that on 2006 and later models, the screws at the corners have plastic washers. On 2005 and earlier models, the bolts in the center have plastic washers and a 3.5 mm shoulder height **(see illustration)**.
6   Installation is the reverse of the removal steps. If the mounting plates in the screw or bolt holes separated from the windshield, be sure to reinstall them **(see illustration 10.5c)**. Position the holder plate tabs to fit against the fairing stay **(see illustration 10.4a)**.

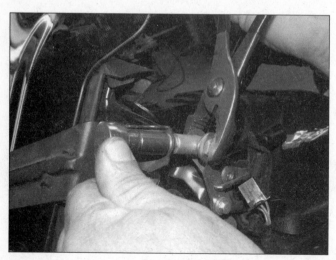

10.4b . . . then support the toggle bolt with pliers so it won't twist and unscrew the nut

10.4c Rotate the holder plate and unscrew the bolt underneath it (arrow)

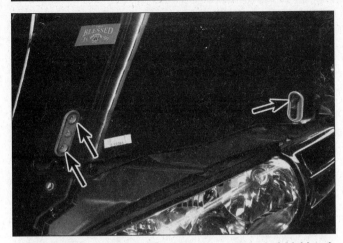

10.5a Remove the Allen bolt at the center of the windshield and the screw at each outer corner (arrows) - 2001 and 2002 models have an additional screw on each side between the Allen bolts and corner screw

10.5b The Allen bolts are shouldered

11 Fairing - removal and installation

Note: *The bank angle sensor (tipover switch) is attached to the headlight assembly. If the headlight assembly or upper fairing is removed, the bank angle sensor must be reinstalled for the engine to restart. The engine will turn over, but it won't start if the switch is not installed or is at the wrong angle.*

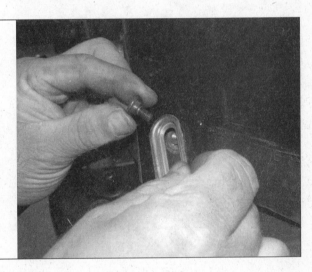

10.5c Note which way the reinforcing plates face so you can install them the correct way

Meter panel

2001 through 2005

1   Carefully disengage the tabs that secure the speaker covers (four tabs per cover) and lift them off **(see illustration)**. This will expose the trim clip at the upper inner corner of each speaker and the bolt at the lower outer corner **(see illustration)**. Remove the bolts and trim clips.

2   Lift the rear of the meter panel to disengage the rear posts from the grommets

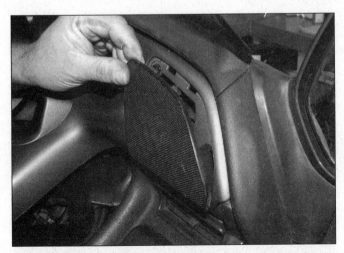

11.1a Pull down on the speaker cover to disengage the tabs at the top . . .

11.1b . . . then disengage the tabs at the bottom and lift the cover off

11.2a Lift the rear of the meter panel to disengage its posts and grommets . . .

11.2b . . . then reach under the panel with a long, narrow screwdriver, unlock the connector tab (arrow) . . .

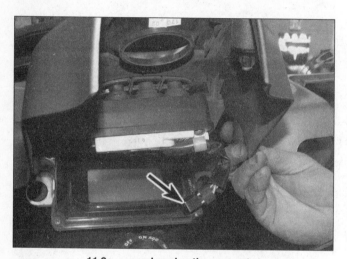

11.2c . . . and unplug the connector

11.3 Lift the meter panel to disengage the remaining posts and grommets (arrows)

(see illustration). Insert a screwdriver from the left side to unlock the tab of the electrical connector and unplug the connector **(see illustrations)**.

3   Lift the meter panel again, disengaging the posts from the grommets on each side of the digital display **(see illustration)**.

4   Pull the panel rearward to disengage the tabs at the top front from their slots **(see illustration)**.

5   Take the meter panel off.

6   Pull the two posts at the top center of the meter panel out of their grommets, lift the panel and unplug the electrical connector. Remove the panel from the bike.

2006 and later

7   Carefully pry up the ignition switch cover, taking care not to scratch the panel.

8   Disengage the meter panel tabs that connect the panel to the top cover. These are located on each side of the meter display.

9   Carefully pull up on the rearward edge of the meter panel to free the two posts from their grommets.

10   Disengage the four speaker opening tabs at the corners of the two speaker openings.

11   Lift the panel and disconnect the meter connector (all models) and two tweeter connectors (US models). **Note:** *Use a long narrow screwdriver to disengage the connector locking tab.* Take the panel off.

All models

12   Installation is the reverse of the removal steps.

Front fairing trim panel and inner fairing

13   Remove the fairing front cover and windshield trim panel (see Sections 5 and 10).

11.4 Disengage the tabs at the top of the meter panel from the fairing slots

11.14a Slide the molding back and disengage the tab at the front . . .

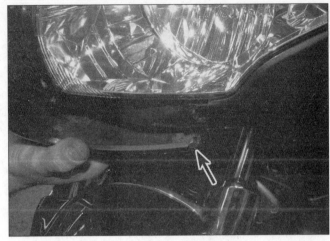

11.14b . . . then disengage the remaining tabs and take the molding off

14   Remove the bolt at the top and two screws at the bottom, then disengage the tab at each corner and take the front fairing trim panel off **(see illustrations).**
15   Remove three trim clips and one screw. Lift the inner fairing off the bike.
16   Installation is the reverse of the removal steps.

Fairing moldings

17   Slide the front end of the molding toward the rear to disengage the front molding tab from the fairing, then slide the molding forward to disengage the remaining tabs **(see illustrations).** Lift the molding off. The top three fasteners under the molding have a 5 mm thread diameter; the bottom one has a 6 mm thread diameter. Remove the other molding (left or right) in the same way.
18   Installation is the reverse of the removal steps.

11.17a Disengage the tab at the front of the molding . . .

11.17b . . . and along the length of the molding

Fairing pockets

19   To remove the left fairing pocket, open it and remove the four fasteners (four trim clips on 2001 and 2006 and later models; two trim clips and two screws with washers on 2002 through 2005 models) **(see illustrations).**

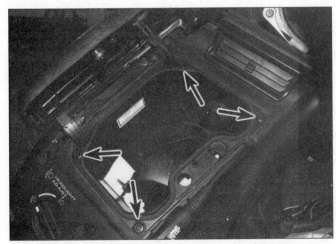

11.19a To remove the left fairing pocket, remove its fasteners (arrows) . . .

11.19b . . . lift the pocket out, unplug its wiring connector and remove it

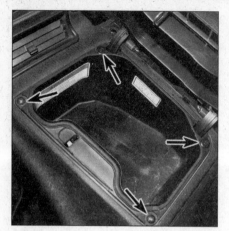

11.20a To remove the right fairing pocket, remove its fasteners (arrows) . . .

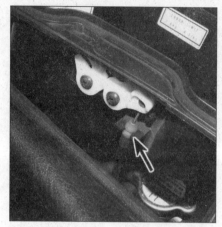

11.20b . . . unclip the cable from its bracket (arrow) . . .

11.20c . . . then rotate the cable out of the slot and slip and the end plug out of the lever

Lift the pocket out of the fairing, disconnect the accessory socket wiring connector and remove the pocket.

20   To remove the right fairing pocket (non-airbag models only), open it and remove the four fasteners (screws or trim clips). Lift the pocket out, disconnect the opener cable and remove the pocket **(see illustrations)**.

Meter panel visor

2001 through 2005

21   Remove the windshield and both inner fairings as described above. Remove the bolt, screws and trim clips and take the visor off **(see illustrations)**. All Allen bolts except the lower center have a 4 mm shoulder; the lower center bolt on each side has a 6 mm shoulder. The outer lower bolt holes have nut clips.

2006 and later

22   Remove the meter panel as described above.

23   If the motorcycle has a navigation sys-

tem or XM radio, unplug the connector(s).

24   Remove the fuel tank top cover's right inner cover (see Section 12).

25   If the bike has cruise control, unbolt the cruise control actuator and move it out of the way.

Caution: Don't bend the cable.

26   If the bike has a tire pressure monitoring system, free the system receiver's wiring harness from its retainer and unplug it from the receiver. Unbolt the receiver and move it out of the way.

27   Remove the screw or trim clip that secures the right air intake duct. Move the duct out of the way.

28   Free the GPS antenna and XM radio antenna wires from the retainers, and disconnect the wires.

29   Rotate both side mirrors forward.

All models

30   Remove two trim clips, two long bolts and six short bolts. Remove four screws (2001 through 2005) or six screws (2006 and later). On 2006 and later models, disengage

the lever boots from their grooves and the tab at each lower corner of the meter panel visor.

31   Lift the meter panel visor off the motorcycle.

32   Installation is the reverse of the removal steps. If you removed the right air intake duct, be sure its rubber seal is properly engaged with the air cleaner cover.

Fairing

33   Remove the fairing pockets as described above for access to air duct trim clips.

34   Remove the fairing moldings, inner fairings and meter panel visor as described above.

35   Remove the fuel tank top cover (see Section 12).

36   If you're working on a 2006 or later model, remove the left panel switch (see Chapter 9).

37   If you're working on a non-airbag model, unscrew the bolt from the right top cover trim panel, disengage three tabs and take the panel off.

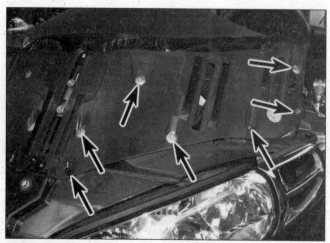

11.21a Remove the bolt, screws and trim clips (arrows) to detach the meter panel visor (2001 through 2005)

11.21b Make sure the clip nuts are in position (arrows) before you install the visor

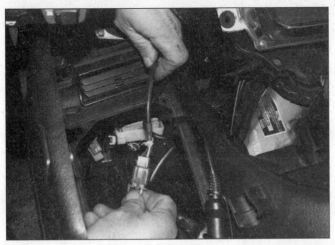

12.4 Unplug the electrical connectors inside the fairing

12.5a Remove the fairing mounting bolts at the top center (arrows) . . .

12.5b . . . along the sides under the fairing molding . . .

12.5c . . . and the nuts or bolts at each rear corner (arrows) - on the right side, the bolt secures a wiring harness

12.5d Remove the center Allen bolt on each side of the cover (arrow)

38 On all 2007 and later models, remove the trim clip at the top and bottom of each ventilation duct, then remove the ducts.

39 If you're working on an airbag model, remove the right side of the fuel tank top cover (see Section 12).

40 Disconnect the connectors for the headlight motors and headlights (see Chapter 9). If the bike has an ambient air temperature sensor and bank angle sensor, disconnect their connectors as well. Free the wiring harness from the fairing.

41 Remove the following fasteners:

a) Flange bolt with collar at front center
b) Flange bolts with washers on each side at the front (the right bolt has a collar on 2006 and later models)
c) Two 5x12 mm bolts on each side of the fairing (non-airbag models)
d) One 5x12 mm bolts and one trim clip on each side of the fairing (airbag models)
e) One 6x14 mm bolts at each lower rear corner of the fairing

42 Have an assistant support the fairing. Spread it carefully to clear the top cover. Free the headlight wiring harnesses from

the retainers. If the bike has cruise control, unplug both connectors from the cruise control module. Take the fairing off the bike.

43 Installation is the reverse of the removal steps.

12 Fuel tank top cover - removal and installation

Non-airbag models

1 Remove the seat and side covers (see Sections 2, 6 and 7).

2 Remove the fairing pockets, meter panel and fairing moldings (see Section 11).

3 Free the headset connector from its holder.

4 Unplug the connector for the left panel switch (and the right panel switch connector if equipped) (see illustration). If the bike is equipped with a foot warmer ventilation cable, disconnect it also.

5 Remove the top cover mounting bolts

(see illustrations). If you need to leave the seat bracket in position, you can remove the nut from each side and spread the top cover to remove it from the studs as you lift the top cover off.

12.5e Remove two screws to detach the cover from the ignition switch support

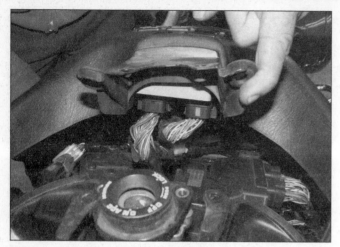

12.6a Lift the cover and disconnect the radio wiring connectors . . .

12.6b . . . and the antenna connector

6   Lift the top cover far enough to disconnect the radio antenna and wiring harness connectors **(see illustrations)**, then lift the top cover off the bike.

7   Installation is the reverse of the removal steps. Be sure to align the ventilation louvers with their air ducts.

Airbag models

8   The fuel tank top cover on airbag models consists of center, left and right sections, as well as the fuel filler cap cover and inner cover.

 Warning: If the motorcycle is equipped with an airbag, refer to the airbag precautions in Chapter 9 before beginning any work.

Center front cover

9   Remove the meter panel (see Section 11).

10   Remove two screws and pull the post from its grommet. Lift the panel off.

11   Installation is the reverse of the removal steps.

Filler cap cover

12   Unlock and open the filler cap lid.

13   Remove the trim clip from each side of the cover.

14   Disengage the tabs that secure the covers for the airbag tethers (one on each side of the filler cap cover). Lift the covers off. They're secured by cords; don't remove these.

15   Unhook the Velcro that keeps the airbag tethers folded. Unfold the tethers to provide access to the four cover bolts.

16   Unscrew the four bolts and lift the cover off.

17   Installation is the reverse of the removal steps, with the following additions:

a) *Fold the airbag tethers into their original positions and secure them with the Velcro pads.*

b) *When you tighten the four cover bolts, be sure not to catch the airbag tethers between the cover and the airbag housing. The tethers must be free to move if the airbag deploys.*

c) *When you install the tether covers, guide the cords that secure the tether covers into their openings, using your fingers.*

Left top cover

18   Remove the center front cover and filler cap cover as described above.

19   Remove the left side cover and left panel switch (see Section 7 and Chapter 9).

20   Disengage the headset connector from its holder on the right side of the left top cover.

21   Work the ventilation lever boot out of its groove in the cover.

22   Free the foot warmer ventilation cable from its retainer inside the cover, then disconnect the end of the cable.

23   Remove the cover mounting bolts **(see illustrations)**. Remove the nut and collar from the stud at the lower rear corner of the cover.

24   Slide the grommet off of the stud at the lower rear corner, then disengage the two tabs on the underside of the cover and lift the cover off the bike.

25   Installation is the reverse of the removal steps. Engage the tabs with their slots and engage the ventilation louver with its duct.

Right top cover

26   Remove the center front cover and filler cap cover as described above.

27   Remove the right side cover (see Section 7).

28   Remove the right lower panel switch (see Chapter 9).

29   Work the ventilation lever boot out of its groove in the cover.

30   Free the amplifier/headset wiring harness from its retainer.

31   Remove six bolts that secure the cover to the motorcycle. At the right rear corner, remove the nut, wiring harness retainer and grommet.

32   Slide the grommet off of the stud at the lower rear corner, then disengage the two tabs on the underside of the cover and lift the cover off the bike.

33   Installation is the reverse of the removal steps. Engage the tabs with their slots and engage the ventilation louver with its duct.

13 Top cover inner cover (2006 and later)

1   Remove the fuel tank top cover (on airbag models, remove the center, left and right components) (see Section 12).

2   Remove the inner cover trim clip and lift the cover out.

3   If necessary, remove the ignition switch cover.

4   Installation is the reverse of the removal steps.

14 Rear fender - removal and installation

2001 through 2005 US, all Canada/UK/Europe

Rear section

1   Remove the mounting bolts **(see illustration)**. All models have four Allen bolts; 2001 through 2005 US models and all Cana-

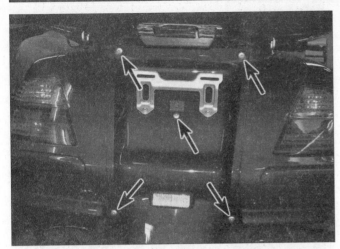

14.1 Remove the Allen bolt at each corner and the flange bolt at the center (if equipped) (arrows)

14.5 Note how the wiring harnesses are routed

dian, UK and European models also have a flange bolt in the center of the fender section.

2   Disengage the tabs that secure the rear fender section to the saddlebags and lift it off the bike.

3   Installation is the reverse of the removal steps.

Front section

4   Remove the saddlebags (see Section 16).

5   Note how the wiring is routed for installation (see illustration). Detach the following electrical components from the fender (see Chapter 9 if necessary): Relay box, ABS control unit (if equipped), reverse relays, three individual relays on the left side of the fender and the starter relays on the left side of fender. Free the electrical connector from the bracket on the fender.

6   Unbolt one side of the crossbar at the rear of the rear subframe. Loosen the bolt on the other side and pivot the crossbar downward to provide removal clearance.

14.7a Remove the fender-to-frame bolt on each side (arrow)

7   Unbolt the fender from the subframe, detach the retaining strap, disengage the mounting hooks and tab and pull the fender

14.7b Remove the retaining strap that secures the left side of the fender to the frame

rearward to remove it (see illustrations).

8   Installation is the reverse of the removal steps.

14.7c Disengage the right side of the fender (arrow) from the frame

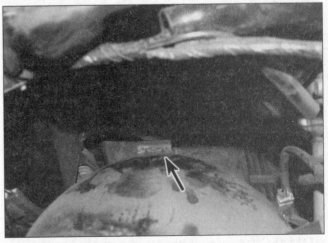

14.7d Separate the tab and slot at the front of the fender

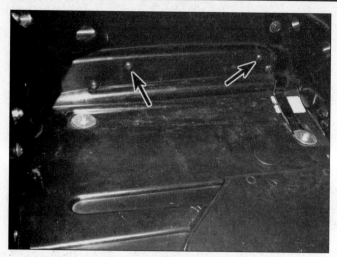

15.1a Inside the trunk, remove the two side molding screws (arrows)

15.1b Disengage the tab at the rear of the side molding . . .

2006 and later US, Australia, New Zealand and Brazil

Rear section

9   This is the same as for 2005 and earlier models, described in Steps 1 through 3 above.

Center section

10   Remove the seat (see Section 2).
11   Remove the rear section of the fender as described in Steps 1 through 3 above.
12   Unplug the amplifier connector and free the wiring harness from its retainers.
13   Free the drain hose from the support bracket. Unbolt the bracket crossmember behind the fender and take it off.
14   Have an assistant support the fender section and remove its two mounting bolts. Lift the fender off, freeing the amplifier harness from any remaining retainers as you do so.
15   Installation is the reverse of the removal steps.

Front section

16   Remove the saddlebags (see Section 16).
17   If you're working on a US model, remove the center section as described above.
18   If you're working on a Canadian model, unbolt the end piece from the stay bracket.
19   Free the wiring harness connector boots from the retainers on the fender. Detach the relay box from the front of the fender (see Chapter 9 if necessary).
20   Detach the following electrical components from the left side of the fender (see Chapter 9 if necessary): Starter relay switches, reverse regulator and heater control unit.
21   Remove the mounting bolt from each side of the fender (see illustration 14.7a).
22   Detach the retaining strap and disengage the hook at the front of the fender from its tab on the motorcycle (see illustrations 14.7b and 14.7d). Lift the fender off.
23   Installation is the reverse of the removal steps.

15 Trunk - removal and installation

Lower cover

1   With the trunk lid open, remove the two screws that secure each side molding to the trunk (see illustrations). Disengage the tab at the rear of each side molding from the center molding and remove the side moldings.
2   Remove two screws and detach the center molding from the trunk (see illustrations).
3   Remove the seven screws (two on each side and three across the back) that secure the lower cover to the trunk (see illustrations), slide it partway outward to free it, then remove it.
4   Installation is the reverse of the removal steps.

15.1c . . . and the tab at the front, then remove the molding

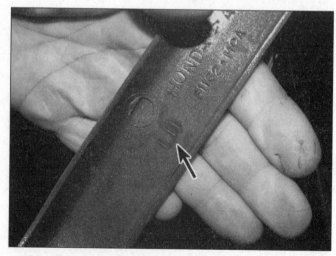

15.1d The moldings are marked LH and RH for left and right sides of the bike

Trunk lid

5   Remove the seat (see Section 2).
6   With the trunk lid open, disconnect its wiring harnesses and free them from their retainers **(see illustration)**.
7   Have an assistant support the trunk lid. Remove the mounting bolts and take the trunk lid off **(see illustration 15.6)**.

Trunk opener cover

8   With the trunk lid open, remove the five screws that secure the opener cover to the trunk lid and take the cover off **(see illustration)**.
9   Installation is the reverse of the removal steps.

Trunk

10   Remove the seat (see Section 2).
11   Remove the rear section of the rear fender (see Section 14).
12   Remove the trunk lower cover and trunk opener cover as described above.

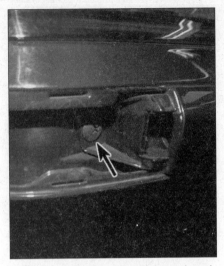

15.2a Remove the screw from each end of the center molding . . .

15.2b . . . then disengage the tabs along the center and take the molding off

15.3a Inside the trunk, remove two lower cover screws (arrows) from each side of the bike

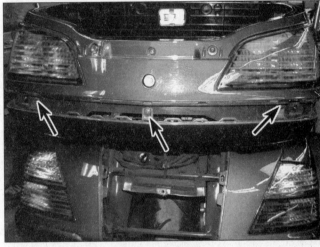

15.3b Remove three screws along the back edge of the lower cover (arrows) and pull the cover out

15.6 Free the wiring harness from its retainers and remove the hinge bolts (arrows)

15.8 Remove the opener cover screws (arrows)

15.14 Note how the wiring harnesses are routed under the trunk and unplug the connectors

15.15 Remove two bolts from each side of the trunk floor (left side shown)

15.16 Align the helmet lock handle shaft with the lock mechanism slot when installing the trunk (there's a helmet lock on each side of the trunk)

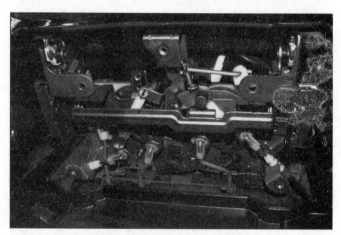

16.5a Trunk/saddlebag opener mechanism details

13   Detach the headset connector from its holder on the left side of the trunk. Free the harnesses from their retainers.

14   Under the trunk, disconnect the wiring harness connectors **(see illustration)**. Free

the harness from its retainers.

15   Inside the trunk, remove four mounting bolts and their washers from the trunk floor **(see illustration)**. Lift the trunk off.

16   Installation is the reverse of the removal

steps. Align the helmet lock shafts with the helmet locks as you lower the trunk into position **(see illustration)**.

16 Saddlebags - removal and installation

Saddlebag

1   Remove the seat (see Section 2).

2   Remove the side cover (see Section 7).

3   Remove the rear section of the rear fender (see Section 14).

4   Remove the trunk lower cover and opener cover (see Section 15).

5   Disconnect the saddlebag wiring connectors and opener cable, then free them from their retainers **(see illustrations)**.

6   Remove the saddlebag mounting bolts **(see illustration)**.

7   Lift the saddlebag off, remove its rubber mounts and bolt collars as you do so.

8   Installation is the reverse of the removal steps.

16.5b To disconnect an opener cable, release the end clip and swivel it away from the cable (arrow) . . .

16.5c . . . pull the cable end out with pliers and pull the cable fitting out of the bracket (arrow)

16.6 Saddlebag mounting bolt locations (arrows)

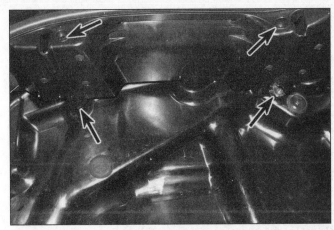

16.10 To remove a saddlebag latch, remove four screws (arrows) and take the inner cover out together with the latch mechanism . . .

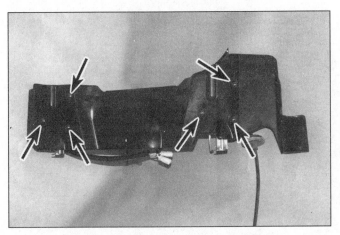

16.12a . . . remove six screws (arrows) . . .

16.12b . . . and separate the latch mechanism from the cover

Saddlebag latches

9   Remove the saddlebag as described above.
10   Remove the latch cover screws and take the latch cover off the upper inside of the saddlebag (see illustration).
11   Disconnect the saddlebag opener cable

(see illustrations 16.5b and 16.5c). Remove the latch cover, together with the latch mechanism.
12   Remove the screws and detach the latch mechanism from the inner cover (see illustrations). Installation is the reverse of the removal steps.

Saddlebag lower molding

13   The saddlebag lower molding is secured by three pull-type trim clips (see illustration). Pull the pins of the clips up, then pull the clips out of their holes (see illustration). Separate the molding from the saddlebag.

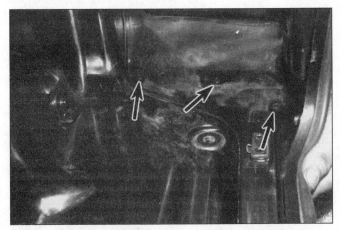

16.13a Working inside the saddlebag, pry the saddlebag lower molding clips up (arrows) . . .

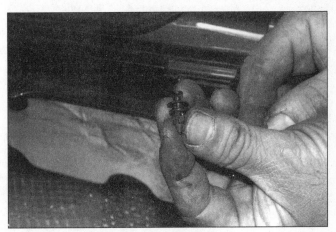

16.13b . . . and pull them out of the holes to free the molding from the saddlebag

16.16a Remove the liner-to-saddlebag clip . . .

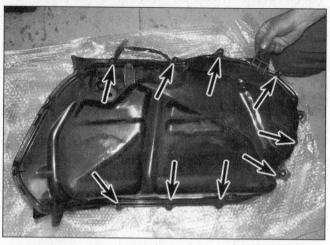

16.16b . . . and the screws that secure the liner to the saddlebag (arrows)

16.16c Pull the grommet out of the bolt hole

16.16d Push the wiring harness grommet into the hole and pull the harness through

6   If you're working on a Canadian model, remove two rear fender bolts.
7   Remove the rearmost muffler mounting bolts and their washers (see Chapter 4 if necessary). Support the mufflers with blocks of wood or straps.
8   Remove the six bolts and two nuts that secure the subframe and lift it off the bike.
9   Installation is the reverse of the removal steps.

18 Sidestand and centerstand - removal and installation

Sidestand

1   Make sure the motorcycle is securely supported before performing this procedure.
2   To remove the sidestand from the motorcycle, disconnect the switch wiring and free the harness from its retainer (see Chapter 9 if necessary). Remove the bracket bolts **(see illustration)** and take the sidestand off the motorcycle.
3   To remove the sidestand from the bracket, unhook the spring and remove it. Remove the switch (see Chapter 9), then

14   Installation is the reverse of the removal steps.

Saddlebag liner

15   Remove the saddlebag.
16   Remove the clip from the ridge at the bottom rear of the liner-to-saddlebag joint **(see illustration)**. Remove the screws that secure the liner to the outer saddlebag **(see illustration)**. Remove the grommet at the upper front mounting bolt hole **(see illustration)**. Push the wiring harness grommet through the hole into the saddlebag **(see illustration)**.
17   Installation is the reverse of the removal steps. Check the liner gasket and replace it if it's damaged or deteriorated **(see illustration)**.

17 Saddlebag and trunk subframe - removal and installation

1   Remove the trim cover from beneath each rear footrest (see Section 3).

2   Remove the trunk (see Section 15).
3   Remove the saddlebags (see Section 16).
4   On 2006 and later US, Australia, New Zealand and Brazil models, remove the center section of the rear fender (see Section 14).
5   Unbolt the rear crash bars (see Section 8).

16.17 If the seal between the liner and saddlebag is damaged or deteriorated, pull it out of its groove and push a new one in

18.2 Unplug the switch wiring and remove the bracket bolts (arrows) to remove the sidestand from the motorcycle

18.3 Unhook the spring from the posts, then remove the nut (arrow) and bolt (beneath the switch) to detach the sidestand from the bracket

18.6a Remove the Allen bolt (arrow) . . .

18.6b . . . and hex bolt (arrow) to detach the centerstand from the motorcycle

remove the nut and bolt that secure the sidestand to the bracket **(see illustration)**.

4   Installation is the reverse of the removal steps.

Centerstand

5   Make sure the motorcycle is securely supported before performing this procedure.

6   Remove the Allen bolt on the spring side (left side of the motorcycle) and the hex bolt on the right side **(see illustrations)**. Take the centerstand off.

7   Installation is the reverse of the removal steps.

Notes

Chapter 9
Electrical system

Contents

Degrees of difficulty

Easy, suitable for novice with little experience	**Fairly easy,** suitable for beginner with some experience	**Fairly difficult,** suitable for competent DIY mechanic	**Difficult,** suitable for experienced DIY mechanic	**Very difficult,** suitable for expert DIY or professional

Specifications

Battery

Capacity/type	
2008 and earlier	12 volts, 18 amp-hours
2009 and later	12 volts, 20 amp-hours
Specific gravity	Maintenance free
Maximum current leakage	5 milliamps
Open circuit voltage	
Standard (fully charged)	13.0 to 13.2 volts
Needs charging	12.3 volts or less
Charging current	
Normal charge	2.0 amps for 5 to 10 hours
Quick charge	10.0 amps for one hour

Charging system
Output .... 1.2 kw @ 500 rpm

Starter motor
Brush length
    Standard .... 12.5 mm (0.49 inch)
    Minimum .... 6.0 mm (0.24 inch)

Trunk opener
Transmitter battery CR2025

Bulb specifications
Headlight (high and low beam).. 55W
Front turn signal/position lights (US, Canada) 21/5W
Front turn signals (except US, Canada) 21W
Rear turn signals 21W
Taillights, tail/brake lights 21/5W
License plate light 3CP
Switch illumination lights.. 1.4W
Instrument cluster... LED

Torque specifications
Oil pressure switch... 12 Nm (108 inch-lbs)
Reverse switch .... 12 Nm (108 inch-lbs)
Alternator mounting bolts... 29 Nm (22 ft-lbs)
Starter mounting bolts.. Not specified
Airbag crash sensor mounting and cover bolts .... 12 Nm (108 inch-lbs)

1 General information

The motorcycles covered by this manual are equipped with a 12-volt electrical system.

The charging system uses a three-phase alternator with an integrated circuit regulator built in. The regulator maintains the charging system output within the specified range to prevent overcharging. The alternator diodes (rectifier) convert the AC (alternating current) output of the alternator to DC (direct current) to power the lights and other components and to charge the battery. The alternator is similar to an automotive alternator, with the field current being produced electromagnetically, rather than by permanent magnets as is common on smaller motorcycles.

An electric starter mounted to the back of the engine is standard equipment. The starting system includes the motor, the battery, the relay and the various wires and switches. If the engine kill switch and the ignition switch are both in the On position, the starting circuit allows the starter motor to operate only if the transmission is in Neutral (gear position switch indicating Neutral) or the clutch lever is pulled to the handlebar (clutch switch on) and the sidestand is up (sidestand switch on).

Note: *Keep in mind that electrical parts, once purchased, can't be returned. To avoid unnecessary expense, make very sure the faulty component has been positively identified before buying a replacement part.*

2.8 Several ground connections are at this terminal under the fuel tank (arrow)

3.2 Remove the bolt at the top of the battery retainer (arrow), then pivot the retainer downward

2 Electrical troubleshooting

A typical electrical circuit consists of an electrical component, the switches, relays, etc. related to that component and the wiring and connectors that hook the component to both the battery and the frame. To aid in locating a problem in any electrical circuit, refer to the wiring diagrams at the end of this Chapter.

Before tackling any troublesome electrical circuit, first study the appropriate diagrams thoroughly to get a complete picture of what makes up that individual circuit. Trouble spots, for instance, can often be narrowed down by noting if other components related to that circuit are operating properly or not. If several components or circuits fail at one time, chances are the fault lies in the fuse or ground connection, as several circuits often are routed through the same fuse and ground connections.

Electrical problems often stem from simple causes, such as loose or corroded connections or a blown fuse. Prior to any electrical troubleshooting, always visually check the condition of the fuse, wires and connections in the problem circuit. Intermittent failures can be especially frustrating, since you can't always duplicate the failure when it's convenient to test. In such situations, a good practice is to clean all connections in the affected circuit, whether or not they appear to be good. All of the connections and wires should also be wiggled to check for looseness which can cause intermittent failure. Unplug the electrical connectors in the circuit completely, then clean the terminals and reconnect them securely.

If testing instruments are going to be utilized, use the diagrams to plan where you will make the necessary connections in order to accurately pinpoint the trouble spot.

The basic tools needed for electrical troubleshooting include a test light or voltmeter, a continuity tester (which includes a bulb, battery and set of test leads) and a jumper wire, preferably with a circuit breaker incorporated, which can be used to bypass electrical components. Specific checks described later in this Chapter may also require an ohmmeter.

Voltage checks should be performed if a circuit is not functioning properly. Connect one lead of a test light or voltmeter to either the negative battery terminal or a known good ground. Connect the other lead to a connector in the circuit being tested, preferably nearest to the battery or fuse. If the bulb lights, voltage is reaching that point, which means the part of the circuit between that connector and the battery is problem-free. Continue checking the remainder of the circuit in the same manner. When you reach a point where no voltage is present, the problem lies between there and the last good test point. Most of the time the problem is due to a loose connection. Keep in mind that some circuits only receive voltage when the ignition key is in the On position.

One method of finding short circuits is to remove the fuse and connect a test light or voltmeter in its place to the fuse terminals. There should be no load in the circuit (it should be switched off). Move the wiring harness from side-to-side while watching the test light. If the bulb lights, there is a short to ground somewhere in that area, probably where insulation has rubbed off a wire. The same test can be performed on other components in the circuit, including the switch.

A ground check should be done to see if a component is grounded properly. Disconnect the battery and connect one lead of a self-powered test light (continuity tester) to a known good ground. Connect the other lead to the wire or ground connection being tested. If the bulb lights, the ground is good. If the bulb does not light, the ground is not good.

HAYNES HiNT *Several ground wires meet at a single location beneath the fuel tank (see illustration). This is a good place to look for circuit problems. Make sure all the terminals are free of corrosion and securely connected.*

A continuity check is performed to see if a circuit, section of circuit or individual component is capable of passing electricity through it. Disconnect the battery and connect one lead of a self-powered test light (continuity tester) to one end of the circuit being tested and the other lead to the other end of the circuit. If the bulb lights, there is continuity, which means the circuit is passing electricity through it properly. Switches can be checked in the same way.

Remember that all electrical circuits are designed to conduct electricity from the battery, through the wires, switches, relays, etc. to the electrical component (light bulb, motor, etc.). From there it is directed to the frame (ground) where it is passed back to the battery. Electrical problems are basically an interruption in the flow of electricity from the battery or back to it.

3 Battery - inspection and maintenance

1   Most battery damage is caused by heat, vibration, and/or low electrolyte levels, so make sure the battery is securely mounted, check the electrolyte level frequently (if the battery is a fillable unit) and make sure the charging system is functioning properly.

Removal and installation

2   Remove the left side cover (see Chapter 8). Remove the trim clip that secures the cover on the right side of the battery (the positive terminal side), then unbolt the top of the battery retainer and pivot it downward **(see illustration)**.

3.3a The negative battery cable terminal is bolted from the side like this . . .

3.3b . . . and the positive terminal fits like this - be sure to install the plastic cover over the terminal after it's connected

3   Pull back the cover from the battery positive terminal and disconnect the battery cables from the battery terminals, negative cable first, then positive **(see illustrations)**.
4   Remove the battery from the battery box and inspect it (see below).
5   Clean the inside of the battery box. If the battery box is damaged, remove it from the motorcycle for replacement.
6   Installation is the reverse of removal. Be sure to attach the positive cable first, then negative **(see illustrations 3.3a and 3.3b)**. Tighten the cables securely. Don't forget to put the protective cap back on the positive terminal **(see illustration 3.3b)**.

Inspection and maintenance

7   All machines covered in this manual are originally equipped with maintenance-free batteries.
8   Check around the base inside of the battery for sediment, which is the result of sulfation caused by low electrolyte levels. These deposits will cause internal short circuits, which can quickly discharge the battery. Look for cracks in the case and replace the battery if either of these conditions is found.
9   Check the battery terminals and cable ends for tightness and corrosion. If corrosion is evident, remove the cables from the battery and clean the terminals and cable ends with a wire brush or knife and emery paper. Reconnect the cables and apply a thin coat of petroleum jelly to the connections to slow further corrosion.
10   The battery case should be kept clean to prevent current leakage, which can discharge the battery over a period of time (especially when it sits unused). Wash the outside of the case with a solution of baking soda and water. Do not get any baking soda solution in the battery cells. Rinse the battery thoroughly, then dry it.
11   If acid has been spilled on the frame or battery box, neutralize it with the baking soda and water solution, dry it thoroughly, then touch up any damaged paint.
12   If the motorcycle sits unused for long

periods of time, disconnect the cables from the battery terminals. Charge the battery about once a month (see Section 4).

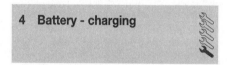

4   Battery - charging

1   If the machine sits idle for extended periods or if the charging system malfunctions, the battery can be charged from an external source.
2   Charging the maintenance-free battery used on these models requires a charger with a built-in ammeter.
3   When charging the battery, always remove it from the machine.
4   Disconnect the battery cables (negative cable first), then connect a digital voltmeter between the battery terminals and measure the voltage.
5   If terminal voltage is 13.0 volts or higher, the battery is fully charged. If it's lower, recharge the battery.
6   A quick charge can be used in an emergency, provided the maximum charge rates

5.1a Fuse functions and ratings are printed on the fuse block cover

and times listed in this Chapter's Specifications are not exceeded (exceeding the maximum rate or time may ruin the battery). A quick charge should always be followed as soon as possible by a charge at the standard rate and time.
7   Hook up the battery charger leads (positive lead to battery positive terminal, negative lead to battery negative terminal), then, and only then, plug in the battery charger.

⚠️ *Warning: The hydrogen gas escaping from a charging battery is explosive, so keep open flames and sparks well away from the area. Also, the electrolyte is extremely corrosive and will damage anything it comes in contact with.*

8   Allow the battery to charge for the specified time listed in this Chapter's Specifications. If the battery overheats or gases excessively, the charging rate is too high. Either disconnect the charger or lower the charging rate to prevent damage to the battery.
9   After the specified time, unplug the charger first, then disconnect the leads from the battery.
10   Wait 30 minutes, then measure voltage between the battery terminals. If it's 13.0 volts or higher, the battery is fully charged. If it's less than 12.3 volts, charge the battery again (refer to this Chapter's Specifications for charge rate and time). If it's less than 12.0 volts, it's time for a new battery.
11   When the battery is fully charged, unplug the charger first, then disconnect the leads from the battery. Wipe off the outside of the battery case and install the battery in the bike.

5   Fuses and relays - check and replacement

Fuses

1   These motorcycles have a fuse block containing accessory fuses and spares **(see**

5.1b Spare fuses are located inside the cover

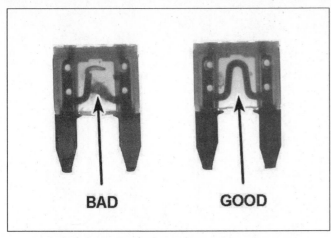

5.3 When the fuse blows, the element between the terminals melts

5.9a The relay box is under the seat - relay functions and ratings are printed on the box

5.9b Release the latches and lift the cover off . . .

5.9c . . . for access to the relays

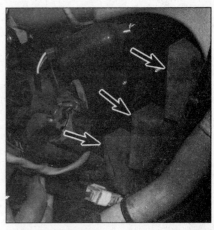

5.9d On 2001 through 2005 models, the speed limiter relay (top), power control relay no. 1 (center) and power control relay no. 2 (bottom) are located on the left side of the bike

illustrations). Fuse ratings and functions are printed on the cover. Spare fuses are mounted inside the cover.

2   If you have a test light, the fuses can be checked without removing them. Turn the ignition key to the On position, connect one end of the test light to a good ground, then probe each terminal on top of the fuse. If the fuse is good, there will be voltage available at both terminals. If the fuse is blown, there will only be voltage present at one of the terminals.

3   A blown fuse can usually be identified by a visible break in the element **(see illustration)**.

4   The accessory and main fuses can also be tested with an ohmmeter or self-powered test light. Remove the fuse and connect the tester to the ends of the fuse. If the ohmmeter shows continuity or the test lamp lights, the fuse is good. If the ohmmeter shows infi-

nite resistance or the test lamp stays out, the fuse is blown.

5   The accessory fuses can be removed and checked visually. If you can't pull the fuse out with your fingertips, use a fuse puller (available at auto parts stores) or a pair of needle-nose pliers. A blown fuse is easily identified by a break in the element.

6   If a fuse blows, be sure to check the wiring harnesses very carefully for evidence of a short circuit. Look for bare wires and chafed, melted or burned insulation. If a fuse is replaced before the cause is located, the new fuse will blow immediately.

7   Never, under any circumstances, use a higher rated fuse or bridge the fuse block terminals, as damage to the electrical system, including fire, could result.

8   Occasionally a fuse will blow or cause an open circuit for no obvious reason. Corrosion of the fuse ends and fuse block termi-

nals may occur and cause poor fuse contact. If this happens, remove the corrosion with a wire brush or emery paper, then spray the fuse end and terminals with electrical contact cleaner.

Relays

9   Most of the relays are located in a block under the seat **(see illustrations)**. In addition, there's a turn signal relay under the instrument panel visor **(see illustration 5.18)**. Remove the seat for access to the relay block or the instrument panel visor for access to the turn signal relay (see Chapter 8). The two starter relays are covered in Section 22. The power control relays and speed limiter relay on 2001 through 2005 models (used for the reverse system) are located next to the starter relays **(see illustration)**.

10   Relay functions and amperage ratings are printed on the outside of the relay box **(see illustration 5.9a)**.

5.11 Part numbers and continuity diagrams are printed on the relays

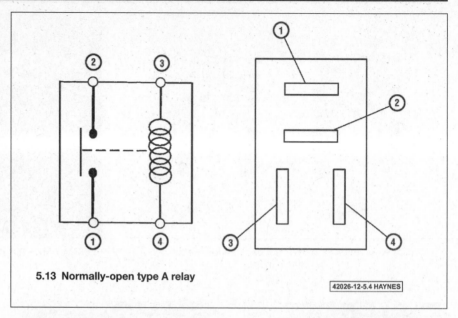

5.13 Normally-open type A relay

42026-12-5.4 HAYNES

11   The relays in the relay box have continuity diagrams and part numbers printed on them **(see illustration)**. Relays with the same part number are interchangeable with each other. On 2001 through 2005 models, the two power control relays and the speed limiter relay are all interchangeable with each other. The quickest way to test a relay is to remove the suspect relay and switch one of the other relays (with the same part number) into the suspect relay's position.

12   Relays can be tested with an ohmmeter or continuity tester and a 12-volt battery. You'll need a pair of jumper wires to connect the battery to the relay terminals. You can easily make these with spring clips and automotive wire, available at auto parts and hardware stores.

4-terminal relays (relay box)

13   These relays have four external spade terminals **(see illustration)**, arranged in two parallel rows, with two terminals per row.

14   To test a 4-terminal relay from the relay box, verify that there is no continuity between terminals no. 1 and 2 when the battery is not

connected to the relay. Then verify that there *is* continuity when the battery positive and negative terminals are connected to terminals no. 3 and 4, respectively.

Power control and speed limiter relays (2001 through 2005)

15   These relays **(see illustration 5.9d)** are normally-open 4-terminal relays, but their terminal arrangement is different from the relays in the relay box **(see illustration)**. To test a power control or speed limiter relay, verify that there is no continuity between terminals no. 1 and 2 when the battery is not connected to the relay. Then verify that there *is* continuity when the battery positive and negative terminals are connected to terminals no. 3 and 4, respectively.

5-terminal relays (relay box and position light relay)

16   Most of the 5-terminal relays are located

in the relay box. In addition, the position light relay is mounted at the front of the motorcycle under the instrument panel visor **(see illustration)**. This relay is the same type as the 5-terminal relays in the relay block, so you can test it by swapping a known-good 5-terminal relay from the relay block into the position light relay's location.

17   To test a 5-terminal relay, verify that there is continuity between terminal 1 and terminal 4 when the battery is not connected to the relay **(see illustration)**. Then, verify that there is continuity between terminals 1 and 2 when the battery positive and negative terminals are connected to relay terminals 3 and 5, respectively.

Turn signal relay

18   The turn signal relay is located under the instrument cluster on the right side. To locate it, remove the instrument panel visor (see Chapter 8). Follow the three pin connec-

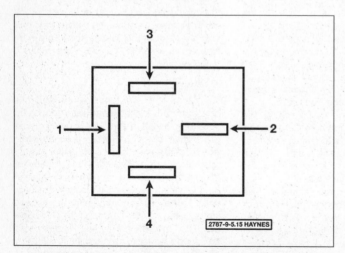

5.15 Power control and speed limiter relay terminals (2001 through 2005)

2787-9-5.15 HAYNES

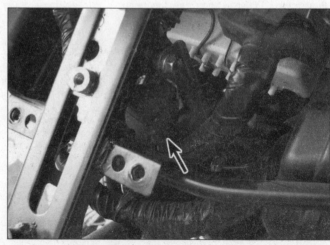

5.16 The position light relay (if equipped) is under the instrument panel visor on the left side (arrow)

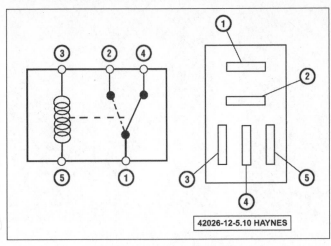

5.17 Five-terminal type B relay

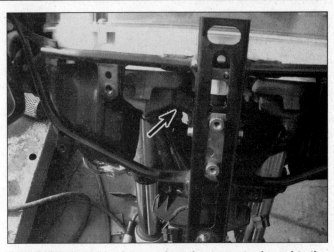

5.18 Follow the wiring harness from the connector (arrow) to the turn signal relay

tor (natural color on 2005 and earlier models; black on 2006 and later models) to the relay **(see illustration)**.

19   Disconnect the connector. Connect a voltmeter between the light-green/black wire's terminal in the harness side of the connector and a good ground (nearby bare metal). The voltmeter should indicate battery voltage. If not, check the fuse and circuit (see the earlier part of this Section and the wiring diagrams at the end of the manual).

20   With the ignition switch in the Off position and the relay connected to the connector, backprobe the blue-green wire's terminal with a jumper wire. Connect the end of the wire to a good ground. Turn the ignition on and operate the turn signals. The turn signals should blink. If not, check the ground side of the circuit. If it's good, replace the relay.

6   Lighting system - check

1   The battery provides power for operation of the headlight, position light, taillight, brake light, license plate light, instrument cluster lights and optional accessory lights. If none of the lights operate, always check battery voltage before proceeding. Low battery voltage indicates either a faulty battery, low battery electrolyte level or a defective charging system. Refer to Chapter 1 for battery checks and Sections 24 and 25 for charging system tests. Also, check the condition of the fuses and relays and replace any that are blown or not working correctly.

Headlight

2   If the headlight is out when the engine is running, check the fuse first with the key On (see Section 5), then unplug the electrical connector for the headlight and use jumper wires to connect the bulb directly to the battery terminals. If the light comes on, the prob-

lem lies in the wiring or one of the switches or relays in the circuit. Refer to Section 12 for the switch testing procedures, and also the wiring diagrams at the end of this Chapter.

Taillight/license plate light

3   If the taillight fails to work, check the bulbs and the bulb terminals first, then check for battery voltage at the taillight electrical connector. If voltage is present, check the ground circuit for an open or poor connection.

4   If no voltage is indicated, check the fuse and the wiring between the taillight and the ignition switch, then check the switch. Check the taillight relay as well.

Brake light

5   See Section 11 for the brake light switch checking procedure.

Neutral indicator light

6   If the neutral light fails to operate when the transmission is in Neutral, check the wiring for breaks or bad connections, referring to the wiring diagrams at the end of this

7.2a   Disconnect the wiring connector from the bulb housing . . .

manual. If the wires are good, refer to Chapter 4 and check the gear position sensor.

7   Headlight bulbs and housings - replacement

Bulb replacement

⚠ **Warning: If the bulb has just burned out, allow it to cool. It will be hot enough to burn your fingers.**

1   For access to the high beam bulbs, remove the fairing pocket (see Chapter 8). If the bike is an airbag model equipped with cruise control and you're replacing a right high beam, remove the cruise control actuator from the frame (see Section 31).

2   Unplug the electrical connector from the headlight **(see illustration)**. Note the position of the mark that indicates the top of the rubber dust cover and remove the dust cover from the headlight assembly **(see illustration)**.

7.2b   . . . and pull off the dust cover - the arrow or line (arrow) indicates the top

7.3a Release the clip (arrow) . . .

7.3b . . . and take out the bulb socket together with the bulb (don't touch the glass with your fingers) . . .

7.3c . . . then pull the bulb out of the socket

3   Lift up the retaining clip and swing it out of the way, then remove the bulb (see illustrations).

4   When installing the new bulb, reverse the removal procedure. Be sure not to touch the bulb with your fingers - oil from your skin will cause the bulb to overheat and fail prematurely. If you do touch the bulb, wipe it off with a clean rag dampened with rubbing alcohol.

Headlight assembly

5   Remove the front fairing from the motorcycle (see Chapter 8).

6   For access to the left headlight on an airbag model with cruise control, remove the reverse/cruise module from the fairing.

7   For access to the right headlight, remove the bank angle sensor (see Section 27).

8   Remove the headlight housing bolts and take the headlight assembly off (see illustration).

9   Installation is the reverse of the removal steps.

8   Headlight aim - check and adjustment

1   An improperly adjusted headlight may cause problems for oncoming traffic or provide poor, unsafe illumination of the road ahead. Before adjusting the headlight, be sure to consult with local traffic laws and regulations.

2   The headlight beam can be adjusted both vertically and horizontally. Before performing the adjustment, make sure the fuel tank is at least half full, and have an assistant sit on the seat.

3   Adjust the headlights to the maximum vertical position by turning the adjusting knob (non-airbag models) or by operating the adjuster switch (airbag models).

4   Vertical and horizontal adjustments can be made with the vertical and horizontal adjusting screws (see illustration).

9   Turn signals, taillight and trunk light bulbs - replacement

Front turn signal bulbs

1   Remove the screw from the underside of the mirror housing. Disengage the two tabs at the top and pull out the mirror.

2   Turn the bulb socket counterclockwise and remove it from the housing.

3   Pull the bulb straight out of the socket. Check the socket terminals for corrosion and clean them if necessary. Push the new bulb in the socket

4   The remainder of installation is the reverse of the removal steps.

Brake and taillights

Trunk-mounted

5   Working inside the trunk, remove three nuts that secure the light housing and take it off (see illustrations).

7.8 Remove the screws (arrows) and take the headlight housing off

8.4 Adjust the headlight with the vertical adjusting screw (left) and horizontal adjusting screw (right)

6   Turn the bulb socket counterclockwise and remove it from the housing (see illustrations). Pull the bulb straight out of the socket to remove it (see illustration). Check the socket terminals for corrosion and clean them if necessary.

Saddlebag-mounted

7   Working inside the trunk or saddlebag, remove three nuts that secure the light housing and take it off (see illustrations). Turn the bulb socket counterclockwise and remove it from the housing (see illustration). Pull the bulb straight out of the socket to remove it. Check the socket terminals for corrosion and clean them if necessary.

Rear turn signal bulbs

8   The rear turn signal bulbs are contained in the saddlebag combination light housings. They're replaced in the same manner as the brake and taillights, described above (see illustrations 9.7a, 9.7b and 9.7c).

9.5a Inside the trunk, remove the nuts (arrows) that secure the taillight housing . . .

9.5b . . . pull the housing out and if necessary, disconnect the wring connector

9.6a Twist the socket counterclockwise from its closed position (right arrows aligned as shown) until the pointer aligns with the round dot (left arrow) . . .

9.6b . . . then pull the socket out of the housing . . .

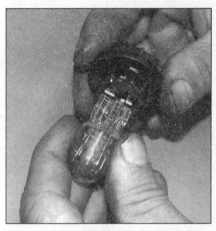

9.6c . . . and pull the bulb straight out of the socket

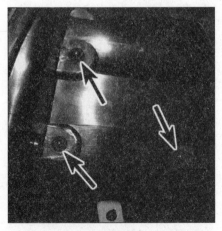

9.7a Inside the saddlebag, remove the nuts that secure the taillight housing (arrows)

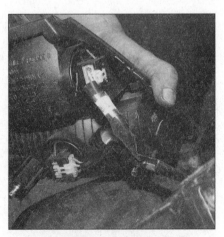

9.7b Remove the housing from the saddlebag . . .

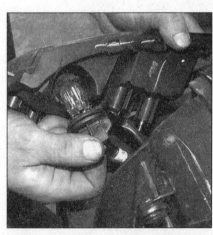

9.7c . . . twist the bulb socket and take it out, then pull the bulb straight out of the socket

License plate light

9   Remove the lens screws and take off the lens **(see illustration)**. Pull the bulb out of the socket, push in a new one and reinstall the lens **(see illustration)**.

Trunk light

10   Open the trunk lid. Squeeze the tab on the lens and lower it away from the lamp housing **(see illustration)**. Align the lever knob with the hole in the lens and take the lens off.
11   Carefully pry the bulb from the clips and push in a new one **(see illustration)**. Reinstall the lens.

10 Turn signal circuit - check

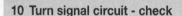

1   The battery provides power for operation of the signal lights, so if they do not operate, always check the battery voltage first. Low battery voltage indicates either a faulty battery or a defective charging system. Refer to Chapter 1 for battery checks and Sections 24 and 25 for charging system tests.
2   Most turn signal problems are the result of a burned out bulb or corroded socket. This is especially true when the turn signals function properly in one direction, but fail to flash in the other direction. Check the bulbs and the sockets (see Section 9).
3   Check the fuses and relay (see Section 5).
4   If the fuses and relay are okay, check the wiring in the turn signal circuit (see the wiring diagrams at the end of this Chapter). Make sure the connectors are clean and tight.

Self-canceling turn signal unit circuit check

5   Make sure the battery is fully charged and the fuses and wiring are in good condition before starting this test. You'll need an ohmmeter and a voltmeter.

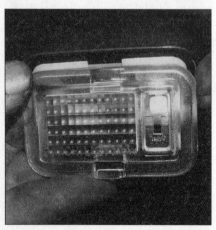

9.10 Squeeze the tab and take the trunk light lens off . . .

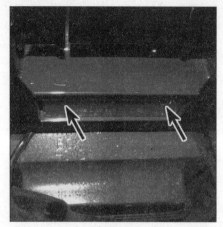

9.9a Remove the license plate light lens screws (arrows) . . .

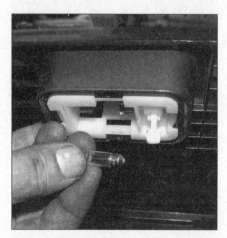

9.11 . . . then carefully pry the bulb out of its clips and push a new one in

6   Remove the instrument cluster (see Section 20). Remove the handlebar center cover and the cap from the steering stem nut (see Chapter 6).
7   Unplug the green connector (inside the steering stem) from the self-canceling unit.
8   Connect an ohmmeter between the green wire terminal and ground. It should indicate continuity. If not, follow the green wire to the ground terminal and check for breaks or bad connections.
9   Connect a voltmeter between the white-green terminal in the harness side of the connector and ground. When the ignition switch is turned on, the voltmeter should indicate battery voltage. If not, follow the wire to the horn/turn relay and check it for breaks or bad connections. If the wire is good, test the relay (see Section 5).
10   Connect an ohmmeter between the pink terminal and ground. With the turn signal switch in the left or right position, there should be continuity (little or no resistance). If not, check the turn signal switch (see Section 12).
11   Move the ohmmeter to the light green-white terminal. Now there should be continu-

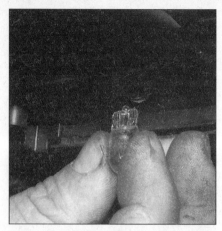

9.9b . . . take off the lens and pull the bulb straight out of the socket

ity with the switch pushed. If not, check the turn signal switch.
12   Place the bike on its centerstand so the rear wheel is slightly off the ground. Shift into neutral. Connect a voltmeter between the white-black terminal and ground. Turn the ignition switch on (but don't start the engine), then spin the rear wheel slowly. The voltmeter should cycle between zero and 5 volts. If not, follow the white/black wire from the green connector to the instrument cluster and check it for breaks or bad connections.
13   Once any problems found in Steps 8 through 12 have been corrected, reconnect the seven-pin green connector, then remove the front fairing (see Chapter 8). Locate the left 14-pin blue connector. Connect the voltmeter between the back side of the blue-black wire's terminal and ground and turn the ignition switch on. With the turn signal switch in the right or left position, the voltmeter should indicate zero volts. In the pushed position, it should indicate battery voltage.
14   If there is battery voltage in all switch positions (left, right and pushed), replace the turn signal canceling unit as described below. If there is no voltage, check the wiring for breaks or bad connections. If the wiring is good, check the turn signal diode as described below.

Self-canceling turn signal unit removal and installation

15   Disconnect the self-canceling unit's electrical connector as described in Steps 6 and 7 above.
16   Remove the angle sensor support plate screw.
17   Remove the self-canceling unit's retaining screws and take it off the bike **(see illustration)**.
18   Separate the upper and lower plates **(see illustration)**. Check all parts for wear and damage and replace the unit if problems are found.
19   Installation is the reverse of the removal steps.

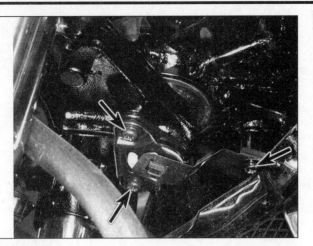

10.17 Remove the self-canceling unit's screws (arrows) and lower it out of the steering stem

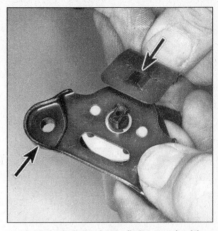

10.18 Install the boss (left arrow) with its flanges upward; fit the sensor plate (right arrow) securely over the end of the control unit

a) *Install the lower plate with its raised flanges upward (toward the control unit)* **(see illustration 10.18)**.
b) *Make sure the angle sensor plate fits tightly over the lower plate.*

Turn signal diode testing and replacement

20 Diode location varies depending on model and year. On 2005 and earlier models, it's under the seat **(see illustration)**. The diode looks like other diodes in the area, but it can be identified by its 3-pin natural-color connector. On 2006 and later non-airbag models, it's inside the left side of the fairing, wrapped in tape at the point the main wiring harness branches into three parts. It can be identified by its 3-pin orange connector. Remove the fuel tank top cover for access to the diode (see Chapter 8). On airbag models, the diode is behind the throttle body. Remove the fuel tank (see Chapter 4).
21 With the ignition switch off, unplug the diode from the harness.
22 Connect the positive probe of an ohmmeter to the center terminal and the negative probe to each of the side terminals in turn and note the readings. Reverse the ohm-meter connections (negative probe to center terminal; positive probe to each side terminal). The readings should be very low in one direction and very high in the other direction. If they're high or low in both directions, replace the diode with a new one.

11 Brake light switches - check and replacement

Circuit check

1 Before checking any electrical circuit, check the fuses and relays (see Section 5).
2 Using a test light connected to a good ground, check for voltage at the brake light switch **(see illustrations)**. If there's no voltage present, check the wire between the switch and the fuse box (see the wiring diagrams at the end of this Chapter). Note that on the front brake light switch, the upper (small) terminals are for the brake light - the lower (large) terminals, if equipped, are for the cruise control cancel switch.
3 If voltage is available, touch the probe of the test light to the other terminal of the

10.20 The turn signal diode can be identified by its connector (see text) - 2001 through 2005 diode shown (arrow)

switch, then pull the brake lever or depress the brake pedal - if the test light doesn't light up, replace the switch.

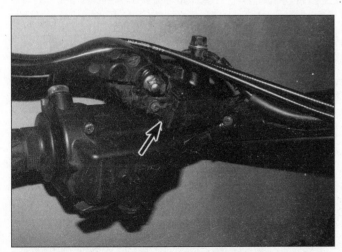

11.2a Check for voltage at the brake light switch (arrow) - the smaller (upper) switch terminals are for the brake light switch

11.2b Follow the wiring harness from the rear brake light switch (arrow) up to the connector and check for voltage

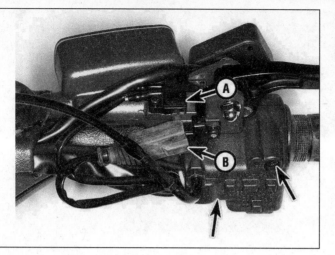

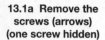

13.1a Remove the screws (arrows) (one screw hidden)

A   Clutch switch
B   Cruise cancel switch

13.1b Separate the upper and lower halves to expose the switches

4   If the test light does light, check the wiring between the switch and the brake lights (see the wiring diagrams at the end of this Chapter).

Switch replacement

Front brake lever switch

5   Remove the mounting screw and unplug the electrical connectors from the switch **(see illustration 11.2a)**.
6   Installation is the reverse of the removal procedure. The brake lever switch isn't adjustable.

Rear brake pedal switch

7   Remove the fuel tank top cover (non-airbag models), right top cover (airbag models) and right ventilation air duct (all models) (see Chapter 8). Unplug the electrical connector in the switch harness.
8   Unhook the switch spring **(see illustration 7.7 in Chapter 7)**.
9   Remove the switch screws and take the switch off the master cylinder **(see illustration 11.2b)**.
10   Install the switch by reversing the removal procedure, then adjust the switch by following the procedure described in Chapter 1.

12 Handlebar switches - check

1   Generally speaking, the switches are reliable and trouble-free. Most troubles, when they do occur, are caused by dirty or corroded contacts, but wear and breakage of internal parts is a possibility that should not be overlooked. If breakage does occur, the entire switch and related wiring harness will have to be replaced with a new one, since individual parts are not usually available.
2   The switches can be checked for continuity with an ohmmeter or a continuity test light. Always disconnect the battery negative cable, which will prevent the possibility of a

short circuit, before making the checks.
3   Trace the wiring harness of the switch in question and unplug the electrical connectors (you'll probably need to remove fairing panels to do this; see Chapter 8).
4   Using the ohmmeter or test light, check for continuity between the terminals of the switch harness with the switches in the various positions. Continuity should exist between the terminals connected by a solid line when the switch is in the indicated position.
5   If the continuity check indicates a problem exists, refer to Section 13, remove the switch and spray the switch contacts with electrical contact cleaner. If they are accessible, the contacts can be scraped clean with a knife or polished with crocus cloth. If switch components are damaged or broken, it will be obvious when the switch is disassembled.

Left handlebar switches

Headlight dimmer switch

6   Lo position - continuity between blue-white and white.
7   Hi position - continuity between blue-white and blue.

Horn switch

8   Free position - no continuity.
9   Pushed - continuity between white/green and light green.

Turn signal switch

10   Right turn position - continuity between gray and light blue; brown/white and orange/white; green and pink.
11   Left turn position - continuity between gray and orange; brown-white and light blue/white; green and pink.
12   Pushed (neutral) position - continuity between green and light green-white.

Right handlebar switches

Brake light switch

13   Lever pulled - continuity.
14   Lever released - no continuity.

Cruise main switch (if equipped)

15   Free position - no continuity.
16   Pushed and locked position - continuity between black/light green and black/yellow.

Cruise control resume-accel switch (if equipped)

17   Free position - no continuity.
18   Pushed position - continuity between white/blue and black/yellow.

Cruise control set-decel switch (if equipped)

19   Free position - no continuity.
20   Pushed position - continuity between white/blue and black/yellow.

Cruise cancel switch (if equipped)

21   Free position - no continuity.
22   Pushed position - continuity between white/blue and black/yellow.

Starter/reverse switch

23   Free position - continuity between brown/red and blue/white.
24   Pushed position - continuity between black/white and yellow/red.

Engine stop switch

25   On position - continuity between white and black/white.
26   Off positions - no continuity.

13 Handlebar switches - removal and installation

1   The handlebar switches are composed of two halves that clamp around the bars. They are easily removed for cleaning or inspection by taking out the clamp screws and pulling the switch halves away from the handlebars **(see illustrations)**.
2   To completely remove the switches, the electrical connectors in the wiring harness should be unplugged.
3   When installing the switches, make sure

15.2 Pull the rubber boot off the oil pressure switch, remove the terminal screw and disconnect the wire - unscrew the switch from the engine to remove it

16.9 The reverse position switch is on the right side of the engine, above the engine oil dipstick

the wiring harnesses are properly routed to avoid pinching or stretching the wires.

14 Clutch switch - check and replacement

Check

1 Disconnect the electrical connector from the clutch switch (see illustration 13.1a).
2 Connect an ohmmeter between the terminals in the clutch switch. With the clutch lever pulled in, the ohmmeter should show continuity (little or no resistance). With the lever out, the ohmmeter should show infinite resistance.
3 If the switch doesn't check out as described, replace it.

Replacement

4 If you haven't already done so, unplug the wiring connector. Remove the mounting screw and take the switch off (see illustration 13.1a).
5 Installation is the reverse of removal.

15 Oil pressure switch - removal, check and installation

Check

1 Remove the left horn (see Section 19).
2 Pull the rubber boot off the switch and disconnect the wire (see illustration).

Light doesn't come on

3 Connect the switch wire to ground (nearby bare metal), using a jumper wire if necessary. With the ignition switch in the On position, the light should come on.
4 If the light doesn't come on, check the wire from the switch to the instrument cluster

for breaks or bad connections.
5 If the light does come on, replace the switch with a new one as described below.

Light stays on or comes on while the engine is running

6 Connect an ohmmeter between ground (nearby bare metal) and the oil pressure switch wire. There should be no continuity with the engine running. If there is, check the switch wire for a short to ground. If there isn't, check the oil pressure (see Chapter 2). If the oil pressure is good, replace the switch.

Replacement

7 Unscrew the switch from the engine and clean the threads in the engine case.
8 Coat the threads of the new switch with sealant, but don't get any sealant on the last 1/8-inch of threads (those that go farthest into the engine). Thread the switch into the engine and tighten it to the torque listed in this Chapter's Specifications.
9 Connect the wire and reinstall the fairing under cover.
10 Refer to Chapter 1 and check the oil level.

16 Reverse actuator and position switch - check and replacement

Reverse actuator

1 Remove the air cleaner housing (see Chapter 4).
2 Disconnect the actuator electrical connectors (refer to the removal procedure in Chapter 2 if necessary).
3 Connect a voltmeter between ground and the brown wire's terminal in the wiring harness side of the red three-pin connector. Turn the ignition key to On (but don't start the engine). There should be battery voltage. If not, follow the brown wire to the reverse shift

actuator fuse in the fuse box and check it for breaks or bad connections.
4 Connect an ohmmeter between the brown and black/white wires' terminals in the actuator side of the three-pin connector.
5 With the actuator in the neutral position (see Chapter 2), there should be continuity (little or no resistance).
6 Place the actuator in the reverse position. To do this, use a pair of jumper wires to connect the motorcycle's battery positive terminal to the blue wire's terminal in the actuator side of the two-pin connector, and the battery negative terminal to the blue/red wire's terminal in the actuator side of the connector (if it won't shift when the battery is connected to it, replace the actuator as described below). With the actuator in the reverse position, there should be continuity between the brown and white/blue terminals in the actuator side of the three-pin connector.
7 If the actuator fails any test, replace the reverse shift actuator as described in Chapter 2. If it's good, check the reverse system wiring for breaks or bad connections. Refer to Chapter 2 and check the reverse system mechanical components.

Reverse position switch

8 Remove the right engine cover (see Chapter 8).
9 Pull back the rubber cover from the switch (see illustration). Unscrew the switch nut and disconnect the wire.
10 Unscrew the switch from the engine.
11 Push on the switch shaft (the part that protrudes from the threaded body). It should move freely and extend by itself. If not, replace the switch.
12 Connect an ohmmeter between the switch terminal and the end of the switch shaft. There should be continuity (little or no resistance). If not, replace the switch.
13 Installation is the reverse of the removal steps. Use a new sealing washer and tighten the switch to the torque listed in this Chapter's Specifications.

17.1a Here's the ignition switch connector . . .

17.1b . . . release the latch with a screwdriver to disconnect it

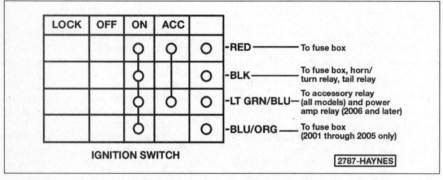

	LOCK	OFF	ON	ACC			
			○	○		○	—RED———— To fuse box
			○			○	—BLK———— To fuse box, horn/turn relay, tail relay
			○	○		○	—LT GRN/BLU— To accessory relay (all models) and power amp relay (2006 and later)
			○			○	—BLU/ORG —— To fuse box (2001 through 2005 only)

IGNITION SWITCH

2787-HAYNES

17.3 Ignition switch continuity diagram

equipped with an engine immobilizer system, remove the immobilizer receiver from the top of the ignition switch.

7   Disconnect the 10-pin black wiring connector. Remove the two ignition switch mounting bolts **(see illustration 17.6b)**. On 2006 and later models, remove the instrument cluster bracket and mounting plate. On all models, remove the ignition switch.

8   Installation is the reverse of the removal steps.

18 Sidestand switch - check and replacement

Check

1   Remove the left engine cover (see Chapter 8).

2   Follow the wiring harness from the sidestand switch at the top of the sidestand to the three-pin connector above the footpeg, then unplug the connector **(see illustration)**. Use an ohmmeter or test lamp to check for continuity between the pairs of terminals listed in the following steps (test the switch side of the connector, not the harness side).

   a) *Sidestand down - no continuity between green-white and green; continuity between yellow-black and green.*

   b) *Sidestand up - continuity between green-white and green; no continuity between yellow-black and green.*

3   If the switch fails either of these tests, replace it.

Replacement

4   Refer to Chapter 8 and remove the left engine cover (if not already done).

5   Undo the switch mounting bolt **(see illustration 18.2)**. Free the harness from its retainers and disengage it from the locating pin, then take it off the motorcycle.

6   Installation is the reverse of the removal procedure. Engage the switch slot with the locating pin.

17 Ignition main (key) switch - check and replacement

Check

1   If you're working on a non-airbag model, remove the fuel tank top cover (see Chapter 8). Disconnect the electrical connector from the switch and free the ignition switch wiring harness from its retainer **(see illustrations)**.

2   If you're working on an airbag model, remove the BARO sensor (see Chapter 4). Remove the cover from the ignition switch, free the wiring harness from its retainer and disconnect the electrical connector from the switch.

3   Using an ohmmeter, check the continuity between the terminal pairs indicated in the following steps **(see illustration)**. Test the switch side of the connector, not the wiring harness side.

   a) *Lock or off position - no continuity.*

   b) *Acc position - continuity between red and light-green black.*

   c) *On position - continuity between red, light green-black and black (all models) and blue/orange (2001 through 2005).*

4   If the switch fails any of the tests, replace it.

Replacement

5   If you haven't already done so, perform Step 1 or Step 2 above, then remove the top cover inner covers (see Chapter 8).

6   Remove two screws that secure the instrument cluster bracket and take it off **(see illustration)**. Remove two screws that secure the mounting plate under the ignition switch **(see illustration)**. Note that one of the bolts secures a wiring harness retainer. If you're working on a UK or European model

17.6a Remove the screws (arrows) and take off the instrument cluster bracket

17.6b Remove the mounting bolts (arrows) and take the ignition switch off

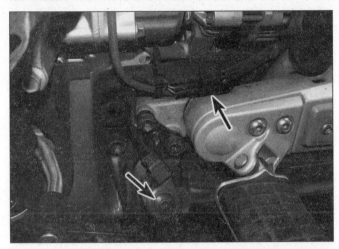

18.2 Disconnect the connector (upper arrow) to check continuity; remove the mounting bolt (lower arrow) to remove the switch

19.2 Disconnect the electrical connectors (arrows) from the horn (left horn shown)

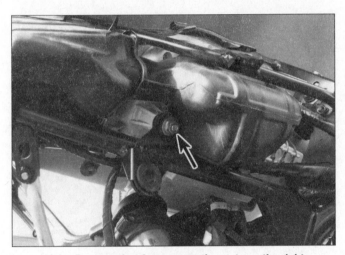

20.2a Remove the cluster mounting nuts on the right side (arrow) . . .

20.2b . . . on the left side (arrow) . . .

19 Horn - check and replacement

20 Instrument cluster - removal and installation

Check

1   Remove the lower front portion of the fairing for access (see Chapter 8).

2   Unplug the electrical connectors from the horn **(see illustration)**. Using two jumper wires, apply battery voltage directly to the terminals on the horn. If the horn sounds, check the switch (see Section 13) and the wiring between the switch and the horn (see the wiring diagrams at the end of this Chapter).

3   If the horn doesn't sound, replace it.

Replacement

4   Unbolt the horn from the motorcycle **(see illustration 19.2)** and detach the electrical connectors.

5   Installation is the reverse of removal.

2001 through 2005

1   Remove the front fairing (see Chapter 8).

2   Remove three nuts from the back side of the instrument cluster **(see illustrations)**.

2006 and later

3   Remove the instrument panel visor (see Chapter 8).

4   Remove the nut and washer from the back side of the instrument cluster.

5   Remove the mounting bolts from the front side of the cluster. The upper two bolts have washers.

All models

6   Pull the connector boots off the back of the instrument cluster to expose the wiring connectors **(see illustration 20.2c)**. Unplug

the connectors and lift the instrument cluster off the bracket.

7   Installation is the reverse of the removal steps.

20.2c . . . and in the center (lower arrow) - disconnect the wiring connectors (upper arrows) to free the cluster

21.3 Disconnect the fuel sender wiring connector (arrow)

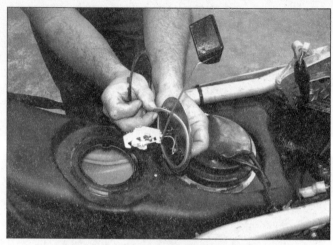

21.10 Lift out the sender unit and remove the gasket

---

21 Meters and gauges - check

Fuel level gauge

1   Check the speedometer, tachometer can coolant temperature gauge. If they're not working either, check the power and ground lines to the instrument cluster, referring to the wiring diagrams at the end of this manual.

2   If the other gauges are working, make sure the ignition key is in the Off position, then remove the seat (see Chapter 8).

3   Disconnect the wiring connector from the fuel level sender **(see illustration)**. Turn the key to On. The low fuel light should come on and the fuel gauge needle should point to E.

4   Turn the ignition key to Off. Connect a length of wire between the gray/black wire's terminal in the sender harness and ground (nearby bare metal). The low fuel light should stay out and the fuel gauge needle should point to F.

5   If, at this point, the low fuel light and the gauge indicate different fuel levels (for example, the low fuel light is on but the gauge needle points to F), remove the instrument cluster from the housing and replace it with a new cluster.

6   If the gauge has tested properly so far, continue testing as described in the following steps.

7   Follow the wires from the fuel level sensors to the instrument cluster and check the for breaks or bad connections. Make any necessary repairs and test the gauge again.

8   If you haven't already done so, disconnect the wiring connector from the fuel level sensor in the forward part of the fuel tank **(see illustration 21.3)**. Unbolt the top shelter bracket and lift it off the fuel tank.

9   Turn the retaining ring counterclockwise **(see illustration 21.3)**. Honda makes a special tool for this, but if you don't have

one, you can turn the ring by tapping it counterclockwise with a brass or hardwood drift positioned against one of its tabs.

10   Once the retaining ring is loose, lift out the fuel level sensor and remove the base gasket **(see illustration)**.

11   Connect an ohmmeter between the sensor terminals. Measure the resistance with the float in the down position, then in the raised position. Compare the readings with the values listed in this Chapter's Specifications. If they're not within the specified range, replace the sensor.

12   There's another fuel level sensor attached to the fuel pump unit. To check it, remove the fuel pump as described in Chapter 4. Connect an ohmmeter to the sensor terminals in the fuel pump connector and measure the resistance as described above. If it isn't within specifications, replace the fuel pump unit.

13   Installation is the reverse of the removal steps. Use a new fuel level sensor gasket and fit it securely into its groove **(see illustration)**.

Coolant temperature gauge

14   Refer to Chapter 3 for coolant temperature gauge checking procedures.

Tachometer and speedometer

15   Special instruments are required to properly check the operation of these meters. Take the instrument cluster to a Honda dealer service department or other qualified repair shop for diagnosis.

---

22 Starter relays - check and replacement

Check

1   Make sure the battery is fully charged and the relay wiring connections are clean

21.13 Place a new gasket in the groove before installing the sender unit

and tight. To prevent accidental movement of the motorcycle, make sure the kill switch and reverse shift switch are in the Off positions.

Starter relay A

2   Remove the left saddlebag (see Chapter 8).

3   Locate starter relay A on the left rear side of the bike **(see illustration)**. Turn the ignition switch to the on position, then press the starter-reverse button. The relay should click as the wire is connected and disconnected.

4   If the relay doesn't click, disconnect the wires and remove it from its mount **(see illustrations)**. Connect an ohmmeter to the two threaded posts on the relay. The ohmmeter should indicate no continuity (infinite resistance).

5   Connect the motorcycle's battery to the two flat terminals nearest the threaded posts. The ohmmeter should now indicate continuity (little or no resistance).

6   If the relay doesn't test correctly, replace it. If it does, but there's still a problem, check

22.3 The starter relays are located on the left side of the bike behind the battery

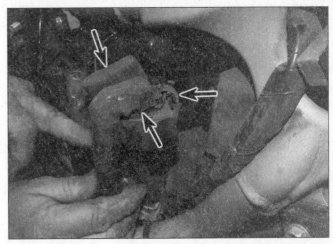

22.4a Pull starter relay B off its mounting bracket - lift the plastic caps and unscrew the terminal nuts, then follow the wiring harness to its connector and disconnect it

the wiring to the relay for breaks or bad connections, referring to wiring diagrams at the end of this Chapter.

Starter relay B

Note: *Test starter relay A and replace it if necessary before testing starter relay B.*

7   Remove the left saddlebag (see Chapter 8).
8   Turn the ignition switch to the on position, then press the starter-reverse button. The relay should click as the button is pressed and released **(see illustration 22.3)**.
9   If the relay doesn't click, disconnect the wires and remove it from its mount. Connect an ohmmeter to the two threaded posts on the relay. The ohmmeter should indicate no continuity (infinite resistance).
10   Connect the motorcycle's battery to the two terminals in the relay's wiring harness. The ohmmeter should now indicate continuity (little or no resistance).
11   If the relay doesn't test correctly, replace it. If it does, but there's still a problem, check

the wiring to the relay for breaks or bad connections, referring to wiring diagrams at the end of this Chapter.

Replacement

12   If you haven't already done so, remove the left saddlebag. Unplug the electrical connector from the relay and detach it from its mount **(see illustration 22.3)**.
13   Installation is the reverse of the removal steps.

---

23 Starter motor - removal and installation

⚠️ *Warning: Some models are equipped with an optional Supplemental Restraint System (SRS), more commonly known as an airbag. Whenever you're working in*

the vicinity of the fairing, fuel tank or the front forks, the system must be disarmed (see Section 32).

Removal

1   Remove the fuel tank (see Chapter 4).
2   Remove the right engine cover (see Chapter 8).
3   Unbolt the reverse cable bracket (and the ground cable terminal that's secured by one of the bracket bolts) **(see illustration 17.5 in Chapter 2)**. Unbolt the cable retainer that also secures the rear master cylinder reservoir bracket. Move the cables aside far enough to give access to the lower right starter mounting bolt.
4   Pull back the rubber cover, remove the nut retaining the starter cable to the starter and disconnect the cable **(see illustration)**.
5   Remove the starter mounting bolts **(see illustration 23.4 and the accompanying illustration)**.

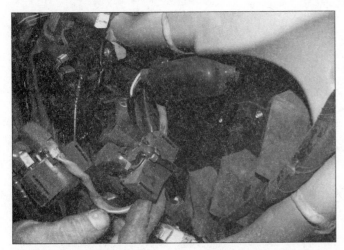

22.4b Remove starter relay A in the same way

23.4 Pull back the cover and unscrew the terminal nut (right arrow) - remove the top mounting bolt (upper arrow) and left mounting bolt (left arrow)

23.5 You'll need a ratchet, extension and universal adapter to reach the right mounting bolt (arrow)

23.6a Pull the starter to the rear until it clears the engine and inspect the O-ring (arrow) . . .

TOOL TiP *The lower right bolt can be reached from behind with a long extension and universal or an extension with a wobble socket (universal socket).*

6   Pull the starter backward out of the engine case **(see illustration)**. Tilt the rear end up and to the left and lift the starter out of the frame **(see illustration)**.

7   Check the condition of the O-ring on the end of the starter and replace it if necessary **(see illustration 23.6a)**. Also check the starter pinion gear and the driven gear inside the engine for chipped or worn teeth.

Installation

8   Apply a little engine oil to the O-ring and install the starter by reversing the removal procedure.

24 Charging system testing - general information and precautions

1   If the performance of the charging system is suspect, the system as a whole should be checked first, followed by testing of the individual components (alternator and regulator). **Note:** *Before beginning the checks, make sure the battery is fully charged and that all system connections are clean and tight.*

2   Checking the output of the charging system and the performance of the various components within the charging system requires the use of special electrical test equipment. A voltmeter and ammeter or a multimeter are the absolute minimum tools required. In addition, an ohmmeter is generally required for checking the remainder of the system.

3   When making the checks, follow the procedures carefully to prevent incorrect connections or short circuits, as irreparable damage to electrical system components

may result if short circuits occur. Because of the special tools and expertise required, it is recommended that the job of checking the charging system be left to a dealer service department or a reputable motorcycle repair shop.

Caution: Never disconnect the battery cables from the battery while the engine is running. If the battery is disconnected, the alternator will be damaged.

25 Charging system - leakage and output test

1   If a charging system problem is suspected, perform the following checks. Start by removing the left rear side cover for access to the battery (see Chapter 8).

Leakage test

2   Turn the ignition switch off and disconnect the cable from the battery negative terminal.

3   Set the multimeter to the a high range, then switch it down to the mA (milliamps) function and connect its negative probe to the battery negative terminal, and the positive probe to the disconnected negative cable.

Caution: Don't connect the ammeter between the battery terminals or the ammeter fuse will blow. Compare the reading to the value listed in this Chapter's Specifications.

4   If the reading is too high there is probably a short circuit in the wiring. Thoroughly check the wiring between the various components (see the wiring diagrams at the end of the book).

5   If the reading is satisfactory, disconnect the meter and connect the negative cable to the battery, tightening it securely. Check the alternator output as described below.

23.6b . . . then tilt the rear of the starter up and to the left and lift it out

Output test

6   Warm the engine to normal operating temperature, then shut it off.

7   Connect the positive terminal of a voltmeter to the battery positive terminal and the voltmeter's negative terminal to the battery negative terminal (leave the cables connected to the battery). The reading (with the engine off) is battery voltage. It should be at or above the minimum listed in this Chapter's Specifications. If not, refer to Sections 3 and 4 to check and charge the battery.

8   Start the engine. Switch on the high beam headlight and raise engine speed to 2000 rpm. With the voltammeter connected as it was in Step 7, measure charging voltage. It should be higher than battery voltage, but less than 15.5 volts.

9   If voltage doesn't increase above battery voltage, the charging system isn't charging the battery.

10   If voltage increases to more than 15.5 volts, the regulator has probably failed. Replace the alternator (see Section 26).

25.13a Disconnect the four-pin alternator connector (top) and pull back the rubber cover (bottom) . . .

25.13b . . . then unscrew the nut and disconnect the cable

Wiring harness check

11   Remove the left side cover and left engine cover (see Chapter 8).

12   Disconnect the negative cable from the battery. This is necessary to prevent sparks when the wires are disconnected in the next step.

13   Disconnect the cable and four-pin connector from the alternator **(see illustrations)**.

14   Reconnect the negative cable to the battery.

15   Connect a voltmeter between the battery terminals and note the reading (battery voltage).

16   Connect the voltmeter between the disconnected alternator cable and ground. It should indicate battery voltage at all times.

17   Connect the voltmeter between the black/yellow wire and ground. It should indicate battery voltage when the ignition switch is turned to the On position and the kill switch is turned to Run.

18   If you don't get the correct voltmeter readings, check the wires for breaks or poor connections.

26 Alternator - removal and installation

TOOL TiP *Access to the alternator bolts is restricted. A gear-type ratcheting wrench (see illustration) will be easier to use than a ratchet and socket. If you use a ratchet and socket, the total length of the socket and extension should be 108 mm (4-1/4 inches) (not counting the ratchet handle). This length is necessary to reach past the thermostat housing to remove the upper right bolt.*

1   Remove the fuel tank (see Chapter 4) and left engine cover (see Chapter 8). Disconnect the cable from the negative terminal of the battery.

2   Disconnect the alternator cable and 4-pin connector **(see illustrations 25.13a and 25.13b)**.

3   Remove the alternator mounting bolts

26.1 A ratcheting wrench will make it easier to remove the upper left bolt

(see illustration 26.1 and the accompanying illustrations).

4   Pull the alternator rearward into the

26.3a Remove the lower left bolt (arrow) . . .

26.3b . . . and the upper right bolt (arrow)

26.4a Pull the alternator straight back until it clears the engine and inspect the O-ring . . .

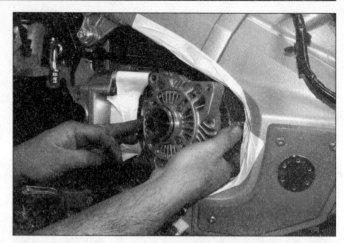

26.4b Then turn the front of the alternator toward the left side of the bike and take it out

frame, then lift it out of the bike **(see illustrations)**.

5   Inspect the alternator O-ring and replace if it's damaged or brittle.

6   If the alternator bearing is loose, rough or noisy, refer to Chapter 2 and replace it.

7   Installation is the reverse of the removal steps with the following additions:

a) *Coat the O-ring with multi-purpose grease* **(see illustration 26.4a)**.

b) *Tighten the alternator mounting bolts to the torques listed in this Chapter's Specifications.*

27 Bank angle sensor - removal and installation

Warning: The bank angle sensor is designed to shut off the fuel pump if the bike is tipped over. If it's defective, it can shut off the engine during a turn, possibly causing a crash. Have the sensor tested by a

Honda dealer if there's any doubt about its condition.

1   Remove the front fairing (see Chapter 8).

2   Locate the bank angle sensor and follow its wiring harness to the connector. Unplug the connector and remove the sensor mounting screws **(see illustration)**.

3   Take the air pressure sensor off the rear fender stay, then undo the bank angle sensor mounting screws and take it off the bike.

4   Installation is the reverse of the removal steps. Don't install the bank angle sensor upside down or the starter motor won't operate.

28 Radio and antenna - removal and installation

Antenna

Removal

1   To separate the antenna from the base pole, loosen the locknut and unscrew the antenna.

2   To remove the antenna cable, remove the seat (see Chapter 8). Locate the antenna cable connector **(see illustration)**. Unplug the connector and remove the cable).

3   To remove the base pole from the bike, remove the seat (see Chapter 8). Free the antenna cable and ground wire from their retainers, then follow them to the jack and connector and unplug them. Working inside the trunk, remove the trunk side pocket for access, then remove the base mounting bolts, washer and bracket and take the base off.

Installation

4   Installation is the reverse of the removal steps. Tighten the base bolts securely, but don't overtighten them and crack the base.

Radio

Non-airbag models

5   Remove the fuel tank top cover (see Chapter 8).

6   Remove ten screws that hold the front and rear halves of the top cover together.

7   Remove the radio screws **(see illustra-**

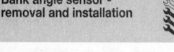

27.2 The bank angle sensor is secured by two screws (arrow)

28.2 Unplug the antenna cable connector (arrow) from the radio

28.7 Remove the screws (arrows) and detach the radio from the top cover

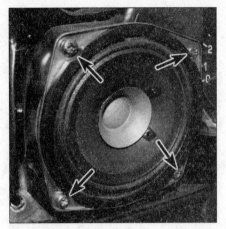

29.1a Remove the speaker screws (arrows), lift it out . . .

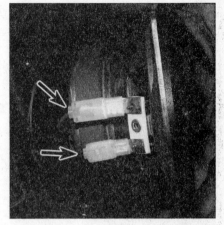

29.1b . . . and disconnect the wires (arrows)

tion). Take the radio off of the top shelter.
8   Installation is the reverse of the removal steps.

Airbag models

9   Remove the fuel tank top cover inner covers, the BARO sensor and the ECM (see Chapters 8 and 4). Remove the trim clip that secures the left intake air duct and remove it.
10   Remove the nut and bolt that secure the ECM bracket and taker it off the radio.
11   Disengage the radio from the airbag module and remove it toward the left side of the motorcycle.
12   Installation is the reverse of the removal steps.

29 Speakers - removal, check and installation

Removal

1   To remove a front speaker or tweeter, remove the instrument panel cover (see Chapter 8). Remove the retaining screws (front speaker) or tabs (tweeter), take the speaker out and disconnect its wires **(see illustrations)**.
2   To remove a rear speaker (if equipped), remove the inner cover from the trunk lid. Remove the armrest and unplug the speaker connectors. Release the tabs that secure the cover to the armrest, take it off, remove the speaker screws and take the speaker out.

Check

3   Connect a voltmeter to the wiring harness side of the speaker connector and set it to AC. With the radio on, there should be voltage. The reading should increase as radio volume is turned up. If not, check the

wiring from the speakers to the power amplifier, referring to wiring diagrams at the end of the manual.
4   Connect an ohmmeter to the speaker wire terminals. Resistance should be 3.8 ohms on all except Canadian models and 3 ohms on Canadian models.

Installation

5   Installation is the reverse of the removal steps. Position the drain slots in the edge of the speaker at top and bottom.

30 Tire pressure monitoring system - general information and precautions

General information

1   This system, used on 2009 and later models, monitors air pressure in the motorcycle's tires and illuminates a warning light on the instrument panel if the pressure drops too low.
2   The system consists of special wheels with tire pressure sensors built into the air valves, a receiver and two indicators on the instrument panel. The sensors send radio signals to the receiver (mounted on the right-hand radiator), which relays the signals to the instrument panel.
3   If air pressure in one of the tires drops too low, the low pressure light on the instrument panel will illuminate (the light doesn't indicate which tire is low). It starts blinking when tire pressure drops 10 per cent below the specified minimum, and stays on constantly when tire pressure drops 20 per cent below the specified minimum. If there's a problem with the system, the TPMS light will illuminate and stay on.
4   Both lights should illuminate briefly when the motorcycle is started, then turn off.

Precautions

5   Don't use aerosol tire sealants. They can interfere with the operation of the sensors.
6   The special wheels used with the system should never be replaced with wheels not designed for use with the system.
7   Changing tires requires a bead breaker and special techniques to prevent damage to the pressure sensors. Have the job done by a dealer service department or other qualified shop.

31 Cruise control system - general information and cable adjustment

General information

1   The cruise control system maintains the speed that you select until the depress the brake pedal or lever, squeeze the clutch lever, or turn the system off. The cruise control system consists of the following components:

   Cruise control switch (on the fairing)
   Front brake cancel switch (at the front brake lever)
   Clutch cancel switch (at the clutch lever)
   Rear brake cancel switch (at the brake pedal)
   Cruise/reverse control module (inside the fairing)
   Cruise/reverse control module (inside the fairing)
   Cruise actuator (inside the fairing)

2   The cruise control system is under the direct control of the cruise/reverse control module. When you select the speed that you want, the module takes control of the throttle plates within the throttle body. It maintains the selected speed with the cruise control actuator, which is connected to the throttle pulley on the throttle body by the actuator

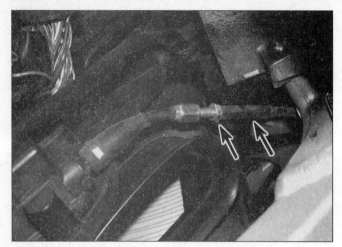

31.7 Loosen the locknut (left arrow) and turn the adjuster (right arrow) to adjust the cruise control cable

31.11 The tab (left arrow) and notch (right arrow) should line up when the cable is adjusted correctly

cable. The system maintains the selected speed until you turn it off, operate the brake or clutch lever, or press the brake pedal.

3   The diagnostic procedures for troubleshooting the cruise control system are beyond the scope of this manual, but the following troubleshooting procedures will help you identify common problems.

4   Check the fuses and relays (see Section 5).

5   Visually inspect the actuator cable between the cruise control actuator and the throttle body for freedom of movement. The cable should move freely, without sticking or binding. If the cable is kinked or frayed, replace it.

6   Test ride the motorcycle to determine if the cruise control is now working. It isn't, take the bike to a dealer service department or other qualified shop for further diagnosis.

Cable adjustment

7   Cable adjustment is checked at the throttle cable pulleys (on the left side of the throttle body). Adjustment is done at the adjuster near the cruise control actuator (see illustration).

8   If you're working on a 2005 or earlier model, remove the fuel tank top cover (see Chapter 8).

9   If you're working on a 2006 or later non-airbag model, remove the right inner fairing cover (see Chapter 8). Move the ECM and ABS control module out of the way.

10   If you're working on an airbag model, remove the left fuel tank top cover (see Chapter 8).

11   Look at the cable pulleys on the left side of the throttle body (see illustration). If the cable is adjusted correctly, the pointer on the cruise pulley will align with the notch in the throttle cable pulley. If not, locate the cable adjuster (see illustration 31.7). Loosen the locknut and turn the adjusting nut to align the notch and pulley, then tighten the locknut.

| 32 | Airbag system - general information |

General information

1   Some models are equipped with an optional Supplemental Restraint System (SRS), more commonly known as an airbag. This system is designed to protect the rider from serious injury in the event of a head-on or frontal collision. It uses four crash sensors, two on each side of the front fork. The airbag assembly is mounted on top of the fuel tank.

Airbag module

2   The airbag inflator module contains a housing incorporating the airbag and inflator unit. It's under a cover on top of the fuel tank. When a collision is detected, the inflator's electronic igniter causes nitrogen gas to fill the airbag. The airbag pushes through the cover as it expands. The airbag is secured to the bike's frame by tethers so it stays with the bike. The tethers unfold as the bag expands. The airbag is V-shaped at the rear to keep the rider in position.

SRS control unit

3   This unit supplies the current to the airbag system in the event of a collision, even if battery power is cut off. It checks this system every time the motorcycle is started, causing the SRS light to go on, then off, if the system is operating correctly. If there is a fault in the system, the light will go on and stay on, or it will flash. The control unit will store a diagnostic code to aid in locating the fault. If the airbag light stays on, take the motorcycle to a dealer immediately for service.

Disarming the system and other precautions

Warning: Failure to follow these precautions could result in accidental deployment of the airbag and personal injury.

4   Whenever you're working in the vicinity of the fairing, fuel tank or the front forks, the system must be disarmed. To disarm the system:

a) Turn the ignition switch to the Off position.

b) Disconnect the cable from the negative battery terminal.

c) WAIT AT LEAST THREE MINUTES FOR THE BACK-UP POWER SUPPLY TO BE DEPLETED.

5   Whenever you handle an airbag module, always keep the airbag opening side (the cover, or upper side) pointed away from your body. Never place the airbag module on a workbench or other surface with the airbag opening facing the surface. Always place the airbag module in a safe, dry location with the airbag module facing up.

6   Never measure the resistance of any SRS component of use any electrical test equipment on any of the wiring or components. An ohmmeter has a built-in battery (power supply) that could accidentally deploy the airbag.

7   Never use electrical welding equipment on a motorcycle equipped with an airbag without first disconnecting the airbag electrical connectors. These connectors - and all SRS component connectors - are bright yellow for easy identification.

8   Don't place any accessories, such as a compass or tank bag, on top of the airbag module cover or anywhere in the space between the seat and handlebars, even temporarily. These might prevent the airbag from opening properly, or they might cause injury if they're launched by a deploying airbag.

9   Never dispose of a live airbag module. Return it to a dealer service department or other qualified repair shop for safe deployment and disposal.

Airbag module removal and installation

10   Deactivate the airbag system as described in Step 4 above.
11   Move the ECM and radio out of the way (see Chapter 4 and Section 28). Remove the right intake air duct.
12   Disconnect the 4-pin electrical connector for the airbag inflator.
13   Unbolt the airbag ECU and cruise actuator from the right side of the airbag. Free their wiring harnesses from the retainers, disconnect the electrical connectors and set the airbag ECU and cruise actuator aside.
14   Unbolt the top cover support bracket (the one that straddles the fuel tank). The airbag tethers are attached to it.
15   Remove three Torx bolts that secure the airbag module and lift it off.
16   Installation is the reverse of the removal steps.

Crash sensor removal and installation

17   Deactivate the airbag system as described in Step 4 above.

Right crash sensors

18   Remove the right brake disc cover (see Chapter 8).
19   Free the crash sensor wiring harness from its retainers on the sensor cover, then unbolt the cover and take it off the fork leg.
20   Unbolt the caliper from the fork leg and support it out of the way (see Chapter 7).
21   Unplug the sensor wiring connectors (there are two sensors, upper and lower). Unbolt the sensors and remove them from the fork leg.
22   Installation is the reverse of the removal steps. Align the crash sensor locating pins with their holes. Tighten the crash sensor and cover mounting bolts to the torque listed in this Chapter's Specifications.

Left crash sensors

23   Remove the left brake disc cover for access to the lower sensor and the rear section of the front fender for access to the upper fender (see Chapter 8).
24   Remove the brake components (caliper, secondary master cylinder, lines and hoses) from the left fork leg and support them out of the way (see Chapter 7). Remove the secondary master cylinder's pivot bushings from the fork leg and caliper bracket.
25   Unplug the sensor wiring connectors (there are two sensors, upper and lower). Unbolt the sensors and remove them from the fork leg.
26   Installation is the reverse of the removal steps. Align the crash sensor locating pins with their holes. Tighten the crash sensor and cover mounting bolts to the torque listed in this Chapter's Specifications.

33 Power trunk lock system - testing and programming the transmitter

1   Here's how the system should work:
When you unlock the saddlebags or trunk lid with the transmitter, the turn signals will flash twice. When you lock them with the transmitter, the turn signals will flash once.

The turn signals won't flash at all if you lock or unlock the saddlebags or trunk lid, using the transmitter, while the ignition key is in the On or Acc position.

If a saddlebag or the trunk lid is open, you can't lock the lids with the transmitter. If you push the lock button, the turn signals will blink 10 times.

If you unlock the trunk lid or saddlebags with the transmitter, but don't open one of them within 30 seconds, they all re-lock automatically.

Holding down the CALL button on the transmitter for more than 1/2-second with the ignition key in the Off position will cause the horn to sound twice and the turn signals to flash twice. If the ignition key is in the On or Acc position, the CALL button will not cause the horns to sound or the turn signals to flash.

The POP-UP function won't work if the ignition key is in the On or Acc position.

Testing the transmitter

2   Aim the transmitter at the trunk and press the LOCK and UNLOCK buttons. If it doesn't work, try the other transmitter (if you have one). If the other transmitter works, go to Step 3.
3   Open the transmitter as described below and inspect it for water damage. If you see water damage, replace the transmitter. If there is no water damage, go to Step 4.
4   Replace the transmitter battery with a new battery as described below, then try to lock and unlock the trunk by pressing the LOCK and UNLOCK buttons five or six times. If the trunk lid locks and unlocks, the transmitter is OK. If not, go to the next Step.
5   Reprogram the transmitter as described below, then try to lock and unlock the trunk. If the trunk locks and unlocks, the transmitter is OK. If not, program the transmitter as described below.

Transmitter battery replacement

6   The battery cover is located on the opposite side of the transmitter from the buttons. Open it by turning slightly counterclockwise with a coin, then take the cover off.
7   Dump out the battery (don't touch it with fingers) and check the inside of the transmitter for corrosion and wetness. If these are found, try cleaning and drying the inside of the transmitter. If that doesn't help, replace the transmitter with a new one.
8   Install a new battery with its positive

terminal (labeled with a + mark) toward the cover (use a rag or paper towel and don't touch the battery with bare fingers). Place the cover on the transmitter so the arrowhead on the cover points to the double circle mark on the transmitter body. Turn the cover clockwise with a coin until the arrowhead aligns with the single circle mark on the transmitter body.

Programming the transmitter

9   This involves several steps, each of which must be done in not less than one second, but not more than four seconds. If you do any step too soon (before one second has elapsed) or too late (after four seconds have elapsed), the transmitter codes stored in the opener unit will be erased. Up to three transmitters can be programmed for one motorcycle. The trunk and saddlebags must be closed.
10   Place the key in the ignition. Operate the key with one hand and have the transmitter ready in the other hand. If you have additional transmitters that you want to program, place them where you can pick them up quickly.
11   Turn the ignition key to On, and between one and four seconds later, point the transmitter at the trunk and press the opener button.
12   One to four seconds later, turn the ignition key to Off.
13   One to four seconds later, turn the ignition key to On, point the transmitter at the trunk and press the opener button.
14   One to four seconds later, turn the ignition key to Off.
15   One to four seconds later, turn the ignition key to On, point the transmitter at the trunk and press the opener button.
16   One to four seconds later, turn the ignition key to Off.
17   One to four seconds later, turn the ignition key to On, point the transmitter at the trunk and press the opener button. This time, the turn signals should flash twice. Within 10 seconds, pick up any additional transmitter that you want to program, point the transmitter at the trunk and press the opener button. Do this with as many as two additional transmitters. Each time you press the opener button on an additional transmitter, the turn signals should flash.
18   Once you've programmed as many transmitters as you want, test them all the ignition switch in the Off position. The turn signals should flash, the trunk should lock and unlock, and the pop-up trunk lid function should work.

34 Engine immobilizer (UK and Europe) - general information and precautions

1   This system (which Honda calls the Honda Ignition Security System, or HISS) is used on UK and European models to pre-

vent theft. The ignition key is equipped with a transponder that activates the engine control module. A key of the proper pattern will turn the ignition switch, but if the correct transponder signal is not detected, the ECM will prevent the engine from starting. Diagnosing the system and programming new keys requires special equipment and should be done by a Honda dealer service department or other qualified shop.

2   The transponder built into the key requires special treatment to keep it from being ruined.

a) *Do not drop the key or strike it against a hard surface.*

b) *Do not expose the key to heat, such as sunlight coming through glass.*

c) *Do not expose the key to water (such as letting it go through the wash).*

d) *Keep other transponder-type keys (for other vehicles) away from the ignition key when you're starting the engine. The transponder signal from the other key may prevent the ECM from allowing the engine to start.*

3   Lost keys can be replaced, but the new key must be programmed to work with the ECM (it's not enough to cut the new key to the correct pattern). This requires an old key.

Caution: If all of the motorcycle's ignition keys are lost, the ECM must be replaced with a new one, in addition to replacing the keys. It isn't possible to program new keys without an old key.

Since the ECM is a very expensive component, it's a good idea to keep a spare key in a safe location, such as a safety deposit box.

4   If a new key is programmed using an old key, any other spare keys must be reprogrammed at the same time, since their transponder codes will no longer work.

5   As many as four keys can be programmed to work with the ECM.

35 Wiring diagrams

Prior to troubleshooting a circuit, check the fuses to make sure they're in good condition. Make sure the battery is fully charged and check the cable connections.

When checking a circuit, make sure all connectors are clean, with no broken or loose terminals or wires. When unplugging a connector, don't pull on the wires; pull only on the connector housings themselves.

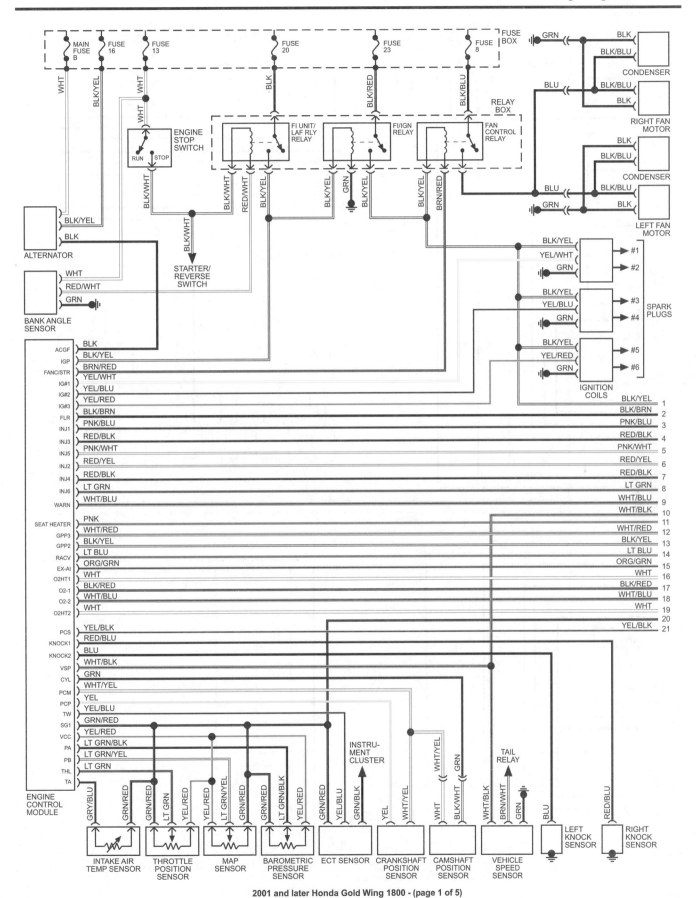

2001 and later Honda Gold Wing 1800 - (page 1 of 5)

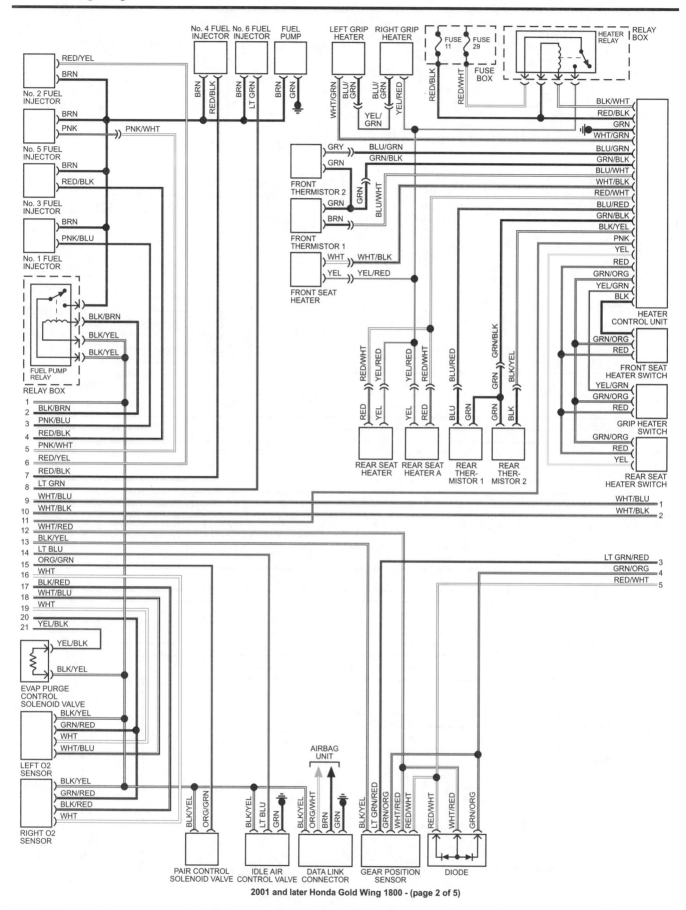

2001 and later Honda Gold Wing 1800 - (page 2 of 5)

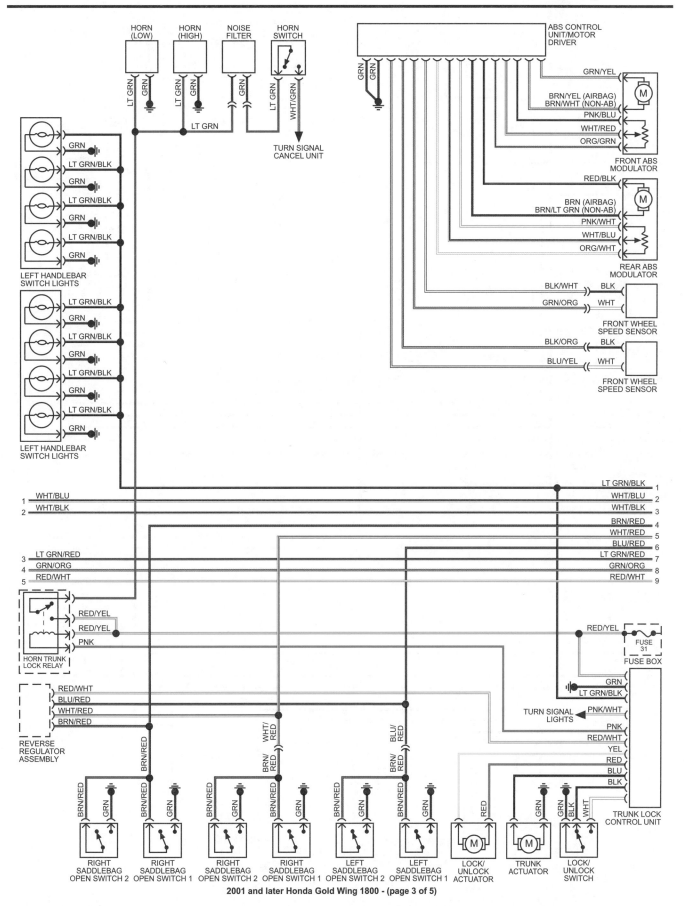

2001 and later Honda Gold Wing 1800 - (page 3 of 5)

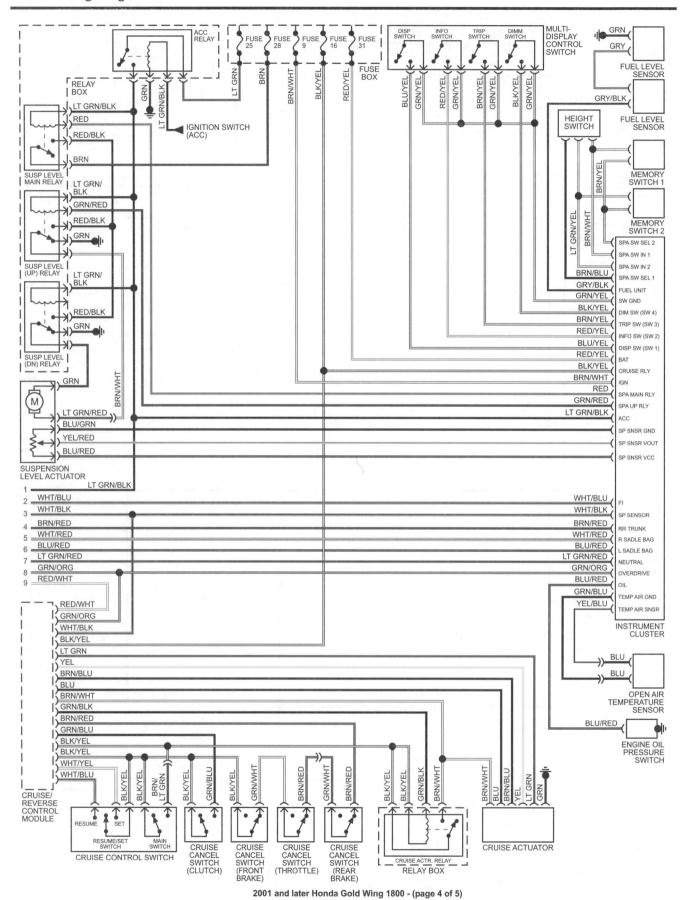

2001 and later Honda Gold Wing 1800 - (page 4 of 5)

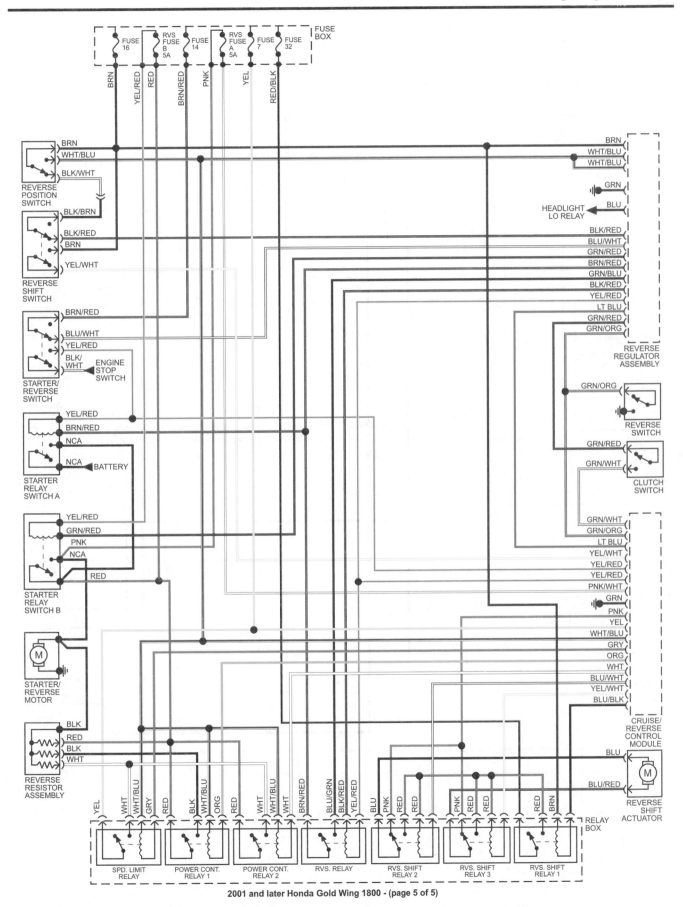

2001 and later Honda Gold Wing 1800 - (page 5 of 5)

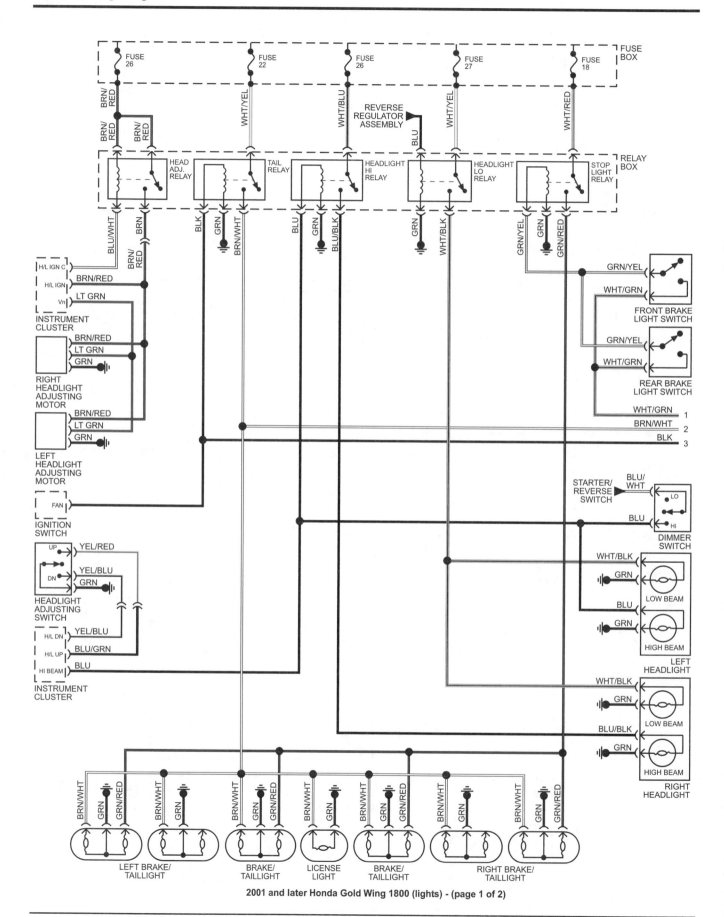

2001 and later Honda Gold Wing 1800 (lights) - (page 1 of 2)

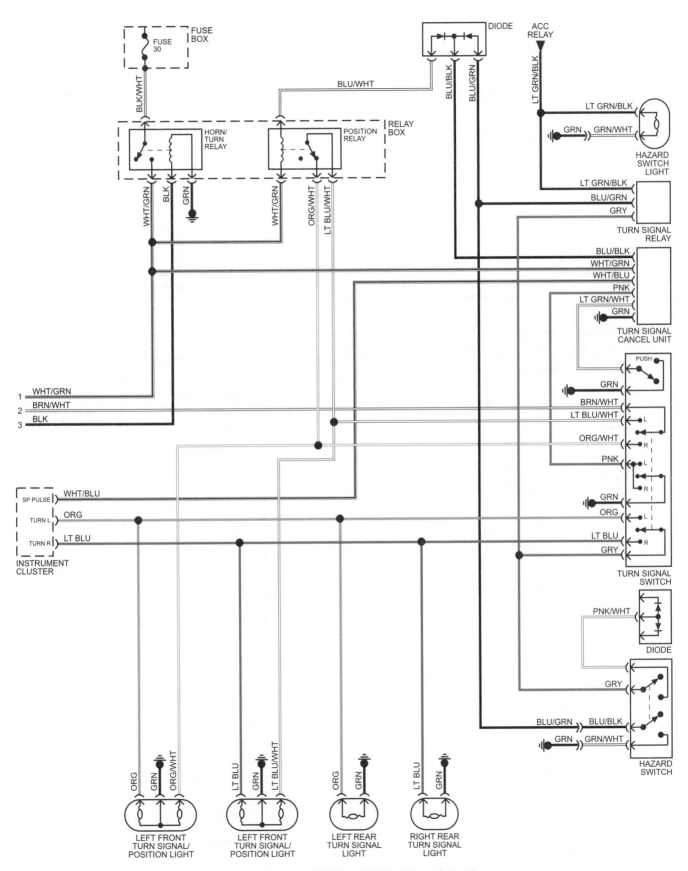

2001 and later Honda Gold Wing 1800 (lights) - (page 2 of 2)

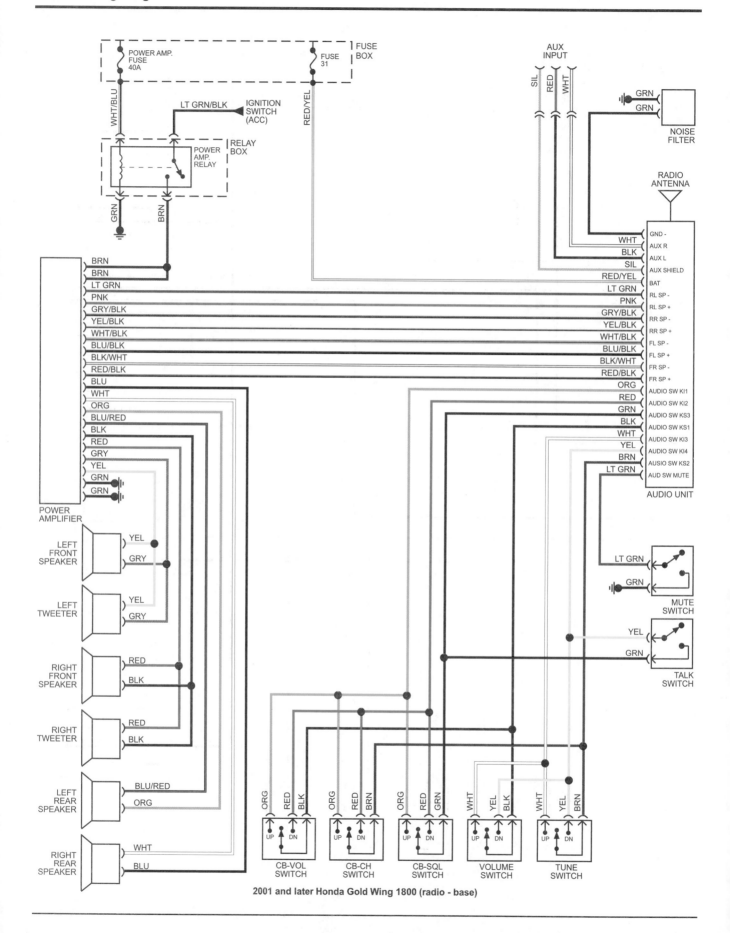

2001 and later Honda Gold Wing 1800 (radio - base)

Dimensions and weights

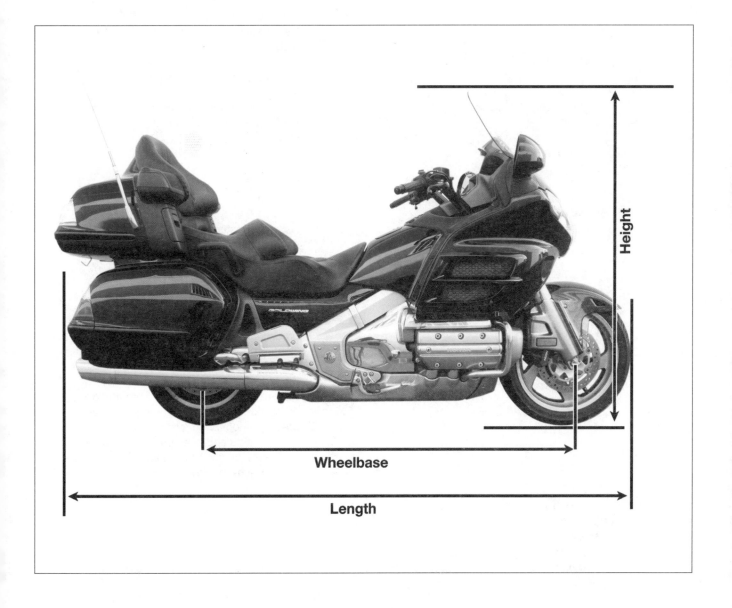

Model codes

On 2006 and later models, model codes are used to identify specific optional equipment.

US and Canada

2006 through 2008

Country codes

A .... US
CM .... Canada

Model and equipment

CM .... Heated grips and seat
IIIA .... Premium audio
IVA .... Heated grips and seat, premium audio
VA .... Heated grips and seat, premium audio, navigation system
VIA .... Heated grips and seat, premium audio, ABS, ultra low emissions
VIIA (US), IICM (Canada) .... Heated grips and seat, premium audio, ABS, ultra low emissions, navigation system
VIIIA (US), IIICM (Canada) .... Heated grips and seat, premium audio, ABS, ultra low emissions, navigation system, airbag

2009 and later

Country codes

A .... US
CM .... Canada

Model and equipment

IICM .... Heated grips and seat, premium audio, navigation system, ABS, tire pressure monitoring system
IIICM .... Heated grips and seat, premium audio, navigation system, ABS, airbag, tire pressure monitoring system
IVA .... Heated grips and seat, premium audio, tire pressure monitoring system
VA .... Heated grips and seat, premium audio, navigation system, XM radio, tire pressure monitoring system
VIIA .... Heated grips and seat, premium audio, navigation system, XM radio, ABS, tire pressure monitoring system
VIIIA .... Heated grips and seat, premium audio, navigation system, XM radio, ABS, airbag, tire pressure monitoring system

Except US and Canada

2006

Model code E

Country or region .... UK
Equipment .... Heated grips and seat, ABS, ultra low emissions

Model code F
- Country or region.. France
- Equipment .... Heated grips and seat, ABS, ultra low emissions

Model code ED
- Country or region.. European direct sales
- Equipment .... ABS, ultra low emissions

Model code IIED
- Country or region.. European direct sales Type II
- Equipment .... Heated grips and seat, ABS, ultra low emissions

Model code EK
- Country or region.. Ireland
- Equipment .... Heated grips and seat, ABS, ultra low emissions

Model code U
- Country or region.. Australia, New Zealand
- Equipment .... Heated grips and seat, ABS, ultra low emissions

Model code BR
- Country or region.. Brazil
- Equipment .... Premium audio, ABS, ultra low emissions

2007 and later

Model code E
- Country or region.. UK
- Equipment .... Heated grips and seat, ABS, ultra low emissions

Model code IIIE
- Country or region.. UK Type III
- Equipment .... Heated grips and seat, navigation system, ABS, airbag, ultra low emissions

Model code F
- Country or region.. France
- Equipment .... Heated grips and seat, ABS, ultra low emissions

Model code IIF
- Country or region.. France Type II
- Equipment .... Heated grips and seat, navigation system, ABS, airbag, ultra low emissions

Model code ED
- Country or region.. European direct sales
- Equipment .... ABS, ultra low emissions

Model code IIED
- Country or region.. European direct sales Type II
- Equipment .... Heated grips and seat, navigation system, ABS, airbag, ultra low emissions

Model code U
- Country or region.. Australia, New Zealand
- Equipment .... Heated grips and seat, ABS, ultra low emissions

Model codes

Except US and Canada (continued)

2007 and later (continued)

Model code IIU

Country or region.. Australia Type II, New Zealand Type II (2007 and 2008)

Equipment .... Heated grips and seat, navigation system (2009 and later Australia Type II), premium audio, ABS, airbag, ultra low emissions

Model code IINZ

Country or region.. New Zealand Type II (2009 and later)

Equipment .... Heated grips and seat, premium audio, navigation system, ABS, airbag, ultra low emissions

Model code BR

Country or region.. Brazil

Equipment .... Premium audio, ABS, airbag, ultra low emissions

Model code SI (2009 and later)

Country or region.. Singapore

Equipment .... Heated grips and seat, premium audio, navigation system, ABS, airbag, ultra low emissions

Model code KO

Country or region.. Korea

Equipment .... Heated grips and seat, premium audio, ABS, airbag, ultra low emissions

Frame and suspension

Wheelbase.. 1690 mm (66.5 inches)
Overall length... 2635 mm (103.7 inches)
Overall width.. 945 mm (37.2 inches)
Overall height... 1455 mm (57.3 inches)
Seat height... 740 mm (29.1 inches)
Dry weight
  2005 and earlier (US and Canada)
    Without ABS .... 359 kg (791 lbs)
    With ABS .... 362 kg (798 lbs)
  2005 and earlier (except US and Canada) .... 363 kg (800 lbs)
  2006 through 2008... Not specified
Curb weight
  2005 and earlier (US and Canada)
    Without ABS .... 399 kg (880 lbs)
    With ABS .... 402 kg (886 lbs)
  2005 and earlier (except US and Canada) .... 399 kg (880 lbs)
  2006 through 2008 (US and Canada)
    IIIA and CM.. 402 kg (886 lbs)
    IVA... 405 kg (893 lbs)
    VA, VIA.. 408 kg (899 lbs)
    VIIA, IICM.. 411 kg (906 lbs)
    VIIIA, IIICM.. 420 kg (926 lbs)

2009 and later (US and Canada)
    IVA.. 406 kg (895 lbs)
    VA .... 409 kg (902 lbs)
    VIIA, IICM.. 412 kg (908 lbs)
    VIIIA, IIICM... 421 kg (928 lbs)
2006 and later (except US and Canada)..................... Not specified
Front suspension .... Telescopic fork
    Left fork leg .... Damper rod
    Right fork leg .... Cartridge
Rear suspension .... Swingarm, single shock absorber/
coil spring with automatic leveling and
progressive rising rate linkage
Front brakes... Dual disc with three-piston sliding calipers
Rear brake .... Single disc with three-piston sliding
caliper
Brake hydraulic system .... Honda Linked Braking System with
optional anti-lock brakes
Fuel capacity.. 25 liters (6.6 US gal, 5.5 Imp gal)

Engine

Type .... Liquid-cooled, 4-stroke, single overhead
cam flat six
Displacement.. 1832 cc (111.8 cubic inches)
Compression ratio .... 9.8 to 1
Ignition system... Transistorized
Fuel system.. Multi-point sequential fuel injection with
dual-bore 40mm throttle body
Transmission.. Five-speed, constant mesh
Clutch .... Hydraulic release, wet multi-plate,
assisted by engine oil pressure

Buying tools

A good set of tools is a fundamental requirement for servicing and repairing a motorcycle. Although there will be an initial expense in building up enough tools for servicing, this will soon be offset by the savings made by doing the job yourself. As experience and confidence grow, additional tools can be added to enable the repair and overhaul of the motorcycle. Many of the special tools are expensive and not often used so it may be preferable to rent them, or for a group of friends or motorcycle club to join in the purchase.

As a rule, it is better to buy more expensive, good quality tools. Cheaper tools are likely to wear out faster and need to be replaced more often, nullifying the original savings.

 Warning: To avoid the risk of a poor quality tool breaking in use, causing injury or damage to the component being worked on, always aim to purchase tools which meet the relevant national safety standards.

The following lists of tools do not represent the manufacturer's service tools, but serve as a guide to help the owner decide which tools are needed for this level of work. In addition, items such as an electric drill, hacksaw, files, soldering iron and a workbench equipped with a vise, may be needed. Although not classed as tools, a selection of bolts, screws, nuts, washers and pieces of tubing always come in useful.

For more information about tools, refer to the Haynes *Motorcycle Workshop Practice Techbook* (Bk. No. 3470).

Manufacturer's service tools

Inevitably certain tasks require the use of a service tool. Where possible an alternative tool or method of approach is recommended, but sometimes there is no option if personal injury or damage to the component is to be avoided. Where required, service tools are referred to in the relevant procedure.

Service tools can usually only be purchased from a motorcycle dealer and are identified by a part number. Some of the commonly-used tools, such as rotor pullers, are available in aftermarket form from mail-order motorcycle tool and accessory suppliers.

Maintenance and minor repair tools

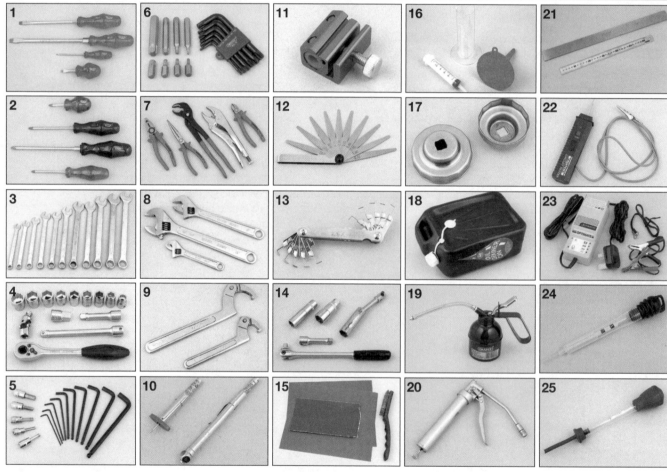

1 Set of flat-bladed screwdrivers
2 Set of Phillips head screwdrivers
3 Combination open-end and box wrenches
4 Socket set (3/8 inch or 1/2 inch drive)
5 Set of Allen keys or bits

6 Set of Torx keys or bits
7 Pliers, cutters and self-locking grips (vise grips)
8 Adjustable wrenches
9 C-spanners
10 Tread depth gauge and tire pressure gauge

11 Cable oiler clamp
12 Feeler gauges
13 Spark plug gap measuring tool
14 Spark plug wrench or deep plug sockets
15 Wire brush and emery paper

16 Calibrated syringe, measuring cup and funnel
17 Oil filter adapters
18 Oil drainer can or tray
19 Pump type oil can
20 Grease gun

21 Straight-edge and steel rule
22 Continuity tester
23 Battery charger
24 Hydrometer (for battery specific gravity check)
25 Antifreeze tester (for liquid-cooled engines)

Repair and overhaul tools

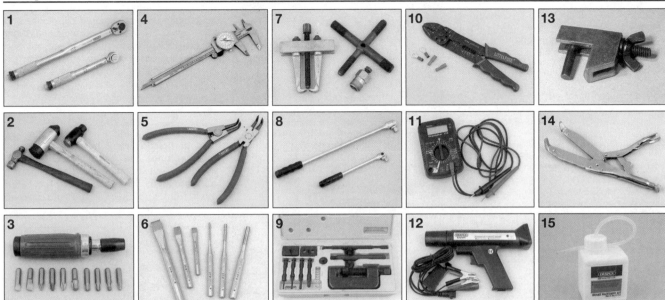

1 Torque wrench
   (small and mid-ranges)
2 Conventional, plastic or
   soft-faced hammers
3 Impact driver set

4 Vernier caliper
5 Snap-ring pliers
   (internal and external, or
   combination)
6 Set of cold chisels
   and punches

7 Selection of pullers
8 Breaker bars
9 Chain breaking/
   riveting tool set
10 Wire stripper and
   crimper tool

11 Multimeter (measures
   amps, volts and ohms)
12 Stroboscope (for
   dynamic timing checks)
13 Hose clamp
   (wingnut type shown)

14 Clutch holding tool
15 One-man brake/clutch
   bleeder kit

Special tools

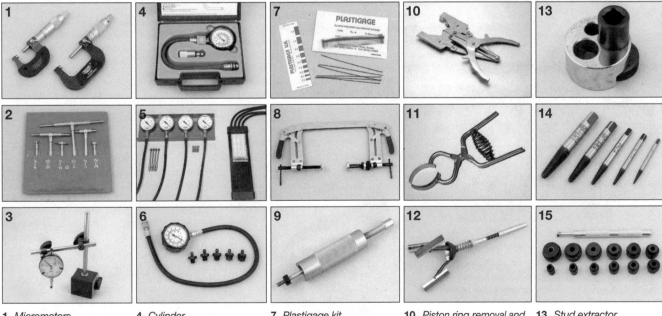

1 Micrometers
   (external type)
2 Telescoping gauges
3 Dial gauge

4 Cylinder
   compression gauge
5 Vacuum gauges (left) or
   manometer (right)
6 Oil pressure gauge

7 Plastigage kit
8 Valve spring compressor
   (4-stroke engines)
9 Piston pin drawbolt tool

10 Piston ring removal and
   installation tool
11 Piston ring clamp
12 Cylinder bore hone
   (stone type shown)

13 Stud extractor
14 Screw extractor set
15 Bearing driver set

1 Workshop equipment and facilities

The workbench

● Work is made much easier by raising the bike up on a ramp - components are much more accessible if raised to waist level. The hydraulic or pneumatic types seen in the dealer's workshop are a sound investment if you undertake a lot of repairs or overhauls **(see illustration 1.1)**.

1.1 Hydraulic motorcycle ramp

● If raised off ground level, the bike must be supported on the ramp to avoid it falling. Most ramps incorporate a front wheel locating clamp which can be adjusted to suit different diameter wheels. When tightening the clamp, take care not to mark the wheel rim or damage the tire - use wood blocks on each side to prevent this.

● Secure the bike to the ramp using tie-downs **(see illustration 1.2)**. If the bike has only a sidestand, and hence leans at a dangerous angle when raised, support the bike on an auxiliary stand.

1.2 Tie-downs are used around the passenger footrests to secure the bike

● Auxiliary (paddock) stands are widely available from mail order companies or motorcycle dealers and attach either to the wheel axle or swingarm pivot **(see illustration 1.3)**. If the motorcycle has a centerstand, you can support it under the crankcase to prevent it toppling while either wheel is removed **(see illustration 1.4)**.

1.3 This auxiliary stand attaches to the swingarm pivot

1.4 Always use a block of wood between the engine and jack head when supporting the engine in this way

Fumes and fire

● Refer to the Safety first! page at the beginning of the manual for full details. Make sure your workshop is equipped with a fire extinguisher suitable for fuel-related fires (Class B fire - flammable liquids) - it is not sufficient to have a water-filled extinguisher.

● Always ensure adequate ventilation is available. Unless an exhaust gas extraction system is available for use, ensure that the engine is run outside of the workshop.

● If working on the fuel system, make sure the workshop is ventilated to avoid a build-up of fumes. This applies equally to fume build-up when charging a battery. Do not smoke or allow anyone else to smoke in the workshop.

Fluids

● If you need to drain fuel from the tank, store it in an approved container marked as suitable for the storage of gasoline **(see illustration 1.5)**. Do not store fuel in glass jars

1.5 Use an approved can only for storing gasoline

or bottles.

● Use proprietary engine degreasers or solvents which have a high flash-point, such as kerosene, for cleaning off oil, grease and dirt - never use gasoline for cleaning. Wear rubber gloves when handling solvent and engine degreaser. The fumes from certain solvents can be dangerous - always work in a well-ventilated area.

Dust, eye and hand protection

● Protect your lungs from inhalation of dust particles by wearing a filtering mask over the nose and mouth. Many frictional materials still contain asbestos which is dangerous to your health. Protect your eyes from spouts of liquid and sprung components by wearing a pair of protective

1.6 A fire extinguisher, goggles, mask and protective gloves should be at hand in the workshop

goggles **(see illustration 1.6)**.

● Protect your hands from contact with solvents, fuel and oils by wearing rubber gloves. Alternatively apply a barrier cream to your hands before starting work. If handling hot components or fluids, wear suitable gloves to protect your hands from scalding and burns.

What to do with old fluids

● Old cleaning solvent, fuel, coolant and oils should not be poured down domestic drains or onto the ground. Package the fluid up in old oil containers, label it accordingly, and take it to a garage or disposal facility. Contact your local disposal company for location of such sites.

Note: It is illegal to dump oil down the drain. Check with your local auto parts store, disposal facility or environmental agency to see if they accept the oil for recycling.

2 Fasteners -
screws, bolts and nuts

Fastener types and applications

Bolts and screws

● Fastener head types are either of hexagonal, Torx or splined design, with internal and external versions of each type **(see illustrations 2.1 and 2.2)**; splined head fasteners are not in common use on motorcycles. The conventional slotted or Phillips head design is used for certain screws. Bolt or screw length is always measured from the underside of the head to the end of the item **(see illustration 2.11)**.

2.1 Internal hexagon/Allen (A), Torx (B) and splined (C) fasteners, with corresponding bits

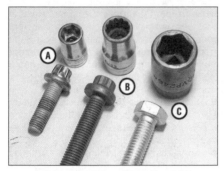

2.2 External Torx (A), splined (B) and hexagon (C) fasteners, with corresponding sockets

● Certain fasteners on the motorcycle have a tensile marking on their heads, the higher the marking the stronger the fastener. High tensile fasteners generally carry a 10 or higher marking. Never replace a high tensile fastener with one of a lower tensile strength.

Washers (see illustration 2.3)

● Plain washers are used between a fastener head and a component to prevent damage to the component or to spread the load when torque is applied. Plain washers can also be used as spacers or shims in certain assemblies. Copper or aluminum plain washers are often used as sealing washers on drain plugs.

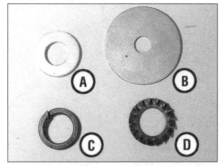

2.3 Plain washer (A), penny washer (B), spring washer (C) and serrated washer (D)

● The split-ring spring washer works by applying axial tension between the fastener head and component. If flattened, it is fatigued and must be replaced. If a plain (flat) washer is used on the fastener, position the spring washer between the fastener and the plain washer.
● Serrated star type washers dig into the fastener and component faces, preventing loosening. They are often used on electrical ground connections to the frame.
● Cone type washers (sometimes called Belleville) are conical and when tightened apply axial tension between the fastener head and component. They must be installed with the dished side against the component and often carry an OUTSIDE marking on their outer face. If flattened, they are fatigued and must be replaced.
● Tab washers are used to lock plain nuts or bolts on a shaft. A portion of the tab washer is bent up hard against one flat of the nut or bolt to prevent it loosening. Due to the tab washer being deformed in use, a new tab washer should be used every time it is removed.
● Wave washers are used to take up endfloat on a shaft. They provide light springing and prevent excessive side-to-side play of a component. Can be found on rocker arm shafts.

Nuts and cotter pins

● Conventional plain nuts are usually six-sided **(see illustration 2.4)**. They are sized by thread diameter and pitch. High tensile nuts carry a number on one end to denote their tensile strength.

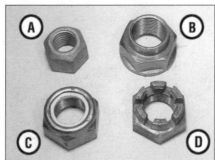

2.4 Plain nut (A), shouldered locknut (B), nylon insert nut (C) and castellated nut (D)

● Self-locking nuts either have a nylon insert, or two spring metal tabs, or a shoulder which is staked into a groove in the shaft - their advantage over conventional plain nuts is a resistance to loosening due to vibration. The nylon insert type can be used a number of times, but must be replaced when the friction of the nylon insert is reduced, i.e. when the nut spins freely on the shaft. The spring tab type can be reused unless the tabs are damaged. The shouldered type must be replaced every time it is removed.
● Cotter pins are used to lock a castellated nut to a shaft or to prevent loosening of a plain nut. Common applications are wheel axles and brake torque arms. Because the cotter pin arms are deformed to lock around the nut a new cotter pin must always be used on installation - always use the correct size cotter pin which will fit snugly in the shaft hole. Make sure the cotter pin arms are correctly located around the nut **(see illustrations 2.5 and 2.6)**.

2.5 Bend cotter pin arms as shown (arrows) to secure a castellated nut

2.6 Bend cotter pin arms as shown to secure a plain nut

Caution: If the castellated nut slots do not align with the shaft hole after tightening to the torque setting, tighten the nut until the next slot aligns with the hole - never loosen the nut to align its slot.

● R-pins (shaped like the letter R), or slip pins as they are sometimes called, are sprung and can be reused if they are otherwise in good condition. Always install R-pins with their closed end facing forwards **(see illustration 2.7)**.

2.7 Correct fitting of R-pin. Arrow indicates forward direction

Snap-rings (see illustration 2.8)

● Snap-rings (sometimes called circlips) are used to retain components on a shaft or in a housing and have corresponding external or internal ears to permit removal. Parallel-sided (machined) snap-rings can be installed either way round in their groove, whereas stamped snap-rings (which have a chamfered edge on one face) must be installed with the chamfer facing the thrust load (see illustration 2.9).

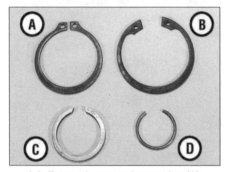

2.8 External stamped snap-ring (A), internal stamped snap-ring (B), machined snap-ring (C) and wire snap-ring (D)

● Always use snap-ring pliers to remove and install snap-rings; expand or compress them just enough to remove them. After installation, rotate the snap-ring in its groove to ensure it is securely seated. If installing a snap-ring on a splined shaft, always align its opening with a shaft channel to ensure the snap-ring ends are well supported and unlikely to catch (see illustration 2.10).

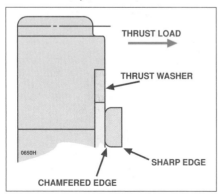

2.9 Correct fitting of a stamped snap-ring

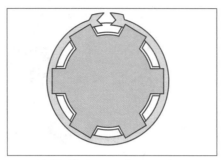

2.10 Align snap-ring opening with shaft channel

● Snap-rings can wear due to the thrust of components and become loose in their grooves, with the subsequent danger of becoming dislodged in operation. For this reason, replacement is advised every time a snap-ring is disturbed.

● Wire snap-rings are commonly used as piston pin retaining clips. If a removal tang is provided, long-nosed pliers can be used to dislodge them, otherwise careful use of a small flat-bladed screwdriver is necessary. Wire snap-rings should be replaced every time they are disturbed.

Thread diameter and pitch

● Diameter of a male thread (screw, bolt or stud) is the outside diameter of the threaded portion (see illustration 2.11). Most motorcycle manufacturers use the ISO (International Standards Organization) metric system expressed in millimeters. For example, M6 refers to a 6 mm diameter thread. Sizing is the same for nuts, except that the thread diameter is measured across the valleys of the nut.

● Pitch is the distance between the peaks of the thread (see illustration 2.11). It is expressed in millimeters, thus a common bolt size may be expressed as 6.0 x 1.0 mm (6 mm thread diameter and 1 mm pitch). Generally pitch increases in proportion to thread diameter, although there are always exceptions.

● Thread diameter and pitch are related for conventional fastener applications and the accompanying table can be used as a guide. Additionally, the AF (Across Flats), wrench or socket size dimension of the bolt or nut (see illustration 2.11) is linked to thread and pitch specification. Thread pitch can be measured with a thread gauge (see illustration 2.12).

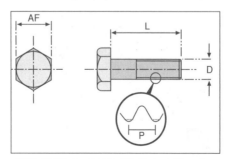

2.11 Fastener length (L), thread diameter (D), thread pitch (P) and head size (AF)

2.12 Using a thread gauge to measure pitch

AF size	Thread diameter x pitch (mm)
8 mm	M5 x 0.8
8 mm	M6 x 1.0
10 mm	M6 x 1.0
12 mm	M8 x 1.25
14 mm	M10 x 1.25
17 mm	M12 x 1.25

● The threads of most fasteners are of the right-hand type, ie they are turned clockwise to tighten and counterclockwise to loosen. The reverse situation applies to left-hand thread fasteners, which are turned counterclockwise to tighten and clockwise to loosen. Left-hand threads are used where rotation of a component might loosen a conventional right-hand thread fastener.

Seized fasteners

● Corrosion of external fasteners due to water or reaction between two dissimilar metals can occur over a period of time. It will build up sooner in wet conditions or in countries where salt is used on the roads during the winter. If a fastener is severely corroded it is likely that normal methods of removal will fail and result in its head being ruined. When you attempt removal, the fastener thread should be heard to crack free and unscrew easily - if it doesn't, stop there before damaging something.

● A smart tap on the head of the fastener will often succeed in breaking free corrosion which has occurred in the threads (see illustration 2.13).

● An aerosol penetrating fluid (such as WD-40) applied the night beforehand may work its way down into the thread and ease removal. Depending on the location, you may be able to make up a modeling-clay well around the fastener head and fill it with penetrating fluid.

2.13 A sharp tap on the head of a fastener will often break free a corroded thread

● If you are working on an engine internal component, corrosion will most likely not be a problem due to the well lubricated environment. However, components can be very tight and an impact driver is a useful tool in freeing them **(see illustration 2.14)**.

2.14 Using an impact driver to free a fastener

● Where corrosion has occurred between dissimilar metals (e.g. steel and aluminum alloy), the application of heat to the fastener head will create a disproportionate expansion rate between the two metals and break the seizure caused by the corrosion. Whether heat can be applied depends on the location of the fastener - any surrounding components likely to be damaged must first be removed **(see illustration 2.15)**. Heat can be applied using a paint stripper heat gun or clothes iron, or by immersing the component in boiling water - wear protective gloves to prevent scalding or burns to the hands.

2.15 Using heat to free a seized fastener

● As a last resort, it is possible to use a hammer and cold chisel to work the fastener head unscrewed **(see illustration 2.16)**. This will damage the fastener, but more importantly extreme care must be taken not to damage the surrounding component.

Caution: Remember that the component being secured is generally of more value than the bolt, nut or screw - when the fastener is freed, do not unscrew it with force, instead work the fastener back and forth when resistance is felt to prevent thread damage.

2.16 Using a hammer and chisel to free a seized fastener

Broken fasteners and damaged heads

● If the shank of a broken bolt or screw is accessible you can grip it with self-locking grips. The knurled wheel type stud extractor tool or self-gripping stud puller tool is particularly useful for removing the long studs which screw into the cylinder mouth surface of the crankcase or bolts and screws from which the head has broken off **(see illustration 2.17)**. Studs can also be removed by locking two nuts together on the threaded end of the stud and using a wrench on the lower nut **(see illustration 2.18)**.

2.17 Using a stud extractor tool to remove a broken crankcase stud

2.18 Two nuts can be locked together to unscrew a stud from a component

● A bolt or screw which has broken off below or level with the casing must be extracted using a screw extractor set. Centerpunch the fastener to centralize the drill bit, then drill a hole in the fastener **(see illustration 2.19)**. Select a drill bit which is approximately half to three-quarters the diameter of the fastener

2.19 When using a screw extractor, first drill a hole in the fastener . . .

and drill to a depth which will accommodate the extractor. Use the largest size extractor possible, but avoid leaving too small a wall thickness otherwise the extractor will merely force the fastener walls outwards wedging it in the casing thread.

● If a spiral type extractor is used, thread it counterclockwise into the fastener. As it is screwed in, it will grip the fastener and unscrew it from the casing **(see illustration 2.20)**.

2.20 . . . then thread the extractor counterclockwise into the fastener

● If a taper type extractor is used, tap it into the fastener so that it is firmly wedged in place. Unscrew the extractor (counter-clockwise) to draw the fastener out.

● Alternatively, the broken bolt/screw can

> ⚠ *Warning: Stud extractors are very hard and may break off in the fastener if care is not taken - ask a machine shop about spark erosion if this happens.*

be drilled out and the hole retapped for an oversize bolt/screw or a diamond-section thread insert. It is essential that the drilling is carried out squarely and to the correct depth, otherwise the casing may be ruined - if in doubt, entrust the work to a machine shop.

● Bolts and nuts with rounded corners cause the correct size wrench or socket to slip when force is applied. Of the types of wrench/socket available always use a six-point type rather than an eight or twelve-point type - better grip

2.21 Comparison of surface drive box wrench (left) with 12-point type (right)

is obtained. Surface drive wrenches grip the middle of the hex flats, rather than the corners, and are thus good in cases of damaged heads **(see illustration 2.21)**.

● Slotted-head or Phillips-head screws are often damaged by the use of the wrong size screwdriver. Allen-head and Torx-head screws are much less likely to sustain damage. If enough of the screw head is exposed you can use a hacksaw to cut a slot in its head and then use a conventional flat-bladed screwdriver to remove it. Alternatively use a hammer and cold chisel to tap the head of the fastener around to loosen it. Always replace damaged fasteners with new ones, preferably Torx or Allen-head type.

A dab of valve grinding compound between the screw head and screwdriver tip will often give a good grip.

Thread repair

● Threads (particularly those in aluminum alloy components) can be damaged by overtightening, being assembled with dirt in the threads, or from a component working loose and vibrating. Eventually the thread will fail completely, and it will be impossible to tighten the fastener.

● If a thread is damaged or clogged with old locking compound it can be renovated with a thread repair tool (thread chaser) **(see illustrations 2.22 and 2.23)**; special thread

2.22 A thread repair tool being used to correct an internal thread

2.23 A thread repair tool being used to correct an external thread

chasers are available for spark plug hole threads. The tool will not cut a new thread, but clean and true the original thread. Make sure that you use the correct diameter and pitch tool. Similarly, external threads can be cleaned up with a die or a thread restorer file **(see illustration 2.24)**.

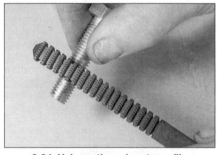

2.24 Using a thread restorer file

● It is possible to drill out the old thread and retap the component to the next thread size. This will work where there is enough surrounding material and a new bolt or screw can be obtained. Sometimes, however, this is not possible - such as where the bolt/screw passes through another component which must also be suitably modified, also in cases where a spark plug or oil drain plug cannot be obtained in a larger diameter thread size.

● The diamond-section thread insert (often known by its popular trade name of Heli-Coil) is a simple and effective method of replacing the thread and retaining the original size. A kit can be purchased which contains the tap, insert and installing tool **(see illustration 2.25)**. Drill out the damaged thread with the size drill specified **(see illustration 2.26)**. Carefully retap the thread **(see illustration 2.27)**. Install the

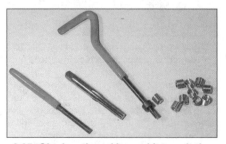

2.25 Obtain a thread insert kit to suit the thread diameter and pitch required

2.26 To install a thread insert, first drill out the original thread . . .

2.27 . . . tap a new thread . . .

2.28 . . . fit insert on the installing tool . . .

2.29 . . . and thread into the component . . .

2.30 . . . break off the tang when complete

insert on the installing tool and thread it slowly into place using a light downward pressure **(see illustrations 2.28 and 2.29)**. When positioned between a 1/4 and 1/2 turn below the surface withdraw the installing tool and use the break-off tool to press down on the tang, breaking it off **(see illustration 2.30)**.

● There are epoxy thread repair kits on the market which can rebuild stripped internal threads, although this repair should not be used on high load-bearing components.

Thread locking and sealing compounds

● Locking compounds are used in locations where the fastener is prone to loosening due to vibration or on important safety-related items which might cause loss of control of the motorcycle if they fail. It is also used where important fasteners cannot be secured by other means such as lockwashers or cotter pins.

● Before applying locking compound, make sure that the threads (internal and external) are clean and dry with all old compound removed. Select a compound to suit the component being secured - a non-permanent general locking and sealing type is suitable for most applications, but a high strength type is needed for permanent fixing of studs in castings. Apply a drop or two of the compound to the first few threads of the fastener, then thread it into place and tighten to the specified torque. Do not apply excessive thread locking compound otherwise the thread may be damaged on subsequent removal.

● Certain fasteners are impregnated with a dry film type coating of locking compound on their threads. Always replace this type of fastener if disturbed.

● Anti-seize compounds, such as copper-based greases, can be applied to protect threads from seizure due to extreme heat and corrosion. A common instance is spark plug threads and exhaust system fasteners.

3 Measuring tools and gauges

Feeler gauges

● Feeler gauges (or blades) are used for measuring small gaps and clearances (see illustration 3.1). They can also be used to measure endfloat (sideplay) of a component on a shaft where access is not possible with a dial gauge.

● Feeler gauge sets should be treated with care and not bent or damaged. They are etched with their size on one face. Keep them clean and very lightly oiled to prevent corrosion build-up.

3.1 Feeler gauges are used for measuring small gaps and clearances - thickness is marked on one face of gauge

● When measuring a clearance, select a gauge which is a light sliding fit between the two components. You may need to use two gauges together to measure the clearance accurately.

Micrometers

● A micrometer is a precision tool capable of measuring to 0.01 or 0.001 of a millimeter. It should always be stored in its case and not in the general toolbox. It must be kept clean and never dropped, otherwise its frame or measuring anvils could be distorted resulting in inaccurate readings.

● External micrometers are used for measuring outside diameters of components and have many more applications than internal micrometers. Micrometers are available in different size ranges, typically 0 to 25 mm, 25 to 50 mm, and upwards in 25 mm steps; some large micrometers have interchangeable anvils to allow a range of measurements to be taken. Generally the largest precision measurement you are likely to take on a motorcycle is the piston diameter.

● Internal micrometers (or bore micrometers) are used for measuring inside diameters, such as valve guides and cylinder bores. Telescoping gauges and small hole gauges are used in conjunction with an external micrometer, whereas the more expensive internal micrometers have their own measuring device.

External micrometer

Note: *The conventional analogue type instrument is described. Although much easier to read, digital micrometers are considerably more expensive.*

● Always check the calibration of the micrometer before use. With the anvils closed (0 to 25 mm type) or set over a test gauge

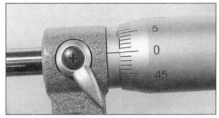

3.2 Check micrometer calibration before use

(for the larger types) the scale should read zero (see illustration 3.2); make sure that the anvils (and test piece) are clean first. Any discrepancy can be adjusted by referring to the instructions supplied with the tool. Remember that the micrometer is a precision measuring tool - don't force the anvils closed, use the ratchet (4) on the end of the micrometer to close it. In this way, a measured force is always applied.

● To use, first make sure that the item being measured is clean. Place the anvil (1) against the item and use the thimble (2) to bring the spindle (3) lightly into contact with the other side of the item (see illustration 3.3). Don't tighten the thimble down because this will damage the micrometer - instead use the ratchet (4) on the end of the micrometer. The ratchet mechanism applies a measured force preventing damage to the instrument.

● The micrometer is read by referring to the linear scale on the sleeve and the annular scale on the thimble. Read off the sleeve first to obtain the base measurement, then add the fine measurement from the thimble to obtain the overall reading. The linear scale on the sleeve represents the measuring range of the micrometer (eg 0 to 25 mm). The annular scale

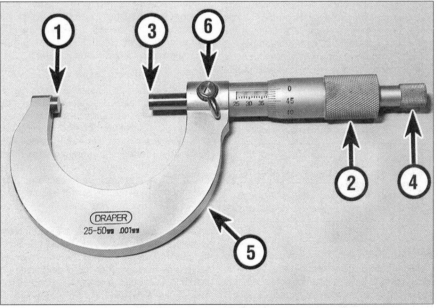

3.3 Micrometer component parts

1 Anvil	3 Spindle	5 Frame
2 Thimble	4 Ratchet	6 Locking lever

on the thimble will be in graduations of 0.01 mm (or as marked on the frame) - one full revolution of the thimble will move 0.5 mm on the linear scale. Take the reading where the datum line on the sleeve intersects the thimble's scale. Always position the eye directly above the scale otherwise an inaccurate reading will result.

In the example shown the item measures 2.95 mm **(see illustration 3.4)**:

Linear scale	2.00 mm
Linear scale	0.50 mm
Annular scale	0.45 mm
Total figure	**2.95 mm**

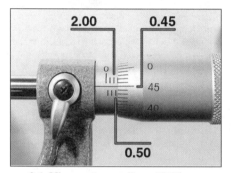

3.4 Micrometer reading of 2.95 mm

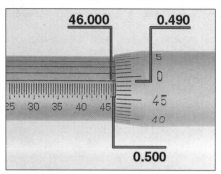

3.5 Micrometer reading of 46.99 mm on linear and annular scales . . .

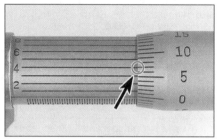

3.6 . . . and 0.004 mm on vernier scale

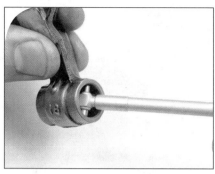

3.7 Expand the telescoping gauge in the bore, lock its position . . .

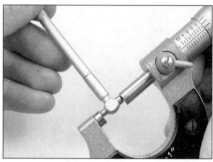

3.8 . . . then measure the gauge with a micrometer

Most micrometers have a locking lever (6) on the frame to hold the setting in place, allowing the item to be removed from the micrometer.
● Some micrometers have a vernier scale on their sleeve, providing an even finer measurement to be taken, in 0.001 increments of a millimeter. Take the sleeve and thimble measurement as described above, then check which graduation on the vernier scale aligns with that of the annular scale on the thimble **Note:** *The eye must be perpendicular to the scale when taking the vernier reading - if necessary rotate the body of the micrometer to ensure this.* Multiply the vernier scale figure by 0.001 and add it to the base and fine measurement figures.

In the example shown the item measures 46.994 mm **(see illustrations 3.5 and 3.6)**:

Linear scale (base)	46.000 mm
Linear scale (base)	00.500 mm
Annular scale (fine)	00.490 mm
Vernier scale	00.004 mm
Total figure	**46.994 mm**

Internal micrometer

● Internal micrometers are available for measuring bore diameters, but are expensive and unlikely to be available for home use. It is suggested that a set of telescoping gauges and small hole gauges, both of which must be used with an external micrometer, will suffice for taking internal measurements on a motorcycle.
● Telescoping gauges can be used to

measure internal diameters of components. Select a gauge with the correct size range, make sure its ends are clean and insert it into the bore. Expand the gauge, then lock its position and withdraw it from the bore **(see illustration 3.7)**. Measure across the gauge ends with a micrometer **(see illustration 3.8)**.
● Very small diameter bores (such as valve guides) are measured with a small hole gauge. Once adjusted to a slip-fit inside the component, its position is locked and the gauge withdrawn for measurement with a micrometer **(see illustrations 3.9 and 3.10)**.

Vernier caliper

Note: *The conventional linear and dial gauge type instruments are described. Digital types are easier to read, but are far more expensive.*
● The vernier caliper does not provide the precision of a micrometer, but is versatile in being able to measure internal and external diameters. Some types also incorporate a depth gauge. It is ideal for measuring clutch plate friction material and spring free lengths.
● To use the conventional linear scale vernier, loosen off the vernier clamp screws (1) and set its jaws over (2), or inside (3), the item to be measured **(see illustration 3.11)**. Slide the jaw into contact, using the thumb-wheel (4) for fine movement of the sliding scale (5) then tighten the clamp screws (1). Read off the main scale (6) where the zero on the sliding scale (5) intersects it, taking the whole number to the left of the zero; this provides the base measurement. View along the sliding scale and select the division which lines up exactly

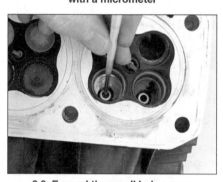

3.9 Expand the small hole gauge in the bore, lock its position . . .

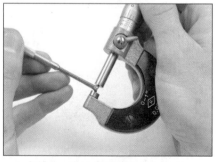

3.10 . . . then measure the gauge with a micrometer

with any of the divisions on the main scale, noting that the divisions usually represents 0.02 of a millimeter. Add this fine measurement to the base measurement to obtain the total reading.

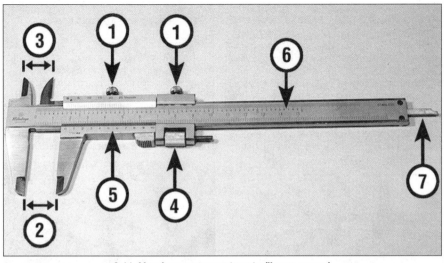

3.11 Vernier component parts (linear gauge)

| 1 | Clamp screws | 3 | Internal jaws | 5 | Sliding scale | 7 | Depth gauge |
| 2 | External jaws | 4 | Thumbwheel | 6 | Main scale | | |

In the example shown the item measures 55.92 mm **(see illustration 3.12)**:

Base measurement	55.00 mm
Fine measurement	00.92 mm
Total figure	**55.92 mm**

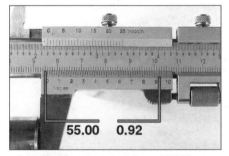

3.12 Vernier gauge reading of 55.92 mm

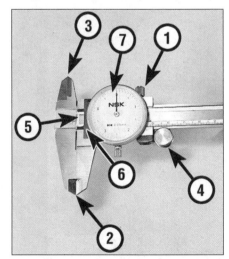

3.13 Vernier component parts (dial gauge)

1	Clamp screw	5	Main scale
2	External jaws	6	Sliding scale
3	Internal jaws	7	Dial gauge
4	Thumbwheel		

● Some vernier calipers are equipped with a dial gauge for fine measurement. Before use, check that the jaws are clean, then close them fully and check that the dial gauge reads zero. If necessary adjust the gauge ring accordingly. Slacken the vernier clamp screw (1) and set its jaws over (2), or inside (3), the item to be measured **(see illustration 3.13)**. Slide the jaws into contact, using the thumbwheel (4) for fine movement. Read off the main scale (5) where the edge of the sliding scale (6) intersects it, taking the whole number to the left of the zero; this provides the base measurement. Read off the needle position on the dial gauge (7) scale to provide the fine measurement; each division represents 0.05 of a millimeter. Add this fine measurement to the base measurement to obtain the total reading.

In the example shown the item measures 55.95 mm **(see illustration 3.14)**:

Base measurement	55.00 mm
Fine measurement	00.95 mm
Total figure	**55.95 mm**

3.14 Vernier gauge reading of 55.95 mm

Plastigage

● Plastigage is a plastic material which can be compressed between two surfaces to measure the oil clearance between them. The width of the compressed Plastigage is measured against a calibrated scale to determine the clearance.

● Common uses of Plastigage are for measuring the clearance between crankshaft journal and main bearing inserts, between crankshaft journal and big-end bearing inserts, and between camshaft and bearing surfaces. The following example describes big-end oil clearance measurement.

● Handle the Plastigage material carefully to prevent distortion. Using a sharp knife, cut a length which corresponds with the width of the bearing being measured and place it carefully across the journal so that it is parallel with the shaft **(see illustration 3.15)**. Carefully install both bearing shells and the connecting rod. Without rotating the rod on the journal tighten its bolts or nuts (as applicable) to the specified torque. The connecting rod and bearings are then disassembled and the crushed Plastigage examined.

3.15 Plastigage placed across shaft journal

● Using the scale provided in the Plastigage kit, measure the width of the material to determine the oil clearance **(see illustration 3.16)**. Always remove all traces of Plastigage after use using your fingernails.

Caution: Arriving at the correct clearance demands that the assembly is torqued correctly, according to the settings and sequence (where applicable) provided by the motorcycle manufacturer.

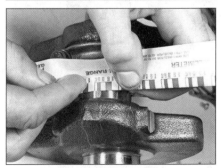

3.16 Measuring the width of the crushed Plastigage

Dial gauge or DTI (Dial Test Indicator)

● A dial gauge can be used to accurately measure small amounts of movement. Typical uses are measuring shaft runout or shaft endfloat (sideplay) and setting piston position for ignition timing on two-strokes. A dial gauge set usually comes with a range of different probes and adapters and mounting equipment.

● The gauge needle must point to zero when at rest. Rotate the ring around its periphery to zero the gauge.

● Check that the gauge is capable of reading the extent of movement in the work. Most gauges have a small dial set in the face which records whole millimeters of movement as well as the fine scale around the face periphery which is calibrated in 0.01 mm divisions. Read off the small dial first to obtain the base measurement, then add the measurement from the fine scale to obtain the total reading.

Base measurement	1.00 mm
Fine measurement	0.48 mm
Total figure	**1.48 mm**

3.17 Dial gauge reading of 1.48 mm

In the example shown the gauge reads 1.48 mm **(see illustration 3.17)**:

● If measuring shaft runout, the shaft must be supported in vee-blocks and the gauge mounted on a stand perpendicular to the shaft. Rest the tip of the gauge against the center of the shaft and rotate the shaft slowly while watching the gauge reading **(see illustration 3.18)**. Take several measurements along the length of the shaft and record the

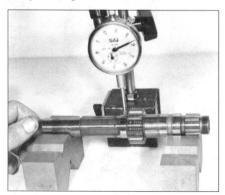

3.18 Using a dial gauge to measure shaft runout

maximum gauge reading as the amount of runout in the shaft. **Note:** *The reading obtained will be total runout at that point - some manufacturers specify that the runout figure is halved to compare with their specified runout limit.*

● Endfloat (sideplay) measurement requires that the gauge is mounted securely to the surrounding component with its probe touching the end of the shaft. Using hand pressure, push and pull on the shaft noting the maximum endfloat recorded on the gauge **(see illustration 3.19)**.

3.19 Using a dial gauge to measure shaft endfloat

● A dial gauge with suitable adapters can be used to determine piston position BTDC on two-stroke engines for the purposes of ignition timing. The gauge, adapter and suitable length probe are installed in the place of the spark plug and the gauge zeroed at TDC. If the piston position is specified as 1.14 mm BTDC, rotate the engine back to 2.00 mm BTDC, then slowly forwards to 1.14 mm BTDC.

Cylinder compression gauges

● A compression gauge is used for measuring cylinder compression. Either the rubber-cone type or the threaded adapter type can be used. The latter is preferred to ensure a perfect seal against the cylinder head. A 0 to 300 psi (0 to 20 Bar) type gauge (for gasoline engines) will be suitable for motorcycles.

● The spark plug is removed and the gauge either held hard against the cylinder head (cone type) or the gauge adapter screwed into the cylinder head (threaded type) **(see illustration 3.20)**. Cylinder compression is measured with the engine turning over, but not running - carry out the compression test as described in

3.20 Using a rubber-cone type cylinder compression gauge

Troubleshooting Equipment. The gauge will hold the reading until manually released.

Oil pressure gauge

● An oil pressure gauge is used for measuring engine oil pressure. Most gauges come with a set of adapters to fit the thread of the take-off point **(see illustration 3.21)**. If the take-off point specified by the motorcycle manufacturer is an external oil pipe union, make sure that the specified replacement union is used to prevent oil starvation.

3.21 Oil pressure gauge and take-off point adapter (arrow)

● Oil pressure is measured with the engine running (at a specific rpm) and often the manufacturer will specify pressure limits for a cold and hot engine.

Straight-edge and surface plate

● If checking the gasket face of a component for warpage, place a steel rule or precision straight-edge across the gasket face and measure any gap between the straight-edge and component with feeler gauges **(see illustration 3.22)**. Check diagonally across the component and between mounting holes **(see illustration 3.23)**.

3.22 Use a straight-edge and feeler gauges to check for warpage

3.23 Check for warpage in these directions

● Checking individual components for warpage, such as clutch plain (metal) plates, requires a perfectly flat plate or piece of plate glass and feeler gauges.

4 Torque and leverage

What is torque?

● Torque describes the twisting force around a shaft. The amount of torque applied is determined by the distance from the center of the shaft to the end of the lever and the amount of force being applied to the end of the lever; distance multiplied by force equals torque.

● The manufacturer applies a measured torque to a bolt or nut to ensure that it will not loosen in use and to hold two components securely together without movement in the joint. The actual torque setting depends on the thread size, bolt or nut material and the composition of the components being held.

● Too little torque may cause the fastener to loosen due to vibration, whereas too much torque will distort the joint faces of the component or cause the fastener to shear off. Always stick to the specified torque setting.

Using a torque wrench

● Check the calibration of the torque wrench and make sure it has a suitable range for the job. Torque wrenches are available in Nm (Newton-meters), kgf m (kilograms-force meter), lbf ft (pounds-feet), lbf in (inch-pounds). Do not confuse lbf ft with lbf in.

● Adjust the tool to the desired torque on the scale (see illustration 4.1). If your torque wrench is not calibrated in the units specified, carefully convert the figure (see *Conversion Factors*). A manufacturer sometimes gives a torque setting as a range (8 to 10 Nm) rather than a single figure - in this case set the tool midway between the two settings. The same torque may be expressed as 9 Nm ± 1 Nm. Some torque wrenches have a method of locking the setting so that it isn't inadvertently altered during use.

4.1 Set the torque wrench index mark to the setting required, in this case 12 Nm

● Install the bolts/nuts in their correct location and secure them lightly. Their threads must be clean and free of any old locking compound. Unless specified the threads and flange should be dry - oiled threads are necessary in certain circumstances and the manufacturer will take this into account in the specified torque figure. Similarly, the manufacturer may also specify the application of thread-locking compound.

● Tighten the fasteners in the specified sequence until the torque wrench clicks, indicating that the torque setting has been reached. Apply the torque again to double-check the setting. Where different thread diameter fasteners secure the component, as a rule tighten the larger diameter ones first.

● When the torque wrench has been finished with, release the lock (where applicable) and fully back off its setting to zero - do not leave the torque wrench tensioned. Also, do not use a torque wrench for loosening a fastener.

Angle-tightening

● Manufacturers often specify a figure in degrees for final tightening of a fastener. This usually follows tightening to a specific torque setting.

● A degree disc can be set and attached to the socket (see illustration 4.2) or a protractor can be used to mark the angle of movement on the bolt/nut head and the surrounding casting (see illustration 4.3).

4.2 Angle tightening can be accomplished with a torque-angle gauge . . .

4.3 . . . or by marking the angle on the surrounding component

Loosening sequences

● Where more than one bolt/nut secures a component, loosen each fastener evenly a little at a time. In this way, not all the stress of the joint is held by one fastener and the components are not likely to distort.

● If a tightening sequence is provided, work in the REVERSE of this, but if not, work from the outside in, in a criss-cross sequence (see illustration 4.4).

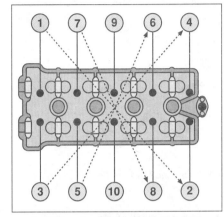

4.4 When loosening, work from the outside inwards

Tightening sequences

● If a component is held by more than one fastener it is important that the retaining bolts/nuts are tightened evenly to prevent uneven stress build-up and distortion of sealing faces. This is especially important on high-compression joints such as the cylinder head.

● A sequence is usually provided by the manufacturer, either in a diagram or actually marked in the casting. If not, always start in the center and work outwards in a criss-cross pattern (see illustration 4.5). Start off by securing all bolts/nuts finger-tight, then set the torque wrench and tighten each fastener by a small amount in sequence until the final torque is reached. By following this practice,

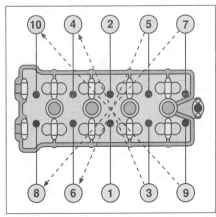

4.5 When tightening, work from the inside outwards

the joint will be held evenly and will not be distorted. Important joints, such as the cylinder head and big-end fasteners often have two- or three-stage torque settings.

Applying leverage

● Use tools at the correct angle. Position a socket or wrench on the bolt/nut so that you pull it towards you when loosening. If this can't be done, push the wrench without curling your fingers around it **(see illustration 4.6)** - the wrench may slip or the fastener loosen suddenly, resulting in your fingers being crushed against a component.

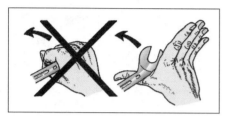

4.6 If you can't pull on the wrench to loosen a fastener, push with your hand open

● Additional leverage is gained by extending the length of the lever. The best way to do this is to use a breaker bar instead of the regular length tool, or to slip a length of tubing over the end of the wrench or socket.
● If additional leverage will not work, the fastener head is either damaged or firmly corroded in place (see *Fasteners*).

5 Bearings

Bearing removal and installation

Drivers and sockets

● Before removing a bearing, always inspect the casing to see which way it must be driven out - some casings will have retaining plates or a cast step. Also check for any identifying markings on the bearing and, if installed to a certain depth, measure this at this stage. Some roller bearings are sealed on one side - take note of the original installed position.
● Bearings can be driven out of a casing using a bearing driver tool (with the correct size head) or a socket of the correct diameter. Select the driver head or socket so that it contacts the outer race of the bearing, not the balls/rollers or inner race. Always support the casing around the bearing housing with wood blocks, otherwise there is a risk of fracture. The bearing is driven out with a few blows on the driver or socket from a heavy mallet. Unless access is severely restricted (as with wheel bearings), a pin-punch is not recommended unless it is moved around the bearing to keep it square in its housing.

● The same equipment can be used to install bearings. Make sure the bearing housing is supported on wood blocks and line up the bearing in its housing. Install the bearing as noted on removal - generally they are installed with their marked side facing outwards. Tap the bearing squarely into its housing using a driver or socket which bears only on the bearing's outer race - contact with the bearing balls/rollers or inner race will destroy it **(see illustrations 5.1 and 5.2)**.
● Check that the bearing inner race and balls/rollers rotate freely.

5.1 Using a bearing driver against the bearing's outer race

5.2 Using a large socket against the bearing's outer race

Pullers and slide-hammers

● Where a bearing is pressed on a shaft a puller will be required to extract it **(see illustration 5.3)**. Make sure that the puller clamp or legs fit securely behind the bearing and are unlikely to slip out. If pulling a bearing

5.3 This bearing puller clamps behind the bearing and pressure is applied to the shaft end to draw the bearing off

off a gear shaft for example, you may have to locate the puller behind a gear pinion if there is no access to the race and draw the gear pinion off the shaft as well **(see illustration 5.4)**.

> **Caution: Ensure that the puller's center bolt locates securely against the end of the shaft and will not slip when pressure is applied. Also ensure that puller does not damage the shaft end.**

5.4 Where no access is available to the rear of the bearing, it is sometimes possible to draw off the adjacent component

● Operate the puller so that its center bolt exerts pressure on the shaft end and draws the bearing off the shaft.
● When installing the bearing on the shaft, tap only on the bearing's inner race - contact with the balls/rollers or outer race will destroy the bearing. Use a socket or length of tubing as a drift which fits over the shaft end **(see illustration 5.5)**.

5.5 When installing a bearing on a shaft use a piece of tubing which bears only on the bearing's inner race

● Where a bearing locates in a blind hole in a casing, it cannot be driven or pulled out as described above. A slide-hammer with knife-edged bearing puller attachment will be required. The puller attachment passes through the bearing and when tightened expands to fit firmly behind the bearing **(see illustration 5.6)**. By operating the slide-hammer part of the tool the bearing is jarred out of its housing **(see illustration 5.7)**.
● It is possible, if the bearing is of reasonable weight, for it to drop out of its housing if the casing is heated as described opposite. If

5.6 Expand the bearing puller so that it locks behind the bearing . . .

5.7 . . . attach the slide hammer to the bearing puller

this method is attempted, first prepare a work surface which will enable the casing to be tapped face down to help dislodge the bearing - a wood surface is ideal since it will not damage the casing's gasket surface. Wearing protective gloves, tap the heated casing several times against the work surface to dislodge the bearing under its own weight **(see illustration 5.8)**.

5.8 Tapping a casing face down on wood blocks can often dislodge a bearing

● Bearings can be installed in blind holes using the driver or socket method described above.

Drawbolts

● Where a bearing or bushing is set in the eye of a component, such as a suspension linkage arm or connecting rod small-end, removal by drift may damage the component. Furthermore, a rubber bushing in a shock absorber eye cannot successfully be driven out of position. If access is available to a hydraulic press, the task is straightforward. If not, a drawbolt can be fabricated to extract the bearing or bushing.

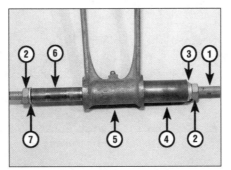

5.9 Drawbolt component parts assembled on a suspension arm

1 Bolt or length of threaded bar
2 Nuts
3 Washer (external diameter greater than tubing internal diameter)
4 Tubing (internal diameter sufficient to accommodate bearing)
5 Suspension arm with bearing
6 Tubing (external diameter slightly smaller than bearing)
7 Washer (external diameter slightly smaller than bearing)

5.10 Drawing the bearing out of the suspension arm

● To extract the bearing/bushing you will need a long bolt with nut (or piece of threaded bar with two nuts), a piece of tubing which has an internal diameter larger than the bearing/bushing, another piece of tubing which has an external diameter slightly smaller than the bearing/bushing, and a selection of washers **(see illustrations 5.9 and 5.10)**. Note that the pieces of tubing must be of the same length, or longer, than the bearing/bushing.
● The same kit (without the pieces of tubing) can be used to draw the new bearing/bushing back into place **(see illustration 5.11)**.

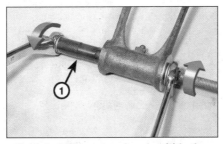

5.11 Installing a new bearing (1) in the suspension arm

Temperature change

● If the bearing's outer race is a tight fit in the casing, the aluminum casing can be heated to release its grip on the bearing. Aluminum will expand at a greater rate than the steel bearing outer race. There are several ways to do this, but avoid any localized extreme heat (such as a blow torch) - aluminum alloy has a low melting point.
● Approved methods of heating a casing are using a domestic oven (heated to 100°C/200°F) or immersing the casing in boiling water **(see illustration 5.12)**. Low temperature range localized heat sources such as a paint stripper heat gun or clothes iron can also be used **(see illustration 5.13)**. Alternatively, soak a rag in boiling water, wring it out and wrap it around the bearing housing.

> ⚠ **Warning: All of these methods require care in use to prevent scalding and burns to the hands. Wear protective gloves when handling hot components.**

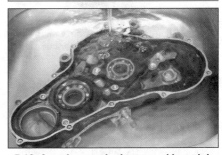

5.12 A casing can be immersed in a sink of boiling water to aid bearing removal

5.13 Using a localized heat source to aid bearing removal

● If heating the whole casing note that plastic components, such as the neutral switch, may suffer - remove them beforehand.
● After heating, remove the bearing as described above. You may find that the expansion is sufficient for the bearing to fall out of the casing under its own weight or with a light tap on the driver or socket.
● If necessary, the casing can be heated to aid bearing installation, and this is sometimes the recommended procedure if the motorcycle manufacturer has designed the housing and bearing fit with this intention.

● Installation of bearings can be eased by placing them in a freezer the night before installation. The steel bearing will contract slightly, allowing easy insertion in its housing. This is often useful when installing steering head outer races in the frame.

Bearing types and markings

● Plain shell bearings, ball bearings, needle roller bearings and tapered roller bearings will all be found on motorcycles (see illustrations 5.14 and 5.15). The ball and roller types are usually caged between an inner and outer race, but uncaged variations may be found.

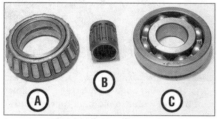

5.14 Shell bearings are either plain or grooved. They are usually identified by color code (arrow)

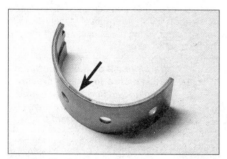

5.15 Tapered roller bearing (A), needle roller bearing (B) and ball journal bearing (C)

● Shell bearings (often called inserts) are usually found at the crankshaft main and connecting rod big-end where they are good at coping with high loads. They are made of a phosphor-bronze material and are impregnated with self-lubricating properties.
● Ball bearings and needle roller bearings consist of a steel inner and outer race with the balls or rollers between the races. They require constant lubrication by oil or grease and are good at coping with axial loads. Taper roller bearings consist of rollers set in a tapered cage set on the inner race; the outer race is separate. They are good at coping with axial loads and prevent movement along the shaft - a typical application is in the steering head.
● Bearing manufacturers produce bearings to ISO size standards and stamp one face of the bearing to indicate its internal and external diameter, load capacity and type (see illustration 5.16).
● Metal bushings are usually of phosphor-bronze material. Rubber bushings are used in suspension mounting eyes. Fiber bushings have also been used in suspension pivots.

5.16 Typical bearing marking

Bearing troubleshooting

● If a bearing outer race has spun in its housing, the housing material will be damaged. You can use a bearing locking compound to bond the outer race in place if damage is not too severe.
● Shell bearings will fail due to damage of their working surface, as a result of lack of lubrication, corrosion or abrasive particles in the oil (see illustration 5.17). Small particles of dirt in the oil may embed in the bearing material whereas larger particles will score the bearing and shaft journal. If a number of short journeys are made, insufficient heat will be generated to drive off condensation which has built up on the bearings.

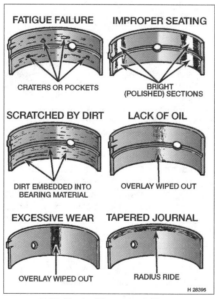

5.17 Typical bearing failures

● Ball and roller bearings will fail due to lack of lubrication or damage to the balls or rollers. Tapered-roller bearings can be damaged by overloading them. Unless the bearing is sealed on both sides, wash it in kerosene to remove all old grease then allow it to dry. Make a visual inspection looking to dented balls or rollers, damaged cages and worn or pitted races (see illustration 5.18).
● A ball bearing can be checked for wear by listening to it when spun. Apply a film of light oil to the bearing and hold it close to the ear - hold the outer race with one hand and spin the

5.18 Example of ball journal bearing with damaged balls and cages

5.19 Hold outer race and listen to inner race when spun

inner race with the other hand (see illustration 5.19). The bearing should be almost silent when spun; if it grates or rattles it is worn.

6 Oil seals

Oil seal removal and installation

● Oil seals should be replaced every time a component is dismantled. This is because the seal lips will become set to the sealing surface and will not necessarily reseal.
● Oil seals can be pried out of position using a large flat-bladed screwdriver (see illustration 6.1). In the case of crankcase seals, check first that the seal is not lipped on the inside, preventing its removal with the crankcases joined.

6.1 Pry out oil seals with a large flat-bladed screwdriver

● New seals are usually installed with their marked face (containing the seal reference code) outwards and the spring side towards the fluid being retained. In certain cases, such as a two-stroke engine crankshaft seal, a double lipped seal may be used due to there being fluid or gas on each side of the joint.

● Use a bearing driver or socket which bears only on the outer hard edge of the seal to install it in the casing - tapping on the inner edge will damage the sealing lip.

Oil seal types and markings

● Oil seals are usually of the single-lipped type. Double-lipped seals are found where a liquid or gas is on both sides of the joint.

● Oil seals can harden and lose their sealing ability if the motorcycle has been in storage for a long period - replacement is the only solution.

● Oil seal manufacturers also conform to the ISO markings for seal size - these are molded into the outer face of the seal (see illustration 6.2).

6.2 These oil seal markings indicate inside diameter, outside diameter and seal thickness

7 Gaskets and sealants

Types of gasket and sealant

● Gaskets are used to seal the mating surfaces between components and keep lubricants, fluids, vacuum or pressure contained within the assembly. Aluminum gaskets are sometimes found at the cylinder joints, but most gaskets are paper-based. If the mating surfaces of the components being joined are undamaged the gasket can be installed dry, although a dab of sealant or grease will be useful to hold it in place during assembly.

● RTV (Room Temperature Vulcanizing) silicone rubber sealants cure when exposed to moisture in the atmosphere. These sealants are good at filling pits or irregular gasket faces, but will tend to be forced out of the joint under very high torque. They can be used to replace a paper gasket, but first make sure that the width of the paper gasket is not essential to the shimming of internal components. RTV sealants should not be used on components containing gasoline.

● Non-hardening, semi-hardening and hard setting liquid gasket compounds can be used with a gasket or between a metal-to-metal joint. Select the sealant to suit the application: universal non-hardening sealant can be used on virtually all joints; semi-hardening on joint faces which are rough or damaged; hard setting sealant on joints which require a permanent bond and are subjected to high temperature and pressure. **Note:** *Check first if the paper gasket has a bead of sealant*

impregnated in its surface before applying additional sealant.

● When choosing a sealant, make sure it is suitable for the application, particularly if being applied in a high-temperature area or in the vicinity of fuel. Certain manufacturers produce sealants in either clear, silver or black colors to match the finish of the engine. This has a particular application on motorcycles where much of the engine is exposed.

● Do not over-apply sealant. That which is squeezed out on the outside of the joint can be wiped off, whereas an excess of sealant on the inside can break off and clog oilways.

Breaking a sealed joint

● Age, heat, pressure and the use of hard setting sealant can cause two components to stick together so tightly that they are difficult to separate using finger pressure alone. Do not resort to using levers unless there is a pry point provided for this purpose (see illustration 7.1) or else the gasket surfaces will be damaged.

● Use a soft-faced hammer (see illustration 7.2) or a wood block and conventional hammer to strike the component near the mating surface. Avoid hammering against cast extremities since they may break off. If this method fails, try using a wood wedge between the two components.

> **Caution: If the joint will not separate, double-check that you have removed all the fasteners.**

7.1 If a pry point is provided, apply gentle pressure with a flat-bladed screwdriver

7.2 Tap around the joint with a soft-faced mallet if necessary - don't strike cooling fins

Removal of old gasket and sealant

● Paper gaskets will most likely come away complete, leaving only a few traces stuck

Most components have one or two hollow locating dowels between the two gasket faces. If a dowel cannot be removed, do not resort to gripping it with pliers - it will almost certainly be distorted. Install a close-fitting socket or Phillips screwdriver into the dowel and then grip the outer edge of the dowel to free it.

on the sealing faces of the components. It is imperative that all traces are removed to ensure correct sealing of the new gasket.

● Very carefully scrape all traces of gasket away making sure that the sealing surfaces are not gouged or scored by the scraper (see illustrations 7.3, 7.4 and 7.5). Stubborn deposits can be removed by spraying with an aerosol gasket remover. Final preparation of

7.3 Paper gaskets can be scraped off with a gasket scraper tool . . .

7.4 . . . a knife blade . . .

7.5 . . . or a household scraper

7.6 Fine abrasive paper is wrapped around a flat file to clean up the gasket face

7.7 A kitchen scourer can be used on stubborn deposits

the gasket surface can be made with very fine abrasive paper or a plastic kitchen scourer **(see illustrations 7.6 and 7.7)**.

● Old sealant can be scraped or peeled off components, depending on the type originally used. Note that gasket removal compounds are available to avoid scraping the components clean; make sure the gasket remover suits the type of sealant used.

8 Chains

Breaking and joining final drive chains

● Drive chains for all but small bikes are continuous and do not have a clip-type connecting link. The chain must be broken using a chain breaker tool and the new chain securely riveted together using a new soft rivet-type link. Never use a clip-type connecting link instead of a rivet-type link, except in an emergency. Various chain breaking and riveting tools are available, either as separate tools or combined as illustrated in the accompanying photographs - read the instructions supplied with the tool carefully.

⚠️ **Warning: The need to rivet the new link pins correctly cannot be overstressed - loss of control of the motorcycle is very likely to result if the chain breaks in use.**

● Rotate the chain and look for the soft link. The soft link pins look like they have been

8.1 Tighten the chain breaker to push the pin out of the link . . .

8.2 . . . withdraw the pin, remove the tool . . .

8.3 . . . and separate the chain link

deeply center-punched instead of peened over like all the other pins **(see illustration 8.9)** and its sideplate may be a different color. Position the soft link midway between the sprockets and assemble the chain breaker tool over one of the soft link pins **(see illustration 8.1)**. Operate the tool to push the pin out through the chain **(see illustration 8.2)**. On an O-ring chain, remove the O-rings **(see illustration 8.3)**. Carry out the same procedure on the other soft link pin.

Caution: Certain soft link pins (particularly on the larger chains) may require their ends to be filed or ground off before they can be pressed out using the tool.

● Check that you have the correct size and strength (standard or heavy duty) new soft link - do not reuse the old link. Look for the size marking on the chain sideplates **(see illustration 8.10)**.
● Position the chain ends so that they are

8.4 Insert the new soft link, with O-rings, through the chain ends . . .

8.5 . . . install the O-rings over the pin ends . . .

8.6 . . . followed by the sideplate

engaged over the rear sprocket. On an O-ring chain, install a new O-ring over each pin of the link and insert the link through the two chain ends **(see illustration 8.4)**. Install a new O-ring over the end of each pin, followed by the sideplate (with the chain manufacturer's marking facing outwards) **(see illustrations 8.5 and 8.6)**. On an unsealed chain, insert the link through the two chain ends, then install the sideplate with the chain manufacturer's marking facing outwards.

● Note that it may not be possible to install the sideplate using finger pressure alone. If using a joining tool, assemble it so that the plates of the tool clamp the link and press the sideplate over the pins **(see illustration 8.7)**. Otherwise, use two small sockets placed over

8.7 Push the sideplate into position using a clamp

8.8 Assemble the chain riveting tool over one pin at a time and tighten it fully

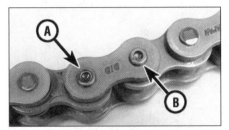

8.9 Pin end correctly riveted (A), pin end unriveted (B)

the rivet ends and two pieces of the wood between a C-clamp. Operate the clamp to press the sideplate over the pins.

● Assemble the joining tool over one pin (following the manufacturer's instructions) and tighten the tool down to spread the pin end securely **(see illustrations 8.8 and 8.9)**. Do the same on the other pin.

> ⚠ **Warning: Check that the pin ends are secure and that there is no danger of the sideplate coming loose. If the pin ends are cracked the soft link must be replaced.**

Final drive chain sizing

● Chains are sized using a three digit number, followed by a suffix to denote the chain type **(see illustration 8.10)**. Chain type is either standard or heavy duty (thicker sideplates), and also unsealed or O-ring/X-ring type.

● The first digit of the number relates to the pitch of the chain, ie the distance from the center of one pin to the center of the next pin **(see illustration 8.11)**. Pitch is expressed in eighths of an inch, as follows:

8.10 Typical chain size and type marking

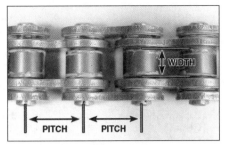

8.11 Chain dimensions

| Sizes commencing with a 4 (for example 428) have a pitch of 1/2 inch (12.7 mm) |
| Sizes commencing with a 5 (for example 520) have a pitch of 5/8 inch (15.9 mm) |
| Sizes commencing with a 6 (for example 630) have a pitch of 3/4 inch (19.1 mm) |

● The second and third digits of the chain size relate to the width of the rollers, for example the 525 shown has 5/16 inch (7.94 mm) rollers **(see illustration 8.11)**.

9 Hoses

Clamping to prevent flow

● Small-bore flexible hoses can be clamped to prevent fluid flow while a component is worked on. Whichever method is used, ensure that the hose material is not permanently distorted or damaged by the clamp.

a) A brake hose clamp available from auto parts stores **(see illustration 9.1)**.
b) A wingnut type hose clamp **(see illustration 9.2)**.

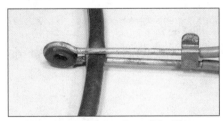

9.1 Hoses can be clamped with an automotive brake hose clamp . . .

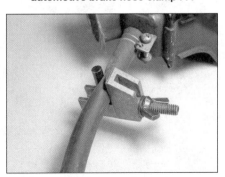

9.2 . . . a wingnut type hose clamp . . .

c) Two sockets placed on each side of the hose and held with straight-jawed self-locking pliers **(see illustration 9.3)**.
d) Thick card stock on each side of the hose held between straight-jawed self-locking pliers **(see illustration 9.4)**.

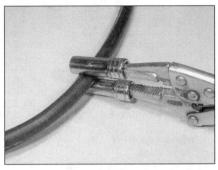

9.3 . . . two sockets and a pair of self-locking grips . . .

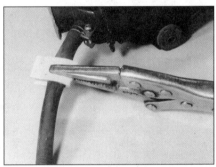

9.4 . . . or thick card and self-locking grips

Freeing and fitting hoses

● Always make sure the hose clamp is moved well clear of the hose end. Grip the hose with your hand and rotate it while pulling it off the union. If the hose has hardened due to age and will not move, slit it with a sharp knife and peel its ends off the union **(see illustration 9.5)**.

● Resist the temptation to use grease or soap on the unions to aid installation; although it helps the hose slip over the union it will equally aid the escape of fluid from the joint. It is preferable to soften the hose ends in hot water and wet the inside surface of the hose with water or a fluid which will evaporate.

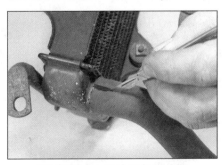

9.5 Cutting a coolant hose free with a sharp knife

Conversion Factors

Length (distance)

Inches (in)	X	25.4	= Millimeters (mm)	X	0.0394	= Inches (in)
Feet (ft)	X	0.305	= Meters (m)	X	3.281	= Feet (ft)
Miles	X	1.609	= Kilometers (km)	X	0.621	= Miles

Volume (capacity)

Cubic inches (cu in; in³)	X	16.387	= Cubic centimeters (cc; cm³)	X	0.061	= Cubic inches (cu in; in³)
Imperial pints (Imp pt)	X	0.568	= Liters (l)	X	1.76	= Imperial pints (Imp pt)
Imperial quarts (Imp qt)	X	1.137	= Liters (l)	X	0.88	= Imperial quarts (Imp qt)
Imperial quarts (Imp qt)	X	1.201	= US quarts (US qt)	X	0.833	= Imperial quarts (Imp qt)
US quarts (US qt)	X	0.946	= Liters (l)	X	1.057	= US quarts (US qt)
Imperial gallons (Imp gal)	X	4.546	= Liters (l)	X	0.22	= Imperial gallons (Imp gal)
Imperial gallons (Imp gal)	X	1.201	= US gallons (US gal)	X	0.833	= Imperial gallons (Imp gal)
US gallons (US gal)	X	3.785	= Liters (l)	X	0.264	= US gallons (US gal)

Mass (weight)

Ounces (oz)	X	28.35	= Grams (g)	X	0.035	= Ounces (oz)
Pounds (lb)	X	0.454	= Kilograms (kg)	X	2.205	= Pounds (lb)

Force

Ounces-force (ozf; oz)	X	0.278	= Newtons (N)	X	3.6	= Ounces-force (ozf; oz)
Pounds-force (lbf; lb)	X	4.448	= Newtons (N)	X	0.225	= Pounds-force (lbf; lb)
Newtons (N)	X	0.1	= Kilograms-force (kgf; kg)	X	9.81	= Newtons (N)

Pressure

Pounds-force per square inch (psi; lbf/in²; lb/in²)	X	0.070	= Kilograms-force per square centimeter (kgf/cm²; kg/cm²)	X	14.223	= Pounds-force per square inch (psi; lbf/in²; lb/in²)
Pounds-force per square inch (psi; lbf/in²; lb/in²)	X	0.068	= Atmospheres (atm)	X	14.696	= Pounds-force per square inch (psi; lbf/in²; lb/in²)
Pounds-force per square inch (psi; lbf/in²; lb/in²)	X	0.069	= Bars	X	14.5	= Pounds-force per square inch (psi; lbf/in²; lb/in²)
Pounds-force per square inch (psi; lbf/in²; lb/in²)	X	6.895	= Kilopascals (kPa)	X	0.145	= Pounds-force per square inch (psi; lbf/in²; lb/in²)
Kilopascals (kPa)	X	0.01	= Kilograms-force per square centimeter (kgf/cm²; kg/cm²)	X	98.1	= Kilopascals (kPa)

Torque (moment of force)

Pounds-force inches (lbf in; lb in)	X	1.152	= Kilograms-force centimeter (kgf cm; kg cm)	X	0.868	= Pounds-force inches (lbf in; lb in)
Pounds-force inches (lbf in; lb in)	X	0.113	= Newton meters (Nm)	X	8.85	= Pounds-force inches (lbf in; lb in)
Pounds-force inches (lbf in; lb in)	X	0.083	= Pounds-force feet (lbf ft; lb ft)	X	12	= Pounds-force inches (lbf in; lb in)
Pounds-force feet (lbf ft; lb ft)	X	0.138	= Kilograms-force meters (kgf m; kg m)	X	7.233	= Pounds-force feet (lbf ft; lb ft)
Pounds-force feet (lbf ft; lb ft)	X	1.356	= Newton meters (Nm)	X	0.738	= Pounds-force feet (lbf ft; lb ft)
Newton meters (Nm)	X	0.102	= Kilograms-force meters (kgf m; kg m)	X	9.804	= Newton meters (Nm)

Vacuum

Inches mercury (in. Hg)	X	3.377	= Kilopascals (kPa)	X	0.2961	= Inches mercury
Inches mercury (in. Hg)	X	25.4	= Millimeters mercury (mm Hg)	X	0.0394	= Inches mercury

Power

Horsepower (hp)	X	745.7	= Watts (W)	X	0.0013	= Horsepower (hp)

Velocity (speed)

Miles per hour (miles/hr; mph)	X	1.609	= Kilometers per hour (km/hr; kph)	X	0.621	= Miles per hour (miles/hr; mph)

Fuel consumption*

Miles per gallon, Imperial (mpg)	X	0.354	= Kilometers per liter (km/l)	X	2.825	= Miles per gallon, Imperial (mpg)
Miles per gallon, US (mpg)	X	0.425	= Kilometers per liter (km/l)	X	2.352	= Miles per gallon, US (mpg)

Temperature

Degrees Fahrenheit = (°C x 1.8) + 32   Degrees Celsius (Degrees Centigrade; °C) = (°F - 32) x 0.56

*It is common practice to convert from miles per gallon (mpg) to liters/100 kilometers (l/100km), where mpg (Imperial) x l/100 km = 282 and mpg (US) x l/100 km = 235

A number of chemicals and lubricants are available for use in motorcycle maintenance and repair. They include a wide variety of products ranging from cleaning solvents and degreasers to lubricants and protective sprays for rubber, plastic and vinyl.

• **Contact point/spark plug cleaner** is a solvent used to clean oily film and dirt from points, grim from electrical connectors and oil deposits from spark plugs. It is oil free and leaves no residue. It can also be used to remove gum and varnish from carburetor jets and other orifices.

• **Carburetor cleaner** is similar to contact point/spark plug cleaner but it usually has a stronger solvent and may leave a slight oily residue. It is not recommended for cleaning electrical components or connections.

• **Brake system cleaner** is used to remove brake dust, grease and brake fluid from the brake system, where clean surfaces are absolutely necessary. It leaves no residue and often eliminates brake squeal caused by contaminants.

• **Silicone-based lubricants** are used to protect rubber parts such as hoses and grommets, and are used as lubricants for hinges and locks.

• **Multi-purpose grease** is an all purpose lubricant used wherever grease is more practical than a liquid lubricant such as oil. Some multi-purpose grease is colored white and specially formulated to be more resistant to water than ordinary grease.

• **Gear oil** (sometimes called gear lube) is a specially designed oil used in transmissions and final drive units, as well as other areas where high friction, high temperature lubrication is required. It is available in a number of viscosities (weights) for various applications.

• **Motor oil** is the lubricant formulated for use in engines. It normally contains a wide variety of additives to prevent corrosion and reduce foaming and wear. Motor oil comes in various weights (viscosity ratings) from 0 to 50. The recommended weight of the oil depends on the season, temperature and the demands on the engine. Light oil is used in cold climates and under light load conditions. Heavy oil is used in hot climates and where high loads are encountered. Multi-viscosity oils are designed to have characteristics of both light and heavy oils and are available in a number of weights from 0W-20 to 20W-50.

• **Gasoline additives** perform several functions, depending on their chemical makeup. They usually contain solvents that help dissolve gum and varnish that build up on carburetor and inlet parts. They also serve to break down carbon deposits that form on the inside surfaces of the combustion chambers. Some additives contain upper cylinder lubricants for valves and piston rings.

• **Brake and clutch fluid** is a specially formulated hydraulic fluid that can withstand the heat and pressure encountered in break/clutch systems. Care must be taken that this fluid does not come in contact with painted surfaces or plastics. An opened container should always be resealed to prevent contamination by water or dirt.

• **Chain lubricants** are formulated especially for use on motorcycle final drive chains. A good chain lube should adhere well and have good penetrating qualities to be effective as a lubricant inside the chain and on the side plates, pins and rollers. Most chain lubes are either the foaming type or quick drying type and are usually marketed as sprays. Take care to use a lubricant marked as being suitable for O-ring chains.

• **Degreasers** are heavy duty solvents used to remove grease and grime that may accumulate on the engine and frame components. They can be sprayed or brushed on and, depending on the type, are rinsed with either water or solvent.

• **Solvents** are used alone or in combination with degreasers to clean parts and assemblies during repair and overhaul. The home mechanic should use only solvents that are non-flammable and that do not produce irritating fumes.

• **Gasket sealing compounds** may be used in conjunction with gaskets, to improve their sealing capabilities, or alone, to seal metal-to-metal joints. Many gasket sealers can withstand extreme heat, some are impervious to gasoline and lubricants, while others are capable of filling and sealing large cavities. Depending on the intended use, gasket sealers either dry hard or stay relatively soft and pliable. They are usually applied by hand, with a brush or are sprayed on the gasket sealing surfaces.

• **Thread locking compound** is an adhesive locking compound that prevents threaded fasteners from loosening because of vibration. It is available in a variety of types for different applications.

• **Moisture dispersants** are usually sprays that can be used to dry out electrical components such as the fuse block and wiring connectors. Some types an also be used as treatment for rubber and as a lubricant for hinges, cables and locks.

• **Waxes and polishes** are used to help protect painted and plated surfaces from the weather. Different types of pain may require the use of different types of wax polish. Some polishes utilize a chemical or abrasive cleaner to help remove the top layer of oxidized (dull) paint on older vehicles. In recent years, many non-wax polishes (that contain a wide variety of chemicals such as polymers and silicones) have been introduced. These non-wax polishes are usually easier to apply and last longer than conventional waxes and polishes.

Preparing for storage

Before you start

If repairs or an overhaul is needed, see that this is carried out now rather than left until you want to ride the bike again.

Give the bike a good wash and scrub all dirt from its underside. Make sure the bike dries completely before preparing for storage.

Engine

● Remove the spark plug(s) and lubricate the cylinder bores with approximately a teaspoon of motor oil using a spout-type oil can **(see illustration 1)**. Reinstall the spark plug(s). Crank the engine over a couple of times to coat the piston rings and bores with oil. If the bike has a kickstart, use this to turn the engine over. If not, flick the kill switch to the OFF position and crank the engine over on the starter **(see illustration 2)**. If the nature of the ignition system prevents the starter operating with the kill switch in the OFF position, remove the spark plugs and fit them back in

their caps; ensure that the plugs are grounded against the cylinder head when the starter is operated **(see illustration 3)**.

> ⚠️ *Warning: It is important that the plugs are grounded away from the spark plug holes otherwise there is a risk of atomized fuel from the cylinders igniting.*

> **HAYNES HINT** *On a single cylinder four-stroke engine, you can seal the combustion chamber completely by positioning the piston at TDC on the compression stroke.*

● Drain the carburetor(s) otherwise there is a risk of jets becoming blocked by gum deposits from the fuel **(see illustration 4)**.

● If the bike is going into long-term storage, consider adding a fuel stabilizer to the fuel in the tank. If the tank is drained completely, corrosion of its internal surfaces may occur if left unprotected for a long period. The tank can be treated with a rust preventative especially for this purpose. Alternatively, remove the tank and pour half a liter of motor oil into it, install the filler cap and shake the tank to coat its internals with oil before draining off the excess. The same effect can also be achieved by spraying WD40 or a similar water-dispersant around the inside of the tank via its flexible nozzle.

● Make sure the cooling system contains the correct mix of antifreeze. Antifreeze also contains important corrosion inhibitors.

● The air intakes and exhaust can be sealed off by covering or plugging the openings. Ensure that you do not seal in any condensation; run the engine until it is hot, then switch off and allow to cool. Tape a

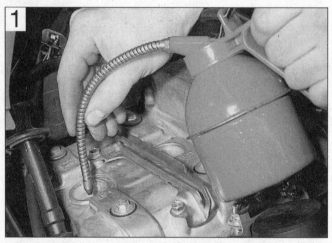

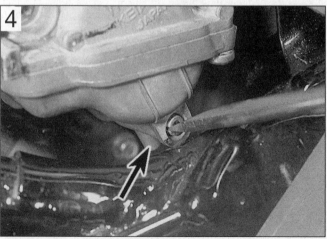

1 Squirt a drop of motor oil into each cylinder

2 Flick the kill switch to OFF . . .

3 . . . and ensure that the metal bodies of the plugs (arrows) are grounded against the cylinder head

4 Connect a hose to the carburetor float chamber drain stub (arrow) and unscrew the drain screw

Exhausts can be sealed off with a plastic bag

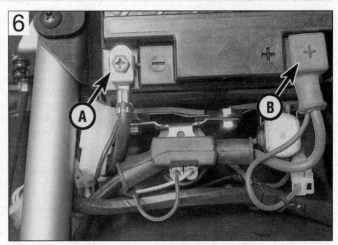

Disconnect the negative lead (A) first, followed by the positive lead (B)

piece of thick plastic over the silencer end(s) **(see illustration 5)**. Note that some advocate pouring a tablespoon of motor oil into the silencer(s) before sealing them off.

Battery

● Remove it from the bike - in extreme cases of cold the battery may freeze and crack its case **(see illustration 6)**.
● Check the electrolyte level and top up if necessary (conventional refillable batteries). Clean the terminals.
● Store the battery off the motorcycle and away from any sources of fire. Position a wooden block under the battery if it is to sit on the ground.
● Give the battery a trickle charge for a few hours every month **(see illustration 7)**.

Tires

● Place the bike on its centerstand or an auxiliary stand which will support the motorcycle in an upright position. Position wood blocks under the tires to keep them off the ground and to provide insulation from damp. If the bike is being put into long-term

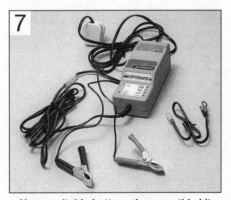

Use a suitable battery charger - this kit also assesses battery condition

storage, ideally both tires should be off the ground; not only will this protect the tires, but will also ensure that no load is placed on the steering head or wheel bearings.
● Deflate each tire by 5 to 10 psi, no more or the beads may unseat from the rim, making subsequent inflation difficult on tubeless tires.

Pivots and controls

● Lubricate all lever, pedal, stand and footrest pivot points. If grease nipples are fitted to the rear suspension components, apply lubricant to the pivots.
● Lubricate all control cables.

Cycle components

● Apply a wax protectant to all painted and plastic components. Wipe off any excess, but don't polish to a shine. Where fitted, clean the screen with soap and water.
● Coat metal parts with Vaseline (petroleum jelly). When applying this to the fork tubes, do not compress the forks otherwise the seals will rot from contact with the Vaseline.
● Apply a vinyl cleaner to the seat.

Storage conditions

● Aim to store the bike in a shed or garage which does not leak and is free from damp.
● Drape an old blanket or bedspread over the bike to protect it from dust and direct contact with sunlight (which will fade paint). Beware of tight-fitting plastic covers which may allow condensation to form and settle on the bike.

Getting back on the road

Engine and transmission

● Change the oil and replace the oil filter. If this was done prior to storage, check that the oil hasn't emulsified - a thick whitish substance which occurs through condensation.
● Remove the spark plugs. Using a spout-type oil can, squirt a few drops of oil into the cylinder(s). This will provide initial lubrication as the piston rings and bores comes back into contact. Service the spark plugs, or buy new ones, and install them in the engine.

● Check that the clutch isn't stuck on. The plates can stick together if left standing for some time, preventing clutch operation. Engage a gear and try rocking the bike back and forth with the clutch lever held against the handlebar. If this doesn't work on cable-operated clutches, hold the clutch lever back against the handlebar with a strong rubber band or cable tie for a couple of hours **(see illustration 8)**.
● If the air intakes or silencer end(s) were blocked off, remove the plug or cover used.
● If the fuel tank was coated with a rust

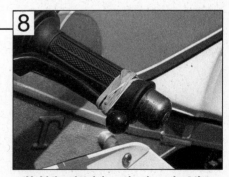

Hold the clutch lever back against the handlebar with rubber bands or a cable tie

preventative, oil or a stabilizer added to the fuel, drain and flush the tank and dispose of the fuel sensibly. If no action was taken with the fuel tank prior to storage, it is advised that the old fuel is disposed of since it will go bad over a period of time. Refill the fuel tank with fresh fuel.

Frame and running gear

● Oil all pivot points and cables.
● Check the tire pressures. They will definitely need inflating if pressures were reduced for storage.
● Lubricate the final drive chain (where applicable).
● Remove any protective coating applied to the fork tubes (stanchions) since this may well destroy the fork seals. If the fork tubes weren't protected and have picked up rust spots, remove them with very fine abrasive paper and refinish with metal polish.
● Check that both brakes operate correctly. Apply each brake hard and check that it's not possible to move the motorcycle forwards, then check that the brake frees off again once released. Brake caliper pistons can stick due to corrosion around the piston head, or on the sliding caliper types, due to corrosion of the slider pins. If the brake doesn't free off after repeated operation, take the caliper off for examination. Similarly drum brakes can stick

due to a seized operating cam, cable or rod linkage.
● If the motorcycle has been in long-term storage, replace the brake fluid and clutch fluid (where applicable).
● Depending on where the bike has been stored, the wiring, cables and hoses may have been nibbled by rodents. Make a visual check and investigate disturbed wiring loom tape.

Battery

● If the battery has been previously removed and given top up charges it can simply be reconnected. Remember to connect the positive cable first and the negative cable last.
● On conventional refillable batteries, if the battery has not received any attention, remove it from the motorcycle and check its electrolyte level. Top up if necessary then charge the battery. If the battery fails to hold a charge and a visual check show heavy white sulfation of the plates, the battery is probably defective and must be replaced. This is particularly likely if the battery is old. Confirm battery condition with a specific gravity check.
● On sealed (MF) batteries, if the battery has not received any attention, remove it from the motorcycle and charge it according to the information on the battery case - if the battery fails to hold a charge it must be replaced.

Starting procedure

● If a kickstart is fitted, turn the engine over a couple of times with the ignition OFF to distribute oil around the engine. If no kickstart is fitted, flick the engine kill switch OFF and the ignition ON and crank the engine over a couple of times to work oil around the upper cylinder components. If the nature of the ignition system is such that the starter won't work with the kill switch OFF, remove the spark plugs, fit them back into their caps and ground their bodies on the cylinder head. Reinstall the spark plugs afterwards.
● Switch the kill switch to RUN, operate the choke and start the engine. If the engine won't start don't continue cranking the engine - not only will this flatten the battery, but the starter motor will overheat. Switch the ignition off and try again later. If the engine refuses to start, go through the troubleshooting procedures in this manual. **Note:** *If the bike has been in storage for a long time, old fuel or a carburetor blockage may be the problem. Gum deposits in carburetors can block jets - if a carburetor cleaner doesn't prove successful the carburetors must be dismantled for cleaning.*

● Once the engine has started, check that the lights, turn signals and horn work properly.

● Treat the bike gently for the first ride and check all fluid levels on completion. Settle the bike back into the maintenance schedule.

This Section provides an easy reference-guide to the more common faults that are likely to afflict your machine. Obviously, the opportunities are almost limitless for faults to occur as a result of obscure failures, and to try and cover all eventualities would require a book. Indeed, a number have been written on the subject.

Successful troubleshooting is not a mysterious 'black art' but the application of a bit of knowledge combined with a systematic and logical approach to the problem. Approach any troubleshooting by first accurately identifying the symptom and then checking through the list of possible causes, starting with the simplest or most obvious and progressing in stages to the most complex. Take nothing for granted, but above all apply liberal quantities of common sense.

The main symptom of a fault is given in the text as a major heading below which are listed the various systems or areas which may contain the fault. Details of each possible cause for a fault and the remedial action to be taken are given. Further information should be sought in the relevant Chapter.

1 Engine problems

Starter turns engine over but engine will not start
- [ ] Fuel tank empty
- [ ] Battery discharged (engine rotates slowly)
- [ ] Battery terminal connections loose or corroded
- [ ] Leaking fuel injector(s), faulty fuel pump, pressure regulator, etc.
- [ ] Fuel not reaching fuel rail
- [ ] Ignition components damp or damaged
- [ ] Worn, faulty or incorrectly gapped spark plugs
- [ ] Broken, loose or disconnected wiring in the starting circuit
- [ ] Broken timing chain or stripped sprocket
- [ ] Defective fuel system relay or harness at relay

Engine hard to start when cold
- [ ] Battery discharged or low
- [ ] Malfunctioning fuel system
- [ ] Injector(s) leaking

Engine hard to start when hot
- [ ] Air filer clogged
- [ ] Fuel not reaching the fuel injection system
- [ ] Corroded battery connections, especially ground
- [ ] Malfunctioning EVAP system

Engine starts but stops immediately
- [ ] Loose or faulty electrical connections at coils or alternator
- [ ] Insufficient fuel reaching the fuel injector(s)
- [ ] Vacuum leak at the gasket between the intake manifold and throttle body

Engine lopes while idling or idles erratically
- [ ] Vacuum leakage
- [ ] Air filter clogged
- [ ] Fuel pump not delivering sufficient fuel to the fuel injection system
- [ ] Leaking head gasket
- [ ] Timing chain or sprockets worn
- [ ] Camshaft lobes worn

Engine misses at idle speed
- [ ] Spark plugs worn or not gapped properly
- [ ] Vacuum leaks
- [ ] Uneven or low compression

Engine misses throughout driving speed range
- [ ] Fuel filter clogged or impurities in the fuel system
- [ ] Low fuel pressure
- [ ] Faulty or incorrectly gapped spark plugs
- [ ] Faulty emission system components
- [ ] Low or uneven cylinder compression pressures
- [ ] Weaker faulty ignition system
- [ ] Vacuum leak in fuel injection system, intake manifold or vacuum hoses.

Engine stumbles on acceleration
- [ ] Spark plugs fouled
- [ ] Fuel injection system faulty
- [ ] Fuel filter clogged
- [ ] Incorrect ignition timing
- [ ] Intake air leak

Engine surges while holding throttle steady
- [ ] Intake air leak
- [ ] Fuel pump faulty
- [ ] Loose fuel injector wiring harness connectors
- [ ] Defective ECU or information sensor

Engine stalls
- [ ] Fuel filter clogged and/or water and impurities in the fuel system
- [ ] Faulty emission system components
- [ ] Faulty or incorrectly gapped spark plugs
- [ ] Vacuum leak in the intake manifold or vacuum hoses
- [ ] Valve clearances incorrectly set

Engine lacks power
- [ ] Faulty or incorrectly gapped spark plugs
- [ ] Fuel injection system malfunction
- [ ] Faulty ignition coil(s)
- [ ] Brakes binding
- [ ] Clutch slipping
- [ ] Fuel filter clogged or impurities in the fuel system
- [ ] Emission control system not functioning properly
- [ ] Low or uneven cylinder compression pressures
- [ ] Obstructed exhaust system

Engine backfires
- [ ] Pulse secondary air system not functioning properly
- [ ] Fuel injection system malfunction
- [ ] Vacuum leak at the fuel injector(s), intake manifold or vacuum hoses
- [ ] Valve clearances incorrectly set or valves sticking

Pinging or knocking sounds during acceleration and uphill
- [ ] Incorrect grade of fuel
- [ ] Fuel injection system faulty
- [ ] Knock sensor(s) faulty
- [ ] Vacuum leak

Engine runs with oil pressure light on
- [ ] Low oil level
- [ ] Short in wiring circuit
- [ ] Faulty oil pressure switch
- [ ] Worn engine bearings or oil pump

2 Clutch problems

- ☐ Clutch slipping
- ☐ Clutch not disengaging completely

3 Gearchanging problems

- ☐ Doesn't go into gear, or lever doesn't return
- ☐ Jumps out of gear
- ☐ Overselects

4 Abnormal engine noise

- ☐ Knocking or pinging
- ☐ Piston slap or rattling
- ☐ Valve noise
- ☐ Other noise

5 Abnormal driveline noise

- ☐ Clutch noise
- ☐ Transmission noise
- ☐ Final drive noise

6 Abnormal frame and suspension noise

- ☐ Front end noise
- ☐ Shock absorber noise
- ☐ Brake noise

7 Excessive exhaust smoke

- ☐ White smoke
- ☐ Black smoke

8 Poor handling or stability

- ☐ Handlebar hard to turn
- ☐ Handlebar shakes or vibrates excessively
- ☐ Handlebar pulls to one side
- ☐ Poor shock absorbing qualities

9 Braking problems

- ☐ Brakes are spongy, don't hold
- ☐ Brake lever or pedal pulsates
- ☐ Brakes drag

10 Electrical problems

- ☐ Battery dead or weak
- ☐ Battery overcharged

1 Engine problems

Starter motor doesn't rotate

- [ ] Engine kill switch OFF.
- [ ] Fuse blown or relay defective. Check main fuse, starter circuit fuse and relays (see Chapter 9).
- [ ] Battery voltage low. Check and recharge battery (Chapter 9).
- [ ] Starter motor defective. Make sure the wiring to the starter is secure. Make sure the starter relay clicks when the start button is pushed. If the relay clicks, then the fault is in the wiring or motor.
- [ ] Starter relay faulty. Check it according to the procedure in Chapter 9.
- [ ] Starter switch not contacting. The contacts could be wet, corroded or dirty. Disassemble and clean the switch (Chapter 9).
- [ ] Wiring open or shorted. Check all wiring connections and harnesses to make sure that they are dry, tight and not corroded. Also check for broken or frayed wires that can cause a short to ground (see wiring diagram, Chapter 9).
- [ ] Ignition (main) switch defective. Check the switch according to the procedure in Chapter 9. Replace the switch with a new one if it is defective.
- [ ] Engine kill switch defective. Check for wet, dirty or corroded contacts. Clean or replace the switch as necessary (Chapter 9).
- [ ] Faulty neutral, side stand or clutch switch. Check the wiring to each switch and the switch itself according to the procedures in Chapter 9.

Starter motor rotates but engine does not turn over

- [ ] Starter motor clutch defective. Inspect and repair or replace (Chapter 2).
- [ ] Damaged idler or starter gears. Inspect and replace the damaged parts (Chapter 2).

Starter works but engine won't turn over (seized)

- [ ] Seized engine caused by one or more internally damaged components. Failure due to wear, abuse or lack of lubrication. Damage can include seized valves, followers/rocker arms, camshafts, pistons, crankshaft, connecting rod bearings, or transmission gears or bearings. Refer to Chapter 2 for engine disassembly.

No fuel flow

- [ ] No fuel in tank.
- [ ] Fuel tank breather hose obstructed.
- [ ] Fuel filter is blocked (see Chapter 1).
- [ ] Leaking fuel injectors, faulty fuel pump, pressure regulator, etc. (see Chapter 4).
- [ ] Fuel not reaching fuel rail (see Chapter 4).
- [ ] Defective fuel pump relay or harness at relay (see Chapter 4).

Starter turns engine over but engine will not start

- [ ] Fuel tank empty.
- [ ] Battery discharged (engine rotates slowly) (see Chapter 9).
- [ ] Battery terminal connections loose or corroded (see Chapter 1)
- [ ] Leaking fuel injector(s), faulty fuel pump, pressure regulator, etc. (see Chapter 4).
- [ ] Fuel not reaching fuel rail (see Chapter 4).
- [ ] Ignition components damp or damaged (see Chapter 5).
- [ ] Worn, faulty or incorrectly gapped spark plugs (see Chapter 1).
- [ ] Broken, loose or disconnected wiring in the starting circuit (see Chapter 9).
- [ ] Broken timing chain or stripped sprocket (see Chapter 2).
- [ ] Defective fuel system relay or harness at relay (see Chapter 9).

Engine hard to start when cold

- [ ] Battery discharged or low (see Chapters 1 and 9).
- [ ] Malfunctioning fuel system (see Chapter 4).
- [ ] Injector(s) leaking (see Chapter 4).

Engine hard to start when hot

- [ ] Air filer clogged (see Chapter 1).
- [ ] Fuel not reaching the fuel injection system (see Chapter 4).
- [ ] Corroded battery connections, especially ground (see Chapters 1 and 9).
- [ ] Malfunctioning EVAP system (see Chapter 4).

Engine starts but stops immediately

- [ ] Loose or faulty electrical connections at coils or alternator (see Chapters 5 and 9).
- [ ] Insufficient fuel reaching the fuel injector(s) (see Chapter 4).
- [ ] Vacuum leak at the gasket between the intake manifold and throttle body (see Chapters 2 and 4).

Engine lopes while idling or idles erratically

- [ ] Vacuum leakage (Chapters 2 and 4).
- [ ] Air filter clogged (see Chapter 1).
- [ ] Fuel pump not delivering sufficient fuel to the fuel injection system (see Chapter 4).
- [ ] Leaking head gasket (see Chapter 2).
- [ ] Timing chain or sprockets worn (see Chapter 2).
- [ ] Camshaft lobes worn (see Chapter 2).

Engine misses at idle speed

- [ ] Spark plugs worn or not gapped properly (see Chapter 1).
- [ ] Vacuum leaks (see Chapter 1).
- [ ] Uneven or low compression (see Chapter 2).

1 Engine problems (continued)

Engine misses throughout driving speed range

- ☐ Fuel filter clogged or impurities in the fuel system (see Chapter 2).
- ☐ Low fuel pressure (see Chapter 4).
- ☐ Faulty or incorrectly gapped spark plugs (see Chapter 1).
- ☐ Faulty emission system components (see Chapter 4).
- ☐ Low or uneven cylinder compression pressures (see Chapter 2).
- ☐ Weaker faulty ignition system (see Chapter 5).
- ☐ Vacuum leak in fuel injection system (see Chapter 4), intake manifold (see Chapter 2) or vacuum hoses.

Engine stumbles on acceleration

- ☐ Spark plugs fouled (see Chapter 1).
- ☐ Fuel injection system faulty (see Chapter 4).
- ☐ Fuel filter clogged (see Chapter 4).
- ☐ Incorrect ignition timing (see Chapter 5).
- ☐ Intake air leak (see Chapters 2 and 4).

Engine surges while holding throttle steady

- ☐ Intake air leak (see Chapter 4).
- ☐ Fuel pump faulty (see Chapter 4).
- ☐ Loose fuel injector wiring harness connectors (see Chapter 4).
- ☐ Defective ECU or information sensor (see Chapter 4).

Engine stalls

- ☐ Fuel filter clogged and/or water and impurities in the fuel system (see Chapter 4).
- ☐ Faulty emission system components (see Chapter 4).
- ☐ Faulty or incorrectly gapped spark plugs (see Chapter 1).
- ☐ Vacuum leak in the intake manifold or vacuum hoses (see Chapters 2 and 4).
- ☐ Valve clearances incorrectly set (see Chapter 1).

Engine lacks power

- ☐ Faulty or incorrectly gapped spark plugs (see Chapter 1).
- ☐ Fuel injection system malfunction (see Chapter 4).
- ☐ Faulty ignition coil(s) (see Chapter 5).
- ☐ Brakes binding (see Chapter 9).
- ☐ Clutch slipping (see Chapter 2).
- ☐ Fuel filter clogged or impurities in the fuel system (see Chapter 2).
- ☐ Emission control system not functioning properly (see Chapter 4).
- ☐ Low or uneven cylinder compression pressures (see Chapter 2).
- ☐ Obstructed exhaust system (see Chapter 4).

Engine backfires

- ☐ Pulse secondary air system not functioning properly (see Chapter 4).
- ☐ Fuel injection system malfunction (see Chapter 4).
- ☐ Vacuum leak at the fuel injector(s), intake manifold or vacuum hoses (see Chapters 2 and 4).
- ☐ Valve clearances incorrectly set or valves sticking (see Chapter 1 or 2).

Pinging or knocking sounds during acceleration and uphill

- ☐ Incorrect grade of fuel
- ☐ Fuel injection system faulty (see Chapter 4).
- ☐ Knock sensor(s) faulty (see Chapter 4).
- ☐ Vacuum leak (see Chapter 4).

Engine runs with oil pressure light on

- ☐ Low oil level (see Chapter 1).
- ☐ Short in wiring circuit (see Chapter 9).
- ☐ Faulty oil pressure switch (see Chapter 9).
- ☐ Worn engine bearings or oil pump (see Chapter 9).

Compression low

- ☐ Spark plugs loose. Remove the plugs and inspect their threads. Reinstall and tighten to the specified torque (Chapter 1).
- ☐ Cylinder head not sufficiently tightened down. If the cylinder head is suspected of being loose, then there's a chance that the gasket or head is damaged if the problem has persisted for any length of time. The head bolts should be tightened to the proper torque in the correct sequence (Chapter 2).
- ☐ Improper valve clearance. This means that the valve is not closing completely and compression pressure is leaking past the valve. Check and adjust the valve clearances (Chapter 1).
- ☐ Cylinder and/or piston worn. Excessive wear will cause compression pressure to leak past the rings. This is usually accompanied by worn rings as well. A top-end overhaul is necessary (Chapter 2).
- ☐ Piston rings worn, weak, broken, or sticking. Broken or sticking piston rings usually indicate a lubrication or fuelling problem that causes excess carbon deposits or seizures to form on the pistons and rings. Top-end overhaul is necessary (Chapter 2).
- ☐ Piston ring-to-groove clearance excessive. This is caused by excessive wear of the piston ring lands. Piston replacement is necessary (Chapter 2).
- ☐ Cylinder head gasket damaged. If a head is allowed to become loose, or if excessive carbon build-up on the piston crown and combustion chamber causes extremely high compression, the head gasket may leak. Retorquing the head is not always sufficient to restore the seal, so gasket replacement is necessary (Chapter 2).
- ☐ Cylinder head warped. This is caused by overheating or improperly tightened head bolts. Machine shop resurfacing or head replacement is necessary (Chapter 2).
- ☐ Valve spring broken or weak. Caused by component failure or wear; the springs must be replaced (Chapter 2).
- ☐ Valve not seating properly. This is caused by a bent valve (from over-revving or improper valve adjustment), burned valve or seat (improper fuelling) or an accumulation of carbon deposits on the seat (from fuelling or lubrication problems). The valves must be cleaned and/or replaced and the seats serviced if possible (Chapter 2).

Miscellaneous causes

- ☐ Throttle valve doesn't open fully. Adjust the throttle grip freeplay (Chapter 1).
- ☐ Clutch slipping. May be caused by loose or worn clutch components. Refer to Chapter 2 for clutch overhaul procedures.
- ☐ Engine oil viscosity too high. Using a heavier oil than the one recommended in Chapter 1 can damage the oil pump or lubrication system and cause drag on the engine.
- ☐ Brakes dragging. Usually caused by debris which has entered the brake piston seals, or from a warped disc, out-of-round drum or bent axle. Repair as necessary.

Engine overheats

- ☐ Coolant level low. Check and add coolant (Chapter 1).
- ☐ Leak in cooling system. Check cooling system hoses and radiator for leaks and other damage. Repair or replace parts as necessary (Chapter 3).
- ☐ Thermostat sticking open or closed. Check and replace as described in Chapter 3.
- ☐ Faulty pressure cap. Remove the cap and have it pressure tested (Chapter 3).
- ☐ Coolant passages clogged. Have the entire system drained and flushed, then refill with fresh coolant.
- ☐ Water pump defective. Remove the pump and check the components (Chapter 3).

- ☐ Clogged radiator fins. Clean them by blowing compressed air through the fins from the backside.
- ☐ Cooling fan or fan switch fault (Chapter 3).

Firing incorrect

- ☐ Spark plugs fouled, defective or worn out. See Chapter 1 for spark plug maintenance.
- ☐ Incorrect spark plugs.
- ☐ ECM defective. See Chapter 4.
- ☐ Camshaft position sensor coil faulty. See Chapter 4.
- ☐ Faulty ignition coils. See Chapter 5.

Fuel/air mixture incorrect

- ☐ Fuel system fault. Check the fuel injection system (Chapter 4).
- ☐ Air filter clogged, poorly sealed, or missing (Chapter 1).
- ☐ Air filter housing poorly sealed. Look for cracks, holes or loose clamps, and replace or repair defective parts.
- ☐ Fuel tank breather hose obstructed.
- ☐ Intake air leak. Check for damaged intake manifold gasket and damaged/disconnected vacuum hoses.

Compression too high

- ☐ Carbon build-up in combustion chamber. Use of a fuel additive that will dissolve the adhesive bonding the carbon particles to the piston crown and chamber is the easiest way to remove the build-up. Otherwise, the cylinder head will have to be removed and decarbonized (Chapter 2).
- ☐ Improperly machined head surface or installation of incorrect gasket during engine assembly.

Engine load excessive

- ☐ Clutch slipping. Can be caused by damaged, loose or worn clutch components. Refer to Chapter 2 for overhaul procedures.
- ☐ Engine oil level too high. The addition of too much oil will cause pressurization of the crankcase and inefficient engine operation. Check Specifications and drain to proper level (Chapter 1).
- ☐ Engine oil viscosity too high. Using a heavier oil than the one recommended in Chapter 1 can damage the oil pump or lubrication system as well as cause drag on the engine.
- ☐ Brakes dragging. Usually caused by debris which has entered the brake piston seals, or from a warped disc or drum or bent axle. Repair as necessary.

Lubrication inadequate

- ☐ Engine oil level too low. Friction caused by intermittent lack of lubrication or from oil that is overworked can cause overheating. The oil provides a definite cooling function in the engine. Check the oil level (Chapter 1).
- ☐ Poor quality engine oil or incorrect viscosity or type. Oil is rated not only according to viscosity but also according to type. Some oils are not rated high enough for use in this engine. Check the Specifications section and change to the correct oil (Chapter 1).

Miscellaneous causes

- ☐ Modification to exhaust system. Most aftermarket exhaust systems cause the engine to run leaner, which makes it run hotter.

2 Clutch problems

Clutch slipping

- ☐ Clutch cable freeplay incorrectly adjusted (cable clutch models) (Chapter 1).
- ☐ Friction plates worn or warped. Overhaul the clutch assembly (Chapter 2).
- ☐ Plain plates warped (Chapter 2).
- ☐ Clutch springs broken or weak. Old or heat-damaged (from slipping clutch) springs should be replaced with new ones (Chapter 2).
- ☐ Clutch pushrod bent. Check and, if necessary, replace (Chapter 2).
- ☐ Clutch center or housing unevenly worn. This causes improper engagement of the plates. Replace the damaged or worn parts (Chapter 2).
- ☐ Wrong type of oil used. Make sure oil with anti-friction additives (such as molybdenum disulfide) is NOT used in an engine/transmission with a wet clutch.

Clutch not disengaging completely

- ☐ Clutch cable freeplay incorrectly adjusted (Chapter 1).
- ☐ Air in clutch hydraulic system (hydraulic clutch models). Bleed the system (Chapter 2).
- ☐ Worn master or slave cylinder (hydraulic clutch models). Inspect and repair or replace as necessary (Chapter 2).

- ☐ Clutch plates warped or damaged. This will cause clutch drag, which in turn will cause the machine to creep. Overhaul the clutch assembly (Chapter 2).
- ☐ Clutch spring tension uneven. Usually caused by a sagged or broken spring. Check and replace the springs as a set (Chapter 2).
- ☐ Engine oil deteriorated. Old, thin, worn out oil will not provide proper lubrication for the plates, causing the clutch to drag. Replace the oil and filter (Chapter 1).
- ☐ Engine oil viscosity too high. Using a heavier oil than recommended in Chapter 1 can cause the plates to stick together, putting a drag on the engine. Change to the correct weight oil (Chapter 1).
- ☐ Clutch housing bearing seized. Lack of lubrication, severe wear or damage can cause the bearing to seize on the input shaft. Overhaul of the clutch, and perhaps transmission, may be necessary to repair the damage (Chapter 2).
- ☐ Loose clutch center nut. Causes housing and center misalignment putting a drag on the engine. Engagement adjustment continually varies. Overhaul the clutch assembly (Chapter 2).

3 Gearchanging problems

Doesn't go into gear or lever doesn't return

- [ ] Clutch not disengaging. See Section 5.
- [ ] Shift fork(s) bent or seized. Often caused by dropping the machine or from lack of lubrication. Overhaul the transmission (Chapter 2).
- [ ] Gear(s) stuck on shaft. Most often caused by a lack of lubrication or excessive wear in transmission bearings and bushings. Overhaul the transmission (Chapter 2).
- [ ] Gear shift drum binding. Caused by lubrication failure or excessive wear. Replace the drum and bearing (Chapter 2).
- [ ] Gear shift lever pawl spring weak or broken (Chapter 2).
- [ ] Gear shift lever broken. Splines stripped out of lever or shaft, caused by allowing the lever to get loose or from dropping the machine. Replace necessary parts (Chapter 2).
- [ ] Gear shift mechanism stopper arm broken or worn. Full engagement and rotary movement of shift drum results. Replace the arm (Chapter 2).
- [ ] Stopper arm spring broken. Allows arm to float, causing sporadic shift operation. Replace spring (Chapter 2).

Jumps out of gear

- [ ] Shift fork(s) worn. Overhaul the transmission (Chapter 2).
- [ ] Gear groove(s) worn. Overhaul the transmission (Chapter 2).
- [ ] Gear dogs or dog slots worn or damaged. The gears should be inspected and replaced. No attempt should be made to service the worn parts.

Overselects

- [ ] Stopper arm spring weak or broken (Chapter 2).
- [ ] Return spring post broken or distorted (Chapter 2).

4 Abnormal engine noise

Knocking or pinging

- [ ] Carbon build-up in combustion chamber. Use of a fuel additive that will dissolve the adhesive bonding the carbon particles to the piston crown and chamber is the easiest way to remove the build-up. Otherwise, the cylinder head will have to be removed and decarbonized (Chapter 2).
- [ ] Incorrect or poor quality fuel. Old or improper fuel can cause detonation. This causes the pistons to rattle, thus the knocking or pinging sound. Drain the old fuel and always use the recommended grade fuel (Chapter 4).
- [ ] Spark plug heat range incorrect. Uncontrolled detonation indicates that the plug heat range is too hot. The plug in effect becomes a glow plug, raising cylinder temperatures. Install the proper heat range plug (Chapter 1).
- [ ] Improper air/fuel mixture. This will cause the cylinders to run hot and lead to detonation. Blocked carburetor jets or an air leak can cause this imbalance. See Chapter 4.

Piston slap or rattling

- [ ] Cylinder-to-piston clearance excessive. Caused by improper assembly. Inspect and overhaul top-end parts (Chapter 2).
- [ ] Connecting rod bent. Caused by over-revving, trying to start a badly flooded engine or from ingesting a foreign object into the combustion chamber. Replace the damaged parts (Chapter 2).
- [ ] Piston pin or piston pin bore worn or seized from wear or lack of lubrication. Replace damaged parts (Chapter 2).
- [ ] Piston ring(s) worn, broken or sticking. Overhaul the top-end (Chapter 2).
- [ ] Piston seizure damage. Usually from lack of lubrication or overheating. Replace the pistons and cylinders, as necessary (Chapter 2).
- [ ] Connecting rod bearing clearance excessive. Caused by excessive wear or lack of lubrication. Replace worn parts.

Valve noise

- [ ] Incorrect valve clearances. Adjust the clearances by referring to Chapter 1.
- [ ] Valve spring broken or weak. Check and replace weak valve springs (Chapter 2).
- [ ] Camshaft or cylinder head worn or damaged. Lack of lubrication at high rpm is usually the cause of damage. Insufficient oil or failure to change the oil at the recommended intervals are the chief causes. Since there are no replaceable bearings in the head, the head itself will have to be replaced if there is excessive wear or damage (Chapter 2).

Other noise

- [ ] Cylinder head gasket leaking.
- [ ] Exhaust pipe leaking at cylinder head connection. Caused by improper fit of pipe(s) or loose exhaust nuts. All exhaust fasteners should be tightened evenly and carefully. Failure to do this will lead to a leak.
- [ ] Crankshaft runout excessive. Caused by a bent crankshaft (from over-revving) or damage from an upper cylinder component failure. Can also be attributed to dropping the machine on either of the crankshaft ends.
- [ ] Engine mounting bolts loose. Tighten all engine mount bolts (Chapter 2).
- [ ] Crankshaft bearings worn (Chapter 2).
- [ ] Cam chain, tensioner or guides worn. Replace according to the procedure in Chapter 2.

5 Abnormal driveline noise

Clutch noise

- [ ] Clutch outer drum/friction plate clearance excessive (Chapter 2).
- [ ] Loose or damaged clutch pressure plate and/or bolts (Chapter 2).

Transmission noise

- [ ] Bearings worn. Also includes the possibility that the shafts are worn. Overhaul the transmission (Chapter 2).
- [ ] Gears worn or chipped (Chapter 2).
- [ ] Metal chips jammed in gear teeth. Probably pieces from a broken clutch, gear or shift mechanism that were picked up by the gears. This will cause early bearing failure (Chapter 2).
- [ ] Engine oil level too low. Causes a howl from transmission. Also affects engine power and clutch operation (Chapter 1).

Final drive noise

- [ ] Chain or drive belt not adjusted properly (Chapter 1).
- [ ] Front or rear sprocket loose. Tighten fasteners (Chapter 6).
- [ ] Sprockets worn. Replace sprockets (Chapter 6).
- [ ] Rear sprocket warped. Replace sprockets (Chapter 6).
- [ ] Differential worn or damaged. Have it repaired or replace it (Chapter 7).

6 Abnormal frame and suspension noise

Front end noise

- [ ] Low fluid level or improper viscosity oil in forks. This can sound like spurting and is usually accompanied by irregular fork action (Chapter 6).
- [ ] Spring weak or broken. Makes a clicking or scraping sound. Fork oil, when drained, will have a lot of metal particles in it (Chapter 6).
- [ ] Steering head bearings loose or damaged. Clicks when braking. Check and adjust or replace as necessary (Chapters 1 and 6).
- [ ] Triple clamps loose. Make sure all clamp bolts are tightened to the specified torque (Chapter 6).
- [ ] Fork tube bent. Good possibility if machine has been dropped. Replace tube with a new one (Chapter 6).
- [ ] Front axle bolt or axle pinch bolts loose. Tighten them to the specified torque (Chapter 7).
- [ ] Loose or worn wheel bearings. Check and replace as needed (Chapter 7).

Shock absorber noise

- [ ] Fluid level incorrect. Indicates a leak caused by defective seal. Shock will be covered with oil. Replace shock or seek advice on repair from a dealer (Chapter 6).
- [ ] Defective shock absorber with internal damage. This is in the body of the shock and can't be remedied. The shock must be replaced with a new one (Chapter 6).
- [ ] Bent or damaged shock body. Replace the shock with a new one (Chapter 6).
- [ ] Loose or worn suspension linkage components (EX250 models). Check and replace as necessary (Chapter 6).

Brake noise

- [ ] Squeal caused by dust on brake pads. Usually found in combination with glazed pads. Clean using brake cleaning solvent (Chapter 7).
- [ ] Contamination of brake pads. Oil, brake fluid or dirt causing brake to chatter or squeal. Clean or replace pads (Chapter 7).
- [ ] Pads glazed. Caused by excessive heat from prolonged use or from contamination. Do not use sandpaper/emery cloth or any other abrasive to roughen the pad surfaces as abrasives will stay in the pad material and damage the disc. A very fine flat file can be used, but pad replacement is suggested as a cure (Chapter 7).
- [ ] Disc warped. Can cause a chattering, clicking or intermittent squeal. Usually accompanied by a pulsating lever and uneven braking. Replace the disc (Chapter 7).
- [ ] Loose or worn wheel bearings. Check and replace as needed (Chapter 7).

7 Excessive exhaust smoke

White smoke

- [ ] Piston oil ring worn. The ring may be broken or damaged, causing oil from the crankcase to be pulled past the piston into the combustion chamber. Replace the rings with new ones (Chapter 2).
- [ ] Cylinders worn, cracked, or scored. Caused by overheating or oil starvation. Install a new cylinder block (Chapter 2).
- [ ] Valve oil seal damaged or worn. Replace oil seals with new ones (Chapter 2).
- [ ] Valve guide worn. Perform a complete valve job (Chapter 2).
- [ ] Engine oil level too high, which causes the oil to be forced past the rings. Drain oil to the proper level (Chapter 1).
- [ ] Head gasket broken between oil return and cylinder. Causes oil to be pulled into the combustion chamber. Replace the head gasket and check the head for warpage (Chapter 2).
- [ ] Abnormal crankcase pressurization, which forces oil past the rings. Clogged breather is usually the cause.

Black smoke

- [ ] Air filter clogged. Clean or replace the element (Chapter 1).
- [ ] Carburetor flooding. Remove and overhaul the carburetor(s) (Chapter 4).
- [ ] Main jet too large. Remove and overhaul the carburetor(s) (Chapter 4).
- [ ] Choke cable stuck (Chapter 4).
- [ ] Fuel level too high. Check the fuel level (Chapter 4).
- [ ] Fuel injector problem (Chapter 4).

8 Poor handling or stability

Handlebar hard to turn

- ☐ Steering head bearing adjuster nut too tight. Check adjustment as described in Chapter 1.
- ☐ Bearings damaged. Roughness can be felt as the bars are turned from side-to-side. Replace bearings and races (Chapter 6).
- ☐ Races dented or worn. Denting results from wear in only one position (e.g., straight ahead), from a collision or hitting a pothole or from dropping the machine. Replace races and bearings (Chapter 6).
- ☐ Steering stem lubrication inadequate. Causes are grease getting hard from age or being washed out by high pressure car washes. Disassemble steering head and repack bearings (Chapter 6).
- ☐ Steering stem bent. Caused by a collision, hitting a pothole or by dropping the machine. Replace damaged part. Don't try to straighten the steering stem (Chapter 6).
- ☐ Front tire air pressure too low (Chapter 1).

Handlebar shakes or vibrates excessively

- ☐ Tires worn or out of balance (Chapter 7).
- ☐ Swingarm bearings worn. Replace worn bearings (Chapter 6).
- ☐ Wheel rim(s) warped or damaged. Inspect wheels for runout (Chapter 7).
- ☐ Spokes loose (see Chapter 1).
- ☐ Wheel bearings worn. Worn front or rear wheel bearings can cause poor tracking. Worn front bearings will cause wobble (Chapter 7).
- ☐ Handlebar clamp bolts loose (Chapter 6).
- ☐ Fork yoke bolts loose. Tighten them to the specified torque (Chapter 6).
- ☐ Engine mounting bolts loose. Will cause excessive vibration with increased engine rpm (Chapter 2).

Handlebar pulls to one side

- ☐ Frame bent. Definitely suspect this if the machine has been dropped. May or may not be accompanied by cracking near the bend. Replace the frame (Chapter 8).
- ☐ Wheels out of alignment. Caused by improper location of axle spacers or from bent steering stem or frame (Chapters 6 and 8).
- ☐ Swingarm bent or twisted. Caused by age (metal fatigue) or impact damage. Replace the arm (Chapter 6).
- ☐ Steering stem bent. Caused by impact damage or by dropping the motorcycle. Replace the steering stem (Chapter 6).
- ☐ Fork tube bent. Disassemble the forks and replace the damaged parts (Chapter 6).
- ☐ Fork oil level uneven. Check and add or drain as necessary (Chapter 1).

Poor shock absorbing qualities

Too hard:
- a) Fork oil level excessive (Chapter 1).
- b) Fork oil viscosity too high. Use a lighter oil (see the Specifications in Chapter 1).
- c) Fork tube bent. Causes a harsh, sticking feeling (Chapter 6).
- d) Shock shaft or body bent or damaged (Chapter 6).
- e) Fork internal damage (Chapter 6).
- f) Shock internal damage.
- g) Tire pressure too high (Chapter 1).

Too soft:
- a) Fork or shock oil insufficient and/or leaking (Chapter 1).
- b) Fork oil level too low (Chapter 6).
- c) Fork oil viscosity too light (Chapter 6).
- d) Fork springs weak or broken (Chapter 6).
- e) Shock internal damage or leakage (Chapter 6).

9 Braking problems

Brakes are spongy, don't hold

- ☐ Air in brake line. Caused by inattention to master cylinder fluid level or by leakage. Locate problem and bleed brakes (Chapter 7).
- ☐ Pad or disc worn (Chapters 1 and 7).
- ☐ Brake fluid leak. See paragraph 1.
- ☐ Contaminated pads. Caused by contamination with oil, grease, brake fluid, etc. Clean or replace pads. Clean disc thoroughly with brake cleaner (Chapter 7).
- ☐ Brake fluid deteriorated. Fluid is old or contaminated. Drain system, replenish with new fluid and bleed the system (Chapter 7).
- ☐ Master cylinder internal parts worn or damaged causing fluid to bypass (Chapter 7).
- ☐ Master cylinder bore scratched by foreign material or broken spring. Repair or replace master cylinder (Chapter 7).
- ☐ Disc warped. Replace disc (Chapter 7).

Brake lever or pedal pulsates

- ☐ Disc warped. Replace disc (Chapter 7).

- ☐ Axle bent. Replace axle (Chapter 7).
- ☐ Brake caliper bolts loose (Chapter 7).
- ☐ Wheel warped or otherwise damaged (Chapter 7).
- ☐ Wheel bearings damaged or worn (Chapter 7).
- ☐ Brake drum out of round. Replace brake drum.

Brakes drag

- ☐ Master cylinder piston seized. Caused by wear or damage to piston or cylinder bore (Chapter 7).
- ☐ Lever binding. Check pivot and lubricate (Chapter 7).
- ☐ Brake caliper piston seized in bore. Caused by wear or ingestion of dirt past deteriorated seal (Chapter 7).
- ☐ Brake caliper mounting bracket pins corroded. Clean off corrosion and lubricate (Chapter 7).
- ☐ Brake pad or shoe damaged. Material separated from backing plate. Usually caused by faulty manufacturing process or from contact with chemicals. Replace pads or shoes (Chapter 7).
- ☐ Pads improperly installed (Chapter 7).
- ☐ Drum brake springs weak. Replace springs

10 Electrical problems

Battery dead or weak

- ☐ Battery faulty. Caused by sulfated plates which are shorted through sedimentation. Also, broken battery terminal making only occasional contact (Chapter 9).
- ☐ Battery cables making poor contact (Chapter 9).
- ☐ Load excessive. Caused by addition of high wattage lights or other electrical accessories.
- ☐ Ignition (main) switch defective. Switch either grounds internally or fails to shut off system. Replace the switch (Chapter 9).
- ☐ Regulator/rectifier defective (Chapter 9).
- ☐ Alternator stator coil open or shorted (Chapter 9).
- ☐ Wiring faulty. Wiring grounded or connections loose in ignition, charging or lighting circuits (Chapter 9).

Battery overcharged

- ☐ Regulator/rectifier defective. Overcharging is noticed when battery gets excessively warm (Chapter 9).
- ☐ Battery defective. Replace battery with a new one (Chapter 9).
- ☐ Battery amperage too low, wrong type or size. Install manufacturer's specified amp-hour battery to handle charging load (Chapter 9).

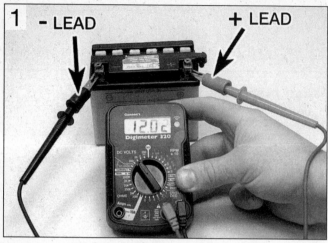

1 – LEAD   + LEAD

Measuring open-circuit battery voltage

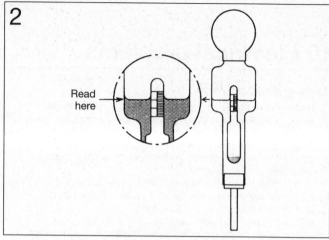

2 Read here

Float-type hydrometer for measuring battery specific gravity

Checking engine compression

● Low compression will result in exhaust smoke, heavy oil consumption, poor starting and poor performance. A compression test will provide useful information about an engine's condition and if performed regularly, can give warning of trouble before any other symptoms become apparent.

● A compression gauge will be required, along with an adapter to suit the spark plug hole thread size. Note that the screw-in type gauge/adapter set up is preferable to the rubber cone type.

● Before carrying out the test, first check the valve clearances as described in Chapter 1.

● Compression testing procedures for the motorcycles covered in this manual are described in Chapter 2C.

Checking battery open-circuit voltage

Warning: The gases produced by the battery are explosive - never smoke or create any sparks in the vicinity of the battery. Never allow the electrolyte to contact your skin or clothing - if it does, wash it off and seek immediate medical attention.

● Before any electrical fault is investigated the battery should be checked.

● You'll need a dc voltmeter or multimeter to check battery voltage. Check that the leads are inserted in the correct terminals on the meter, red lead to positive (+), black lead to negative (-). Incorrect connections can

damage the meter.

● A sound, fully-charged 12 volt battery should produce between 12.3 and 12.6 volts across its terminals (12.8 volts for a maintenance-free battery). On machines with a 6 volt battery, voltage should be between 6.1 and 6.3 volts.

1 Set a multimeter to the 0 to 20 volts dc range and connect its probes across the battery terminals. Connect the meter's positive (+) probe, usually red, to the battery positive (+) terminal, followed by the meter's negative (-) probe, usually black, to the battery negative terminal (-) **(see illustration 1)**.

2 If battery voltage is low (below 10 volts on a 12 volt battery or below 4 volts on a six volt battery), charge the battery and test the voltage again. If the battery repeatedly goes flat, investigate the motorcycle's charging system.

Checking battery specific gravity (SG)

Warning: The gases produced by the battery are explosive - never smoke or create any sparks in the vicinity of the battery. Never allow the electrolyte to contact your skin or clothing - if it does, wash it off and seek immediate medical attention.

● The specific gravity check gives an indication of a battery's state of charge.

● A hydrometer is used for measuring specific gravity. Make sure you purchase one which has a small enough hose to insert in the aperture of a motorcycle battery.

● Specific gravity is simply a measure of the electrolyte's density compared with that of water. Water has an SG of 1.000 and

fully-charged battery electrolyte is about 26% heavier, at 1.260.

● Specific gravity checks are not possible on maintenance-free batteries. Testing the open-circuit voltage is the only means of determining their state of charge.

1 To measure SG, remove the battery from the motorcycle and remove the first cell cap. Draw some electrolyte into the hydrometer and note the reading **(see illustration 2)**. Return the electrolyte to the cell and install the cap.

2 The reading should be in the region of 1.260 to 1.280. If SG is below 1.200 the battery needs charging. Note that SG will vary with temperature; it should be measured at 20°C (68°F). Add 0.007 to the reading for every 10°C above 20°C, and subtract 0.007 from the reading for every 10°C below 20°C. Add 0.004 to the reading for every 10°F above 68°F, and subtract 0.004 from the reading for every 10°F below 68°F.

3 When the check is complete, rinse the hydrometer thoroughly with clean water.

Checking for continuity

● The term continuity describes the uninterrupted flow of electricity through an electrical circuit. A continuity check will determine whether an **open-circuit** situation exists.

● Continuity can be checked with an ohmmeter, multimeter, continuity tester or battery and bulb test circuit **(see illustrations 3, 4 and 5)**.

● All of these instruments are self-powered by a battery, therefore the checks are made with the ignition OFF.

● As a safety precaution, always disconnect the battery negative (-) lead before making checks, particularly if ignition switch checks are being made.

● If using a meter, select the appropriate

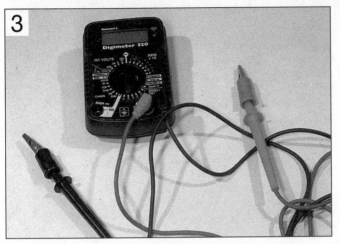

3

Digital multimeter can be used for all electrical tests

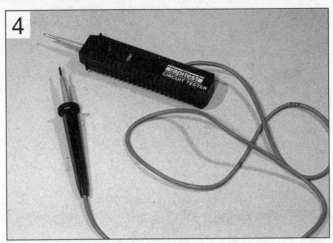

4

Battery-powered continuity tester

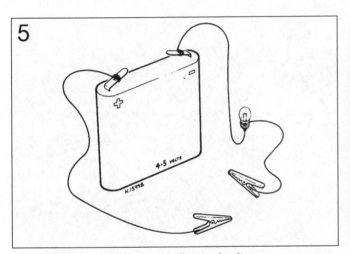

5

Battery and bulb test circuit

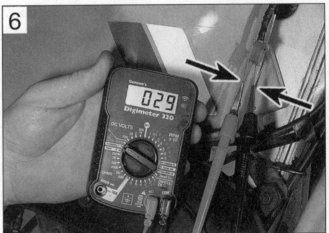

6

Continuity check of front brake light switch using a meter - note cotter pins used to access connector terminals

ohms scale and check that the meter reads infinity (∞). Touch the meter probes together and check that meter reads zero; where necessary adjust the meter so that it reads zero.

● After using a meter, always switch it OFF to conserve its battery.

Switch checks

1 If a switch is at fault, trace its wiring up to the wiring connectors. Separate the wire connectors and inspect them for security and condition. A build-up of dirt or corrosion here will most likely be the cause of the problem - clean up and apply a water dispersant such as WD40.

2 If using a test meter, set the meter to the ohms x 10 scale and connect its probes across the wires from the switch **(see illustration 6)**. Simple ON/OFF type switches, such as brake light switches, only have two wires whereas combination switches, like the ignition switch, have many internal links. Study

the wiring diagram to ensure that you are connecting across the correct pair of wires. Continuity (low or no measurable resistance - 0 ohms) should be indicated with the switch ON and no continuity (high resistance) with it OFF.

3 Note that the polarity of the test probes doesn't matter for continuity checks, although care should be taken to follow specific test procedures if a diode or solid-state component is being checked.

4 A continuity tester or battery and bulb circuit can be used in the same way. Connect its probes as described above **(see illustration 7)**. The light should come on to indicate continuity in the ON switch position, but should extinguish in the OFF position.

Wiring checks

● Many electrical faults are caused by damaged wiring, often due to incorrect routing or chaffing on frame components.

● Loose, wet or corroded wire connectors

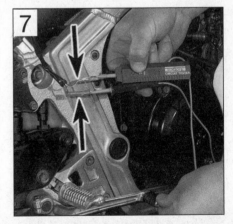

7

Continuity check of rear brake light switch using a continuity tester

can also be the cause of electrical problems, especially in exposed locations.

Continuity check of front brake light switch sub-harness

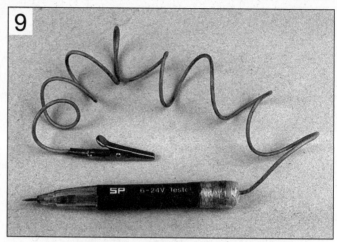

A simple test light can be used for voltage checks

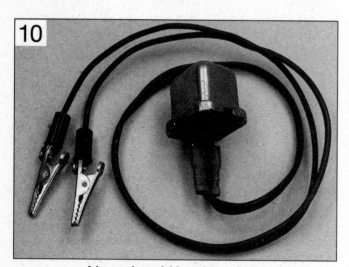

A buzzer is useful for voltage checks

Checking for voltage at the rear brake light power supply wire
using a meter . . .

1 A continuity check can be made on a single length of wire by disconnecting it at each end and connecting a meter or continuity tester across both ends of the wire **(see illustration 8)**.

2 Continuity (low or no resistance - 0 ohms) should be indicated if the wire is good. If no continuity (high resistance) is shown, suspect a broken wire.

Checking for voltage

● A voltage check can determine whether current is reaching a component.

● Voltage can be checked with a dc voltmeter, multimeter set on the dc volts scale, test light or buzzer **(see illustrations 9 and 10)**. A meter has the advantage of being able to measure actual voltage.

● When using a meter, check that its leads

are inserted in the correct terminals on the meter, red to positive (+), black to negative (-). Incorrect connections can damage the meter.

● A voltmeter (or multimeter set to the dc volts scale) should always be connected in parallel (across the load). Connecting it in series will destroy the meter.

● Voltage checks are made with the ignition ON.

1 First identify the relevant wiring circuit by referring to the wiring diagram at the end of this manual. If other electrical components share the same power supply (ie are fed from the same fuse), take note whether they are working correctly - this is useful information in deciding where to start checking the circuit.

2 If using a meter, check first that the meter leads are plugged into the correct terminals on the meter (see above). Set the meter to the dc volts function, at a range suitable for the battery voltage. Connect the meter red probe (+) to the power supply wire and the black probe to a good metal ground on the

motorcycle's frame or directly to the battery negative (-) terminal **(see illustration 11)**. Battery voltage should be shown on the meter with the ignition switched ON.

3 If using a test light or buzzer, connect its positive (+) probe to the power supply terminal and its negative (-) probe to a good ground on the motorcycle's frame or directly to the battery negative (-) terminal **(see illustration 12)**. With the ignition ON, the test light should illuminate or the buzzer sound.

4 If no voltage is indicated, work back towards the fuse continuing to check for voltage. When you reach a point where there is voltage, you know the problem lies between that point and your last check point.

Checking the ground

● Ground connections are made either

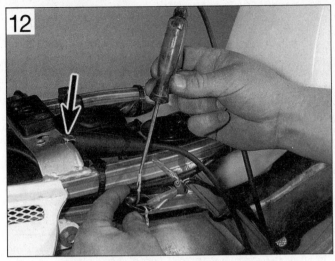

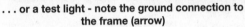

... or a test light - note the ground connection to the frame (arrow)

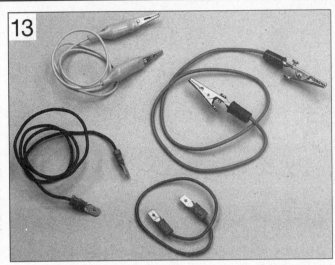

A selection of jumper wires for making ground checks

directly to the engine or frame (such as sensors, neutral switch etc. which only have a positive feed) or by a separate wire into the ground circuit of the wiring harness. Alternatively a short ground wire is sometimes run directly from the component to the motor-cycle's frame.

● Corrosion is often the cause of a poor ground connection.

● If total failure is experienced, check the security of the main ground lead from the negative (-) terminal of the battery and also the main ground point on the wiring harness. If corroded, dismantle the connection and clean all surfaces back to bare metal.

1 To check the ground on a component, use an insulated jumper wire to temporarily bypass its ground connection **(see illustration 13)**. Connect one end of the jumper wire between the ground terminal or metal body

of the component and the other end to the motorcycle's frame.

2 If the circuit works with the jumper wire installed, the original ground circuit is faulty. Check the wiring for open-circuits or poor connections. Clean up direct ground connections, removing all traces of corrosion and remake the joint. Apply petroleum jelly to the joint to prevent future corrosion.

Tracing a short-circuit

● A short-circuit occurs where current shorts to ground bypassing the circuit components. This usually results in a blown fuse.

● A short-circuit is most likely to occur where the insulation has worn through due to wiring chafing on a component, allowing a direct path to ground on the frame.

1 Remove any body panels necessary to access the circuit wiring.

2 Check that all electrical switches in the circuit are OFF, then remove the circuit fuse and connect a test light, buzzer or voltmeter (set to the dc scale) across the fuse terminals. No voltage should be shown.

3 Move the wiring from side to side while observing the test light or meter. When the test light comes on, buzzer sounds or meter shows voltage, you have found the cause of the short. It will usually shown up as damaged or burned insulation.

4 Note that the same test can be performed on each component in the circuit, even the switch.

Introduction

In less time than it takes to read this introduction, a thief could steal your motorcycle. Returning only to find your bike has gone is one of the worst feelings in the world. Even if the motorcycle is insured against theft, once you've got over the initial shock, you will have the inconvenience of dealing with the police and your insurance company.

The motorcycle is an easy target for the professional thief and the joyrider alike and the

official figures on motorcycle theft make for depressing reading; on average a motorcycle is stolen every 16 minutes in the UK!

Motorcycle thefts fall into two categories, those stolen 'to order' and those taken by opportunists. The thief stealing to order will be on the look out for a specific make and model and will go to extraordinary lengths to obtain that motorcycle. The opportunist thief on the other hand will look for easy targets which can be stolen with the minimum of effort and risk.

While it is never going to be possible to make your machine 100% secure, it is estimated that around half of all stolen motorcycles are taken by opportunist thieves. Remember that the opportunist thief is always on the look out for the easy option: if there are two similar motorcycles parked side-by-side, they will target the one with the lowest level of security. By taking a few precautions, you can reduce the chances of your motorcycle being stolen.

Security equipment

There are many specialized motorcycle security devices available and the following text summarizes their applications and their good and bad points.

Once you have decided on the type of security equipment which best suits your needs, we recommended that you read one of the many equipment tests regularly carried

out by the motorcycle press. These tests compare the products from all the major manufacturers and give impartial ratings on their effectiveness, value-for-money and ease of use.

No one item of security equipment can provide complete protection. It is highly recommended that two or more of the items described below are combined to increase the security of your motorcycle (a lock and chain plus an alarm system is just about ideal). The more security measures fitted to the bike, the less likely it is to be stolen.

Lock and chain

Pros: *Very flexible to use; can be used to secure the motorcycle to almost any immovable object. On some locks and chains, the lock can be used on its own as a disc lock (see below).*

Cons: *Can be very heavy and awkward to carry on the motorcycle, although some types*

will be supplied with a carry bag which can be strapped to the pillion seat.

● Heavy-duty chains and locks are an excellent security measure **(see illustration 1)**. Whenever the motorcycle is parked, use the lock and chain to secure the machine to a solid, immovable object such as a post or railings. This will prevent the machine from being ridden away or being lifted into the back of a van.

● When fitting the chain, always ensure the chain is routed around the motorcycle frame or swingarm **(see illustrations 2 and 3)**. Never merely pass the chain around one of the wheel rims; a thief may unbolt the wheel and lift the rest of the machine into a van, leaving you with just the wheel! Try to avoid having excess chain free, thus making it difficult to use cutting tools, and keep the chain and lock off the ground to prevent thieves attacking it with a cold chisel. Position the lock so that its lock barrel is facing downwards; this will make it harder for the thief to attack the lock mechanism.

Ensure the lock and chain you buy is of good quality and long enough to shackle your bike to a solid object

Pass the chain through the bike's frame, rather than just through a wheel . . .

. . . and loop it around a solid object

U-locks

Pros: *Highly effective deterrent which can be used to secure the bike to a post or railings. Most U-locks come with a carrier which allows the lock to be easily carried on the bike.*

Cons: *Not as flexible to use as a lock and chain.*

● These are solid locks which are similar in use to a lock and chain. U-locks are lighter than a lock and chain but not so flexible to use. The length and shape of the lock shackle limit the objects to which the bike can be secured **(see illustration 4)**.

Disc locks

Pros: *Small, light and very easy to carry; most can be stored underneath the seat.*

Cons: *Does not prevent the motorcycle being lifted into a van. Can be very embarrassing if*

U-locks can be used to secure the bike to a solid object - ensure you purchase one which is long enough

you forget to remove the lock before attempting to ride off!

● Disc locks are designed to be attached to the front brake disc. The lock passes through one of the holes in the disc and prevents the wheel rotating by jamming against the fork/brake caliper **(see illustration 5)**. Some are equipped with an alarm siren which sounds if the disc lock is moved; this not only acts as a theft deterrent but also as a handy reminder if you try to move the bike with the lock still fitted.

● Combining the disc lock with a length of cable which can be looped around a post or railings provides an additional measure of security **(see illustration 6)**.

Alarms and immobilisers

Pros: *Once installed it is completely hassle-free to use. If the system is 'Thatcham' or 'Sold Secure-approved', insurance companies may give you a discount.*

Cons: *Can be expensive to buy and complex to install. No system will prevent the motorcycle from being lifted into a van and taken away.*

● Electronic alarms and immobilizers are available to suit a variety of budgets. There are three different types of system available: pure alarms, pure immobilizers, and the more expensive systems which are combined alarm/immobilizers **(see illustration 7)**.
● An alarm system is designed to emit an audible warning if the motorcycle is being tampered with.
● An immobilizer prevents the motorcycle being started and ridden away by disabling its electrical systems.
● When purchasing an alarm/immobilizer system, check the cost of installing the system unless you are able to do it yourself. If the motorcycle is not used regularly, another consideration is the current drain of the system. All alarm/immobilizer systems are powered by the motorcycle's battery; purchasing a system with a very low current drain could prevent the battery losing its charge while the motorcycle is not being used.

A typical disc lock attached through one of the holes in the disc

A disc lock combined with a security cable provides additional protection

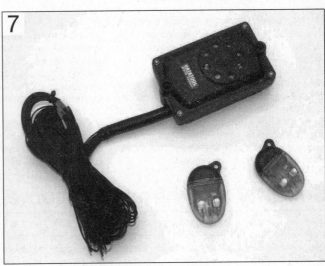

A typical alarm/immobilizer system

Indelible markings can be applied to most areas of the bike – always apply the manufacturer's sticker to warn off thieves

Chemically-etched code numbers can be applied to main body panels . . .

. . . again, always ensure that the kit manufacturer's sticker is applied in a prominent position

Security marking kits

Pros: *Very cheap and effective deterrent. Many insurance companies will give you a discount on your insurance premium if a recognized security marking kit is used on your motorcycle.*

Cons: *Does not prevent the motorcycle being stolen by joyriders.*

● There are many different types of security marking kits available. The idea is to mark as many parts of the motorcycle as possible with a unique security number **(see illustrations 8, 9 and 10)**. A form will be included with the kit to register your personal details and those of the motorcycle with the kit manufacturer. This register is made available to the police to help them trace the rightful owner of any motorcycle or components which they recover should all other forms of identification have been removed. Always apply the warning stickers provided with the kit to deter thieves.

Ground anchors, wheel clamps and security posts

Pros: *An excellent form of security which will deter all but the most determined of thieves.*

Cons: *Awkward to install and can be expensive.*

● While the motorcycle is at home, it is a good idea to attach it securely to the floor or a solid wall, even if it is kept in a securely locked garage. Various types of ground anchors, security posts and wheel clamps are available for this purpose **(see illustration 11)**. These security devices are either bolted to a solid concrete or brick structure or can be cemented into the ground.

Permanent ground anchors provide an excellent level of security when the bike is at home

Security at home

A high percentage of motorcycle thefts are from the owner's home. Here are some things to consider whenever your motorcycle is at home:

✔ Where possible, always keep the motorcycle in a securely locked garage. Never rely solely on the standard lock on the garage door, these are usual hopelessly inadequate. Fit an additional locking mechanism to the door and consider having the garage alarmed. A security light, activated by a movement sensor, is also a good investment.

✔ Always secure the motorcycle to the ground or a wall, even if it is inside a securely locked garage.

✔ Do not regularly leave the motorcycle outside your home, try to keep it out of sight wherever possible. If a garage is not available, fit a motorcycle cover over the bike to disguise its true identity.

✔ It is not uncommon for thieves to follow a motorcyclist home to find out where the bike is kept. They will then return at a later date. Be aware of this whenever you are returning

home on your motorcycle. If you suspect you are being followed, do not return home, instead ride to a garage or shop and stop as a precaution.

✔ When selling a motorcycle, do not provide your home address or the location where the bike is normally kept. Arrange to meet the buyer at a location away from your home. Thieves have been known to pose as potential buyers to find out where motorcycles are kept and then return later to steal them.

Security away from the home

As well as fitting security equipment to your motorcycle here are a few general rules to follow whenever you park your motorcycle.

✔ Park in a busy, public place.

✔ Use car parks which incorporate security features, such as CCTV.

✔ At night, park in a well-lit area, preferably directly underneath a street light.

✔ Engage the steering lock.

✔ Secure the motorcycle to a solid, immovable object such as a post or railings with an additional lock. If this is not possible,

secure the bike to a friend's motorcycle. Some public parking places provide security loops for motorcycles.

✔ Never leave your helmet or luggage attached to the motorcycle. Take them with you at all times.

A

ABS (Anti-lock braking system) A system, usually electronically controlled, that senses incipient wheel lockup during braking and relieves hydraulic pressure at wheel which is about to skid.

Aftermarket Components suitable for the motorcycle, but not produced by the motorcycle manufacturer.

Allen key A hexagonal wrench which fits into a recessed hexagonal hole.

Alternating current (ac) Current produced by an alternator. Requires converting to direct current by a rectifier for charging purposes.

Alternator Converts mechanical energy from the engine into electrical energy to charge the battery and power the electrical system.

Ampere (amp) A unit of measurement for the flow of electrical current. Current = Volts ÷ Ohms.

Ampere-hour (Ah) Measure of battery capacity.

Angle-tightening A torque expressed in degrees. Often follows a conventional tightening torque for cylinder head or main bearing fasteners **(see illustration)**.

Angle-tightening cylinder head bolts

Antifreeze A substance (usually ethylene glycol) mixed with water, and added to the cooling system, to prevent freezing of the coolant in winter. Antifreeze also contains chemicals to inhibit corrosion and the formation of rust and other deposits that would tend to clog the radiator and coolant passages and reduce cooling efficiency.

Anti-dive System attached to the fork lower leg (slider) to prevent fork dive when braking hard.

Anti-seize compound A coating that reduces the risk of seizing on fasteners that are subjected to high temperatures, such as exhaust clamp bolts and nuts.

API American Petroleum Institute. A quality standard for 4-stroke motor oils.

Asbestos A natural fibrous mineral with great heat resistance, commonly used in the composition of brake friction materials. Asbestos is a health hazard and the dust created by brake systems should never be inhaled or ingested.

ATF Automatic Transmission Fluid. Often used in front forks.

ATU Automatic Timing Unit. Mechanical device for advancing the ignition timing on early engines.

ATV All Terrain Vehicle. Often called a Quad.

Axial play Side-to-side movement.

Axle A shaft on which a wheel revolves. Also known as a spindle.

B

Backlash The amount of movement between meshed components when one component is held still. Usually applies to gear teeth.

Ball bearing A bearing consisting of a hardened inner and outer race with hardened steel balls between the two races.

Bearings Used between two working surfaces to prevent wear of the components and a build-up of heat. Four types of bearing are commonly used on motorcycles: plain shell bearings, ball bearings, tapered roller bearings and needle roller bearings.

Bevel gears Used to turn the drive through 90°. Typical applications are shaft final drive and camshaft drive **(see illustration)**.

BHP Brake Horsepower. The British measurement for engine power output. Power output is now usually expressed in kilowatts (kW).

Bevel gears are used to turn the drive through 90°

Bias-belted tire Similar construction to radial tire, but with outer belt running at an angle to the wheel rim.

Big-end bearing The bearing in the end of the connecting rod that's attached to the crankshaft.

Bleeding The process of removing air from a hydraulic system via a bleed nipple or bleed screw.

Bottom-end A description of an engine's crankcase components and all components contained therein.

BTDC Before Top Dead Center in terms of piston position. Ignition timing is often expressed in terms of degrees or millimeters BTDC.

Bush A cylindrical metal or rubber component used between two moving parts.

Burr Rough edge left on a component after machining or as a result of excessive wear.

C

Cam chain The chain which takes drive from the crankshaft to the camshaft(s).

Canister The main component in an evap-orative emission control system (California market only); contains activated charcoal granules to trap vapors from the fuel system rather than allowing them to vent to the atmosphere.

Castellated Resembling the parapets along the top of a castle wall. For example, a castellated wheel axle or spindle nut.

Catalytic converter A device in the exhaust system of some machines which

Cush drive rubber segments dampen out transmission shocks

converts certain pollutants in the exhaust gases into less harmful substances.

Charging system Description of the components which charge the battery, ie the alternator, rectifer and regulator.

Clearance The amount of space between two parts. For example, between a piston and a cylinder, between a bearing and a journal, etc.

Coil spring A spiral of elastic steel found in various sizes throughout a vehicle, for example as a springing medium in the suspension and in the valve train.

Compression Reduction in volume, and increase in pressure and temperature, of a gas, caused by squeezing it into a smaller space.

Compression damping Controls the speed the suspension compresses when hitting a bump.

Compression ratio The relationship between cylinder volume when the piston is at top dead center and cylinder volume when the piston is at bottom dead center.

Continuity The uninterrupted path in the flow of electricity. Little or no measurable resistance.

Continuity tester Self-powered bleeper or test light which indicates continuity.

Cp Candlepower. Bulb rating commonly found on US motorcycles.

Crossply tire Tire plies arranged in a criss-cross pattern. Usually four or six plies used, hence 4PR or 6PR in tire size codes.

Cush drive Rubber damper segments fitted between the rear wheel and final drive sprocket to absorb transmission shocks **(see illustration)**.

D

Degree disc Calibrated disc for measuring piston position. Expressed in degrees.

Dial gauge Clock-type gauge with adapters for measuring runout and piston position. Expressed in mm or inches.

Diaphragm The rubber membrane in a master cylinder or carburetor which seals the upper chamber.

Diaphragm spring A single sprung plate often used in clutches.

Direct current (dc) Current produced by a dc generator.

Decarbonization The process of removing carbon deposits - typically from the combustion chamber, valves and exhaust port/system.

Detonation Destructive and damaging explosion of fuel/air mixture in combustion chamber instead of controlled burning.

Diode An electrical valve which only allows current to flow in one direction. Commonly used in rectifiers and starter interlock systems.

Disc valve (or rotary valve) An induction system used on some two-stroke engines.

Double-overhead camshaft (DOHC) An engine that uses two overhead camshafts, one for the intake valves and one for the exhaust valves.

Drivebelt A toothed belt used to transmit drive to the rear wheel on some motorcycles. A drivebelt has also been used to drive the camshafts. Drivebelts are usually made of Kevlar.

Driveshaft Any shaft used to transmit motion. Commonly used when referring to the final driveshaft on shaft drive motorcycles.

E

ECU (Electronic Control Unit) A computer which controls (for instance) an ignition system, or an anti-lock braking system.

EGO Exhaust Gas Oxygen sensor. Sometimes called a Lambda sensor.

Electrolyte The fluid in a lead-acid battery.

EMS (Engine Management System) A computer controlled system which manages the fuel injection and the ignition systems in an integrated fashion.

Endfloat The amount of lengthways movement between two parts. As applied to a crankshaft, the distance that the crankshaft can move side-to-side in the crankcase.

Endless chain A chain having no joining link. Common use for cam chains and final drive chains.

EP (Extreme Pressure) Oil type used in locations where high loads are applied, such as between gear teeth.

Evaporative emission control system Describes a charcoal filled canister which stores fuel vapors from the tank rather than allowing them to vent to the atmosphere. Usually only fitted to California models and referred to as an EVAP system.

Expansion chamber Section of two-stroke engine exhaust system so designed to improve engine efficiency and boost power.

F

Feeler blade or gauge A thin strip or blade of hardened steel, ground to an exact thickness, used to check or measure clearances between parts.

Final drive Description of the drive from the transmission to the rear wheel. Usually by chain or shaft, but sometimes by belt.

Firing order The order in which the engine cylinders fire, or deliver their power strokes, beginning with the number one cylinder.

Flooding Term used to describe a high fuel level in the carburetor float chambers, leading to fuel overflow. Also refers to excess fuel in the combustion chamber due to incorrect starting technique.

Free length The no-load state of a component when measured. Clutch, valve and fork spring lengths are measured at rest, without any preload.

Freeplay The amount of travel before any action takes place. The looseness in a linkage, or an assembly of parts, between the initial application of force and actual movement. For example, the distance the rear brake pedal moves before the rear brake is actuated.

Fuel injection The fuel/air mixture is metered electronically and directed into the engine intake ports (indirect injection) or into the cylinders (direct injection). Sensors supply information on engine speed and conditions.

Fuel/air mixture The charge of fuel and air going into the engine. See Stoichiometric ratio.

Fuse An electrical device which protects a circuit against accidental overload. The typical fuse contains a soft piece of metal which is calibrated to melt at a predetermined current flow (expressed as amps) and break the circuit.

G

Gap The distance the spark must travel in jumping from the center electrode to the side electrode in a spark plug. Also refers to the distance between the ignition rotor and the pickup coil in an electronic ignition system.

Gasket Any thin, soft material - usually cork, cardboard, asbestos or soft metal - installed between two metal surfaces to ensure a good seal. For instance, the cylinder head gasket seals the joint between the block and the cylinder head.

Gauge An instrument panel display used to monitor engine conditions. A gauge with a movable pointer on a dial or a fixed scale is an analog gauge. A gauge with a numerical readout is called a digital gauge.

Gear ratios The drive ratio of a pair of gears in a gearbox, calculated on their number of teeth.

Glaze-busting see Honing

Grinding Process for renovating the valve face and valve seat contact area in the cylinder head.

Ground return The return path of an electrical circuit, utilizing the motorcycle's frame.

Gudgeon pin The shaft which connects the connecting rod small-end with the piston. Often called a piston pin or wrist pin.

H

Helical gears Gear teeth are slightly curved and produce less gear noise that straight-cut gears. Often used for primary drives.

Helicoil A thread insert repair system. Commonly used as a repair for stripped spark plug threads **(see illustration)**.

Installing a Helicoil thread insert in a cylinder head

Honing A process used to break down the glaze on a cylinder bore (also called glaze-busting). Can also be carried out to roughen a rebored cylinder to aid ring bedding-in.

HT (High Tension) Description of the electrical circuit from the secondary winding of the ignition coil to the spark plug.

Hydraulic A liquid filled system used to transmit pressure from one component to another. Common uses on motorcycles are brakes and clutches.

Hydrometer An instrument for measuring the specific gravity of a lead-acid battery.

Hygroscopic Water absorbing. In motorcycle applications, braking efficiency will be reduced if DOT 3 or 4 hydraulic fluid absorbs water from the air - care must be taken to keep new brake fluid in tightly sealed containers.

I

lbf ft Pounds-force feet. A unit of torque. Sometimes written as ft-lbs.

lbf in Pound-force inch. A unit of torque, applied to components where a very low torque is required. Sometimes written as inch-lbs.

IC Abbreviation for Integrated Circuit.

Ignition advance Means of increasing the timing of the spark at higher engine speeds. Done by mechanical means (ATU) on early engines or electronically by the ignition control unit on later engines.

Ignition timing The moment at which the spark plug fires, expressed in the number of crankshaft degrees before the piston reaches the top of its stroke, or in the number of millimeters before the piston reaches the top of its stroke.

Infinity (∞) Description of an open-circuit electrical state, where no continuity exists.

Inverted forks (upside down forks) The sliders or lower legs are held in the yokes and the fork tubes or stanchions are connected to the wheel axle (spindle). Less unsprung weight and stiffer construction than conventional forks.

J

JASO Japan Automobile Standards Organization. JASO MA is a standard for motorcycle oil equivalent to API SJ, but designed to prevent problems with wet-type motorcycle clutches.

Joule The unit of electrical energy.

Journal The bearing surface of a shaft.

K

Kickstart Mechanical means of turning the engine over for starting purposes.

Only usually fitted to mopeds, small capacity motorcycles and off-road motorcycles.

Kill switch Handebar-mounted switch for emergency ignition cut-out. Cuts the ignition circuit on all models, and additionally prevent starter motor operation on others.

km Symbol for kilometer.

kmh Abbreviation for kilometers per hour.

L

Lambda sensor A sensor fitted in the exhaust system to measure the exhaust gas oxygen content (excess air factor). Also called oxygen sensor.

Lapping see **Grinding**.

LCD Abbreviation for Liquid Crystal Display.

LED Abbreviation for Light Emitting Diode.

Liner A steel cylinder liner inserted in an aluminum alloy cylinder block.

Locknut A nut used to lock an adjustment nut, or other threaded component, in place.

Lockstops The lugs on the lower triple clamp (yoke) which abut those on the frame, preventing handlebar-to-fuel tank contact.

Lockwasher A form of washer designed to prevent an attaching nut from working loose.

LT Low Tension Description of the electrical circuit from the power supply to the primary winding of the ignition coil.

M

Main bearings The bearings between the crankshaft and crankcase.

Maintenance-free (MF) battery A sealed battery which cannot be topped up.

Manometer Mercury-filled calibrated tubes used to measure intake tract vacuum. Used to synchronize carburetors on multi-cylinder engines.

Tappet shims are measured with a micrometer

Micrometer A precision measuring instrument that measures component outside diameters **(see illustration)**.

MON (Motor Octane Number) A measure of a fuel's resistance to knock.

Monograde oil An oil with a single viscosity, eg SAE80W.

Monoshock A single suspension unit linking the swingarm or suspension linkage to the frame.

mph Abbreviation for miles per hour.

Multigrade oil Having a wide viscosity range (eg 10W40). The W stands for Winter, thus the viscosity ranges from SAE10 when cold to SAE40 when hot.

Multimeter An electrical test instrument with the capability to measure voltage, current and resistance. Some meters also incorporate a continuity tester and buzzer.

N

Needle roller bearing Inner race of caged needle rollers and hardened outer race. Examples of uncaged needle rollers can be found on some engines. Commonly used in rear suspension applications and in two-stroke engines.

Nm Newton meters.

NOx Oxides of Nitrogen. A common toxic pollutant emitted by gasoline engines at higher temperatures.

O

Octane The measure of a fuel's resistance to knock.

OE (Original Equipment) Relates to components fitted to a motorcycle as standard or replacement parts supplied by the motorcycle manufacturer.

Ohm The unit of electrical resistance. Ohms = Volts ÷ Current.

Ohmmeter An instrument for measuring electrical resistance.

Oil cooler System for diverting engine oil outside of the engine to a radiator for cooling purposes.

Oil injection A system of two-stroke engine lubrication where oil is pump-fed to the engine in accordance with throttle position.

Open-circuit An electrical condition where there is a break in the flow of electricity - no continuity (high resistance).

O-ring A type of sealing ring made of a special rubber-like material; in use, the O-ring is compressed into a groove to provide the sealing action.

Oversize (OS) Term used for piston and ring size options fitted to a rebored cylinder.

Overhead cam (sohc) engine An engine with single camshaft located on top of the cylinder head.

Overhead valve (ohv) engine An engine with the valves located in the cylinder head, but with the camshaft located in the engine block or crankcase.

Oxygen sensor A device installed in the exhaust system which senses the oxygen content in the exhaust and converts this information into an electric current. Also called a Lambda sensor.

P

Plastigage A thin strip of plastic thread, available in different sizes, used for measuring clearances. For example, a strip of Plastigage is laid across a bearing journal. The parts are assembled and dismantled; the width of the crushed strip indicates the clearance between journal and bearing.

Polarity Either negative or positive ground, determined by which battery lead is connected to the frame (ground return). Modern motorcycles are usually negative ground.

Pre-ignition A situation where the fuel/air mixture ignites before the spark plug fires. Often due to a hot spot in the combustion chamber caused by carbon build-up. Engine has a tendency to 'run-on'.

Pre-load (suspension) The amount a spring is compressed when in the unloaded state. Preload can be applied by gas, spacer or mechanical adjuster.

Premix The method of engine lubrication on some gasoline two-stroke engines. Engine oil is mixed with the gasoline in the fuel tank in a specific ratio. The fuel/oil mix is sometimes referred to as "petrol".

Primary drive Description of the drive from the crankshaft to the clutch. Usually by gear or chain.

PS Pferdestärke - a German interpretation of BHP.

PSI Pounds-force per square inch. Imperial measurement of tire pressure and cylinder pressure measurement.

PTFE Polytetrafluroethylene. A low friction substance.

Pulse secondary air injection system A process of promoting the burning of excess fuel present in the exhaust gases by routing fresh air into the exhaust ports.

Q

Quartz halogen bulb Tungsten filament surrounded by a halogen gas. Typically used for the headlight **(see illustration)**.

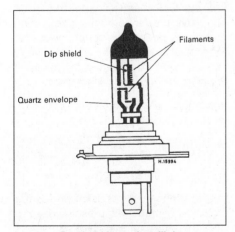

Quartz halogen headlight bulb construction

R

Rack-and-pinion A pinion gear on the end of a shaft that mates with a rack (think of a geared wheel opened up and laid flat). Sometimes used in clutch operating systems.

Radial play Up and down movement about a shaft.

Radial ply tires Tire plies run across the tire (from bead to bead) and around the circumference of the tire. Less resistant to tread distortion than other tire types.

Radiator A liquid-to-air heat transfer device designed to reduce the temperature of the coolant in a liquid cooled engine.

Rake A feature of steering geometry - the angle of the steering head in relation to the vertical **(see illustration)**.

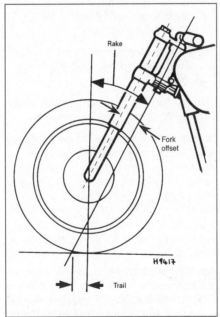

Steering geometry

Rebore Providing a new working surface to the cylinder bore by boring out the old surface. Necessitates the use of oversize piston and rings.

Rebound damping A means of controlling the oscillation of a suspension unit spring after it has been compressed. Resists the spring's natural tendency to bounce back after being compressed.

Rectifier Device for converting the ac output of an alternator into dc for battery charging.

Reed valve An induction system commonly used on two-stroke engines.

Regulator Device for maintaining the charging voltage from the generator or alternator within a specified range.

Relay A electrical device used to switch heavy current on and off by using a low current auxiliary circuit.

Resistance Measured in ohms. An electrical component's ability to pass electrical current.

RON (Research Octane Number) A measure of a fuel's resistance to knock.

rpm revolutions per minute.

Runout The amount of wobble (in-and-out movement) of a wheel or shaft as it's rotated. The amount a shaft rotates "out-of-true." The out-of-round condition of a rotating part.

S

SAE (Society of Automotive Engineers) A standard for the viscosity of a fluid.

Sealant A liquid or paste used to prevent leakage at a joint. Sometimes used in conjunction with a gasket.

Service limit Term for the point where a component is no longer useable and must be replaced.

Shaft drive A method of transmitting drive from the transmission to the rear wheel.

Shell bearings Plain bearings consisting of two shell halves. Most often used as big-end and main bearings in a four-stroke engine. Often called bearing inserts.

Shim Thin spacer, commonly used to adjust the clearance or relative positions between two parts. For example, shims inserted into or under tappets or followers to control valve clearances. Clearance is adjusted by changing the thickness of the shim.

Short-circuit An electrical condition where current shorts to ground bypassing the circuit components.

Skimming Process to correct warpage or repair a damaged surface, eg on brake discs or drums.

Slide-hammer A special puller that screws into or hooks onto a component such as a shaft or bearing; a heavy sliding handle on the shaft bottoms against the end of the shaft to knock the component free.

Small-end bearing The bearing in the upper end of the connecting rod at its joint with the gudgeon pin.

Snap-ring A ring-shaped clip used to prevent endwise movement of cylindrical parts and shafts. An internal snap-ring is installed in a groove in a housing; an external snap-ring fits into a groove on the outside of a cylindrical piece such as a shaft. Also known as a circlip.

Spalling Damage to camshaft lobes or bearing journals shown as pitting of the working surface.

Specific gravity (SG) The state of charge of the electrolyte in a lead-acid battery. A measure of the electrolyte's density compared with water.

Straight-cut gears Common type gear used on gearbox shafts and for oil pump and water pump drives.

Stanchion The inner sliding part of the front forks, held by the yokes. Often called a fork tube.

Stoichiometric ratio The optimum chemical air/fuel ratio for a gasoline engine, said to be 14.7 parts of air to 1 part of fuel.

Sulphuric acid The liquid (electrolyte) used in a lead-acid battery. Poisonous and extremely corrosive.

Surface grinding (lapping) Process to correct a warped gasket face, commonly used on cylinder heads.

T

Tapered-roller bearing Tapered inner race of caged needle rollers and separate tapered outer race. Examples of taper roller bearings can be found on steering heads.

Tappet A cylindrical component which transmits motion from the cam to the valve stem, either directly or via a pushrod and rocker arm. Also called a cam follower.

TCS Traction Control System. An electronically-controlled system which senses wheel spin and reduces engine speed accordingly.

TDC Top Dead Center denotes that the piston is at its highest point in the cylinder.

Thread-locking compound Solution applied to fastener threads to prevent loosening. Select type to suit application.

Thrust washer A washer positioned between two moving components on a shaft. For example, between gear pinions on gearshaft.

Timing chain See **Cam Chain**.

Timing light Stroboscopic lamp for carrying out ignition timing checks with the engine running.

Top-end A description of an engine's cylinder block, head and valve gear components.

Torque Turning or twisting force about a shaft.

Torque setting A prescribed tightness specified by the motorcycle manufacturer to ensure that the bolt or nut is secured correctly. Undertightening can result in the bolt or nut coming loose or a surface not being sealed. Overtightening can result in stripped threads, distortion or damage to the component being retained.

Torx key A six-point wrench.

Tracer A stripe of a second color applied to a wire insulator to distinguish that wire from another one with the same color insulator. For example, Br/W is often used to denote a brown insulator with a white tracer.

Trail A feature of steering geometry. Distance from the steering head axis to the tire's central contact point.

Triple clamps The cast components which extend from the steering head and support the fork stanchions or tubes. Often called fork yokes.

Turbocharger A centrifugal device, driven by exhaust gases, that pressurizes the intake air. Normally used to increase the power output from a given engine displacement.

TWI Abbreviation for Tire Wear Indicator. Indicates the location of the tread depth indicator bars on tires.

U

Universal joint or U-joint (UJ) A double-pivoted connection for transmitting power from a driving to a driven shaft through an angle. Typically found in shaft drive assemblies.

Unsprung weight Anything not supported by the bike's suspension (ie the wheel, tires, brakes, final drive and bottom (moving) part of the suspension).

V

Vacuum gauges Clock-type gauges for measuring intake tract vacuum. Used for carburetor synchronization on multi-cylinder engines.

Valve A device through which the flow of liquid, gas or vacuum may be stopped, started or regulated by a moveable part that opens, shuts or partially obstructs one or more ports or passageways. The intake and exhaust valves in the cylinder head are of the poppet type.

Valve clearance The clearance between the valve tip (the end of the valve stem) and the rocker arm or tappet/follower. The valve clearance is measured when the valve is closed. The correct clearance is important - if too small the valve won't close fully and will burn out, whereas if too large noisy operation will result.

Valve lift The amount a valve is lifted off its seat by the camshaft lobe.

Valve timing The exact setting for the opening and closing of the valves in relation to piston position.

Vernier caliper A precision measuring instrument that measures inside and outside dimensions. Not quite as accurate as a micrometer, but more convenient.

VIN Vehicle Identification Number. Term for the bike's engine and frame numbers.

Viscosity The thickness of a liquid or its resistance to flow.

Volt A unit for expressing electrical "pressure" in a circuit. Volts = current x ohms.

W

Water pump A mechanically-driven device for moving coolant around the engine.

Watt A unit for expressing electrical power. Watts = volts x current.

Wet liner arrangement

Wear limit see **Service limit**

Wet liner A liquid-cooled engine design where the pistons run in liners which are directly surrounded by coolant **(see illustration)**.

Wheelbase Distance from the center of the front wheel to the center of the rear wheel.

Wiring harness or loom Describes the electrical wires running the length of the motorcycle and enclosed in tape or plastic sheathing. Wiring coming off the main harness is usually referred to as a sub harness.

Woodruff key A key of semi-circular or square section used to locate a gear to a shaft. Often used to locate the alternator rotor on the crankshaft.

Wrist pin Another name for gudgeon or piston pin.

Notes

Note: *References throughout this index are in the form, "Chapter number"•"Page number"*